*This book is sponsored by the Theological
Commission of the World Evangelical Fellowship*

THE UNIQUE CHRIST
IN OUR PLURALIST WORLD

*Titles produced by the Faith and
Church Study Unit of the Theological Commission of the
World Evangelical Fellowship:*

BIBLICAL INTERPRETATION AND THE CHURCH:
Text and Context

THE CHURCH IN THE BIBLE AND THE WORLD:
An International Study

TEACH US TO PRAY:
Prayer in the Bible and the World

RIGHT WITH GOD:
Justification in the Bible and the World

WORSHIP:
Adoration and Action

THE UNIQUE CHRIST
IN OUR PLURALIST WORLD

edited by

Bruce J. Nicholls

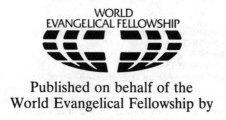

Published on behalf of the
World Evangelical Fellowship by

THE PATERNOSTER PRESS
Carlisle UK

BAKER
BOOK HOUSE
Grand Rapids, Michigan

Copyright © 1994 World Evangelical Fellowship

First published 1994 jointly by The Paternoster Press,
P.O. Box 300, Carlisle, Cumbria CA3 0QS, U.K.,
and Baker Book House, Box 6287, Grand Rapids,
MI 49516–6287, U.S.A.

All Rights Reserved. No part of this publication may
be reproduced, stored in a retrieval system, or
transmitted in any form or by any means, electronic,
mechanical, photocopying, recording or otherwise,
without the prior permission of the publisher
or a licence permitting restricted copying.
In the U.K. such licences are issued by the
Copyright Licensing Agency, 90 Tottenham Court Road,
London W1P 9HE

Unless otherwise stated, Scripture quotations in this
publication are from the Holy Bible, New International Version.
Copyright © 1973, 1978, 1984 International Bible Society.
Published by Zondervan and Hodder & Stoughton.

This book is sold subject to the condition that it shall
not, by way of trade or otherwise be lent, re-sold,
hired out, or otherwise circulated without the
publisher's prior consent in any form of binding or
cover other than that in which it is published and
without a similar condition including this condition
being imposed on the subsequent purchaser.

British Library Cataloguing in Publication Data

Unique Christ in our Pluralist World
I. Nicholls, Bruce J.
232

ISBN 0–85364–574–4

Library of Congress Cataloging-in-Publication Data

The unique Christ in our pluralist world / edited by Bruce J.
Nicholls.
        p.   cm.
    Papers originally presented at an international meeting in Manila,
June 16–20, 1992.
    Includes bibliographical references.
    ISBN 0–8010–2013–1
    1. Jesus Christ—Person and offices—Congresses. 2. Christianity
and other religions—Congresses. 3. Religious pluralism–
–Evangelicalism—Congresses. 4. Evangelistic work—Philosophy–
–Congresses. I. Nicholls, Bruce. II. World Evangelical
Fellowship. Theological Commission.
BT202.U55   1995.
232—dc20   94–36248
                                                                CIP

Typeset by Photoprint, Torquay, Devon
and printed in the UK by
The Cromwell Press, Melksham, Wiltshire
for the publishers.

Contents

Foreword

Leaders representing the world's principal religions and interfaith groups gathered in Chicago September 1993 for the Parliament of the World's Religions. The goals of the Parliament were to promote cooperation among the world's religious institutions, renew the role of the religions of the world in relation to personal spiritual growth, and develop interfaith programmes which will continue inter-faith cooperation into the 21st Century.

The participants of the Parliament were the leading religious figures representing Baha'is, Buddhists, Confucianists, Hindus, Jains, Jews, Muslims, Native Americans, Shintos, Sikhs, Taoists, Unitarians and Zoroastrians as well as Protestants and Roman Catholics. Evangelical leaders are alarmed by the increasing religious pluralism and syncretistic influence within and outside the Church; moreover, this religious pluralism has crept into the evangelical church in a subtle way in recent years to cause divisions among evangelical Christians and to arouse theologians to be concerned.

Is Christ the unique and only Saviour? Is Christianity unique? Do we as evangelicals have a theology of religions? What do we mean by 'uniqueness'? Eighty-five evangelical theologians from 28 countries met in Manila, June 16–20, 1992 to discuss similar questions and hear summaries of twenty papers presented on the theme, 'the Unique Christ in Our Pluralistic World'.

The drafting committee of fifteen scholars produced a 'Manila Declaration on the Unique Christ in Our Pluralistic World' which was approved by the participants. This document is available as the WEF Theological Commission's monograph series, No. 5. We in the Theological Commission are very grateful to Dr. Bruce Nicholls for editing this volume. Since this topic of pluralism and syncretism is intimately related to evangelism, missions, justice and peace, political ideologies, and eschatology and other areas of the Christian church, I trust that this book would be widely distributed around the world in vernacular languages in order to help many Christians, pastors, and theological students to understand clearly the challenge of the unique Christ in our pluralistic society, to find the biblical answer to this theological issue of pluralism, and to see where the differences of interpretation lie even within evangelical Christianity. To God be the glory!

BONG RIN RO, TH.D.
WEF Theological Commission Director

7

1

Bruce Nicholls

INTRODUCTION

OUR THEOLOGICAL TASK

We who belong to the post World War II generation are living in a world in which ways of thinking and value systems are changing more rapidly than in any comparable period of history. The rate of exchange is accelerating. Life is becoming more complex. In this context God is calling us to 'contend for the faith that was once entrusted to the saints' (Jude 3), and to pass on this historic evangelical legacy to future generations.

OUR RELIGIOUS AND IDEOLOGICAL CONTEXT

Pluralism is the mark of our age. Multi-media communication and education, air travel and tourism, migration and refugees have brought the world's Faiths into direct dialogue and confrontation with each other. Religion has become an exchangeable commodity in our free market world. The traditional religions of Hinduism, Buddhism and primitive folk religions are providing the religious base for the New Age movements of cosmic consciousness which are challenging the Christian claim to Truth. Saving the planet Earth from ecological death is becoming the central issue of religious concern. Paganism is no longer a term of disrepute. Fundamentalist Islam and now fundamentalist Hinduism are offering a religious, encultured and politicised ethic and life style to save society from degenerate Christianity and secular humanism.

Religious and cultural pluralism is claiming that it is axiomatic that no one religion can claim uniqueness and finality; no one religious founder can claim to be the only saviour of the world. The Indian theologian Stanley Samartha, former Director of the WCC programme on Dialogue with People of Living

Rev. Dr Bruce J Nicholls was formerly director of WEF Theological Commission. He has relocated from New Delhi to Auckland, New Zealand.

Faiths and Ideologies writes, 'To claim that one religious tradition has the only answer to such global problems sounds preposterous.' (*International Review of Missions, July 1988, p. 315*). The impact of pluralism on sections of the Christian Church has been profound. Since Vatican II the Roman Catholic church has moved closer to an inclusive position, affirming the possibility of salvation in other Faiths, as seen in the writings of Karl Rahner, Raimundo Panikkar and Paul Knitter. Among Protestants, John Robinson, John Hick, Wilfred Cantwell Smith and others have pressed for religious pluralism and the relativity of truth and ethical behaviour. Pluralistic Christianity is very congenial to the modern secular mind, both western and eastern.

A second characteristic of our one world is the universal impact of modernity on religious faiths. The world view, value systems and life style of the dominant European and North American secular and materialistic society have penetrated every corner of the globe. Beginning with the urbanized and industrial cities, modernity is spreading to the villages and to the marginalized communities. Modern communication technology brooks no boundaries. Neither the fundamentalist Islamic states nor the remaining marxist regimes are able to contain it. The new gods are science, technology, pleasure and self preservation. The secular humanistic debate is no longer one of atheism versus theism, for since God has been shown to be irrelevant to modern life this debate is now meaningless. Modern man is the master of his destiny. The realization of global consciousness and of human potentiality replaces any sense of need for religious conversion. Jesus Christ is no longer unique because he is no longer relevant to human life.

A third fact of our times is the escalation of violence and of human suffering. It is the preoccupation of the media, the obsession of our newspapers and TV programmes. Both rich and poor are caught up in the web of violence which increases economic and social poverty. Today the unborn child, women and children, ethnic minorities, marginalized religious communities and political refugees are among those who suffer the most. Police brutality, terrorism, civil war, fear of a nuclear holocaust suggest that the age of the Lawless One is upon us. We believe that unless the Lord intervenes humankind is drifting powerlessly towards self-destruction. People are crying 'peace, peace' but there is no peace. People cry for justice but there is no justice for those who deny God as the source of justice. We believe that Christ who is the prince of peace and justice is our only hope. This hope enables us to accept Christ's claim as to who he is and what he claimed to accomplish on the cross.

Again, the modern world is also the arena of competing ideologies and political utopias. Fascism, nazi-ism, marxism have been tried and found wanting. The fusion of religious fundamentalism and political dictatorship has led to increased bondage of spirit, oppression and widespread suffering – not to freedom, justice and peace. The Church can no longer stand aside from involvement in this arena of political and economic oppression. To maintain a ghetto mentality is to vote for the continuance of the status quo. We believe that Jesus Christ is the one who will judge all ideologies and utopias according to the divinely established laws of God. He came as a prophet and suffered the consequences of his uncomfortable message as did the prophets before him. His disciples, the Church, are called to a prophetic ministry of conscientising people about their sin, rebuking evil and pointing to the Light who alone can redeem the world.

FACTORS IN THE HERMENEUTICAL PROCESS

Our theological task is to exegete correctly the revealed Word of God in its own cultural context and to interpret it through the guidance and power of the Holy Spirit, so that it speaks authentically and authoritatively to the issues of our time. Exegesis and interpretation are the two distinct but inter-dependent sides of the one hermeneutical process. Luther is reported to have said, 'If you preach the Gospel in all aspects except the issues that deal specifically with your time, you are not preaching the Gospel at all.' If we are giving theological answers to questions people are not asking we are failing in our task.

Hermeneutics is a three way conversation. It involves a dialogue between a final and unchanging text as the Word of God and a relative and ever-changing context of human thought and practice. Between the text and the context stand the exegete and the communicator. They may be one and the same person or different persons. Rightly interpreting the Word of God to the issues of our time may be undertaken by an individual or better by a skilled team, as in the *Asia Bible Commentary* series which I am editing. We are looking for each volume to be the combined work of an exegete, a theologian and a pastor. The combined insights and wisdom of the faculty of a theological school are greater than those of any one member. This is equally true of our missiological task. As we listen to the people of God through the history of the Church, our understanding of God's Word is clarified and illumined. We do not put tradition on the same level as the Word itself but accept it as a subordinate and confirming standard of the Faith.

This hermeneutical task is not an endless circle of uncertainties and relative truth, but a progressive movement towards the knowledge of God and his will. Our theological task is both an academic and a spiritual one. The symbol of a *spiral* is more appropriate to our task, for it points to a process which is an ongoing dialogue moving to an eschatological direction towards the knowledge of the will of God and the completion of his Kingdom on earth. In terms of theological education our hermeneutical task can be symbolized by holding together in partnership the chapel, the classroom, the local church and the market place. The fear of the Lord is the beginning of wisdom and of knowledge. Our task is God-centred from beginning to end.

CHRISTOLOGY THE CENTRE OF THE STORM

The central theological issue of our times is the Christological one, 'Who do you say that I am?'. Jesus left us in no doubt as to who he, the Son of man, is. He came from the Father, returned to the Father and will return a second time to the earth in the power of the Father. He acknowledged that his power over nature, demonic spirits and over death came from the Father. His disciples slowly came to understand this truth which he revealed to them. John concludes his Gospel, 'These (words) are written that you may believe that Jesus is Christ, the son of God, and that by believing you may have life in his name' (Jn. 20:31).

Christ was not only the Lord from heaven; he was 'the man for others'. He came to serve and not to be served. He identified with his Jewish religion and culture, but not uncritically, and with both the rich and the poor, the healthy and the diseased. He is unique because he never confused his dual identity from above and from below, but neither did he isolate one from the other. The Early Church recognized this complementary truth and clarified the issues. The creeds restated the dual nature of Christ's person and work without solving the dilemma. They affirmed that he was 'true God from true God' and 'for us men and for our salvation he came down from heaven: by the power of the Holy Spirit he was born of the Virgin Mary and became man'. (Nicene Creed).

Our theological task is to hold together in creative tension a theology from above and a theology from below. Evangelicals have always been in danger of proclaiming a docetic Christ who had no human limitations and Liberals speak of an adoptionist Christ who as revolutionary liberates from poverty and oppression. The divine mystery of the Incarnation is revealed only to those with ears to hear. It is not the object of scientific or rational analysis. In our theological methodology we follow Anselm: 'I believe so that I may understand'. Faith precedes rational knowledge. To reduce the Incarnation to the myth of religious experience as Hick and Knitter do, is to deny the gospel itself. The logical conclusion is to reject the cross as God's act of atonement and the resurrection of Christ as an historical reality. The Early Church overcame the gnostic and oriental heresies of their time with a Christology that was faithful to Scripture and yet clothed in language that was relevant to their cultural and philosophical world. Today we face a similar challenge from the mythology of Western Enlightenment and the mysticism of eastern New Age.

Thus our theological task begins with our commitment to Christ and our openness to the Holy Spirit. It demands the faithful exegesis of Scripture as the Word of God. It is enriched by listening to and sharing with the Church as the people of God and takes shape in the context of participation with Christ in his mission to the world. It is both personal and communal, academic and spiritual, rational and mystical. No man or woman could have a higher calling.

CONCLUSION

The Theological Commission of the World Evangelical Fellowship has come a long way since its founding in 1976 – or 1969 if we go back to the launching of the Theological Assistance Programme. The issue of world evangelization – the whole Church taking the whole gospel to the whole world – has been clarified thanks to the Lausanne Committee for World Evangelization.

Evangelicals have begun to discover their theological identity having recovered from the impact of a century of liberal theology and the more recent criticism of fundamentalism. It would be true to say that evangelicals 'have come of age'.

Our theological task has broadened as we have become aware of cultural factors that impinge on every aspect of our work. Issues of contextualisation and syncretism have been foremost in our concerns. New structures have emerged and national theological commissions and theological societies have been formed. New patterns of regional co-operation in each continent have taken shape and regular international consultations held.

Many new theological schools have been started, standards raised and evaluated, new faculty trained, many with doctorates. Journals have been launched, monographs and books written and published.

Where Do We Go From Here?

Of the many theological tasks before us today I will draw attention to seven.

1. The issue of Christology will not end with this consultation. It will always remain a central task.
2. Understanding the uniqueness of salvation in Christ in the context of religious pluralism will continue to be a critical issue in world evangelization.
3. A prophetic response to the social issues of violence, poverty, corruption, and oppression will continue to be the concern of our churches.
4. Personal and social ethics, Christian and community lifestyle will call for increasing attention.
5. Theological foundations for Christian environmental stewardship is an issue demanding immediate attention.
6. The unity and diversity of the Church and her agencies in Christ's mission to the world call for constant re-evaluation.
7. The Church's response to political power and to religious persecution will call for increasing action in a world of escalating violence, suffering and oppression.

As we set our hands to our theological task may we never turn back, but press on for the high calling of God in Christ Jesus.

2

The WEF Manila Declaration

I. THE UNIQUE CHRIST IN THE PLURALITY OF RELIGIONS

We live in a pluralistic world. There have always been many different cultures, languages, worldviews, moral codes, scientific systems, and religions. What is new is the modern world in which religions must live side by side in non-traditional combinations. And what is new is the extent to which many people are aware of alternatives both in their immediate context and in the larger world.

A. Diversity and Pluralism

We affirm that God desires diversity in his creation. We must learn to accept, and even celebrate, that diversity. We therefore affirm freedom of conscience, practice, propagation, and witness in the areas of culture, worldview, scientific investigation, and religion. We note that secular governments, by encouraging mutual tolerance and by supporting freedom to choose in these areas, often protect the rights of cultural minorities, religious believers, creative thinkers, and others from persecution and tyranny.

Beyond these legitimate functions, pluralism as a way of thinking is sometimes extended from a mere description of existing diversity to the affirmation that all religious beliefs – or, at least, those of the major religious traditions – are more-or-less equally valid and equally true and that all religious beliefs have a rough parity with each other. This we reject.

Against such pluralism, we affirm that God has acted decisively, supremely, and normatively in the historical Jesus of Nazareth. In his person and work, Jesus is unique such that no one comes to the Father except through him. All salvation in the biblical sense of eternal life, life in the kingdom, reconciliation with God and forgiveness of sins comes solely from the person and work of Jesus Christ.

To the pluralist's claim that all religious beliefs are more-or-less equally valid and equally true, we have several additional objections. Among them are these: (1) Such pluralism results in an abstract view of God lacking spiritual power and inconsistent with scripture. To the extent that pluralists

---

The Manila Declaration was drafted and approved by the participants at the consultation June 16–20, 1992, at Manila.

offer a specific view of God, that specific view often has been surreptitiously dderived from a particular religion such as Christianity or Hinduism. (2) Pluralism turns the New Testament and credal affirmations about Jesus into mere myths, lacking any historical and factual foundation. (3) Pluralism thus renders the Christian faith and worship of Jesus Christ ultimately idolatrous. (4) Some forms of pluralism not only deny the centrality of Jesus Christ and of a personal God but even deny the centrality of a vague and abstract 'ultimate'. These forms of pluralism have placed human 'salvation' as the heart and norm of all religion, thereby making the human self the decisive centre of all meaning and value. Such pluralism is ego-centric and fundamentally similar to monistic religions such as Hinduism and the New Age Philosophy. (5) Pluralism can become a dogmatic exclusivism that, under the guise of humility and tolerance, is arrogant and intolerant of existing religious traditions. (6) Pluralism gives too much authority to relativistic views of revelation, denying Christianity's witness to God's non-relativistic action in the world in Jesus Christ. We note that other religions may have a similar problem with pluralism from their points of view. (7) Some forms of pluralism would restrict each religion to working solely with its traditional adherents thus denying the universal message that is so central to scripture and, thus, to Christianity's self-identity. Again we note that some other religions may have a similar objection to pluralism based on their own self-understanding. (8) Pluralism is no help at all, pastorally or evangelically, in ministering to those in our congregations or in proclaiming Jesus Christ to all peoples of every tribe, nation, and people group.

B. Other Religions and Salvation

In our modern pluralistic world, many Christians ask: 'Is it not possible that there might be salvation in other religions?' This question is misleading because it implies that religions have the power to save us. This is not true. Only God saves. All people have sinned, all people deserve condemnation, all salvation stems solely from the person and atoning work of Jesus Christ, and this salvation can be appropriated solely through trust in God's mercy.

The question, therefore, should be rephrased as: 'Can those who have never heard of Jesus Christ be saved?' Old Testament saints, who did not know the name Jesus, nevertheless found salvation. Is it possible that others also might find salvation through the blood of Jesus Christ although they do not consciously know the name of Jesus? We did not achieve a consensus on how to answer this question. More study is needed.

We did agree that salvation is to be found nowhere else than in Jesus Christ. The truth to be found in other religious teachings is not sufficient, in and of itself, to provide salvation. We further agreed that universalism (that all people without exception will be saved) is not biblical. Lastly, we agreed that our discussion of this issue must not in any way undercut the passion to proclaim, without wavering, faltering, or tiring, the good news of salvation through trust in Jesus Christ.

C. Plea For an Evangelical Theology of Religions

We evangelicals need a more adequate theology of religions. As a prologue to that theology of religions, we observe the following. The term 'religion' refers to a complex phenomenon, and it is important to distinguish between its various aspects. In many societies, religion forms an important part of their identity. As such, a diversity of religions – or, more accurately, a diversity of certain aspects of the religions – may be affirmed as a part of the richness of God's good creation, although it must be immediately added that people have often sinfully used these religions, including Christianity, to create a false ultimacy and superiority for their own cultures and religious groups.

Religions may also be understood as expressions of the longing for communion with God, which is an essential human characteristic since we are created in the image of God for the purpose of service to him, fellowship with him, and praise for him. Here also, while always corrupted by sin in practice, we may affirm in principle the goodness of a diversity of some aspects of the religions.

We are not able, however, to affirm the diversity of religions without qualification because religions teach a path to salvation, or a concept of salvation, that is not consistent with God's saving action in Jesus Christ as recorded in the Bible. To the extent that a religion points away from Jesus Christ, we deny the validity of that religion. We would also deny the validity of the Christian religion should it fail to proclaim Jesus as the Christ, the Lord of all creation, and the sole saviour of the world.

We wish to explore the trinitarian basis of a Christian theology of religions. Remembering that the Father and Spirit created the world through the Word, and remembering also that the Holy Spirit is the Spirit of Jesus and always points to him, it is possible to affirm that God draws people who live far beyond the religious boundaries of Christianity towards salvation while at the same time denying that God saves any one 'beyond' or 'apart from' Jesus Christ. Thus the true aspects of the world's religions stem from God's creative power or from the work of the Holy Spirit as he prepares individuals, people groups, and even whole cultures to hear about Jesus Christ. Moreover this same trinitarian basis undergirds the decisive, normative, and unique work and person of the historical Jesus Christ.

II. THE UNIQUE CHRIST IN THE CHALLENGE OF MODERNITY

Modernity refers to that particular way of thinking, and feeling, that emerged in the West in the wake of the disintegration of medieval culture. Its influence, however, is now worldwide. Some people claim that modernity is itself in the process of disintegration and that a postmodern world is now emerging. Our particular concerns with modernity, however, also apply to the postmodern world. In many cases, the most troubling features of modernity may be becoming even more prominent in our postmodern world.

A. Modernity's Positive Contributions

God has used modernity to provide many blessings such as the recognition of the dignity and inalienable rights of each person, the separation of state control from institutionalized religion, powerful methods of economic production that have increased material well-being in many places of the world, opportunities for creative work through technology, a deepened understanding of the created world through science, advances in public health, increased opportunity for education, and liberation from superstition and fear.

We note the positive contribution of Christianity to the origins of modern science through its doctrines of revelation and creation. And we note the positive contribution of Christianity to the growing sense of individual dignity and worth through its teachings that each person is made in God's image and that God loves each person deeply enough to sacrifice his own Son for that person's salvation. We repent for those times when Christians, invoking the authority of the church and the Bible, retarded the growth of scientific knowledge and of the expansion of human dignity and liberation.

B. Modernity's Harm

Modernity, however, has also produced much that is threatening and destructive, creating a crisis that deepens as each decade passes. The destructive elements are often distortions of – the shadow side of – those very blessings of modernity that we prize so highly. The concern for the individual's dignity and worth has degenerated into a rampant individualism that focuses on one's own rights at the expense of one's neighbour, on orienting the world around one's own gratification at the expense of service, and the pursuit of one's own happiness at the expense of the health of the larger community.

Rather than using modernity's economic power to satisfy our material needs and thus to obtain the freedom to pursue higher values, we have often engaged in an incessant materialism and consumerism that is now destroying our planet as well as our souls. The engine of economic growth that has raised the standard of living for many hundreds of millions of people has also left many other people in poverty and hunger, forcing them to sell their labour for wages that cannot sustain life, to sell their daughters into prostitution, and to sell or abandon their traditional lands and homes.

The science and technology of modernity, rather than leading us to awe-filled praise of our Creator, have produced weapons that can destroy all life, and they have legitimized a mechanistic view of neighbour, self, and nature that leaves no room for authentic personhood. The same medicine that heals can both destroy the unborn and yet, paradoxically, encourage an explosion of the human population that the earth cannot sustain. The same secular cultures of modernity that often allow the preservation of free thought and intellectual exploration have also made it impossible to control pornography, sexual deviance, moral relativism, official graft, exploitation, and nihilism that destroy families, communities, and nations.

C. Modernity and Relativism

We affirm modernity's search for truth, through the sciences, social sciences and humanities. Yet, too often this search – based on a view of humanity as the centre of knowledge, value, and significance – led to a radical relativism and scepticism that has caused many to despair of ever finding genuine knowledge, real values, or objective significance.

We note that relativism gives contemporary religious pluralism its plausibility and urgency. Christians have always been aware of other religious options – sometimes intensely so as in the first four centuries in the Roman

Empire or as in the case of countries such as India, China, or Japan. What makes the modern pluralism different is precisely the influence of relativism, the denial of objective truth, and the loss of significance and value as genuine, objective parts of the world. This loss creates in modern people the sense that religious differences concern not truth but taste. Since, in matters of taste, one person's preference is as good as any other person's, modern people often see the choice between religions as an individual and private affair or, at most, as a matter of one's cultural orientation. It would thus appear ungracious, intolerant, or even dangerously anti-social to insist that one's own religious option is 'truer' or objectively 'better' than the others. In this way, pluralism matches one of the least positive aspects of modernity.

D. Jesus Christ as the Answer for Modernity

Against the challenges of modernism, relativism, and pluralism, we affirm that Jesus Christ is the way, the truth, and the life. To preach Jesus Christ results in pastoral, prophetic, and evangelistic ministries to the modern world. Jesus is the pastor whose yoke is light and whose burden is easy, who offers God's love and healing to maimed and hurt people. Jesus Christ calls each congregation to be a community of acceptance, of compassion, of wholeness, of concern for the well-being of each of its members, and of moral integrity. We confess that often individuals and congregations fail to obey this call. But it is only as we fulfil this mandate that we witness to God's alternative to the soul-destruction so deeply rooted in modernity.

Jesus Christ is also the prophet. In Jesus Christ, God has acted richly and fully, providing a contrast with the spiritual poverty of the modern world. The presence of God in Jesus Christ reveals the banality, triviality, and hollowness of modern materialistic societies which have lost the capacity to sense the presence of God or to experience any form of sacred mystery. The divine purpose operating in Jesus' life, which sustained him even as he set his face towards the cross outside the walls of Jerusalem, highlights the moral vacuum and loss of significance in the relativism of modern societies. While Jesus' love of banquets, festivals, and shared meals shows a deep sense of community and appreciation of God's physical gifts, nonetheless his freedom not to pursue wealth or treasure on earth gives the lie to the modern teaching that happiness consists in endless acquisition of material objects.

As prophet, Jesus calls us to a prophetic ministry to our own generation, a ministry both of preaching in words and of witnessing through an appropriate life-style. We must, therefore, be especially careful not to compete with those religions – for example, the New Age Movement or certain other 'new' religions – that simply confirm the negative aspects of modernity such as its self-centredness, its moral permissiveness, and materialistic drive for cease-less consumption. Jesus calls us to prophetic ministry in which we present him as Lord, thereby condemning all the false idols of our age which demand final and ultimate allegiance for themselves. God does not call Christians, whether individually or congregationally, to success as the world counts success but to radical faithfulness to Jesus Christ. True blessedness comes from obedience to God and not from the rewards of the modern world.

Jesus Christ is the evangelist to the modern and postmodern world. God loves modern people and desires their salvation. Against the hollow world of modernity, Jesus Christ offers true life, blessedness, and everlasting purpose, value, and significance. Evangelism among modern people is not easy. A relativistic and pluralistic environment tempts many people to go 'shopping' for a religion 'that meets their needs'. Modern people often do not hesitate to combine various religions into a mix that elevates themselves to the centre of value and meaning. And yet they do hesitate to acknowledge any Lord beyond their own egoistic demand for gratification. Therefore God calls his church to that ministry of evangelism in which we proclaim and affirm that Jesus Christ is Lord and that the confession of Jesus as Lord brings us to the very heart of salvation.

III. THE UNIQUE CHRIST AND POLITICAL IDEOLOGIES

The modern world has been the arena of competing ideologies and utopian dreams.

A. Positive Byproducts of Ideology in the Modern World

We recognize that the terms, 'ideology' and 'utopia,' primarily carry negative connotations. But we also recognize that the struggle of ideologies has had some positive byproducts. In particular, they have provided analyses of society's problems so that improvement becomes an option. Utopian dreams have provided alternative visions by which to measure and test the justice and desirability of current political and economic arrangements.

B. Jesus Christ as the Answer to Ideology

The collapse of Marxist and socialist political systems in the former Soviet Union and eastern European spotlights the earlier collapse of their sustaining ideologies. The disillusionment with these ideologies, while long obvious to those living there, has now become self-evident throughout the world.

We are hesitant however to offer uncritical support to the victorious ideologies of capitalism, individualism, and pluralism. All ideologies have an inner tendency to become idolatrous. This is because they deal with our personal, familial, and national well-being, where this well-being is constantly under pressure from the uncontrollable events of history and from the threat of economic insecurity. To guarantee their own well-being, people are always tempted to give final and unqualified loyalty to political, economic, and national 'saviours'. Against the idolization of any ideology, political system, or economic scheme, we affirm the supreme Lordship of Jesus Christ. We affirm that the gospel of Jesus Christ is not an ideology; rather to preach the gospel is to proclaim what God has done and will continue to do for us. We also affirm that just as religions cannot save us, even less can political systems or economic plans save us, whether or not they are called 'ideological' or 'utopian'. Only God can save us. We further affirm that only Jesus Christ can give meaning to history and that the cross and resurrection of Jesus Christ reveal the final goal and outcome of history, which is the kingdom of God in its fullness. Lastly, we affirm that Jesus Christ gives us access to knowledge of reality and that the Bible gives us a standard by which to correct self-deception, ideologies, and utopias.

C. Jesus Christ as the Norm by which to Uncover the Ideological Distortions in Our Work as Christian Leaders

In addition to being the standard by which to correct ideologies and utopias in the political and economic areas, God's revelation in Jesus Christ is also the standard by which we should examine our own Christian work. One benefit of the modern discussion of ideology is to alert us to the distortions that creep into our theology, preaching, church administration, and teaching from our economic, nationalistic, political, and even psychological interests. These interests are often hidden from ourselves as much as from other people. No person can claim total freedom from their distorting effects. Thus in relation to these interests, there is a kind of limitation to our preaching and theology. Christian leaders from different cultures need each other to correct the distortions from their own interests.

As proclaimers of the gospel, we claim only a provisional certainty. The certainty comes from the gospel of Jesus Christ which is truly present in our Christian witness and proclamation. The provisionality comes from our fallibility as human beings. Thus we affirm not ourselves but God's act in Jesus Christ which is sure and certain, without any distortion or limitation of class, economic, or social interest, and the only basis for the salvation of the whole world.

IV.   THE UNIQUE CHRIST IN THE CHURCH'S DIVERSITY AND UNITY

God has gifted the Christian church with a legitimate unity and a legitimate diversity. The church's unity and diversity can, however, both be corrupted by sin.

A. The Church

We understand the church to be the company of those who are born again through personal faith in Jesus Christ, are brought by the Holy Spirit into fellowship both with God and with other Christians, and who are sanctified, empowered, and gifted for witness, service, worship and mutual strengthening in the name of the Lord. The church is the body of Christ, his bride, and the community of the Spirit. The church is called to be a witness of the resurrection of Jesus Christ and to be a sign of the kingdom of God in which people from all the diverse nations and tribes in creation will join together in mutual acceptance, love, affirmation, and everlasting praise of God. All who have faith in Jesus Christ are thereby a part of Christ's church, and God expects them to participate – except in cases where this is physically impossible – in some local congregation. Just as it is natural for fish to swim in water, so it is natural for Christians to live in the community of Christians.

B. The Theological Foundations of Church's Unity and Diversity

The church's proper unity and diversity reflect the perfect harmony of unity and diversity within the Triune God himself. Unity and diversity are further rooted in the goodness of God's creation in which the many different kinds of creatures are all called to join in a polyphonous praise of God. It is also the example of the early church and explicitly taught in scripture (e.g., 1 Cor. 12).

The person and work of Jesus Christ, both in his historical existence as God's supreme act and in his universal rule and authority, give the church its unity. In part, this unity in Christ may be described by the following affirmations: God calls all congregations, and groups of congregations, to join in confessing Jesus Christ – true God and true man, made incarnate and sacrificed for our sins, and resurrected from the dead by God's power – as Lord and Saviour. The congregations are called to acknowledge that God provides salvation only through Jesus Christ and that this salvation can be appropriated only through faith by God's own grace.

The church also recognizes the Hebrew Bible and the New Testament as the only norm and source for its knowledge of Jesus Christ. As Christian congregations we are to proclaim the gospel of Jesus Christ both inside the Christian community through preaching, teaching, and Bible study as well as outside the Christian community in evangelism and witness. As Christian congregations, we are to stand in solidarity with other Christ-centred congregations throughout the world, especially those living in persecution and great need. We are to join with other Christian groups in service, both in word and deed, to our neighbours. The church includes not only individual believers, but also congregations, and ultimately all Christ-centred congregations. And as Christian congregations, we are called to acknowledge that the same Holy Spirit operates throughout all Christian congregations, and associations of congregations, where this Holy Spirit always and everywhere points only to Jesus Christ and where this Holy Spirit brings us through Jesus Christ to the one God our Father.

The church's diversity, grounded and rooted in the nature of God and in the goodness of his creation, will be reflected in the many languages and cultures in which the church ministers. Given the cultural, psychological, and historically diverse contexts of ministry, the church will legimately display a variety of worship styles, a variety of activities in congregational and denominational life, a variety of modes of witness, and a variety of forms of service. We expect, respect, and celebrate such types of diversity among congregations.

C. The Sinful Disruption of the Church's Unity and Diversity

We acknowledge that individual Christians, congregations, and groups of congregations have sinned by allowing false forms of unity and diversity to disturb the peace of the church and the effectiveness of its witness to Jesus Christ. Whenever we admit persons to church membership, or grant positions of leadership, on the basis of economic status, race, ethnic group, or social status, we have placed the unity of the church somewhere else than in the person and work of Jesus Christ and we have created unnecessary and unbiblical divisions within the church. Likewise whenever we claim that all congregations and denominations must follow one particular worship style, one particular pattern of organization or ministry, or one particular way of organizing congregational life, we maintain neither true unity nor true diversity. Lastly, whenever the church accepts and sustains such things as injustice, ignorance, and repression of the innocent, it again loses both its proper unity and its proper diversity.

D. The Church's Allegiance to Christ as Lord Takes Priority Over, and Relativizes All other Loyalties and Relations

God calls Christians to affirm and contribute to the life of the nation, tribe, cultural, or ethnic group in which they live. At the same time, however, it is important to remember that nations and empires, tribes and peoples, can become idolatrous when they are allowed to take priority over Jesus Christ. The life of each congregation, especially as it gathers to worship, must be open to people from outside the local community. It should never be the case that a congregation celebrates its national or ethic identity in such a way that it would be impossible for a Christian visitor from another country to participate in good conscience in their worship and life.

A particular point of concern is cooperation with other religions. It may happen that local Christians conclude that a neighbouring religion forms such a tight-knit pattern that cooperation with that religion at any level is impossible. It may also happen, however, that local Christians identify some aspect of the neighbouring religions – perhaps its service to the poor or its defence of freedom of religion – in which they can freely participate without compromising the Lordship of Jesus Christ.

Before proceeding with such cooperation, however, two conditions must be met. First, the local people, whether Christian or not, should clearly understand that to participate in those specific activities with the neighbouring religions would not affirm any claims to salvation apart from Jesus Christ. Second, the local Christians must be concerned for Christians in other cultures and regions as well. That is, joint participation in activities with the other religions must be of such a character that they are easily explainable to Christians from other countries. The unity of the Body of Christ requires such a concern for the conscience of other Christians.

E. Summary

We affirm the church's unity in and through its head, Jesus Christ. We affirm and celebrate the diversity that God has given within his church. We understand the church's confession of Jesus Christ as the only basis for the salvation of the world as providing the context for the legitimate range of diversity within the church.

V.   THE UNIQUE CHRIST FOR PEACE AND JUSTICE

The cry for peace and justice echoes loudly in our modern world, as it did in Jesus' own generation, and as it does in every age.

A. The Biblical Content of Christ's Peace and Justice

In our eagerness to affirm that Jesus Christ alone gives us the foundation, norm, and goal of all peace and justice, we must carefully watch the content with which those terms are filled in different secular, religious, and biblical contexts.

In a sense, Jesus did not come to give peace but a sword and to set a mother against her daughter and a father against his son (Matt. 10:34–36). In another sense, Jesus gives peace to his disciples, but a different peace from that which the world gives (Jn. 14:27). We must learn the content of Christ's peace from reflecting on the peace which he created on the cross, from Jesus' teachings on the kingdom of God, from the apostle's teachings on the peace of God in Christ, and from the entire biblical revelation of God's shalom. Likewise, the atonement on the cross, the promised judgment, and the proclamation of forgiveness of sins give us our basic understanding of Christian justice.

We affirm that the unique Christ, through his specific actions on the cross outside the city walls of Jerusalem and through his resurrection three days later, provides the deepest and ultimate foundation for peace and justice. We affirm that God calls those whom he has justified through faith in his Son to become a peaceable community in which justice reigns. We further affirm that because the risen, living Christ has universal authority and power, his peace and justice are meant for all people and even for all creation.

In our current situation, it is important to note that one way Christ provides peace and justice is by making possible community with God and with other people as well as by making possible harmony with nature. (Harmony with nature does not mean worship of nature or the gods of nature; rather harmony with nature means the careful stewardship of nature so as to support humanity's God-given needs and so as to preserve the beauty, goodness, and variety with which God endowed nature as he formed it.)

B. The Church as the New Man

Paul teaches (Eph. 2:11–22) that Jesus Christ so unites both Jews and Gentiles in himself, that is, in his body which is the Church, that the two become 'one new man'. This makes peace. And it is as a community, consisting of Jews and Gentiles together, that we are reconciled through the cross to God.

We affirm that because God intends the church to include both Jew and Gentile. God also intends the church to include people from different ethnic and cultural heritages. The church as the complete body of Christ will eventually include members from every people, tongue, and tribe, living in harmony and praising God and his Christ. Each congregation, therefore, must always be open to people from any background.

In this context, we re-affirm the legitimate diversity, grounded in the goodness of God's creation, of different cultural and linguistic groups. This affirmation has an important implication for congregational life. We note that different congregations, therefore, are not obligated to share the same culture. For example, in regions where diverse people groups live side-by-side, local congregations may well worship in different languages. In such a situation, it is important that each congregation maintains an urgent sense of mission for those outside its own linguistic boundaries. It may not be possible for one congregation – especially a monocultural congregation in a multi-cultural area – to express the church's rich diversity as well as its precious unity. It may require groups of congregations to express adequately the opulent multiplicity of Christ's body. We welcome, however, those creative attempts to unite diverse linguistic and cultural groups within a single congregational structure even while maintaining opportunities for worship, fellowship, and service for each group.

C. The People of God as Light and Salt

We affirm that Christians are to be both models (light) as well as agents (salt) of peace and justice. God calls his church to be a witness to the peace of his kingdom. This means that congregations should demonstrate in their own life the reconciling power of Jesus Christ. We sadly confess that congregations and denominations have too often failed in this witness, presenting instead sinful spectacles of strife feuds between families, intolerance, selfishness, and power-grabbing. Nonetheless, we joyfully acknowledge that at other times the Spirit of God has given his church the capacity for peaceful living and that this has been light to the world.

The church is also to be salt. The sheer existence of the church, living in Christ as light to the world, can be an agent for change. This was often true in Marxist countries, where the mere presence of the Christian church declared the reality of God's grace; and in the remaining Marxist regimes, the existence of Christian congregations continues to provide an alternative standard of true justice and the basis for a lively hope. We pray that the existence of church may also be salt in those Islamic and other countries that are officially closed to the gospel. And in places where the church is not persecuted or hindered from evangelism, the church's demonstration of the peace of Christ within its own life may be the salt that encourages greater justice in the larger world.

D. Peace, Justice, and the Future Kingdom of God

It is important not to confuse particular political, social, or economic plans for greater peace and justice with God's promises of perfect peace and justice for his future Kingdom at the end of history. Otherwise, disappointed hopes stirred up by idealistic Christians and Christian groups might turn people away from the gospel and do harm to Christianity as a whole. The church, therefore, is not to 'sanctify' any one political, economic, or social system, because no such system brings salvation and because all such systems can become ideological and repressive. The church recognizes only Jesus Christ as her Lord, and she will not be captive to any system.

We also affirm that some political, economic, and social systems are better than others – that is, more just and more conducive to peace. We affirm the right of all Christians and the obligation of those Christians with the appropriate opportunities, to work with others, individually and in voluntary groups, for provisional visions of peace and justice at particular times and places. When Christians do so, and when they offer their labours to the Lord Jesus, their work for peace and justice becomes worship of our God and of his unique Christ.

VI. THE UNIQUE CHRIST AS THE HOPE AND JUDGE OF THE WORLD

We affirm that Jesus Christ is the hope and judge of the world. He is the hope and judge both in his particularity and in his universality.

A. The Particularity of Christ as God's Own Act in History

Jesus Christ is not merely an image, symbol, idea, or cosmic power, but a particular, historical figure who lived, died, and was resurrected at a datable time and locatable place.

Second, Jesus Christ is God's own action in space and time. Jesus not only has that particularity that attaches to any historical event or figure, but he has a decisive particularity because he is God's own, supreme, unrepeatable, and normative act in history. In Jesus Christ, the medium of revelation (God's action in Jesus Christ) is the content of revelation (God himself). And just as God is one, so his particular revelation in Jesus Christ is one. The gospel of Jesus Christ is not a good idea, or a good experience, but good news. Or, to be more precise, the Christian gospel teaches good ideas and it leads to good experiences only because it is first the good news of what God has done in Jesus of Nazareth.

B. The Universality of Christ's Authority and Significance

The unique Christ, however has universal significance. In the Bible, God uses particular, historical, and factual means – such as his call of Abraham, his speaking through Moses, and his election of Israel – to make his salvation universally available to people in their concrete situations, in their real existence. Thus the historical-factual foundation of God's action in Jesus Christ has an existential-universal application to the salvation of all people, and even of all creation.

C. The Theology of Christian Hope and Judgement

We thus affirm that the unique Jesus Christ brings hope to all people. This hope has many dimensions. Jesus alone provides the basis for the forgiveness of sins of all people and their reconciliation with the Father; Jesus alone offers eternal life to all people; Jesus alone enables true community (the kingdom of God and the church to the extent that it witnesses to that kingdom) to which he invites all people to participate; and Jesus alone inaugurates God's sovereign rule over all creation (the kingdom of God) which he himself will complete at a particular time in the future.

We also affirm, on the same basis, that Jesus Christ is the judge of the world. This judgement has many dimensions reflecting God's rejection of all forms of sin, of all that alienates people from himself and from each other, of all that destroys his creation, and of all that thwarts his purposes for the world. This judgment is both in the present and also a particular event in the future. Jesus did not come into the world to condemn the world, but to redeem it. But without Christ, we are judged and condemned, both now and on the future day of judgment.

The Bible indicates that the final day of judgment will be a day of surprises.

This should be a warning to Christians not to usurp God's prerogative as judge. Our role as Christians is not to condemn others but to proclaim Jesus Christ. At the same time, we must remember that proclaiming Jesus Christ has an eternal significance.

When the gospel is preached, God offers Jesus Christ to those who hear the gospel. And a person's acceptance or rejection of Jesus Christ results in eternal hope or judgement. We also must remember that the Bible does not teach that the day of judgement will be a day of surprises in order to destroy the confidence of those who humbly trust Jesus but to warn against our presuming upon grace and against our hardness of heart towards other people.

D. Christ as the Hope and Judge in Relation to Other Religions

Christ's role as hope and judge not only extends to future events but also includes his sovereignty over all religions. God's revelation in Jesus Christ, as recorded in the Bible, is decisive and normative for our understanding of other religions. To the extent that the religious confirm God's revelation in Jesus Christ, Christ functions as a negative norm. In addition, however, the religions teach many things neither the same as nor in conflict with Jesus Christ. Here, Christ functions as an invitation and guide to inquiry. Here, the insights of the other religions can augment, enrich, enlarge, and deepen our own Christian insight.

We face a tension in this matter. We affirm that it is Christ, as recorded in scripture, who functions as the decisive norm and not merely our understanding of Christ. At the same time, when we interact with people of other religions, or with their teachings and practices, we necessarily bring not only Christ but also our understanding of Christ. Therefore we must depend, constantly and humbly, on the guidance of the Holy Spirit. In addition, we may discover that such interactions with people of other faiths actually correct our understanding of the real message and identity of Jesus. Genuine friendship with people of other faiths and genuine study of their teachings will place our limited understandings of Jesus and the Bible at risk. We should welcome such corrections. We affirm, however, that when such corrections are needed, they are needed because of our human failings and not because of any deficiency in Jesus Christ or in the biblical witness to him.

In short, our discussions with people of other faiths can impact our Christian commitments in two ways. First, in those areas which scripture leaves open, we may find helpful insights in other religions and philosophies which augment our previous understandings. Second, even in those areas where the biblical revelation directly speaks, it may be that our understanding is limited or faulty, and discussions with people of other faiths may have a role in correcting our misunderstanding. We affirm, however, that as our understanding of Jesus grows, he will function ever more effectively as our positive and negative norm (as hope and judge) and as our invitation and guide to exploration with people of other faiths.

The legitimate insights of people of other faiths will come from God's work in and through creation (general revelation, common grace) and from the work of the Holy Spirit. However, because God created the world through his Word, and because the Holy Spirit is the Spirit of Jesus who, always and everywhere, points to Jesus Christ, we affirm that Jesus Christ is the centre, ground, norm, and goal of all religious insight and knowledge. In addition we affirm that the universal message of Christ is essentially dependent on the historical Jesus Christ who, in his particularity, is the very act of God and that therefore it is not appropriate to refer to the Christ principle in other religions, or to the cosmic Christ, or to the hidden Christ, or to the unnamed Christ except in connection with and in dependence on Jesus of Nazareth.

Part One

The Unique Christ in the Plurality of Religions

3

Chris Wright

Dr. Wright gives a masterly and incisive analysis of the issues in the contemporary theological debate on the uniqueness of Christ. He builds a solid foundation for his response on the Old Testament analysis of the human predicament and its solution; the uniqueness of Israel in God's purpose to redeem the nations; and the fulfilment of the uniqueness of Yahweh in Jesus Christ, the promised Messiah.

In this chapter I shall confine my response to two areas of the current inter-religious debate: some critical remarks on religious pluralism, and some biblical perspectives on the uniqueness of Christ which are not often aired in the debate.

THE CASE AGAINST PLURALISM

The debate on the relationship between Christianity and the other world religions has been shaped around three terms that are said to encompass the range of opinion on the matter: exclusivism, inclusivism and pluralism.[1] Nobody is entirely happy with this spectrum. Among evangelicals, who are usually labelled *exclusivist*, there are quite sharp divisions between those who, for example, would argue that no human being can be saved apart from explicit knowledge of and faith in Jesus Christ, and others who, while affirming that salvation is only through Christ, leave open the possibility that God in his grace will save some who have never heard of Christ yet turn to God in some kind of repentance and trust. Among *inclusivists*, there are those who affirm a degree of divine revelation among those of other faiths, but deny that anyone is saved through them, while others would see the saving work of Christ present in hidden and anonymous ways in those other faiths. Neverthe-less, the triple distinction is useful in providing some kind of classification for the sake of the discussion, provided it is recognized that some participants sit uncomfortably in the gaps or overlaps between the three categories. In my view the major and most critical divide is between exclusivist-inclusivist on the one hand and *pluralists* on the other. It seem to me possible for

Dr. Chris Wright is Principal of All Nations Christian College, Ware, England.

fundamental loyalty to the uniqueness and finality of Christ to be held sincerely along with views that could place one at different points between exclusivism and inclusivism, but the shift of pluralism requires either a complete surrender of the uniqueness of Christ or such a radical redefinition of it that it loses all value.

It needs to be said at the outset that the word 'pluralism' is here being used in a strictly theological sense. It should not be confused with sociological plurality. Christians in the West now find themselves living alongside communities of other faiths. They are thus experiencing the kind of plurality of religions that has been a fact of life, of course, for most non-Western Christian communities for centuries. It is perhaps typical of the 'blinkered' nature of Western Christianity that Western theologians tend to imagine that what is a new experience for them is a new phenomenon in the history of Christianity itself when in fact it is as old as the New Testament. But neither changing social patterns, nor increasing and improved factual knowledge about other faiths, can change the objective truths of God's revelation. They may (indeed should) change our perceptions, our theological expressions, and our forms of relating to those of other faiths. But the truth (or otherwise) of the claim that Jesus of Nazareth was unique both as God incarnate and as the only Saviour is not subject to modification merely because of changes in the social and religious contexts in which Christians happen to live in each generation. Either Jesus was God and still is, or he is not God and never has been. It is this theological issue we are concerned about here.

Definition of Pluralism

Exclusivist and inclusivist scholars have in common that they wish to be 'Christocentric', that is, they want to preserve the centrality and normative-ness of Christ himself. More recently some scholars have begun to push much further and to advocate what they call a 'theocentric' theology of religions. That is to say, they want us to see *God* at the centre of the religious universe, not Christ or Christianity. Now this is not merely syncretism. Syncretism is the desire to blend and unite the best in all world religions into one future composite world faith. Syncretism recognizes that certain features of every religion will be incompatible with some features of others, and thus seeks to remove or minimize those incompatible elements and unite what is compatible. Pluralism, on the other hand, is content to accept the validity and complementarity of all the faiths as different responses to the one 'Ultimate Divine Reality'. Even apparent contradictions between different faiths can be seen as merely the result of our human limitations – we simply cannot grasp the whole truth. So it is not necessary to try to resolve those contradictions, or to decide which is true and which is false, for they can all be 'true' at some more profound level of reality not yet understood by us. It is a basic premise of pluralism that no single religious tradition can claim to have or to be 'the truth'.

Alan Race offers the following definition of pluralism:

> . . . the belief that there is not one, but a number of spheres of saving contact between God and man. God's revealing and redeeming activity has elicited response in a number of culturally conditioned ways throughout history. Each

response is partial, incomplete, unique; but they are related to each other in that they represent different culturally focused perceptions of the one ultimate divine reality.[2]

Salvation is thus to be found in any or all faiths, including Christianity but not confined to it. Christ and Christianity, instead of being the centre of the saving and revealing work of God, 'go into orbit' along with other faiths, as one among many planetary responses to the gravitational pull of the sun of divine reality at the centre.

This astronomical metaphor is derived from the leading British exponent of this approach to other faiths, namely John Hick. Hick proposes a 'Copernican Revolution' in theology. It took an enormous adjustment for humanity (and especially the church) to be weaned from the apparently obvious 'fact' that the earth stands at the centre of the universe, surrounded by other moving heavenly bodies, to accept the actual truth that the earth, along with other spinning planets is revolving around the sun at the centre of our solar system. It was no easy thing to accept our own relativity. Similarly, says Hick, it is not easy, but nevertheless essential, for Christians to see that while Jesus Christ may be central for themselves, he is not the centre of the religious universe. Only God is that. Christ is only one among others who have borne valid witness to the divine reality.

> We have to realize that the universe of faiths centres upon *God* and not upon Christianity or any other religion. He is the sun, the originative source of light and life, whom all the religions reflect in their different ways.[3]

Critique of Pluralism

My criticisms of pluralism are directed at its implications regarding God, Jesus, the New Testament and the Christian church itself.

i) An Abstract God

Hick proposes that the church has moved from exclusive 'ecclesiocentrism' (the church at the centre of all salvation) to inclusive 'Christocentrism' (Christ is normative, but he has revealed and/or saved in other religions also). Now we should adopt pluralist 'theocentrism' (neither Christ nor the church at the centre, but only God). However, one marked feature of this conceptual revolution is that the *theos* who is finally left at the centre becomes utterly abstract. Clearly 'he' cannot be identified or named in terms of any specific deity known within the different world faiths, for they are all only partial responses to *theos*. So one finds that the 'sun at the centre' is given other 'names' which are in fact an absence of definition: 'Ultimate Divine Reality' is Hick's favourite. 'Ultimate Truth and Perfection' is another. 'Transcendent Being', or even simply, 'The Real' are others. Furthermore, by using this kind of language you can avoid deciding whether *theos* is personal or impersonal. This is very convenient, but is it likely to meet human perceived need for salvation? Most ordinary people find the abstract conceptualizing of philosophers rather difficult to understand, still less to believe in for their salvation. As Newbigin has put it so strongly, on what grounds are we compelled to believe that an impersonal or undefinable abstraction is a more worthy claimant for the centre of the religious universe than a known person who stands revealed in recorded history? Or that faith in the existence of such a concept is a more reliable starting point for truth-discovering dialogue with other faiths than commitment to a personal God in Christ?[4]

Furthermore, we can point to an epistemological contradiction in the pluralist position. They argue that God cannot be identified with any of the 'names' in various religions, including Christ. Nevertheless, they tend to attribute to their Ultimate Divine Reality some characteristics which are decidedly derived from the Christian tradition. But how do they *know*? Harold Netland has pointed out this problem very clearly.

> Knitter's theocentrism presupposes that we have significant knowledge of God – what he is like and what he expects from humankind – apart from any reference to Jesus Christ. For God is now said to be the norm by which we judge the significance of Jesus. But what then is the source of this other knowledge of God? . . . Knitter offers no clue as to the epistemological source of theocentric theology. . . . If Christ no longer defines what we mean by God, then where do theocentrists get their idea of God? It is difficult to escape the impression that Knitter's God, while ostensibly severed ontologically from the person of Jesus and functioning as an independent norm by which we are to understand Jesus, is actually in significant measure derived from the New Testament picture of Jesus.[5]

In other words, pluralism is parasitic. It presupposes and feeds on the very tradition it undermines.

ii) A Relativized Christ

It seems to me to be impossible, within the framework of the New Testament, to be theocentric without being Christocentric. Some scholars, however, try to drive a wedge between the fact that Jesus preached the kingdom of *God* (i.e. a theocentric proclamation), and the fact that the church, faced with the apparent failure or delay of that kingdom, preached *Jesus*, thus shifting to a Christocentric proclamation which has taken over as the church's dominant position. But the kingdom of God as preached by Jesus, centred on himself. In fact it was because he so persistently put himself at the centre of his teaching about God and his kingdom that he aroused such hostility. There was nothing at all scandalous about being theocentric in Jewish society! But for a man to claim that scriptures concerning the future work of God were fulfilled in himself, that he had power to forgive sins, that he was Lord over the Sabbath, that he was the Son of Man to whom eternal dominion would be given, and many other such claims, was tantamount to blasphemy – unless it was true.

Likewise the first Jewish Christians, as monotheists, already lived in a thoroughly theocentric universe, but with considerable struggle and personal cost, they deliberately put their contemporary, Jesus of Nazareth, at that centre in the crucial affirmation 'Jesus is Lord'. That did not mean that they had given up or even diluted their theocentrism. Rather, their faith in God at the centre was now filled out, redefined, and proclaimed in the light of their encounter with God in the person and action of Jesus the Christ. The whole New Testament is the deposit of the process and struggle by which the God-centred faith of the Old Testament scriptures was seen to be Christ-centred in reality (as we shall see in Part II).

Following from the above point, it seems to me that the pluralist view cannot be reconciled with authentic Christianity, because to relativize Jesus Christ is to deny him. If the New Testament is taken even as a reasonably reliable source, then it is unquestionable that Jesus made some astounding and absolute claims for himself. It is equally clear that his immediate followers in the early Christian church made similar claims concerning him, both explicitly in their preaching, and implicitly in their worship and prayer through his name. So, since biblical and historical Christianity makes such affirmations about Jesus, it follows that whatever kind of 'Christianity' is put into orbit around the 'sun of ultimate divine reality', it is not the 'Christianity' of Christ and his apostles.

Now, pluralists will reply that Jesus remains central for *Christians*, and as such, Jesus is the distinctive Christian gift to the inter-religious dialogue, once he has been freed from absolute claims to uniqueness or finality. Jesus is decisive for those who have chosen to follow him, but not in any universal sense for others. Thus Race says, 'Jesus is "decisive", not because he is the focus of all the light everywhere revealed in the world, but for the vision he has brought in one cultural setting . . . Jesus would still remain central for the Christian faith.'[8]

Another way of making this point is to say that while *Jesus* is *the* name for Christians, '*Christ*' may have other names in other faiths and cultures. This is the view of the Indian scholar R. Panikkar. He argues that Christ is not less than Jesus of Nazareth, but at the same time the Christian cannot say that Christ is only Jesus, for that reduces the Divine Mystery to being exhaustively present in Jesus of Nazareth. Each 'authentic name' enriches and qualifies that mystery. Others may call the mediator of the mystery Yahweh, Krishna, Allah or Buddah; for the Christian it can only be Christ, but this Christ must not be encapsulated in the historical Jesus of Nazareth. Jesus is Lord for Christians, but 'Christ is "the name above all names"'.[7] We thus end up with a kind of universalized Christ but a relativized Jesus. But this is in stark contrast to the actual affirmation of the New Testament in the text which is misused and misquoted by Panikkar. For it is precisely *Jesus* who is given the name that is above every name, 'that at the name of *Jesus* every knee should bow, in heaven and on earth and under the earth, and every tongue confess that *Jesus* Christ is Lord to the glory of God the Father' (Phil. 2:9–11).

One has to probe further yet and ask what kind of 'gift to inter-faith dialogue' this relativized Jesus actually is. If Jesus Christ was not God incarnate, if he was not the final revelation of God and the completion of God's saving work for humanity, if he is not the risen and reigning Lord, then we are faced with two possibilities. Either Jesus himself was mistaken in the claims he made concerning himself (if the New Testament is to be believed), in which case he was either sadly deluded or an arrogant imposter, but certainly not a worthy religious figure whom we can bring to the dialogue table with any confidence. Or, the Church from its earliest period (including the generation of Jesus' own contemporaries) has grossly misinterpreted him, misunderstood his claims, and exaggerated his importance. The pluralist requires us therefore to accept that the Church throughout its history has thus propagated, lived by, and based all its hope upon, a massive self-deluded untruth. A deluded Jesus or a deluded Church, or both. Such seems to be the unavoidable implication of the pluralists' insistence on relativizing Jesus.

The dismal results of this view are quickly clear. A.G. Hunter, for example, arguing for a human Jesus, divinized only by the Church and trinitized at Chalcedon, boldly affirms that it was 'psychologically and religiously impossible for Jesus [to have claimed divinity] and it is historically false to say that he did.'[8] Such confident negative dogmatism about the 'historical' Jesus produces equally negative uncertainty about his value for faith: 'What emerges,' Hunter concludes, 'is that though we are agreed that Jesus is at the heart of our faith as Christians, it is hard to find any clear consensus as to the precise delineation of his importance.'[9] If such paralysed agnosticism is all we are left with, is it worth contributing to the dialogue at all? If, as pluralists urge, we have to relativize Jesus before we can come to the dialogue, then we had better not come at all for we have nothing to come with except a repentant confession that we belong to a worldwide faith which throughout the whole of its history has had an illusion and a falsehood at its fundamental heart and core.

iii) A Mythologised New Testament

Because the pluralist position cannot be reconciled with the New Testament on any face-value reading of it, it can be deemed a 'Christian' option only by means of a radical re-interpretation of central New Testament teaching in terms of *myth*. Many scholars (and not only evangelical ones) have exposed the weakness of the myth school of interpretation, so I want only to add a few points relevant to this issue.

First, commitment to a mythic interpretation of the New Testament affirmations about Jesus rules out *a priori* the possibility of the New Testament writers ever asserting anything ontological about him (that is about who and what he actually *is* in his own being). It is presupposed that everything they asserted about his person or nature is to be taken as myth, relating only to his function and his relationship to them (the NT authors) or to us. But supposing that those early witnesses to Jesus actually did wish, consciously and deliberately, to make ontological statements about Jesus, believing them to be not merely figures of speech but transcendently true (even when all allowance has been made for the inadequacy of all human language)? The mythic interpreter will simply not be listening, for he has already decided in advance that all such statements cannot be taken as descriptions of any objective reality (what Jesus truly *is*), but only as subjective, confessional, 'love-language' (What Jesus *means to me*).

Second, this mythic interpretation seems to me historically faulty in not distinguishing between the world of known first-century mythical religions and the strongly historical affirmations of the early Christians about Jesus of Nazareth. It is often asserted that the first Christian witnesses had no other way of expressing what Jesus had meant for them or what they believed he had done for them, except through the medium of the mythical world-view of their day. Their apparently ontological language is simply the way such understandings would naturally and culturally have been expressed in mythical categories. I find this unconvincing. The first-century world was awash with a plurality of mythical and mystical religions, but the New

Testament preachers and writers made their assertions about Jesus and his unique significance on the solid basis of *historical events* witnessed and attested by contemporaries who knew him. Some of these affirmations were made in quite deliberate opposition to and distinction from the mythical world-views, as is the case in Colossians. It seems quite unrealistic to imagine that Paul, in his ontological affirmations about the historical Jesus in that letter, was countering the whole world of mythic dualism by means of yet another kind of myth.

Thirdly, this mythic re-interpretation ends up allowing its adherent to assert the opposite of what the New Testament actually says, while still claiming to be interpreting the New Testament itself. A fairly typical piece of John Hick's writing should illustrate this. After arguing that the incarnation is a 'a mythological idea, a figure of speech, a piece of poetic imagery', he goes on from that 'insight' to draw the following conclusions:

> When we see the Incarnation as a mythological idea applied to Jesus to express the experienced fact that he is our sufficient, effective and saving point of contact with God, we no longer have to draw the negative conclusion that he is man's one and only effective point of contact with God. We can revere Christ as the one through whom we have found salvation, without having to deny other points of reported saving contact between God and man. We can commend the way of Christian faith without having to discommend other ways of faith. We can say that there is salvation in Christ without having to say that there is no salvation other than in Christ.[10]

But that last point, of course, is precisely what the New Testament *does* say!

iv) An Idolatrous Christianity

Pluralism necessarily aligns itself with a 'Christology from below', as it is sometimes referred to; that is, a purely human Jesus. There are many varieties of this view, but essentially it means that, whatever else Jesus may have been, he was ultimately not more than human. Certainly he was not God incarnate in any ontological sense, however much he may have been the vehicle of God's revelatory and saving work as a man. Many scholars in this camp would allow that Jesus was unique in some sense in the depth of his own relationship with God and the extent to which he mediated God to others including ourselves. But they would see this as a uniqueness of degree, not of essence. God may have been specially present and active through Jesus of Nazareth, but Jesus was not (and therefore is not) God. He cannot stand at the centre of the religious universe but, even in his uniqueness as defined, he must go into orbit around the centre along with other great religious figures who have their own unique features also.

The more I reflect on this view, the more surprised I am how reluctant its advocates seem to be to draw the ultimate conclusion from it, which seems quite inescapable. And that is, that Christianity is, and always has been, the worst form of idolatry ever practised on earth. The most serious charge which Jews and Muslims[11] have levelled against Christians all through the centuries would actually be true: we have elevated a human being to the place of God and have worshipped him there. For that is what we do, and have been doing ever since the book of Acts. We ascribed to Jesus honour and glory that belongs only to God; we call on his name as God; we call him Lord and refuse to acknowledge any other; we apply to him the most solemn scriptures that Israel used concerning Yahweh; we sing praises to him that were sung to Yahweh, and have made up bookfuls of our own. All this we have done for two thousand years but with no justification at all, if the pluralists are right. For if Jesus was no more than a remarkable human being, then the whole Christian faith, Christian church and all the generations of Christian worship have been one monstrous, deluded idolatry.

Sometimes such things are best perceived by those who stand outside the Christian fold and observe with some incredulity what apparently Christian intellects are doing to their own religion. So we conclude this section with a comment from the Jewish scholar E.G. Borowitz on the mania to 'universalize' Christ, by seeing him in any and every human religious endeavour and by loosing him from the mooring of the hard historical particularity of the biblical witness to Jesus. He quotes the view of Dawe that Christians now see in Christ 'the fullest disclosure of the relationship of God to the fulfilment of human existence', and then comments:

> But when done translating Christhood into humanization, no particular truth, no special claim attaches to Jesus, the Christ, or to Christians. Instead, again and again we hear that wherever new being generates human fulfilment; wherever life is renewed and virtue expressed, one has the equivalent of the Christian's Christ. Thus, such truth as Christianity has is universal. What is particular about Christianity has been relegated to a second, perhaps valuable, but certainly not essential, level of truth and value . . . But Christianity itself has not previously authorized this emptying out of its particularity . . . To humanize Christianity, he has made it dispensable . . . Would there be any *theological* loss if Christianity should disappear as an identifiable religion?[12]

So we arrive at the end of the pluralists' road. At best, Christ becomes so universal as to be of no real value except as a symbol. At worst, he is exposed as an idol for those who worship him, and as dispensable by those who don't.

SCRIPTURAL PERSPECTIVES ON CHRIST'S UNIQUENESS

Many discussions about the significance of Jesus Christ within the context of world religions virtually cut him off from his historical and scriptural roots and speak of him as the founder of a new religion. Now, of course, if by that is meant merely that Christianity has historically become a separate religion from Judaism, that may be superficially true. But certainly Jesus has no intention of launching another 'religion' as such. Who Jesus was and what he had come to do were both already long prepared for through God's dealings with Israel and their scriptures. It is from the Hebrew Bible that we will gain the richest insight into Jesus' own self-understanding, his sense of identity and his motivating mission, because that is where he himself drew these things from. Indeed, without the Old Testament you cannot understand Jesus since it was the basis of how he understood himself.[13] That is where we must begin if we are to get our view of his uniqueness straight also. Out of all the points one could raise from the riches of the Hebrew Bible, I wish to highlight three.[14]

The Nature of Sin and Salvation[15]

The Bible begins by setting out the basic stage upon which the whole drama of earthly history is played – namely the creation framework of God, the earth, and the human race, each integrally related to the other. It then goes on to show how all three relationships within this framework – between God and humanity, God and the earth and the earth to humanity – have been fractured and distorted by evil. The account of the human rebellion, in its profound simplicity, in Genesis 3, and the following narratives up to the Tower of Babel, in Genesis 11, portray a world in which everything has gone wrong. Human beings are estranged from God and driven from his presence. The earth is subjected to God's curse and resists the dominion and stewardship of humanity. Human beings are in conflict with each other, at every level, from the corruption and inequity of sexual relations since the fall, through family friction, to social arrogance, violence and corruption. Sin entered into and affects every dimension of human life, spiritual, intellectual, physical and social. The result is a world of individuals and nations scattered under God's curse and divided among themselves.

The Hebrew Bible, then, gives us an assessment of the human predicament which is radical and comprehensive in its scope. This means that if God has got any answer it has to be as big as the problem. In other words, it is the Hebrew Bible's realism and honesty about the nature of sin and the reality of judgment which shows us what salvation has to be and that only God can achieve it. If we had space to embark on a full account of the Old Testament concept of salvation, we would indeed find that it too is exceedingly broad and deep – sufficient to cope with all the effects of sin in creation. It is personal and social, spiritual and physical, political and economic, human and ecological, local and cosmic, present and future. God as Saviour meets every dimension of human need, and indeed intends to mend his whole creation. Thus, when we bring the Bible to bear on the issue of different religious claims, the first thing that happens is that we are prevented from peddling facile and superficial concepts of salvation because it shows up the depth and scale of human need and guilt and the seriousness of divine judgment.

I find it a frustrating exercise reading the work of religious pluralists because they tend to be so vague and inadequate on what salvation actually *is*. And that in turn seems to me largely because they ignore the Hebrew Bible's insight on the nature and seriousness of sin. Wilfred Cantwell Smith, for example, can speak of God 'saving' through all religions by using phrases like 'enabling a truly moral life', 'living with a more than mundane reference colouring one's goals', 'keeping the forces of despair and meaninglessness at bay'. It is true that salvation in its biblical sense will do all of these, but more as by-products, not as the essence of salvation in itself. Other scholars question or ridicule the idea of a radical fracture in the relationship between God and humanity (the 'fall'). Once that basic problem is overlooked or minimized, then salvation can be whatever you like, depending on your personal or cultural preference as to the solution to other human needs.

One of the best critiques of this vagueness over what salvation is comes from the pen of Carl Braaten, and is worth quoting at length.

Christian theologians are debating the question whether or not there is salvation in other religions, and taking sides on the issue, without first making clear the model of salvation they have in mind. . . . What is the salvation that theologians expect to find or not to find in other religions? Most of the debate so far has taken us nowhere, because vastly different things are meant by salvation. If salvation is whatever you call it, there is no reason for a Christian to deny that there is salvation in other religions . . .

Braaten then goes on to list a whole range of candidates for the label 'salvation', including illumination, union with the divine, revolution, equality, physical health, peace, justice, etc. He shows how all the religions and even the non-religious philosophies of the world have something to offer on these hopes and desires. Certainly also, the biblical teaching on God's saving work includes these dimensions, but they are not the heart of the matter. For the basic problem is alienation from the living and life-giving God resulting in death.

On a theological level salvation is not whatever you want to call it, the fulfilment of every need or the compensation for every lack . . . Salvation in the Bible is a promise that God offers the world on the horizon of our expectation of personal and universal death. The gospel is the power of God unto salvation because it promises to break open the vicious cycle of death . . . We cannot derive a final meaning for life on this side of death. We can gain the partial salvation we are willing to pay for, but none of these techniques of salvation can succeed in buying off death.

Salvation in the New Testament is what God has done to death in the resurrection of Jesus. Salvation is what happens to you and me and the whole world in spite of death . . . The story of salvation is a drama of death and resurrection, whatever other human, personal and social problems the world might take on . . . Since death is what separates the person from God in the end, only that power which transcends death can liberate the person for eternal life with God. This is the meaning of salvation in the biblical Christian sense.

Theologians who speak of salvation in the non-Christian religions should tell us if it is the same salvation that God has promised the world by raising Jesus from the dead. The resurrection gospel is the criterion of the meaning of salvation in the New Testament sense. When Christian enter into dialogue with persons of other religions, they must do their utmost to communicate what they mean by the assertion that Jesus lives and explain how this gospel intersects the hopes and fears of every person whose fate is to anticipate death as the final eschaton . . . A Christology that is silent about the resurrection of Jesus from the dead is not worthy of the Christian name and should not be called Christology at all.[16]

It needs to be pointed out, in case these extracts give a wrong impression, that it is clear from the rest of the context of what Braaten says that he is not peddling a 'pie in the sky when you die' caricature of salvation, i.e. something which counts only after death. He quite agrees that the Bible has plenty to say about the present experience and reality of salvation in this life. Nor does he exclude the physical, social and environmental dimensions of salvation, which are certainly part of the Old Testament's vision of full salvation. But he rightly insists that unless the fundamental alienation of humanity from God which the Bible calls death and attributes to sin, is dealt with, all other aspects of salvation remain ultimately cosmetic. And he rightly emphasizes that the heart of the matter is resurrection – the historical resurrection of Jesus and the promised resurrection to life of those who believe in him. Resurrection is the crowning New Testament answer. I would simply add that it is the Old Testament which properly sets the question.

The Uniqueness of Israel

Having 'set the question' by its description of the human predicament in Genesis 1–11, the Bible goes on to show how God began answering it through the call of Abraham and the creation of Israel as his people, beginning at Genesis 12. God's covenant with Abraham makes it very clear that what God has in mind is blessing for all nations. Having shown that the effects of sin are universal, the narrative now shows us that God's redemptive intention is equally universal. But at the same time, it shows us that the way God chose to achieve that goal was through a very particular historical means – the nation of Israel.

The NT, from Matthew's opening genealogy, affirms that Jesus completed what God had already begun to work out through Israel. Jesus as an historical, particular man has to be understood against the background of an historical, particular people. His uniqueness is linked to theirs. The Bible is quite clear that God's action in and through Israel was unique. Now this *does* not mean that God was in no way involved and active in the histories of other nations. The Old Testament explicitly asserts that he was. (e.g. Amos 9:7; Deut. 2:20–23; Ex. 9: 13–16; Isa. 10:5–19; Jer. 27:5–7; Isa. 44:28–45:13). It does mean that only in Israel did God work within the terms of a covenant of redemption, initiated and sustained by his grace (e.g. Amos 3:2; Deut. 4:32–34; Ps. 147:19f.; Isa. 43: 8–13; Ex. 19:5–6, 20–26; Num. 23:9; Deut. 7:6).

To stress this truth about Israel does not take away from the other truth, namely that God's purpose was ultimately universal in scope. Israel existed at all only because of God's desire to redeem people from every nation. But in his sovereign freedom he chose to do so by this particular and historical means. The tension between the universal goal and the particular means is found throughout the Bible and cannot be reduced to either pole alone. What it comes down to is that, while God has every nation in view in his redemptive purpose, in no other nation did he act as he did in Israel, for the sake of the nations. That was their uniqueness, which can be seen to be both exclusive (no other nation experienced what they did of God's revelation and redemption), and inclusive (they were created, called and set in the midst of the nations for the sake of the nations).

Now when we come to consider Jesus in the light of this double truth, the vitally important fact is that the New Testament presents him to us as the *Messiah*, Jesus the Christ. And the Messiah 'was' Israel. That is, he represented and personified Israel. The Messiah was the completion of all that Israel had been put in the world for – i.e. God's self-revelation and his work of human redemption. For this reason, Jesus shares in the uniqueness of Israel. In fact, he was the whole point and goal of it. What God had been doing through no other nation he now completed through no other person than the Messiah, Jesus of Nazareth. The paradox is that precisely through the narrowing down of his redemptive work to the unique particularity of the single man, Jesus, God opened the way to the universalizing of his redemptive grace to all nations, which was his purpose from the beginning. The fulfilment of Israel's *historical particularity* in Jesus was at the same time the fulfilment of Israel's *eschatological universality*.

It had been a mystery all through the Old Testament ages how God could bring about for Abraham what he had promised him – namely blessing to all nations. Paul saw this clearly and expounds it in Ephesians 2–3 and Galatians 3 especially. What the gentile nations did not have before, because it was at that time limited to Israel, is now available to them in the Messiah Jesus. It is significant how regularly Paul inverts the normal order and puts Christ before Jesus in these passages, precisely because it is the messiahship of Jesus which both fulfils the Old Testament hope of redemption and extends it to include those of any or all nations who are 'in the Messiah' (Gal. 3:14, 26–29; Eph. 2:11–13, 3:4–6). Unquestionably, then, there is an inclusive dimension to Paul's gospel, because of its roots in the Abraham covenant and its promise to 'all nations'. But it is firmly based on an exclusive foundation – only through the Messiah Jesus, just as it had previously been only through Israel. The uniqueness of Jesus is thus bound to the uniqueness of Israel.

It is not surprising therefore that scholars who want to relativize Jesus or modify his uniqueness are embarrassed by the Old Testament. They either ignore it altogether, which allows them to talk of 'Christ' in vague and universal terms while talking of 'Jesus' as only one manifestation among others. In doing so, they tear apart the indivisible historical unity of 'The Messiah Jesus'.[17] Or they choose to twist the overall thrust of the Old Testament by emphasizing the universal at the expense of the particular. But both dimensions – the universal and the particular, God's intention for all nations and his unique involvement with Israel – are part of the Old Testament witness from the beginning since both are included in the covenant with Abraham.[18]

The Uniqueness of Yahweh

A very important ingredient in Israel's eschatological hopes for the future was the conviction that 'in that day' *God himself* would come and take action in the world. Isaiah 35, for example, announces 'Your God will come' (v. 4), and then goes on to list the signs and blessing that will be proof of his coming (v. 5f.). Jesus himself pointed to these signs (Matt. 11:4–6). In other places, the promise that God himself would 'take over' is linked without explanation to the expected coming and rule of a messianic figure. This is clearest in Ezekiel 34. There God, in response to the failure of Israel's historical kings ('shepherds'), promises a restoration of full theocracy ('I myself will shepherd the flock with justice', v. 16), but at the same time promises the rule of a future 'David' (v. 23f.). The Old Testament closes with the warning that God himself would come, but he would be preceded by 'Elijah' (Mal. 2:1, 4:5). In the light of this text, Jesus could declare that this prophecy about 'Elijah' was fulfilled in John the Baptist. But then, if 'Elijah' was to precede the coming of God himself, and John was 'Elijah', *who must Jesus be*, as the one who so unmistakably came after John? 'If you are willing to accept it', said Jesus (Matt. 11:14). The difficulty of accepting what he was saying lay not so much in the fact of identifying John with 'Elijah' as in what they would mean for the identity of Jesus himself.

For those who *were* willing to accept it, it meant beyond doubt that God himself had indeed come in the person of Jesus of Nazareth, to bring in the new age of his kingdom and salvation. Very soon after the death and resurrection of Jesus we find the early church, referring to him and addressing him in terms which had previously applied only to Yahweh in their scriptures. They called him Lord, the Greek word *Kyrios* being the one regularly used in the Greek version of the Old Testament for the divine name Yahweh. They 'called on his name' in worship and prayer. That was a phrase used in the Old Testament for invoking the presence and power of God in person. Stephen at the point of death declared that he saw Jesus standing at the right hand of God sharing in his divine glory (Acts 7:55). Paul, in an act of instinctive evangelism, called on the Philippian jailer to 'believe on the Lord Jesus Christ', if he wanted to be saved (Acts 16:31). Elsewhere he could theologically justify such confidence by quoting Joel 2:32, 'Everyone who calls on the name of the Lord will be saved'. Joel was unquestionably referring to Yahweh. Paul, just as unquestionably, was referring to Jesus Christ as the agent of God's salvation for Jew and gentile alike (Rom. 10:13).

In my opinion, the most remarkable identification of Jesus with Yahweh comes in Philippians 2:5–11, the hymn of Christ's humility and exaltation. It is widely agreed that these verses were probably not composed by Paul, but were part of a Christian hymn which he incorporates here to make his point. They are thus very early evidence of Christian convictions about Jesus. The hymn concludes by referring to the future acknowledgement of Jesus Christ as Lord.

> . . . that at the name of Jesus every knee should bow,
>   in heaven and on earth and under the earth,
> and every tongue confess that Jesus Christ is Lord
>   to the glory of God the Father.

This is a partial quotation of words which were originally spoken by *Yahweh about himself*, from Isaiah 45:22–3. And in that context the point of the words was to underline Yahweh's unique ability to save.

> Before me every knee will bow;
>   by me every tongue will swear.
> They will say of me, 'In Yahweh alone are righteousness [salvation]
>   and strength'.

This declaration by God comes in the most unambiguously monotheistic section of the whole Old Testament. The magnificent prophecies of Isaiah 40–55 assert again and again that Yahweh is utterly unique as the only living God in his sovereign power over all nations and all history, and in his ability to save. This early Christian hymn, therefore, by deliberately selecting a scripture from such a context and applying it to Jesus, is affirming that *Jesus is as unique as Yahweh* in those same respects. This is clear from the way the 'name' of Jesus is inserted at the crucial point where Yahweh would otherwise have been understood. *Jesus* is Lord, and will ultimately be recognized and acknowledged as such by all.

Another interesting factor here is the context of both texts. It is actually religious pluralism. In Philippians, the uniqueness of Jesus is asserted in the midst of the religious pluralism of the Greek and Roman world of the 1st Century AD, using the same language and terms as the uniqueness of Yahweh himself had been asserted in the midst of the pluralistic, polytheistic environment of Babylon in the 6th century BC. I question, therefore, whether the rediscovered (but not new) religious pluralism of the 20th century AD gives us any adequate reason for departing from affirmations made in both Testaments in similar contexts. At least we should be aware that if we insist on relativizing Jesus out of deference to surrounding religious pluralism, we take leave not only of the New Testament witness to him, but also jettison the Old Testament foundations on which it was built.[19] In Jesus, then, the uniqueness of Israel and the uniqueness of Yahweh flow together for he shares and fulfils the identity and the mission of both by the way he embodied the one and incarnated the other.

CONCLUSION

In conclusion, however, we need to remember that the affirmation of Isaiah 45:23 (that all nations will acknowledge Yahweh as God and saviour) as well as its application to Jesus in Philippians 2:5–11, is eschatological. That is to say,we still look forward to it being demonstrated to all nations and accepted by them. Our claim that Jesus of Nazareth was Yahweh in human flesh, that he is exalted as Lord, that he is unique as God's final act of revelation and salvation, remains the affirmation of faith and hope. It is our hope (in the biblical sense) that the truth we now perceive by faith will be finally and conclusively demonstrated. And the responsibility for that final demonstration and proof rests not with us, for we, like Israel, are simply witnesses in the case. 'You are my witnesses', said Yahweh to Israel (Isa. 43:10). 'You shall be my witnesses', echoed Jesus to his disciples, '. . . to the ends of the earth' (Acts 1:8). The uniqueness of Jesus is not something Christianity invented. It is a truth which has been entrusted to us as stewards and witnesses. The final proof of it rests with God himself who, meanwhile, has exalted him to the highest place and given him his own supreme name.

NOTES

1. The three terms were based on the analysis given by Alan Race in *Christians and Religious Pluralism* (Orbis, 1982). A related set of models is given by Paul Knitter in *No Other Name?* (SCM, 1985). A very helpful discussion of the three terms, which comes to a conclusion broadly in favour of cautious inclusivism, is Gavin D'Costa *Theology and Religious Pluralism* (Blackwell, 1986). I have briefly surveyed and critiqued the three positions in, Chris Wright: *What's So Unique about Jesus* (Monarch, 1990). A very thorough and well-reasoned defence of exclusivism and critique of pluralism is provided by Harold Netland: *Dissonant Voices: Religious Pluralism and the Question of Truth* (Eerdmans, Apollos, 1991).
2. A. Race: *Pluralism*, p. 78.
3. J. Hick: *God Has Many Names*, (Macmillan, 1980), p. 52. Theocentric pluralism is also espoused in various nuanced forms by the Indian theologians R. Panikkar and S. Samartha, by Wilfred Cantwell Smith, Alan Race and Paul Knitter. The pluralist agenda is most thoroughly set out in the symposium, J. Hick and P. Knitter (eds.): *The*

Myth of Christian Uniqueness: Towards a Pluralistic Theology of Religions (Orbis, 1987). A major response and critique of its position from an inclusivist perspective is another symposium, Gavin D'Costa (ed.); *Christian Uniqueness Reconsidered: The Myth of a Pluralistic Theology of Religions* (Orbis, 1990).

4. Newbigin makes the following comment on the abstract nature of the pluralist's 'God'.

> The other stance [referring to Hick] takes as its point of reference, Transcendent Being. (The capital letters are presumably to be taken seriously). This is, of course, not a recorded event in history. It is an idea difficult for one not trained in philosophy to grasp. 'Transcendent' is an adjective which literally refers to the position of something above or beyond something else. 'Being' is a verbal noun from the verb 'to be' which normally only has meaning in association with a subject. The idea of 'being' which is devoid of any reference to something which *is*, seems for most people to be very difficult to grasp. A person untrained in philosophy may be forgiven for asking whether 'Being' which is not being anything is not a figment of the imagination. . . . I know of no basis, no axiom, no necessity of thought which requires me to believe that a historic person [Jesus] and a series of historical events provide a less reliable starting point for the adventure of knowing than does the highly sophisticated mental construct of a philosopher.

L. Newbigin: *The Open Secret* (Eerdmans, 1978) p. 52.

5. H.A. Netland, *Dissonant Voices*, pp. 255f.

6. Race: *Pluralism*, p. 136.

7. R. Panikkar: *The Trinity and the Religious Experience of Man* (Orbis, 1973). For a survey of Panikkar's views, see also Knitter: *No Other Name?* ch. 8.

8. A.G. Hunter: *Christianity and Other Faiths in Britain* (SCM, 1985), p. 55. This theory that the early Christology of the church 'evolved' from an originally 'low' beginning to affirmations of deity only at a much later, post NT, stage has been effectively challenged by C.F.D. Moule: *The Origin of Christology* (Cambridge, 1977), and I.H. Marshall: *The Origins of New Testament Christology* (Apollos, updated edition, 1990). Cf also, R.T. France: 'Development in New Testament Christology', *Themelios* 18.1 (October 1992).

9. *Ibid*. p. 76.

10. Hick and Hebblethwaite (eds.): *Christianity and Other Religions* (Collins 1980, Fortress, 1981), p. 186.

11. Muslims are well aware of the implications of the pluralist developments in Christian theology. A friend from Singapore tells me that *The Myth of God Incarnate* is required reading for Muslim missionaries. Christian missionaries in India report that even in remote rural villages Muslims can counter the Christian gospel with the riposte that even bishops in the Church of England now believe what Muslims have always believed – that Jesus was not really God and did not really rise again.

12 E.G. Borowitz: 'A Jewish Response: The Lure and Limits of Universalizing our Faith', in D.G. Dawe and J.B. Carman (eds.): *Christian Faith in a Religiously Plural World* (Orbis, 1978), pp. 64f.

13. I have tried to present a detailed survey of how Jesus drew his sense of identity, mission and values from his Hebrew scriptures, in, Chris Wright: *Knowing Jesus through the Old Testament* (Harper Collins 1992). This book includes a bibliography of significant works, Jewish and Christian, on the historical Jesus and his relation to the Hebrew scriptures and first century Judaism.

14. Obviously, the range of relevant biblical material is vast. I have tried to give a reasonably comprehensive survey of it in: 'The Christian and other religions: the biblical evidence'. *Themelios*, 9.2 (Jan. 1984), pp. 4–18 (now reprinted as chapter 4 in *What's So Unique about Jesus?*).

15. By starting with a discussion of sin and salvation, I am by no means overlooking the importance of the creation material in the Bible and its relevance to Christian relations with people of other faiths. A lot can be said on the image of God in all

human beings, on the fact that all humans are addressable by and accountable to the one living God, and on the relevance of the Wisdom literature, with its creation orientation, to the inter-faith question. For a fuller discussion, see John Goldingay and Christopher Wright: '"Yahweh our God Yahweh One": The Old Testament and Religious Pluralism', in Andrew D. Clarke and Bruce W. Winter (eds.): *One God, One Lord in a World of Religious Pluralism* (Tyndale House, Cambridge, 1991), pp. 34–52. The focus of our discussion here is the redemptive uniqueness of Christ, not the whole breadth of the Old Testament's contribution to our understanding of other faiths.

16. Carl Braaten: 'The Uniqueness and Universality of Jesus Christ', in G. H. Anderson and T. F. Stransky (eds.), *Faith Meets Faith*, Mission Trends, No. 5, (Paulist Press, and Eerdmans, 1981), pp. 69–89.

17. This separation of the historical Jesus from a cosmic Christ is also a feature of how Jesus is viewed in some new religious movements and New Age philosophies. See, Arild Romarheim, 'The Aquarian Christ', *Bulletin of the John Rylands University Library of Manchester*, 70 (1988), pp. 197–207.

18. This is the subject of the study by Eliya Mohol: 'Particularity and Universality of God in Selected Passages in the Old Testament: A historical survey with special reference to the use of such themes in the context of pluralism in India' (unpublished MTh dissertation, Union Biblical Seminary, Pune, [Serampore university], 1988).

19. The same point is made very persuasively in relation to the 'I am' sayings of John's Gospel and their background in Isaiah 40–55 by David M. Ball: '"My Lord and my God": The Implications of "I am" Sayings for Religious Pluralism', in A. D. Clarke and B. W. Winter, *op. cit.*, pp. 53–71.

4

Kwame Bediako

Dr. Kwame Bediako examines the uniqueness of Christ from the perspective of the spiritual aspirations and fears of people of other faiths. He argues that the biblical affirmations are witnesses to the unique Christ. He calls for a theology of the Holy Spirit in interpreting the incarnation as a unique sign and demonstration of divine vulnerability in history; redemption through the Cross as the logic of divine love; and the Lord's table demonstrating the making of one people out of many peoples. Bediako argues for inclusiveness without exclusiveness (See Christ Wright's introduction).

INTRODUCTION:
CHRIST, UNIQUE IN RELATION TO 'OTHER LORDS'

'Jesus is the Son of God', said the Christian evangelist.
'My shrine-spirit is also a child of God', said the traditionalist.
What is the next line in the discussion?
That sequence in a constructed conversation between a Christian preacher and an African religious traditionalist may be taken to illustrate the kind of issues that are at stake in the Christian affirmation of the uniqueness of Christ in the midst of the plurality of religions. It is not often recognized in Christian circles that theological affirmations about Christ are meaningful ultimately not in terms of what Christians say, but in terms of what persons of other faiths understand those affirmations to imply for them. In other words, our Christian affirmations about the uniqueness of Christ achieve their real impact when they are tested to establish their credentials and validity not only in terms of the religious and spiritual universe in which Christians habitually operate, but also and indeed especially, in terms of the religious and spiritual worlds which persons of other faiths inhabit. For it is, after all, in those 'other worlds' that the true meaning of the unique Christ is meant to become apparent and be validated.
Perhaps I need to stress that the procedure I suggest does not mean that Christian affirmations are to be shaped or determined by the content of other

---

Dr. Kwame Bediako is director of the Akrofi-Christaller Memorial Centre, Akropong-Akuapem, Ghana.

religious faiths, let alone be derived from those sources. The point is rather that by their very nature, Christian affirmations about the unique Christ of our faith arise from their relationship to the claims and presuppositions that are made by persons of other faiths for theirs. There are no real grounds for affirming the uniqueness of Christ where there are no alternatives to be taken seriously. In the words of the apostle Paul:

> For although there may be so-called gods in heaven or on earth – as indeed there are many 'gods' and many 'lords' –, yet for us there is one God, the Father, from whom are all things and for whom they exist, and one Lord Jesus Christ, through whom are all things and through whom we exist. (1 Cor. 8:5–6, RSV).

In the apostle's statement, the very affirmation that there is only one Lord Jesus Christ is made in relation to the other 'so-called many lords'. In other words, affirmation of uniqueness has meaning as it relates to alternative claims. Accordingly, the affirmation about the unique Lord Jesus Christ arises from how he is perceived in his relation to other 'lords'.

The approach I am taking is essentially that adopted by Bishop Kenneth Cragg, a sure guide into our subject, in his book, *The Christ and the Faiths – Theology in Cross-Reference* (London; SPCK, 1986). Bishop Cragg states this quite clearly from the start:

> There would seem to be today a growing recognition that Christian theology must justify its being 'Christian' by undertaking a theology of religion at large and incorporating this into its traditional responsibility for its own distinctiveness. It is there – Christian theology in harness with a theology of religion and tethered around the theme of the Christ – that this book aims to take in hand (xi).

In my view, it is this approach that the New Testament, indeed the Old Testament as well, take in affirming the unique divine self-disclosure that we have been given and which culminates in our Lord Jesus Christ.

CHRISTIAN AFFIRMATIONS – AS RECOGNITION NOT ASSERTIONS

Once the affirmation about the unique Christ is expressed in the terms we have suggested, it may seem to be so self-evident that it might not need to be stated. And yet, in point of fact, it is because the nature of our Christian affirmations is so often misconstrued by Christians and non-Christians alike, that the issue can bear some elaboration.

It is perhaps not an exaggeration to suggest that there is a general tendency in Christian circles to treat Christian affirmations as essentially theological data, as some sort of fixed grid of doctrinal positions which have an inherent meaning in and of themselves, irrespective of their validation in terms other than those in which they are stated. The affirmation about the unique Christ will, accordingly, be one such theological datum. While there may be a case for treating our own formulations of our doctrinal positions in this way, I am certain that we cannot treat biblical affirmations in that way. Biblical affirmations, while they have the character of convictions, nevertheless, are not given as fixed data. Rather, being an integral part of the total biblical revelation, they share in the character and purpose of that revelation, namely, to provide the conditions for humans to make an identical response of faith in the unique Christ, whom they reveal and to whom they bear witness. Within the scriptures this process can be identified in the apostle Paul's statement in 2 Corinthians 4: 13–14:

> Since we have the same spirit of faith as he had who wrote: 'I believed and so I spoke', we too believe, and so we speak, knowing that he who raised the Lord Jesus will raise us also with Jesus and bring us with you into his presence.

The truth of biblical revelation, therefore, is not just truth to be believed in by mere intellectual or mental assent; it is truth to be participated in. Paul by his faith in Christ, finds that he has become a participant in the same truth as motivated the psalmist in Psalm 116:10.

Another way of expressing this view is to say that the truth of biblical revelation is the truth, not of assertion, but of recognition. In that sense, the biblical affirmations concerning the uniqueness of Christ are not arbitrary claims or assertions, made *a priori* in the interests of, or for the benefit of, any particular community, not even of the Christian community. The affirmations too are the fruit of recognition, and are intended, in centrifugal motion, to find their true significance in their application to the human whole. Thus, these affirmations, in reverse centripetal motion, provide the opportunity and the conditions for the perception or recognition by others of their significance for them. It is in this way that it becomes possible to describe the entire biblical revelation as a witness – borne by God, and especially to his Son, but also borne by those who, in response to the divine initiative, became partakers by this recognition, of the truth of the witness of God. The cumulative effect of biblical revelation, understood as witness, is the expectation that it will generate similar recognition of the truth to which it witnesses. Thus, in the well-known words of 1 John 1: 1ff.:

> That which was from the beginning, which we have heard, which we have seen with our eyes, which we have looked upon and touched with our hands, concerning the Word of life – the life was made manifest, and we saw it and testify to it, and proclaim to you the eternal life which was with the Father and was made manifest to us – that which we have seen and heard we proclaim to you, so that you may have the fellowship with us.

The whole of the nature of the biblical revelation may be said to be summarized in these verses. They show that the climactic divine self-disclosure was not in a set of documented religious formulae or theological propositions, but rather in a life – in a human life which could be seen, looked upon and touched. And yet the quality of that human life was such that it provided and continues to provide, clues for its recognition as truly divine in its origin, and it was truly human in its manifestation. Upon this recognition Christian affirmation makes its claim that the human-divine life to which it bears witness is the light of the world and the life and hope of the whole of humankind and of the cosmos itself.

To clarify further our argument, perhaps in contrast to another major religious faith, Islam, we may quote a recent observation by Andrew Walls:

> Much misunderstanding in Christian-Muslim relations has occurred from the assumption that the Bible and the Qur'an have analogous status in the respective faiths. But the true Christian anology with the Qur'an is not the Bible but Christ. Christ for Christians, the Qur'an for Muslims, is the Eternal Word of God; but Christ is Word Translated. That fact is the sign that the contingent Scriptures (also describable as Word of God), unlike the Qur'an, may and should constantly be translated.
>
> Incarnation is translation. When God in Christ became man, Divinity was translated into humanity, as though humanity were a receptor language. Here was a clear statement of what would otherwise be veiled in obscurity or uncertainty, the statement, 'This is what God is like'.[1]

In sum, then, the principle of recognition, focusing as it does on seeing Christ as God incarnate and accessible, becomes of crucial importance for rightly understanding the true character of the Christian affirmation concerning the unique Christ. As Christ himself said to the Pharisees:

> You search the Scriptures, because you think that in them you have eternal life; it is they that bear witness to me; and yet you refuse to come to me that you may have life (Jn. 5:39f.).

THE UNIQUE CHRIST (1):
RELIGIONS AS TRADITIONS OF RESPONSE

Once the point is granted that Christian affirmations about the unique Christ are not assertions, but rather invitations to recognition, it becomes essential to engage the major question: What then is it that in Christ confronts us, which calls for recognition? This is the fundamental question regarding the status of the unique Christ amid the plurality of religions. It is to be answered not by Christian claims alone, but also by conclusions arrived at through working with the inward meanings of the religious worlds of other faiths. This is so because the vindication of the status of the unique Christ is seen, ultimately, as a demonstration that he is able to inhabit those other worlds also as the Lord.

Here we can begin only with the ministry of Jesus on earth, 'in the days of his flesh' (Heb. 5:7, RSV), in other words, as the divine self-disclosure in and through him was offered for recognition to men and women. In this regard, it is important that in Paul's summary of the gospel he focuses, in effect, on the actual events of the life and ministry of Jesus. 'He died for our sins, according to the Scriptures, was buried . . . was raised on the third day, according to the Scriptures . . . He appeared . . . to Cephas, . . . the twelve . . . more than five hundred brethren at one time . . . to James . . . all the apostles . . . last of all to me' (1 Cor. 15:3–9). These actual 'earthly' events in the career of Jesus came to be recognized as soteriologically significant; Paul's own final testimony to the efficacy of the salvific import and reach of those events in vv. 9–11 is the sign that these events, validated by the witness of the Scriptures, did and do contain and offer the conditions which make the recognition of their significance possible.

This concentration on the 'earthly' ministry of Jesus is valid and indeed necessary, since it is in the circumstances of human earthly existence that we are given to discern and understand the religious dimension of human life in the experiences of men and women. In turn, what constitutes the 'stuff of the sacred', the category of the religious in people's experiences, becomes important as the locus of the encounter between Christian affirmation and the plurality of so-called 'non-Christian' religions. This is another way of saying that it would be false to conceive of the meeting of Christian affirmation with the religious meanings of other faiths in terms of mutually exclusive systems, or even of credal formulations. Rather, the encounter takes place in the things that pertain to the Spirit who, like the wind, blows where he wills. In this sense, a discussion of the ways in which the Christian affirmation about the unique Christ relates to the plurality of religions, involves also a theology of the Holy Spirit. As Kenneth Cragg has written:

> In the mystery and the burden of the plurality of religions, there lies, surely, the supreme test of the meaning we intend when we say, 'I believe in the Holy Spirit'.[2]

There is an obvious analogy here with the attempts found in some authors in early patristic theology, particularly Justin Martyr and Clement of Alexandria.[3] However, in place of their notion of the pre-Incarnate Word (Logos) who operated as much in extra-biblical tradition as in the biblical, I evoke the activity of the Holy Spirit.

Since we are concerned with religions, not as 'belief-systems', but as the matrix in which men and women experience and respond to, the 'stuff of the sacred', in their human existence, it is possible to agree with John V. Taylor in how we may regard peoples' religions:

> I believe it is truer to think of a religion as a people's tradition of response to the reality the Holy Spirit has set before their eyes. I am deliberately not saying that any religion is the truth which the Spirit disclosed, nor even that it contains that truth. All we can say without presumption is that this is how men have responded and taught others to respond to what the Spirit made them aware of. It is the history of a particular answer, a series of answers, to the call and claim of him who lies beyond all religions.[4]

Looked at as 'a tradition of response' to the reality and disclosure of the Transcendent, every religion can be probed, therefore, not so much for the measure of truth it contains, as for the truth of the human response to the divine action within the tradition. As a tradition of response, every religion also displays within it, 'the same tension between conservatism and development which characterises all human response to the call of God which comes through the new situation'.[5] It becomes possible, then, to speak also of a plurality within a religion as a tradition of response, and to distinguish strands of response within it. Thus, it is possible to understand how one response to Old Testament religious teaching can lead to the Mishnah and the Talmud whilst another response can lead to the New Testament. The distinction of strands occurs in the process of the encounter with Jesus, who is Christ the Lord.

THE UNIQUE CHRIST (2):
WHAT IS IT THAT, IN CHRIST, CONFRONTS US?

Granted therefore that the Christian affirmation about the unique Christ in the midst of the plurality of religions encounters traditions of response to the disclosure of the Transcendent that the Holy Spirit sets before people, our present task is to demonstrate how the scriptural witness to the life and ministry of Christ, illuminated by the Holy Spirit, is the clue to the yearnings and quests in the religious lives of people. As Kenneth Cragg remarks, 'the critical question for the Christian' is 'how to have the meanings of Christ operative in human hearts'.[5]

There are three aspects of Christian affirmation about the unique Christ which readily stand out for consideration. The first is the affirmation concerning the Incarnation, namely, the affirmation that in Christ, God humbled himself and identified with humankind in Christ's birth as a human baby, born of woman, and endured the conditions of 'normal' human existence – in other words, the Incarnation is supremely the unique sign and demonstration of divine vulnerability in history.

The second aspect relates to the Christian affirmation about the Cross of Christ, showing forth the will to suffer forgivingly and redemptively as the very expression of the divine mind and the logic of the divine love. Accordingly all other attempts to achieve the redemptive ends which Christ sought, apart from the ways of the Cross, are revealed as partial and inadequate.

The third aspect relates to the communion at the Lord's Table, in which the invitation to all who are united to Christ in faith to partake of the holy emblems of bread and wine – symbols of Christ's redemptive achievement through his body and blood – demonstrates the uniqueness of the making of one people out of the many of humankind. Accordingly, the reconciliation of broken relationships across racial, ethnic, national, cultural, social and economic barriers becomes an important test of the nature of a people's response to the disclosure of the Transcendent which the Holy Spirit sets before them.

It is possible to reformulate these three aspects of what confronts us in the ministry of Christ as follows: in Jesus Christ, the Holy Spirit reveals to us a divine paradigm which confronts all religions, challenging men and women in three specific areas – in the understanding of power and weakness, in the response to evil and in the response to cultural enmity and social exclusiveness. It is by these down-to-earth clues to the divine paradigm disclosed in the ministry of Christ that all religions are challenged and invited to make an equally concrete response, in faith, repentance and obedience. In this respect, Christianity too, formally equivalent to the other religions as traditions of response, is challenged to respond to the unique Christ who is the Lord. For,

. . . Man-in-Christianity lies under the wrath of God just as much, and for the same reasons, as man-in-Hinduism.

and,

it is not Christianity that saves, but Christ.[7]

In Jesus Christ, then, we have the threefold paradigm of divine vulnerability, the will to redemptive suffering and reconciling love, not as abstract notions, but as concrete events and deeds in a human life, and achieved in ways which Christian faith reads as expressive of the divine nature itself. As the Gospel records of yet another instance of recognition:

> When the centurion, who stood facing him, saw that he thus breathed his last, he said, 'Truly, this man was the Son of God' (Mk. 15:39, RSV).

What, therefore, in Christ, confronts us, are clues to the recognition of divine self-disclosure and the consequent challenge to become a disciple, one in whose incarnate life that disclosure has been given. Thus the Christian affirmation about the unique Christ in the midst of the plurality of religions does not arise, first and foremost, from theological propositions or credal formulations, but rather from the recognition of the divine nature expressed in actual historical existence. Kenneth Cragg is right to point out:

> Sonship, then, before it becomes a term in creeds, is a reality in deeds. We have to read that central decision of willingness to suffer . . . as the expression in the actual, of that by which it was sustained in the volitional. 'The cup which my Father has given me'; 'Father, glorify thy Name': 'Father, forgive'; 'Father, into thy hands I commend . . .'; these were the prayers within which Jesus suffered. Sonship, in that immediate, existential sense, was the context of his doing. Therefore, we take it also as the secret of his being. If Jesus is 'Son of God' in the music of the *Te Deum* and in the confessions of Nicea and Chalcedon, it is because he was the Son of God beneath the olive branches of Gethsemane and in the darkness of Golgotha.[8]

And, as Cragg further remarks:

> that confession did not, could not, mean adoption, or deification, or divinisation. For it could not be rightly stated except as the divine initiative . . . An acquired Sonship is not a fulfilled one. Only as we can say: 'God was in Christ' can we rightly say: 'Jesus is Lord' (ibid).

What remains important is the realization that the focus of the Christian affirmation is not the assertion of a formula, but the recognition of an achievement in actual history which, in turn, provides clues to the sources of those deeds. As one apostolic precedent of how that history is to be interpreted, says:

> Although he was a Son, he learned obedience through what he suffered, and being made perfect, he became the source of eternal salvation to all who obey him, being designated by God a high priest after the order of Mechizedek (Heb. 5: 8–10).

The consistent New Testament pattern of affirmation about Christ is to work from the actual historical achievement in his life, ministry, death and resurrection, to the theological elaboration of the universal significance and application of that achievement. If we wish to follow the New Testament in our affirmation of the unique Christ in the midst of the plurality of religions, then we can also have what Kenneth Cragg calls a 'sober, critical confidence'[9] that the actual history of the achievement in the ministry of Christ is able to stake its claims in the religious worlds of other faiths, because we hold that 'the "mind of the Christ" generates the mind of the Church about the Christ, and not the other way round'.[10] The 'meanings of Christ' as given in the symbols of the Incarnation, the Cross and the reconciling fellowship at the Lord's Table, can become operative in human hearts because he belongs there, and whatever is ultimate in the religious universe of every 'tradition of response', at least in intention, is Christ.

This means also that the encounter between the unique Christ and the meanings inherent in other religions takes place in the terms of those meanings themselves. Acts 14:15–17 and Acts 17:22–34 indicate that this is a possibility. In the process, it also becomes possible to explore new theological idioms without surrendering the Christian content, which, strictly, is Christ himself. I have attempted to demonstrate that, in relation to the spiritual universe of African primal religions, for instance, it is possible to apply to Christ the religiously significant category of Ancestor, but in a far richer sense than is traditionally held about lineal ancestors:

> Jesus Christ is the only real and true Ancestor and Source of life for all mankind, fulfilling and transcending the benefits believed to be bestowed by lineage ancestors. By his unique achievement in perfect atonement through his own self-sacrifice, and by effective eternal mediation and intercession as God-man in the divine presence, he has secured eternal redemption (Hebrews 9:12) for all those who acknowledge who he is for them and what he has done for them, abandon the blind alleys of merely human traditions and rituals and instead entrust themselves to him. As mediator of a new and better covenant between God and humanity (Hebrews 8:6; 12:24), Jesus brings the redeemed into the experience of a new identity in which he links their human destinies directly and consciously with the eternal gracious will and purpose of a loving and caring God (Hebrews 12:22–24). No longer are human horizons bounded by lineage, clan, tribe or nation. For the redeemed now belong within the community of the living God, in the joyful company of the faithful of all ages and climes. They are united in fellowship which through their union with Christ is infinitely richer than the mere social bonds of lineage, clan, tribe or nation, which exclude the 'stranger' as a virtual 'enemy'.[11]

CONCLUSION: A CHRISTIAN THEOLOGY OF RELIGIOUS PLURALISM – THE CONTINUING ENCOUNTER

Conceivably it may be objected that the approach I propose is too open-ended, and even risky, for leaving many questions unresolved from the start and for holding many Christian theological propositions in abeyance. One response would be that such an approach, through openness and vulnerability, is what Christian witness to the divine vulnerability in Christ demands. How could we bear witness to the divine incognito in Christ if we saw our task as the coercion of belief by the discrediting of the religious values of other faiths as 'traditions of response to the reality of the Transcendent'? On the contrary, our affirmation of the unique Christ in the midst of the plurality of religions, which is the task of a Christian theology of religious pluralism, consists in commending the meanings of Christ as discussed above, to men and women in their own worlds of faith, respecting their personalities as beings created, like ourselves, in the image of the one and the same Creator, and yet seeking to 'move them Christward in the freedom of their personal wills'.[12] Thus, a Christian theology of religious pluralism becomes an exercise in spirituality, in which one affirms a commitment to the ultimacy of Christ, whilst accepting the integrity of other faiths and those who profess them.

A remark by Bishop John Taylor, citing Kenneth Cragg, on what lies at the heart of Christian-Muslim differences, helps to focus our attention again on the encounter which truly takes place 'in the things that pertain to the Spirit', as expressed in actual history:

> . . . the contradictions between Muslim and Christian fidelity can be seen to arise in large part from the different ways in which the Messiah and the Prophet responded to the same situation when it confronted them. Each was sure of his call to show men a new way, preaching, gathering the crowds, training his disciples; and each was faced with the opposition of the religious leaders, rejection and disaffection on his followers. What did he do? Jesus chose to go on in the same way, in the same spirit. He bowed his head to what was coming; he accepted rejection, failure and death, entrusting the outcome to God. In the case of Muhammad, it looked for a moment as if he too would take the way of suffering; but then he decided to *fight back on behalf of the truth. He raised his army and marched on Mecca*: and that was the turning point in his career and the birth of Islam. From these two choices, one can derive the fundamental difference between Christian and Muslim ideas of God's nature . . . The gulf between them is seen, as it were, in cross section; for it is nothing less than the *cross* which is now demanding our decision. Once more we see that the evangelism of the Holy Spirit consists in creating the occasion for choice. The servant of the Gospel can do not less and perhaps need do no more[13] (emphasis mine).

Bishop Taylor's observations bring us full circle: the Christian affirmation about the unique Christ in the midst of the plurality of religions implies the provision in Christ-like humility and vulnerability, of the conditions which make the perception and recognition of Jesus as Christ the Lord, possible.

NOTES

1. Walls, Andrew F. (1990), 'The translation principle in Christian history' in, P.C. Stine (ed.), *Bible translation and the spread of the Church – the last 200 years*, Leiden: E.J. Brill: 24–39.

2. Cragg, Kenneth (1968), *Christianity in World Perspective*, London: Lutterworth Press, p. 71.

3. Bediako, Kwame (1992), *Theology and Identity – the impact of culture upon Christian thought in the second century and modern Africa*, Oxford: Regnum Books.

4. Taylor, J.V. (1972), *The Go-Between God – The Holy Spirit and the Christian Mission*, London: SCM Press, p. 182.

5. *Ibid.*, p. 183.

6. Cragg, Kenneth (1977), *The Christian and other religions – the measure of Christ*, London & Oxford: Mowbrays, p. 116.

7. Walls, Andrew F. (1970), 'The first chapter of the epistle to the Romans and the modern missionary movement' in, W. Gasque & R.P. Martin (eds), *Apostolic History and the Gospel*, Exeter: Paternoster Press: p. 357.

8. Cragg, Kenneth. *The Christian and Other Religions op. cit.*, p. 56.

9. *Ibid.* p. 59.
10. *Ibid.*
11. Bediako, Kwame (1990), *Jesus in African Culture – a Ghanaian perspective*, Accra: Asempa Publishers, p. 41f.
12. Cragg, Kenneth. *The Christian and Other Religions*, p. 116.
13. Taylor, *op. cit.*, p. 188f.

5

Joshua K. Daimoi

In the light of his understanding of the religious world view, values and cultic customs of his own Papua New Guinean people, Joshua Daimoi draws out the significance of the interrelatedness and interdependence of his community in proclaiming the uniqueness of Christ. Then on the basis of his interpretation of scripture in this context, he points to a number of factors necessary for effective witness to animist people.

A CASE STUDY FROM PAPUA NEW GUINEA

I have written this case study from my background as a Papua New Guinean, belonging to that geographical area known as Melanesia, in Oceania.

THE WORLD OF THE ANIMIST

The animist sees his world as an homogeneous totality. For the animist, the human and the non-human, the living and the non-living, the material and the non-material, the visible and the non-visible all belong together; they influence and are influenced by each other's existence. What is said about Papua New Guinean society is also true of other animistic societies.

> The idea of totality or homogeneity does not mean that the New Guinean is unable to distinguish between the various aspects of existence or activity, but he is acutely aware of the interrelatedness and interdependence of all things, an awareness that has, to a considerable extent, been obscured in Western thought because of the analytical, fragmentary point of view. Man and nature, seen and unseen, living and dead, past and present, fragment and whole, natural and supernatural – all belong as an homogeneous totality of life. All of existence is therefore brought together into a cosmic totality. The individual, the community, nature, spirits, are all aspects of the whole and representations of it. Everything is interrelated and inter-dependent, so that nothing can be isolated without losing its identity. There is existence only within the framework of this cosmic totality.[1]

Rev. Joshua K. Daimoi is Principal of the Christian Leaders Training College, Banz, Papua New Guinea.

Existence for the animist can be understood only within this cosmic totality. Our presentation to the animist of Christ's uniqueness must be within this cosmic totality, the world as the animist sees and understands it to be.

The Interrelatedness and Interdependence of All Things

Religious Life: The animist's religious life is a spirit-centred life

The animist sees himself as being surrounded by spirit beings at every moment of his existence. His relationship to these spirit beings governs his conduct in life.

> The animist lives in a world filled with spirit powers, between whom and himself there is a constant communication. Everything around him, the stones, the trees, the very air he breathes, is charged with mystical properties and powers, which may at any time come into his life for good or evil.[2,3]

As children we were warned by our parents not to call each other by our proper names every time we walked past a certain spot in the bush. To call a person by his or her proper name is to hand over that person's life to the spirits. At night the spirit will come and steal his soul; the person then will get sick and eventually die. When planting a new garden, the animist will perform the appropriate rituals for the spirit to make his garden produce a harvest in abundance and of good quality. The animistic life is a ritualistic life. He depends on his rituals for success in hunting, fertility in marriage, strength to conquer the enemy, courage to face the unknown. The animist attributes all the events of his life directly to the spirits. Sickness, misfortune, natural disaster are caused by someone rather than something. From conception to the grave, the animist lives with the consciousness of the spirits. 'The Melanesian is born to the knowledge that he lives and works within a spirit world.'[4]

In our Christian witness to the animist we need to take his view of his world seriously. How he sees and relates to his world is the key into his heart and mind. Living in the consciousness of the spirit beings gives the traditional priests, shamans, magicians and witch doctors authority and influence in their society. For the animist the spirit beings are real. The Siwai people of North Solomons in Papua New Guinea believe that when the *mumiaku* – the clan leader – performs the rituals, the clan god – *Hagoro* – is actually present and will give power to the *mumiaku*. They believe the *Hagoro* knows what the people need and therefore *Hagoro* will grant the *mumiaku* the petitions of the people.

Thought Patterns

The animist view of the world affects his thought patterns. He explains everything he sees and feels in terms of what he believes. For him the known explains the unknown. Since spirit beings are real to him, he understands and explains everything in relation to the spirits. The animist of Papua New Guinea sees everything interrelated and interdependent so that nothing can be isolated without losing its identity. In many ways this mode of understanding is akin to that of the Hebrews, the Africans and many others in the two-thirds world cultures.

> Melanesians do not differentiate religious and non-religious experience. For them, I believe, an experience or experience in general is a total encounter for the living person within the universe that is alive and explosive. In fact, for the Melanesians there are no religious and other experiences. An experience for the Melanesian, I believe, is the person's encounter with the spirits, the law, the economics, the politics, and life's own total whole.[7]

A former Catholic missionary to Papua New Guinea, Louis Luzbetake, makes the same point when he writes: 'The totality of which we speak embraces the overt as well as the covert responses, the manifest as well as the implicit, the theoretical or ideal as well as the actual or real, the universals, alternatives, and specialities.'[8]

Social Interrelationships

The homogeneity discussed so far is seen most clearly in the life of the community where social relationships take place. The community provides security, support and the total well-being of all the people. In this community-centred living, the community concerns take precedent over individual concerns. In the animist community the individual exists for the community. Every one in the community is required to maintain the communal well-being. Their community solidarity is based on the fact that 'to be' means to be a unity, a totality, not a 'fragmentation of disconnected and isolated components'.[9] To put it another way, 'I am' because 'they are'. To be a person in Papua New Guinea is to belong to the community. A man may lose his *mana*, but he cannot afford to lose his community.

The community solidarity we are looking at is a solidarity of men, women, ancestors, spirits and the nature around, beneath and above them. Natural disaster, sickness and death are attributed to the breaking of this relationship or solidarity. Whenever a person is suspected of being responsible for a breach of relationship, the only way to restore that relationship is to put the person to death. Since community harmony means community 'salvation', no one would openly conceal anything that is related to their well-being. A stranger, such as a missionary, being an outsider, cannot be trusted with community secrets, until he can prove to them that he is one of them.

For the animist the community solidarity extends beyond the living members of the community into the realm of the departed members. Generally speaking all non-Western societies have always believed in life after death. These societies have always believed that life continues to exist beyond death in a different form. This concept of life existing beyond death is central to belief in spirit beings. These spirits reside both in animate and inanimate entities. Death provides the life force with the opportunity to shed the old skin and put on the new one like the lobster or the snake.[10]

The animist believes that the present order of things is only the shadow of the real world being enjoyed by those who have left. The belief in the spirit being does not simply lead to a good life in this present world, but is part of a search for that better world enjoyed by the departed members of the society.

The solidarity of the society also plays an important role in the way animistic societies make their decisions. Perhaps the best way to describe their decision-making process is to call it an 'interpersonal interrelated decision making'. All the members of the community participate in the decision-making, because every decision they make is important for their interpersonal relationship and their interrelationship with the world around them. They need to decide not only on what is good for them as living members of the community but the decision they make must benefit the invisible members of their community also.

The best people to judge the feelings of the invisible members of the community are the elders of the community. This council of the elders probably consists of three or four people. One of them, perhaps their traditional priest, will make the final decision after considering all the views expressed by the community. All the elders together with the chief of the village who may or may not be the traditional priest, are the custodians of their world-view. They are the people who have the knowledge of the spirit world and the way to communicate with the spirits. They are the ones who decide on the forms of discipline to be applied to the trouble-makers of their community.

> The authority and power of the chief include the responsibility to maintain harmony and order, to direct the common operations and industries, to represent his people to strangers, to preside at sacrifices, to lead to war, to inflict fines, to order trouble makers to be put to death.[11]

THE BIBLICAL WITNESS: COLOSSIANS 1: 15–20

The animist is a deeply spiritual person. His entire life is centred in the spirit world. He looks to the spirits for provision, protection, and prominence. Unless he is offered a superior alternative to the spirits, he will see no reason for denouncing his allegiance to them. As a Christian I know that the answer my people have been looking for is found in Christ and him alone! In Christ God has provided for the animist of Papua New Guinea and around the world, that superior, unique, incomparable alternative – the only alternative and answer they long for.

Colossians 1: 15–20 holds before us the uniqueness of Christ as the one and only solution to the searching and longing heart of the animist for the real world that is beyond his grasp. This passage describes the uniqueness of Christ in several different ways.

Christ is the Image of the Invisible God v. 15

Christ is the fulness of God in human body (v. 19). He came from the world beyond to become God to us. In his conversation with the woman of Samaria, Jesus said, 'God is spirit, and his worshippers must worship in spirit and in truth' (Jn. 1:24). The animist lives in a world explosive with spirit power and presence. God is spirit; no one has ever seen him or lived in a face-to-face relationship with him. The only person who enjoyed this honour and intimacy is the Lord Jesus Christ (Jn. 1: 1, 18). God is spirit but is not merely the same as or on a par with all the many spirits the animist believes in. God is the creator of the universe and this includes all the spirits and other invisible beings.

To call Jesus the fullness, the total expression of the invisible God, the invisible Spirit, is to acknowledge that Jesus is that God and that Spirit. One of the ways in which young men in Papua New Guinea enter into adulthood is to go through the process of initiation. In some areas during the third and final stage of the initiation, the initiates are inducted into the inner part of the spirit house to view images or representations of the ancestral spirits. These young men, having gone through the initiation process, before they return home to take their places as responsible adults, have to see these representations of the spirits to impress on them their reciprocal obligations.

Jesus Christ as the great eternal Spirit stands alone and far above all the spirits on earth and in heaven. He came from the innermost shrine, from the Most Holy Place, from the very presence of the One who sits on the throne, the one eternal God to whom all the saints and the heavenly hosts offer their unceasing homage saying: 'Holy, holy, holy is the Lord God Almighty, who was, and is, and is to come' (Rev. 4: 8). Jesus is the image of God, the very being of God clothed in flesh. The almighty, holy, invisible God chose to manifest himself through this one person alone; 'For God was pleased to have all his fullness dwell in him' (Col. 1: 19).

As the passage makes clear all the other spirits were created by him and for his glory. No spirit the animist believes in has ever taken on a human body, lived and died. The Bible speaks much about the reality of spirit beings and the spirit world. What kind of shape and form these spirits have we are not told. Jesus Christ on the other hand is a real person of flesh and blood. No spirit, ancestral or otherwise can push Jesus Christ aside. Christ is the fulfilment of the animist search. He fully reveals all the animist is longing to understand about God.

Jesus Christ is the Lord of Life, vv. 15, 16, 17

As the image of the invisible God, Jesus Christ is prior to all other beings and orders of existence. He existed before everything else came into being. 'He is prior to, distinct from, and highly exalted above every creature. As the first born he is the heir and ruler over all.'[12] He is supreme over all creation. Since Christ is prior to and supreme over all created beings it follows that everything in heaven and on earth must bow the knee to his lordship.

All things without exception were created by Christ. All things owe their origin to Christ and exist for his glory.

If the angels, the best of the spirit powers described in the Scriptures, are subject to Christ, then so, too, are all lesser spirit powers of the animist. Christ's supremacy over all creation is an acknowledgement of his lordship over all human cultures. The heart of every culture is religion. The animist is a very religious person. His religion is centred in spirit beings, demonic powers and angelic representations. The animist is not a lower form of human being. He is a dignified person, endowed with intelligence, beauty and creativity. Like the rest of humankind he too is made in the image of God. Many aspects of his culture are beautiful, wholesome and adequate for his survival and the survival of his offspring. There are at the same time many aspects of his culture which are plainly demonic. The god of this world has made him captive to the principalities and rulers of this world. The animist does not know that what he worships are inferior beings, creatures of the one supreme God.

The Willowbank Report states,

> We think it vital in evangelism in all cultures to teach the reality and hostility of demonic powers, and to proclaim that God has exalted Christ as Lord of all and that Christ, who really does possess all power, however we may fail to acknowledge this, can (as we proclaim him) break through any world-view in any mind to make his lordship known and bring about a radical change of heart and outlook.[13]

The Colossian passage encourages us to see that we will succeed in our missionary service because, 'in him all things hold together . . . and through him to reconcile to himself all things, whether things on earth or things in heaven, by making peace through his blood, shed on the cross' (vv. 17, 20). Human powers and cultures are held together by the Lord who makes himself known to them from their cultures. These words assure us that we will succeed in our mission because the Lord who holds all human cultures under his control, goes before us and with us to liberate them from their cultural tyranny.

We will triumph over spirit powers and demonic strong holds because Christ has triumphed over them. 'Having cancelled the written code, with its regulations, that was against us and that stood opposed to us; he took it away, nailing it to the cross. And having disarmed the powers and authorities, he made a public spectacle of them, triumphing over them by the cross' (Col. 2: 14, 15). The death of Jesus on the cross cancelled our past record of guilt and conquered our past captors. On the cross Christ fought a cosmic war against universal cosmic powers. The cross delivered us from bondage to demonic powers. The animist is locked in a double bondage, bondage to his own set of rituals in order to manipulate the spirits and bondage to the powers of the spirits. Christ is indeed the animist's true liberator.

Jesus Christ is Lord of the Church, v. 18

The climax of all missionary service in this present world is to bring the people we minister to into a proper relationship with the Lord Jesus. The formation of the local body of believers – the Church, regardless of the number is the visible manifestation of the triumph of the gospel in the lives of those who have been held captive by Satan and his associates. The goal of missionary service is so to present the gospel in the power of the Holy Spirit that those who respond to it will transfer their loyalty from what formerly dominated them to Jesus Christ. In terms of the animists, our aim is to see the people move from a spirit-dominated world-view to a Christ-centred world-view. Our motive must be to bring those who have been ruled by other powers into an intimate relationship with Christ, where he will be seen as their Lord, the head of their individual and corporate life. The homogeneous, integrated life which previously centred on the tribe, will now, in Christ come to fulness through communal expression through the church.

Christ's headship over the church in the verse under consideration is a headship over the universal church, not just the local church. This places the missionary and the new Christian in equal relationship; they are both servants of Christ and brothers in him.

Jesus is Lord of Death, v. 18

As the 'first-born from the dead' Christ has conclusively defeated death for all mankind in every culture down through the ages. By his resurrection Christ has established himself Lord of life and of death. He is the first one to experience that full, complete resurrection life which all of us will experience one day.

When the Bible says that Jesus is Lord of death, it means that Jesus is Lord of the dead also. The dead cannot control the living or the world of the living. The control of heaven and all the powers associated with them are in the hands of the risen, triumphant Christ of the cosmos.

FACTORS IN OUR WITNESS TO ANIMISTS

Confronting the Spirit World

The first thing we need to recognize is that for the animist the spirit world is real. The animist lives in an homogeneous world where humans, spirits, plants and animals live together, each one influencing and being influenced by the other. Jesus not only recognized the existence of the spirits, but was continually confronted by them. He confronted Satan and his kingdom (Matt. 12: 22–32; Mk. 3: 20–3; Lk. 11: 14–23; 12: 10). Jesus healed people possessed by demons (Matt. 8: 28–34). The apostle Paul also deals with various types of principalities and powers (Eph. 2: 2; 6: 12; 5: 8). The book of Revelation presents the never-ceasing struggle between the powers of darkness and God climaxing in Satan and his angels being eternally banished into utter darkness.

Mission amongst animists must take this aspect of their world-view very seriously. A study in demonology would help us to know our common enemy and his tactics in order to be better prepared for ourselves and others. This study on demonology should be done in the light of Christ's accomplished victory on the cross. We must, however, take care not to give to Satan or any other spirit being that place which Christ alone must occupy. Satan's power is a defeated power. Christ alone is omnipotent!

Presenting Christ to the Whole Community

The animist lives in a closely knitted community. He makes no distinction between the sacred and the secular. Religion permeates every aspect of his life, politics, social, economic and all his interpersonal relationships. Christ needs to be presented as the one person who meets all his aspirations, fears and worries. When he is brought to Christ we need to teach him to practise his faith at home, in the office, in business, on the sport fields, in the community and in church service.

The total person for the animist also means the total community he belongs to. His community is his security. The gospel needs to be presented to him within his community setting. The decision to follow Christ needs to be seen as a community decision. In some Papua New Guinean societies decisions to follow Christ were postponed until the tribe or the elders of the tribe gave their approval.

Living with a New God-Consciousness

In his traditional society the animist lives with spirit consciousness all through his life. Religion is a vital part of his life. Christianity is not an addition to the old religion but a replacement of it. Christ is not an addition to the many spirits the animist believes in but a replacement of them. As Christ becomes the centre of their world-view, they have to relate to him on a very personal level wherever they happen to be. One of the good things our people have learned to do through the influence of times of revival is to speak to God for all their needs, at any time from any place. They look to God to provide all their daily necessities instead of depending on magic and sorcery.

They pray to God while hunting and fishing, for their gardens, for their pigs and dogs, and every aspect of their daily life. Before this revival they would go to church, but once they came out of church they would turn to their magic things for hunting, fishing, gardening, etc. Now they look to God for everything – personal and collective needs. For personal needs they pray by themselves but for collective needs they pray together in the church.[14]

Christ's supremacy over the whole creation means that he controls every part of creation, he desires us to look to him for all our needs. We need to teach the people that unlike the spirits, Christ cannot be manipulated. The truth that he knows our needs before we call to him should encourage us to pray to him at any time and at the same time to be very honest with him.

Knowing and Affirming the Leaders

Every community has its own leaders or elders. These men are the custodians of the people's world-view, the ancestral secrets, and the people's well being. The people will not change their religious allegiance until the elders agree to it. Because the messenger of the gospel is an outsider, it will be important for him or her to affirm the position and authority of the elders and work for their conversion by befriending them. The earlier that relationship is established the easier it will be for the gospel to be presented. When the elders are converted to Christ we should establish them firmly in the faith so that in time they will become custodians of the Christian faith. By the grace of God we hope and pray that they will fully give their allegiance to Jesus Christ and lead their people to walk that same way.

Overcoming in the Spiritual Warfare

The missionary must guard his spiritual life. Working amongst animists is like working in a mine full of explosives. Unless the explosives are rendered lifeless they remain deadly to all who are within their reach. Satan like a wounded lion is roaring around looking for someone to devour. The messenger of the gospel is undoubtedly his number one target. The Holy Spirit warns us against this when he says:

> For our struggle is not against flesh and blood, but against the rulers, against the authorities, against the powers of this dark world and against the spiritual forces of

evil in the heavenly realms. Therefore put on the full armour of God, so that when the day of evil comes, you may be able to stand your ground, and after you have done everything, to stand (Eph. 6: 12–13).

Recent study done amongst Wycliffe Bible Translators around the world showed that the biggest single problem that missionaries found is to maintain a vital, meaningful time with the Lord. For those of us who are involved in preparing men and women for the ministry, daily encounter with the Lord must receive top priority. Unless as staff and students we learn to fight the enemy on our knees while we are together it will be too late to learn the art of waiting on the Lord when the students leave the premises. All missionary candidates should be required to put in writing their daily walk with the Lord. They should be encouraged to indicate their joys and their disappointments as they seek to walk with the Lord. Someone has wisely stated: 'As now so then'.

CONCLUSION

Animists have a system of belief of their own. Their lives are imprisoned by spirit powers. They live under constant fear of the spirits. Those who turn to Christ need a great deal of support and encouragement. Without proper follow-up teaching they would soon turn back to the spirit world. To present Jesus Christ effectively at their World-View level will demand a great deal from the missionary. 'The missionary can know what the people assume about the world only by digging it out through painstaking effort, patience and participation' (Roxburn). The missionary must dig it out. For those of us from an animistic background, the challenge is to develop deeper skills of understanding and exegeting the Scriptures which relate to our heritage and to proclaim the uniqueness of Christ to our people.

NOTES

1. Koschade, Alfred. *New Branches On The Vine, From Mission Field to Church in New Guinea.* Minneapolis, Augsburg Publishing House, 1967, p. 116f.
2. Frerichs, A.C., *Anatu Conquers in New Guinea*, Columbus Ohio, The Wartburg Press, 1957, p. 121.
3. Daimoi, J.K., *Nominalism in Papua New Guiea*, Fuller Theological Seminary, School of World Mission, Pasadena, 1985, p. 49.
4. Narokobi, Bernard M., 'What is Religious Experience for a Melanesian?' in Callick, Rowan, *Christ in Melanesia, Exploring Theological Issues*, 7–12, Goroka, Papua New Guinea, Melanesian Institute, 1977, p. 9.
5. Dawia, Alexander, 'Indigenizing Christian Worship,' Point 1: 13–60, 1980, p. 28.
6. Daimoi, *op. cit.*, p. 74.
7. Narokobi, *op. cit.*, p. 7f.
8. Luzbetak, Louis J., *The Church and Culture*, Pasadena, California, William Carcy Library, 1970, p. 62.
9. Koschade, *op. cit.*, p. 122.
10. Narokobi, *op. cit.*, p. 10.

11. Codrington, R.H., *The Melanesians, Studies in Their Anthropology and Folklore*, Oxford, The Clarendon Press, 1981, p. 47.

12. Hendriksen, William. *Colossians and Philemon*, Baker Book House, Grand Rapids, Michigan, 1964, p. 72.

13. *Lausanne Occasional Papers, No. 2 The Willowbank Report – Gospel and Culture*, Wheaton, Lausanne Committee for World Evangelization, 1978, p. 21.

14. Tamanabae, Richmond. 'The Pentecostal Movement,' *Catalyst, Social Pastoral Magazine for Melanesia*, 11:1: 1–17, Goroka, Papua New Guinea, Melanesian institute, 1981, p. 13.

6

Kim-Sai Tan

INTRODUCTION

In a way every person in the world is unique. No two people are exactly alike. This is true also of religious founders with their respective faiths. In this paper the uniqueness of Christ is taken to mean that Christ is the one and only Saviour of all humankind, that 'Salvation is found in no one else, for there is no other name under heaven given to men by which we must be saved' (Acts 4:12).

This 'salvific' uniqueness of Christ as discussed below is set in the context of the plurality of religions in our world today, with special reference to the issues of a theology of religions. The main concern is this. Confronted with the assertiveness of various resurging world religions, realizing the many failures of historic and contemporary Christianity, and troubled with modern epistemologies and hermeneutics of religious interpretation, is it still possible for Christians to hold on to the dogma of Christ's salvific uniqueness for all people?

CHALLENGE OF THE 'PLURALISTIC' THEOLOGIANS

The publication of *The Myth of Christian Uniqueness* (Orbis Books, 1987), coedited by Presbyterian John Hick and Catholic Paul F. Knitter, was meant to be the launching pad or 'Rubicon crossing' of the 'Pluralist' position, vis-a-vis a Christian theology of religions.[1] Publication of the book was preceded by a symposium of contributing writers.

The recent book of S. J. Samartha, the first and retired director of the Dialogue Programme of the WCC in Geneva, entitled *One Christ, Many Religions* (Orbis Books, 1991) will certainly reinforce this 'monstrous'[2] paradigm shift. Hick, Knitter, and Samartha may be called the 'Pluralistic Trio'.

Other theologians that contribute to *The Myth of Christian Uniqueness* include W. Cantwell Smith (described as a pioneer of the paradigm shift)[3]

Dr. Kim-Sai Tan teaches theology in Seoul, Korea.

Gordon D. Kaufman, Langdon Gilkey, Raimundo Panikkar, Tom F. Driver, Aloysius Pieris and so on. Here is a shift that calls for serious attention, for it will definitely affect Christian mission and evangelism.

The 'Pluralist' paradigm is put in juxtaposition and opposition to the conservative 'Exclusivist' paradigm and the liberal 'Inclusivist' paradigm. It seems to be a new paradigm, and seems to promise a lot. But in fact it is only the old universalism in new dress, armed with more sophisticated weaponry.

Samartha seems to put the blame for many international, interreligious, intercommunal, and interpersonal problems on the unique claims of the Christian faith, as if it is a big theological and moral evil.[4] I really doubt whether but for the exclusivist conviction of men and women of God who brought the unique Christ to India, he would have become a Christian. Such would be the 'fate' of many, myself included.

In contrast to the 'Exclusivist' paradigm, which proclaims Christ as the only Lord and Saviour, and salvation in him alone; and the 'Inclusivist' paradigm, which upholds Christ as the only Lord and Saviour, but claims that salvation is possible for others by the mysterious grace of God; the 'Pluralist' paradigm advocates that other religions, lords or saviours are independently valid ways to salvation.[5] Apparently the Pauline injunction that there is only one God and one Lord is disregarded (1 Cor. 8:4–6).

The 'Pluralist' way is seen as a logical expansion of the 'Inclusivist' position, with one opening the door to the other. John Hick avers,

> As a Christian position this can be seen as an acceptance of the further conclusion to which inclusivism points. If we accept that salvation/liberation is taking place within all the great religious traditions, why not frankly acknowledge that there is a plurality of saving human responses to the ultimate divine reality? . . . There is not merely one way but a plurality of ways of salvation or liberation[6]

UNIQUENESS AND FINALITY OF CHRIST AT STAKE

Focusing on the real issue at stake is needed. We Evangelicals do not argue for the superiority or finality of the Christian church on earth, nor any brand of Christianity;[7] neither do we say that unless a person becomes a church member, he or she cannot be saved. Jesus Christ and his salvific grace has been defined by the Church, but it can never be confined by it. The grace and love of God is certainly broader than we ever realize.

Obviously as individual Christians we dare not claim superiority over non-Christians, realizing that we are merely sinners saved by grace. In fact in the light of Christ's uniqueness, Christians corporately as well as individually deserve a harsher chastisement for our failures (Lk. 12:48; 1 Pet. 4:17). Where we have been able to glorify God and be of help to others, this is not of our own doing, but out of God's mercy and grace in and through Christ.

It is not proper to dogmatize that people who have never had an opportunity of encounter with Christ are automatically lost. However, dogmatizing the other way round is equally inappropriate. So stressing Christ's salvific uniqueness is not to be equated with automatic condemnation of others.

With regard to possible salvific grace of God beyond church walls, passages like Isaiah 19:25, Amos 9:7, Malachi 1:11, Matthew 8:11–12, Acts 10:34–35, Romans 2:5–11; 5:15–17 can be encouraging. But these are not necessarily enlightening, in the sense that they do not tell how God saves, if he does, apart from expressed allegiance to Christ. However, as Christ is (and will be) the only Saviour and Judge, we can be sure whoever is saved is saved only through him (Rev. 20:11–15).

Whatever inclusivist hope may be entertained or speculated, as Evangelicals we need to be constantly reminded of the urgent evangelistic mandate, and to press on with it, until Christ shall return. It would be a mistake to major on speculation and theologization with regard to who might be saved, and minor or minus on the Great Commission entrusted to us.

So the real bone of contention is the uniqueness, finality, and superiority of Jesus Christ and his salvific work, as compared with other lords or saviours and their respective ways. Insofar as it is the salvific uniqueness of Christ that is at stake, the title of the 'Myth' book (which reads 'Christian' uniqueness) is foggy and misleading.

While God has given Christ all the authority in heaven and on earth (Mt. 28:18), and exalted him to the highest place, endowed with the Name that is above every name (Phil. 2:9–11), pluralist theologians seem determined to bring him down, and confine him to Christian circles.

PAROCHIAL OPINION AND PERSONAL SENTIMENTALISM

Nonetheless pluralist theologians do continue to speak of the uniqueness of Christ, but it is a uniqueness that is personal, sentimental, and parochial, confined to intrachristian usage. In an interreligious context its usage would be a hindrance and obnoxious taboo.

According to Knitter, exclusivist Christological language such as 'one and only' is 'much like the language a husband would use of his wife (or vice versa): "you are the most beautiful woman in the world . . . You are the only woman for me".'[8] This is said to be a trait of 'confessional' and 'testimony' language, and not the language of philosophy, science or dogmatics. The implication is that such a claim can be only subjectively and relatively true, and Christians should not seek to preach it to others.

'Confessional' and 'testimony' language it certainly is. As Christians throughout the ages have known, we are commissioned precisely to make this confession and testimony of the Lord Jesus, 'to the ends of the earth' (Acts 1:8). But by the way Knitter, Hick and company treat such a 'confession' it is not 'confessional' and 'testimonial', in the traditional sense of the world. Rather it has become something parochial, personal and sentimental, as the husband and wife analogy above illustrates.

It is also alleged that exclusivist claims in the Bible are in the nature of a 'minority language' or 'survival language'. Says Samartha, 'A minority community was seeking to guard its identity in relation to a large and powerful majority.'[9] This idea seems to be another example of wishy washy personal opinion, probably first suggested by Gregory Baum.[10]

If a minority or survival situation justifies such usage of language, then Christians in India, being a poor and small minority, deserve to use it more. If such language should not be used at all, by majority or minority, then let it be known that it was such language together with the conviction behind it that pushed forward the Christian outreach. If the early apostles and other Christians had adopted the pluralist stand, would the Christian faith have spread beyond the Judean border?

Furthermore, it is said that exclusivist language in the New Testament had been eschatologically conditioned. If the proposition is true, then all Christians who believe the end time has drawn much closer than before certainly should intensify rather than slacken its use.[11]

A personal and sentimental Christology will produce only a personal and sentimental Christianity which will not survive the onslaught of modern secular and 'spiritual' forces. Whatever merits pluralist scholars may have (and I do think we can learn something from them), their major concern does not seem to be that humans everywhere should come to acknowledge Jesus Christ as Lord and Saviour.

Following the publication of *The Myth of God Incarnate* edited by Hick (1977);[12] and *No Other Name?* authored by Knitter (1985); and now with the promotion of *The Myth of Christian Uniqueness*, be not surprised if they publish next a book entitled *The Myth of the Great Commission*!

IS CHRIST'S UNIQUENESS EXCLUSIVIST?

The pluralist view is tailored to meet the challenge of religious plurality. But as far as the uniqueness of Christ is concerned, the New Testament is certainly exclusivist (likewise for Yahweh in the Old Testament).

Knitter himself acknowledges the fact that 'much of what the New Testament says about Jesus is also exclusive, or at least normative'. 1 Tim. 2:5, Acts 4:12, Jn. 1:14, 14:6, 1 Cor. 21–22, and Heb. 9:12 are quoted to illustrate the point. He continues:

> To close one's eyes to such proclamation is either physchologically to repress or dishonestly to deny what one does not wish to see. It is also either dishonest or naive to argue that the early Christians really did not mean or believe what they were saying, as if they were conscious of the 'historical relativity' or 'mythic conditioning' of such language. When the early Jesus-followers announced to the world that Jesus was 'one and only' they meant it.[13]

In fact exclusivist Christology has been the norm not only in the New Testament, but also in all the church traditions, whether Catholic, Orthodox, or Protestant (at least up to the time of the writing of his book), as Knitter's deliberations on these various traditions testify.[14]

THE VATICAN, THE WCC AND THE EVANGELICAL POSITION

Soteriologywise, the Catholic Church seems to have become too inclusive. I do not see valid biblical justification for the broad soteriological inclusiveness which asserts, among other things, that all humans, without exception are redeemed already, in Christ.[15]

But when it comes to Christology, the Catholic church does not compromise at all on the supreme uniqueness of Christ, i.e. it has not gone Pluralist, as Knitter himself expresses it:

> Christ must be proclaimed as the fullest revelation, the definitive savior, the norm above all other norms for all religions. This, they say, is as far as Christians can go. The move beyond this point is to jeopardise the distinctiveness, the essence, of Christianity.[16]

Not only that, according to a 1991 papal Encyclical on Missionary activity named *Redemptoris Missio*, the Pope urges emphatically that missionary evangelization is 'the primary service which the church can render to every individual and to all humanity in the modern world, which . . . seems to have lost its sense of ultimate realities and of existence itself'. He follows by declaring Christ as 'The Only Savior', and affirming 'proclamation as the permanent priority of mission'.[17]

On the other hand, the WCC executives[18] also seem to have gone the way of soteriological inclusiveness. In *resources for Reflections – Preparation for WCC 7th Assembly*, we find the following statement:

> We affirm unequivocally that God the Holy Spirit has been at work in the life and traditions of people of living faiths . . . Our recognition of the mystery of salvation in the men and women of other religious traditions shapes the concrete attitudes with which we Christians must approach them in religious dialogues.

It says as a matter of fact that there are God's other missions in the world, apart from the mission of the Church. These other divine missions are being carried out through the Buddhist movement, the Hindu complex, and the Islamic venture.[19] Has WCC leadership gone Pluralistic?

In the Report of the Central Committee to the 7th. Assembly, very little is said about evangelism. As regards Dialogue with other religions, sharp differences among churches is reported. The urgency to declare Christ as Lord and Saviour of the world, and an unequivocal call to mission and evangelism, such as they are manifested in the papal Encyclical *Redeptoris Missio*, are sadly missing.[20]

The Evangelical position is unequivocally firm and clear. Article 3 of the 1974 Lausanne Covenant declares that 'there is one Saviour and only one gospel'; that 'Jesus Christ has been exalted above every other name; we long for the day when every knee shall bow to him and every tongue shall confess him Lord.' General revelation is said to have no salvific value at all. In article 4 evangelism is defined as 'the proclamation of the historical, biblical Christ as Saviour and Lord, with a view to persuading people to come to him and so be reconciled to God'.[21]

Lausanne II in Manila reiterated this basic commitment. In the Manila Manifesto (article 7) there is the affirmation that 'other religions and ideologies are not alternative paths to God, and that human spirituality, if unredeemed by Christ, leads not to God but to judgement, for Christ is the only way.'[22] To go by the Lausanne Covenant, Evangelical position is exclusivist both Christologically and soteriologically.

AFFIRMATION OF CHRIST'S 'FIVE Cs' UNIQUENESS

I propose to affirm the salvific uniqueness of Christ by a 'Five Cs' affirmation. The 'Five Cs' are as follows: 'Cradle' as the symbol of Christ's incarnation; 'Career' which refers to his life and ministry; 'Cross' meaning his redemptive death; 'Character' referring to his full sanctification and dedication; and 'Crown' as the symbol of Christ's resurrection and glorification.

First, the 'Cradle' as the symbol of Christ's incarnation. Both Matthew and Luke record the virgin birth. John speaks in terms of the incarnation. Taken together there is the threefold affirmation of the unique birth of Christ. How can people 'prove' that the virgin birth or for that matter the incarnation was not literally true? The onus of 'proof' is on those who call it a 'myth' and discredit its literal truthfulness, and I do not see that any critical scholar can ever do that. On the other hand, there is no lack of reputable scholars arguing for its defence.[23]

The significance of the incarnation is in 'Immanuel', meaning 'God with us' (Matt. 1:23). 'The Word became flesh and made his dwelling among us' (Jn. 1:14). It reveals the God who in Christ became human and dwelt in our midst, and who continues to do so, even more intimately, through the indwelling Holy Spirit. The incarnate Christ serves as the ladder between heaven and earth, God and humans (Jn. 1:51). It is also essential for soteriology, so that the substitutionary death of Christ is seen as the 'self-substitution' of God,[24] thus removing the charge of its being immoral.

The second point is the unique Career of Christ, equally set in concrete historical context.[25] There are records of Christ's powerful deeds and authoritative words which can never be hermeneutically explained away. The impact of his career was that the sovereign rule of God has dawned, and history has entered a new era (Matt. 3:16, 12:28). Though Christ's public ministry life was only about three years, his deeds and words continue to inspire and to transform.

No ministerial life has been cut short so soon, so cruelly, and has yet a living legacy that is so fruitful and lasting. It reveals the God who in Christ identifies with human struggles against evils – secular and 'spiritual', as well as seeking and saving the lost. The living struggles of Christ have been specially emulated by modern liberation theologians for social justice and wellbeing (Heb. 12:2–4).

The central and crucial point is the Cross of Christ. It reveals the God who not only comes to live in the midst of humans, helping and saving, but goes to the extent of suffering and dying for humans, bearing human sins on the cross, in Christ. In this respect a growing number of theologians, evangelical and otherwise, have come to speak of the 'suffering God', so much so that theopaschitism (not amounting to patripassionism) is now referred to as the rising chorus of a 'new orthodoxy'.[26]

Others may die for noble ideas or causes, only the perfect Christ is qualified to die for sinners (Rom. 5:8). Others may solve social or political problems, He alone can solve the sin problem (Matt. 1:21; Jn. 1:29). Others may present a heroic death; his death as well as his life (in fact more than his life) is forever redemptive (Mk. 10:45; Eph. 1:7).

The uniqueness of the Cradle, the Career, and the Cross is marked by the most unique Character he exemplified, so much so that he could declare he was one with the Father, that the Father was in him and he was in the Father, that he who sees him sees the Father (Jn. 14:9–11). His oneness with God is both and at the same time ontological and functional.

He had been tempted in all things yet without sin (Heb. 4:15).[27] Such character reveals the very nature of God himself. 'For in Christ all the fulness of the deity lives in bodily form' (Col. 2:9). Through Christ believers are enabled to partake in the divine nature and character, as a branch is joined to the stem of the vine (Rom. 6:1–4; Jn. 15:1–8; Pet. 1:3–4). In him is the union of the human and the divine made possible, and perfect.

The unique death of Christ is followed by his bodily, glorious resurrection. No other religious founder was raised from the dead like him, and exalted to the highest place in Heaven, seated at the right hand of God (Phil. 2:9–11). Resurrection and glorification constitute the unique 'Crown' of Christ, which will be made manifest to all the world at his second coming.

Christ's resurrection was an event attested with 'many convincing proofs' (Acts 1:3) personal, circumstantial, and consequential.[28] The death and resurrection of Christ became the greatest world shaking and changing event that has ever taken place. It shows God's full acceptance of the redemptive life and death of Christ, and his victory (also Christ's victory) over the forces of evil and death. It assures that ultimately the sovereign rule of God will triumph. It is also the concrete basis for our hope of eternity and glory.

THE UNIQUENESS OF A CHRISTIAN WORLDVIEW

Pressing for a pluralist theology of religions, theologians allege that there are various and 'evolutionary' forms of Christology in the New Testament itself, all of which are to some extent culturally conditioned, so why not this biblical pluralism to include also salvific models of other religions?[29]

Granted that there are various Christological perspectives in the Bible, and that there is perceived 'development' (from below to above, functional to ontological) with regard to the understanding of Christ, from the Synoptic, Pauline and the Johannine traditions, the Church has always seen them as supplementary and complementary to one another, and treat all of them as equally divine and canonical.

Pluralists seek to discriminate especially against the 'high' and 'exclusive' Christologies on the basis of their personal favour. This discrimination is lopsided and unacceptable. The high Christology in John's Gospel is perceived as a major stumbling block to interreligious dialogues. However James Dunn, a noted advocate of developmental Christology himself, has the following counsel to offer:

> The Jesus of John is *also* Jesus as he was increasingly seen to be, as the understanding of who Jesus was deepened through the decades of the first century. John's Gospel, we may say, is intended to present the *truth* about Jesus, but not by means of a strictly historical portrayal. The Synoptic Gospels, if you like, are more like a portrait of Jesus; John's Gospel is more like an impressionist painting of Jesus. Both present the real Jesus, but in very different ways.[30]

So in spite of differences in perspectives, there is one Jesus Christ recognized and received by all. The fivefold uniqueness of Christ deliberated above is, as far as I know, generally accepted by all major Church traditions, with the exception of some cultic or liberal partisans.

It seems that based on the unique Christ, with his Cross at the centre, there could be the distillation of a Christian worldview, defined as its core and diehard beliefs and values.

The essence and uniqueness of a Christian worldview, as I see it, is in our God who is holy and is love, who gives himself through his incarnate Word, and the indwelling Spirit, for the salvation and eternal life of humankind. This forms the basis of Christian knowledge of God and redemption.

Everything begins with the infinite God who gives of himself to humanity, supremely manifest in the incarnation and the Cross. Christians are people who have experienced this self-giving and redemptive love of God in Christ, and are inspired and exhorted to share it with others. A. Toynbee sees these as the essential elements of Christian faith.[31]

My perception is that there is no other worldview in the world like it. There may be some pale shadows of it in certain forms of some non-Christian religions, but the reality and fulness of it is found only in Christ.[32]

I would advocate a worldview approach to the presentation of the gospel, in which the goal is the inculcation of a transformational worldview change, based on core beliefs and values as mentioned above, without trying to change the culture or even 'religious' practices of the believers (as in the case of Messianic Jews and Messianic Muslims). But the present paper is not the place to elaborate on this proposition further.

SOME CONCLUDING REMARKS

(1) The pluralist approach to a Christian theology of religions is neither biblical nor Christian, in the traditional sense of the word. It is therefore to be rejected as a well meaning but ill conceived personal opinion and sentiment. Capitulation to it will certainly lead to further erosion of mission and evangelism. God had ordained him to be Saviour and Lord of all, and given him the highest Name. Let no one try to bring him down.

(2) While the sensitivity of pluralist theologians towards other religionists is very commendable, their tactic of publishing shocking 'titles,' the 'Myth' of this and that, seemingly without pastoral consideration for the multitudes of lay Christians, is highly deplorable.

Only God knows the extent of damage they have afflicted on the faithful by such pronouncements, especially on those of us living in the South, in already hostile environments, John Hick seems to be aware of the danger, and he continued to publish one 'Myth' after another.[33]

The use (or misuse) of the term 'myth' causes much confusion,[34] and it is to be employed with extreme care when applied to the Bible. Whatever technical meanings it may have for the experts, I suspect that for the general public and the general believers the connotations would be always negative. We need to be extremely careful about it.

(3) The practice of pluralist theologians to dump the incarnation with all sorts of legends of fairy tales as 'myth' is objectionable. While the 'myth' of virgin birth and the incarnation has long been subjected to the most severe

and often biased dissectation, under the veneer of scholarship, the same kind of treatment is not seen to apply to other 'myths'.

Various 'myths' seem to be given the same value, both on the surface and the deep level. For instance, the historicity of Krishna and Rama is so complicated that Samartha sees it as almost impossible to indicate any date with a measure of certainty (the rounded form of their stories could have been reached from 400 BC–AD 400).[35]

Characterwise, there certainly is a world of difference between Christ and Krisna,[36] yet deities such as this seem to be classed on par with our Christ as viable alternatives. Such approach is intellectually, morally and spiritually offensive, objectively speaking.

(4) To be true to the Bible and the Great Commission, and even more so as Evangelicals, there should be no compromise in the confession and affirmation that Jesus is the Word of God incarnate, and only Saviour of all the world. This is indeed the Christology, biblical, evangelical, ecumenic and historic.[37] New versions of Christology may be formulated; differences of emphasis need to be applied in different contexts, but the unique supremacy of Christ is not something to be compromised.

In the early 60s, the General Secretary of the WCC then, W. A. Visser't Hooft had sensed the challenge of plurality of religions, and expressed the following contention:

> The attitude of the Christian Church to the religions can therefore only be the attitude of the witness who points to the one Lord Jesus Christ as Lord of all men. Where the church ceases to give this witness, it ceases to have a *raison d'etre*, for it came into being to proclaim this good news and not to add one more form of spiritual experience to the many which existed already.[38]

The apostolic mission given to the church is that it should be faithful to the 'news', and not to become renovative in fashionable 'views'. For that matter the 'news' consists precisely in the particularity of Christ as the only Lord and Saviour. If it is a scandal it is one inherent in the Christ-given message and mission itself. The imperative is to be faithful as worthy ambassadors, irrespective of whether one likes the message or the task or not (2 Cor. 5:19–21; 1 Cor. 4:2). Let this conviction be the heart of Evangelicalism.

(5) To be realistic and relevant, Evangelicals do have to take into consideration the writings of pluralist advocates.[39]

After reading through some of them, I remind myself to be more sober and sensitive in my proclamation of the unique Lordship of Christ, so that I do not betray by my deed what my mouth confesses.

Indeed as a matter of 'approach' it may be discreet not to simply 'advertise' Christ's supremacy. But to 'sell' it as a theological principle is a different matter. If Christianity has failed in the past, the need is for a more authentic and radical discipleship (Samartha speaks brilliantly about it),[40] but never to compromise in truth. Two wrongs never make a right.

(6) To be honest with ourselves, we really need to develop an Evangelical theology of religions. While rejecting the Pluralist viewpoint, and upholding the exclusive claims of Christ, how are we to look at other world religions? What do we say of seekers of truth who apparently have not been given an opportunity of encounter with Christ?

If broad soteriological inclusivism is not justifiable, is conservative soterio-logical exclusivism always satisfactory? Is the Spirit of God confined within the church walls? Is general revelation and grace never salvific at all? What are the rules of accountability in judgement? These are some of the issues to grapple with.

(7) The Evangelical circle needs a lot more of scholars, in the areas of biblical exegesis, theology, as well as comparative religious studies and missiology. The need is even more acute in the two-thirds world. What can be done to raise more of such?

NOTES

1. The editors say in the Preface, 'Part of the purpose of this book is to "expose" this new approach, to bring it out into the open so that other theologians, together with the Christian community at large, might better evaluate its content and coherence, and judge how adequate it is to human experience, how appropriate and faithful to Christian tradition', p. VIII.

2. In the words of Langdon Gilkey, Divinity professor of Chicago University, quoted in the above Preface: 'a monstrous shift indeed . . . a position quite new to the churches, even to the liberal churches' (Ibid.).

3. See John Hick, *Problems of Religious Pluralism* (NY: St. Martin's Press, 1983), p. 28.

4. Read *One Christ–Many Religions*, pp. 98–103.

5. Op. cit., in the words of Hick and Knitter, the 'pluralist' position is 'a move away from insistence on the superiority or finality of Christ and Christianity toward a recognition of the independent validity of other ways'.

6. See *Problems of Religious Pluralism*, p. 34.

7. Raimundo Panikkar writes of the inadequacies of the 'superiority' approach, citing three sets of consideration: the psychological/pastoral, the historical, and the theological (*The Unknown Christ of Hinduism*, Orbis Books, 1981), pp. 75–89. As it regards the church, Christianity, or individual Christians, he is right. But the 'superiority' of Christ is a different question.

8. See Paul F. Knitter, *No Other Name?* Maryknoll, NY: Orbis Books, 1986, p. 185.

9. See Samartha, p. 100.

10. See *Christ's Lordship and Religious Pluralism*, edited by Gerald H. Anderson & Thomas F. Stransky (NY: Orbis Books, 1981), p. 88.

11. Ibid., P. 87–88.

12. Published by London: SCM Press Ltd..

13. See *No Other Name*, p. 182.

14. Ibid., Chapter 5–7.

15. See Pope John Paul II, *Redemptor Hominis*, note 14 which says: 'The human person – every person without exception – has been redeemed by Christ; because Christ is in a way united to the human person – every person without exception – even if the individual may not realize this fact.' My question is, in the light of Rev. 21:8, how can it be said that all humans, without exception are redeemed? I find such a position soteriologically unduly broad (Washington: United States Catholic Conference, 1979), p. 44.

16. Ibid., p. 143.

17. See Origins – CNS Documentary Service, Vol. 20: No. 24, Jan. 1991, pp. 543, 554. There is evidence that the emphasis of the Encyclical is at least in part to serve as a response to the Pluralist shift. See Chapter 1, note 4, last paragraph.

18. By WCC executives I mean those who prepare the related document.

19. For the quotation above and related statement, please refer to the *Resources for Reflections*, pp. 69–71. It was published by the WCC in Geneva in 1990, as a preparation for the 1991 Assembly in Canberra, Australia.

20. See *Reading Vancouver to Canberra, 1983–90*, edited by Thomas Best. Geneva: WCC Publications. Read especially pp. 103–106, 130–140.

21. See J. D. Douglas (ed.0, *Proclaim Christ until he Comes*. (Minn.: World Wide Publications, 1990), p. 20.

22. Ibid., p. 26.

23. For the defence of the incarnation, to cite at random, read for instance the works of Thomas F. Torrance (The *Incarnation*, Edinburgh: Handsel Press, 1981; *The Trinitarian Faith*, Edinburgh: T & T Clark, 1988); E. L. Mascall (*Theology and the Gospel of Christ*, London: SPCK, 1977; *Jesus, Who is He and How We Know Him*, London: Darton, Longman and Todd, 1985); John Macquarrie (*The Humility of God*, Philadelphia: The Westminster Press, 1978; *The Search of Deity*, NY: Crossroad, 1984); James Dunn (*The Evidence for Jesus*, KY: The Westminster Press, 1985); Michael Goulder, ed. *The Debate Continued: Incarnation and Myth* (Grand Rapids: Wm. B. Eerdmans, 1979) Brian Hebblethwaite (*The Incarnation, Collected Essays in Christology*. Cambridge: Cambridge University Press, 1987); Robert L. Reymond (*Jesus, Divine Messiah*, 1990); Howard I. Marshall (*The Origin of New Testament Christology*. IL: InterVarsity Press, updated, 1990) etc. Robert L. Reymond's *Jesus, Divine Messiah* should be in the possession of every Evangelical.

24. See John Stott, *The Cross of Christ* (Leicester: InterVarsity Press, 1986), p. 156.

25. For the poverty of historical criticism with regard to the life of Christ, read E. L. Mascall (*Theology and the Gospel of Christ*. London: SPCK, 1977), pp. 63–117. He had written about fact and the Gospels in *The Secularization of Christianity* (London: Darton, Longman and Todd, 1965), pp. 213–282. Noted historian Michael Grant deplores the hostile attitude of liberal scholars in this area (See *Jesus: An Historian's Review of the Gospels*. NY: Charles Scribner's Sons, 1977, pp. 197–204).

Some criticisms from continental 'insiders' include damning works by Gerhard Maier (*The End of the Historical-critical Method*. St. Louis: Concordia Pub. House, 1974. transl. by Leverenz and Norden), Eta Linnemann (*Historical Criticism of the Bible: Methodology or Ideology*. Grand Rapids: Baker Book House, 1990. transl. by Yarbrough), and a more moderate one by Peter Stuhlmacher (Philadelphia: Fortress Press, 1977. transl. by Harrisville).

26. Concept of the 'suffering' or 'crucified' God (not tantamount to patripassionism) is on the ascendance. Ronald Goetz described the phenomenon as 'the rise of a new orthodoxy' (*Christian Century*: Vol. 103, no. 3, pp. 385–389). His list of modern theopaschite thinkers include Barth, Brunner, Cobb, Kung, Moltmann, N. Niebuhr, liberation theologians, etc.

John Stott is strongly in favour of this concept, as can be read in *The Cross of Christ* (Leicester: InterVarsity, 1986), pp. 311–337.

Interestingly old evangelicals like G. Campbell Morgan and A. W. Tozer also held strongly to such view. Read, for instance Campbell Morgan's sermon in *Great Sermons on the Death of Christ* (Wilber Smith, ed. Natwick, Mass.: W. A. Wilde Company, 1965), p. 117; A. W. Tozer (*The Pursuit of God*. Camphill, CA: Christian Publication, Inc., 1982), p. 13.

27. Oxford don Dennis Nineham, a contributor to *The Myth of God Incarnate*, indicates that historically the perfection of Christ can be questionable (See the book, pp. 186–204).

28. John A. T. Robinson seems to attest to the faithfulness of the biblical record on the resurrection. See *Can We Trust the New Testament?* (Grand Rapids: Wm. B. Eerdmans, 1977), pp. 120–129.

In fact, the book affirms the New Testament as a 'faithful' book, in both senses of the quoted word. He writes critically of undue criticism of its historical trust-worthiness.

29. For instance see Knitter, *No Other Name*, pp. 177–182.

30. See James G. D. Dunn, *The Evidence for Jesus* (Louisville, KY: The Westminster Press, 1985), p. 43.

31. Arnold Toynbee seems to capture the core of a Christian worldview when he deliberates on its three 'essential elements', i.e. one, the God who loves his creatures so much that he sacrifices himself for their salvation: two, human beings ought to follow the example God has set them in his incarnation and crucifixion; three, to act on the above conviction as far as one is able ('What Should be the Christian Approach to the Contemporary Non-Christian Faiths'? in *Attitudes Toward Other Religions*, edited by Owen C. Thomas. NY: Harper & Row Publishers, 1969, pp. 167–168).

32. The argument of Toynbee that there are similar elements in nature-worship, Buddhism and so on is poor and muddled (Ibid., pp. 168–169). Islam, of course, does not accept the notion of the incarnation and the God who suffers for and with humans, to the point of divine self-sacrifice.

33. See *Problems of Religious Pluralism*, p. 14. In Malaysia it is common for such statements to be seized by other religionists to attack Christians. Some assert that they are more 'christian' than the clergy and the bishops because they believe in the virgin birth! We are often subjected to such painful exposures.

34. A common definition is that it is 'an explanatory story'. The question is: What explanatory story? Is it true, fictional, or quasi-true? In the Chinese language it seems there is no way of getting round its connotation as a fairy tale (shen hua?).

35. Read Samartha, *One Christ, Many Religions*, pp. 124–31. To compare the 'myth' of Krisna and the 'myth' of Christ, one may compare *Krisna*, by A. C. Bhaktivedanta Swami (Boston: Iskcon Press, 1970) with the Gospels.

36. E. Stanley Jones deliberates on the character and attraction of krisna as follows:

He is the incarnation of the irresponsible. He steps outside all laws and codes. He is a gay figure, standing with one foot crossing the other as he plays his flute; as a baby kicks a cart to pieces, he steals the butter and the curds, plays pranks on everyone, runs away with the clothes of the bathing gopis (milkmaids), and hides in a tree and laughs at their distress. He entrances the wives of the cowherds of Brindaban and gaily dances with sixteen thousand of them at night and marries and consorts with whom he pleases. He walks across all codes and laws and seems to promise freedom from Karma, for he himself seems to be free. He is the incarnation of the gay, the irresponsible, the Karma-free. (See *Christ at the Round Table*. NY: The Abingdon Press, 1928, p. 266).

An influence of such and similar deities on Hindu religious and moral life can be read in *The Unique Christ and the Mystic Gandhi*, by P. V. George (Tiruvalla, India: The Malabar Christian Office). See specially pp. 174–184.

37. Refer Bernard L. Ramm, *An Evangelical Christology: Ecumenic and Historic*, NY: Thomas Nelson Publishers, 1985.

38. See *No other Name* (Philadelphia: The Westminster Press, 1963), p. 116. These words were written as a precaution against religious syncretism; nevertheless they would be equally applicable in the context of pluralism.

39. For an introduction into the subject, besides those titles cited in this Endnote, I offer the following random selection: John Hick and Brian Hebblethwaite (*Christianity and Other Religions*. Philadelphia: Fortress, 1981); Gerald H. Anderson & Thomas F. Stransky, ed. (*Christ's Lordship and Religious Pluralism* NY: Orbis Books, 1981); Kenneth Cragg (*The Christ and the Faiths*. Philadelphia: The Westminster Press, 1986); Stephen Neill (*Christian Faith and Other Faiths*. Oxford: Oxford University Press, 1960; J. N. D. Anderson (*Christianity and Comparative Religion*. IL.: InterVarsity Press, 1971); Hans Kung (*Christianity and the World Religions*. NY: Doubleday and Company, 1986), etc..

40. See Samartha, *One Christ, Many Religions*, p. 142–154.

Part Two

The Unique Christ in the Challenge
of Modernity

7

Yoshiaki Hattori

Dr. Yoshiaki Hattori introduces this section of our theme by reaffirming the classical evangelical position on general and special revelation and on the methods of biblical exegesis and in interpreting from text to context. He surveys the impact of modern communication technology and then calls for a reaffirmation of the primacy of text-orientated exegesis of the Bible.

INTRODUCTION

Regardless of whether we like it or not, the unceasing waves of modernity have been influencing and shifting our way of life in one way or another. Little Kenji was in a store with his mother when he was given a stick of candy by one of the girls working in the store. 'What do you say, Kenji?' asked his mother. 'Charge it!' he replied.

In view of the general theme of this consultation with its focus upon the uniqueness of Christ, there seems to be a very basic prerequisite for our discussion of the theme of the unique Christ. It is the uniqueness of special revelation. Referring to the Old Testament, our Lord Jesus witnessed that the Scripture, in that case the Old Testament, was to reveal the Messiah, who was Jesus Christ himself, as seen in Luke 24:44, '. . . all things which are written about me in the Law of Moses and the prophets and the psalms must be fulfilled.' It is in the New Testament that we come to the revelation which speaks of the uniqueness of Christ when in his own words he said: 'I am the Way, and the Truth and the Life; no one comes to the Father, but through me,' (Jn. 14:6) or in the words of Peter's Spirit-filled proclamation when he said: 'There is salvation in no one else; for there is no other name under heaven that has been given among men, by which we must be saved' (Acts 4:12). Therefore, it is not through general or natural revelation but through special revelation that we come to the full knowledge of the uniqueness of Christ.[1]

Hence, biblical exegesis is to be re-affirmed as the basic necessity for proper understanding of the written form of revelation as the Word of God,

---

Dr. Yoshiaki Hattori teaches Old Testament and Theology at Tokyo Christian University, Japan.

the Bible, in order that the uniqueness of Christ may most adequately be emphasized in our effort to proclaim him as the only Saviour in order to fulfil our ultimate mission.

I. BIBLICAL REVELATION RE-AFFIRMED

At the outset of B.B. Warfield's book *The Inspiration and Authority of the Bible*, the author states, 'the religion of the Bible is a frankly supernatural religion.'[2] While not denying the function of a natural revelation,[3] the fundamental aspect of the Bible, with which the topic of this consultation deals – the gospel message/revelation of Christ's work of redemption – can never be fully revealed by natural revelation. It is only through special revelation given through the Bible, the Word of God, that the full and complete revelation concerning the uniqueness of the redemptive work of Christ becomes available to us. Accordingly the focal point to be emphasized is the divine authority of the written Bible.

Inspiration of the Written Bible

Paul said in his letter to Timothy, 'All Scripture is inspired by God and profitable for teaching, for reproof, for correction, for training in righteousness; that the man of God may be adequate, equipped for every good work' (2 Tim. 3:16–17). 'The Scripture' he referred to was, no doubt in his mind, the written word, the text of the Old Testament.[4]

In terms of special revelation, the efficacy of divine inspiration is to be understood in the realm of 'writing' or 'written-text' rather than in the realms of 'tradition', which might be considered as preceding the written form. If 'tradition' is the medium of divine revelation until the time of its codifying into written-form/text, then the genuine or actual work of divine inspiration is to be properly acknowledged at the point of the 'writing down' of the tradition. One may call the preceding period of time the 'time of oral tradition'.[5]

However, the work of divine inspiration is not to be applied to the time of oral tradition. In that sense, it is necessary to state that biblical inspiration is basically 'linguistic inspiration'. What was actually inspired was the word(s) or text(s), and the divine revelation in terms of the 'message' to us is to be brought by our act of engaging in the labour of 'exegesis' (reading out) of the written text. Although it should be acknowledged that preceding generations have contributed much in the field of biblical interpretation, even forming various kinds of traditional interpretations, it is extremely important, at least from the standpoint of biblical inspiration from an evangelical perspective, to stick closely to the written text for proper exegesis. This is so because the text is the inspired medium for special revelation.[6]

The Uniqueness of Special Revelation

In comparison with general or natural revelation, special revelation reveals to us in a most definite manner the nature of God's self-revelation via his redemptive provision in the person of his son Jesus Christ and his accomplished work of redemption. The revelation is given in the form of the written word, the Bible.[7] In fact, the Bible – the Old and the New Testaments – is the canon of the church, the Protestant church in particular. As in the past, the Protestant church, more specifically the evangelical movement, stresses the importance of the Bible today. The fact that many evangelical churches have added the word 'Bible' to their names such as in the Tokyo International Bible Church and the Dallas Park Street Bible Baptist Church, seems to be a sign of such an attitude of the church toward the Bible.

Through the written Word of God, the Bible, we are able to come to the full knowledge of the decisive and completed work of salvation through the redemptive death of Jesus Christ on the cross and his triumphant resurrection on the third day. God revealed, and still reveals to us, this unique way of salvation in Christ through the inspired written word, the Bible. In this sense, as I. H. Marshall says,[8] God uses the word to reveal himself and his provision.

Therefore, the uniqueness of the special revelation in terms of the Bible is inseparably related to the concept of the uniqueness of Christ in terms of Christian theology.

II. MODERN COMMUNICATION – RE-ASSESSED

The rapid change in today's world, seen in such events as the Gulf War, the collapse of the former Soviet Union and the rising of many independent nations in its stead, illustrates the effectiveness of modern communication media. Events happening in one part of the world are vividly portrayed almost instantaneously in other parts of the world. This is thanks in large part to the fast-growing technology of modern communication science! Indeed, today's modern scientific technology, communication science in particular, has made this world quite small. And we all are the recipients of its influence, good or bad.

Communication via Pictures

One of the most attractive and necessary features of modern communication science is the 'speed' of communication. However, though the 'speed' of communication plays an extremely important role, the 'wholeness' or 'totality' of communication plays a somewhat supplementary or complementary role. Referring to the well-known Chinese proverb, 'seeing once is better than hearing a hundred times',[9] man's ability to obtain information by means of visual aids seems better than by auditory means. Generally speaking, when we visualize a picture or scene we can easily and quickly perceive its overall contents. In contrast, when we hear or read about the same picture it takes more time to perceive its contents.

In our modern society, many people, especially young people, are becoming rapidly image or picture-oriented in their efforts to obtain knowledge or information. Nowadays, more people are using facsimile for fast and economical communication. Although some people send their written message *in letter-form* via facsimile, others prefer to use facsimile because material such as images or pictures or charts or diagrams are transmitted almost instantaneously. The use of computers may be considered in the same category. The effectiveness of visual images on today's television commercials is almost beyond measure, regardless of its contents.

Generally speaking, people, especially young people, are losing their interest as well as their skill in reading written materials. Many people want to get necessary information quickly through modern communication technology instead of reading written materials and contemplating them, something that requires more time. During the past several years in Japan, an evangelical publishing firm, which has been publishing Bibles for many years, has produced and is selling what is called the *Media Bible* on video-casettes. It is a modern version of the old picture Bible.

Data-Accumulation Approach

With global accessibility of modern computer science and technology, we are constantly exposed to enormous amounts of data in every field. This is true not only in the field of natural sciences but also in the field of humanities, such as literature, philosophy and religion. A data-accumulation approach has been well adopted into their research and study.

In biblical study, the use of the concordance and the lexicon or dictionary has been standard for many years. Now the use of various data-bases or data-processing is rapidly taking the place of these older approaches. In addition, various kinds of analytical information out of such data-bases or data-processing are becoming available for research and study; thanks to modern technology in computer science!

With such tremendous and ever increasing amounts of information the scope of biblical research and study may be developed and widened almost unlimitedly. However, a question comes to mind: 'Does this information substantially contribute to our endeavour of bringing out the unique message of salvation in Jesus Christ in terms of exegesis of the inspired written Word of God or not?[10]

Meeting with many local pastors and ministers in a modern and extremely busy society, I am more and more conscious that they have more information or data about various aspects of biblical content using modern technology and data-processing. On the other hand, I am facing again the same simple and frustrating question. 'Does all this information contribute to their effort to up-grade and make more effective their preaching ministry, proclaiming the uniqueness of our Lord Jesus Christ and his gospel in particular?' While admitting there may be some exceptions, my personal answer to that question at present is regrettably somewhat negative.

III.   BIBLICAL EXEGESIS AND INTERPRETATION

Although I have said that my response to the general trend seen around me is somewhat negative, I am nevertheless optimistic in this matter of dealing with the Bible, which reveals the uniqueness of Christ. That perspective is to re-confirm the importance of the grammatico-historical text-oriented approach to exegesis, which has been generally considered 'traditional' among evangelicals.[11]

The Approach of Text-Oriented Exegesis

Text, consisting of words, phrases, sentences and form structure, needs to be treated with careful attention in terms of exegesis. This is because, as discussed already, divine inspiration, which makes any written portion of the Bible infallible and authoritative, is to be considered as linguistic inspiration. The contents of revelation are closely related to the way of expressing both in word and structure.[12] The Hebrew (and Aramaic) in the Old Testament and the Greek in the New Testament are, after all, 'language' and the ideas expressed by these languages are to be expounded linguistically.

In such an approach one must inevitably pay attention to the various aspects of the language of the text such as word(s), phrase(s), sentence(s), structure(s) and other grammatical elements. It is, then, in engaging oneself in serious 'exegesis', instead of 'eisegesis',[13] of the text of the Bible that any revealed message of that particular portion can be best obtained. Although the statistic or numerical information on words, phrases, clauses, sentences, structures is valuable in itself, the significance or the hermeneutical ideas which contribute very substantially to our homiletical endeavour in ministry may not automatically derive from them. There must be text-oriented exegetical words,[14] and out of careful and prayerful observation of the text and application of such exegetical approach we should expect to draw out our homiletical materials, especially for biblical preaching or expository preaching.

Application of the 'From-Text-to-Context' Principle

We recognized both the importance and the role of 'context' in our endeavour to bring the gospel message of the unique Christ to people, especially to those of a different cultural background. Nevertheless, it is necessary to emphasize the primary importance of 'text' more than 'context', as seen in some recent hermeneutical trends in handling the Bible.[15]

As we have observed already, the starting point of divine revelation as far as special revelation is concerned is from the text of the Bible. On that basis, it is our understanding that we, who hold a high view of the Bible as the Word of God, need to re-confirm the basic principle 'from-text-to-context' in our process of hermeneutics. This means that we apply the revealed message, which becomes available through our prayerful and careful text-oriented exegesis, to preaching ministry.

Holding this principle, it is possible to proclaim the biblical world-view and the concept of 'value of judgment' to people in today's multi-cultural societies.

Therefore, it is fundamental to reconfirm that the written divinely inspired Word of God, the Bible, is the final and authoritative source of God's revelation. On the basis of that affirmation, we are then to engage in prayerful and careful text-oriented exegesis trying to observe *what (God) was saying to the original audience at a particular time in history*. Then we proceed to exposition or hermeneutics, applying the message which became available through the exegetical work to the present day situation, asking *what it (text) has to say to us*.[16]

CONCLUSION

First, it is necessary to recognize the reality of fast growing communication technology in modern society and its influence upon the general public, both within and outside the church. In effect, many Christians in modern society seem to have ,a tendency to depart from or dislike the act of reading the written Word of God.

Secondly, people including Christians tend more to an image-oriented way of understanding the Bible than to reading the text of the Bible. Pastors and ministers should more prayerfully and carefully engage in a 'text-oriented' exegesis of the text of the Bible. Therefore, it is becoming more and more necessary for us to reconfirm the necessity of a text-oriented, careful exegesis of the Bible.

Lastly, it should not be forgotten that in spite of all these exegetical efforts, we, the ministers of the Word of God, need to seek humbly the help of the greatest Teacher of all, the Holy Spirit. Otherwise, all our efforts are in vain. Hans Walter Wolff said, 'If the texts stand, by origin or by adoption, in the service of witness to the God of Israel, and if no other than the God of Israel is God today, no hermeneutic principle can force the text to testify to God today. But it is just for this reason that for proper understanding it must be said; no method can replace the Spirit of the Living God as the proper expositor of the texts.'[17]

NOTES

1. Acknowledging the genuine and organic relationship or unity between the general/natural and special/scriptural revelations, it is unconditionally important to make the decisive assessment on the superiority of the latter to the former. 'While the Bible indeed affirms God's general revelation, it invariably correlates general revelation with special redemptive revelation,' says Carl F.H. Henry. Further he says, 'The modern tendency to veer toward a doctrine of revelation whose locus is to be found in an immediate existential response, rather than in an objectively conveyed Scripture, thwarts the theological interest in biblically revealed doctrines and principles from which an explanatory view of the whole of reality and life may be exposited.' Carl F.H. Henry, 'Special Revelation,' *Baker's Dictionary of Theology*, Grand Rapids: Baker Book House, 1960, pp. 457 and 459.

2. Benjamin B. Warfield, *The Inspiration and Authority of the Bible*, Grand Rapids: Baker Book House, 196 reprint, p. 71.

3. Through natural revelation man may come to a general knowledge of God such as his existence. But this may not be complete in terms of man's corrupted influence on or pollution of, at least some areas of the natural world, which form the media for natural revelation. Cf. Geoffrey W. Bromiley, 'Natural Revelation,' *Baker's Dictionary of Theology*, Grand Rapids: Baker Book House, 1960, p. 456.

4. The word used for 'All Scripture' is πᾶσα γραφή, referring to the high view of the Scripture in its entirety in terms of divine inspiration. Cf. Eerdmans Pub. Co., 1957, pp. 19, 22, 88. Referring to the similar wording in preceding vs. 15, W. Lock says, 'γραφή (is) defining more exactly the γράμματα in which Timothy had been trained

from childhood.' Walter Lock, *A Critical and Exegetical Commentary on the Pastoral Epistles (I & II Timothy and Titus)* (ICC), Edinburgh: T. & T. Clark, 1959 impression, p. 110 cf. also p. 109. Referring to 2 Tim. 3:16, H. Marshall says, 'What is being asserted is the activity of God through the whole of the process so that the whole of the product ultimately comes from him. At the same time it allows for the activity of the Spirit in special ways within the process without requiring that we understand all of the Spirit's working in one and the same way.' I. Howard Marshall, *Biblical Inspiration*, Grand Rapids: Wm. B. Eerdmans Pub. Co., 1983, pp. 42–43.

5. In both the Old and New Testaments, therefore, a period prior to the final literary stage of the biblical documents can be recognized. This period has come to be frequently designated the 'oral period', because it is assumed to be a time in which the stories and other traditions which later came to be codified within the text circulated in unwritten form, being used and re-used within the communities of Israel and the church respectively. As they were preserved and transmitted, they took on the quality of 'traditions'; that is, they were thought to be valuable enough, indeed sacred enough, to be passed on from generation to generation. The term tradition, after all simply refers to that which has been handed over, or passed along, whether sacred or not, but in the context of the Old or New Testament, it obviously denotes those stories and materials which the communities of faith regarded as sacred and normative in defining their faith and practice.' Taken from John H. Haynes and Carl R. Holladay, *Biblical Exegesis, A Beginner's Handbook*, Atlanta: John Knox Press, 1987, p. 93.

6. Cf. *ibid.*, p. 17; also Peter Cotterell and Max Turner, *Linguistics and Biblical Interpretation*, Downers Grove, Ill. Inter-Varsity Press, 1989, pp. 67–68.

7. 'Special or particular revelation complements the distortion of any general manifestation of the nature and character of Deity by focusing attention upon divine redemption through the medium of the historical process, culminating in the work of Jesus Christ.' R.K. Harrison, *Introduction to the Old Testament*, London: Tyndale Press, 1970, p. 463.

8. 'I conclude, therefore, that the possibility that God uses words to reveal himself is thoroughly reasonable, and if he does not do so, it is very dubious whether he can reveal himself at all adequately to us.' Marshall, *op. cit.*, p. 15.

9. Usual English rendering: 'Seeing is believing'.

10. Of course to some degree it may depend upon anyone's way of handling the available information.

11. Evaluating this 'grammatico-historical method' of exegesis, I. H. Marshall says, 'It is this approach which is being commended in this book, for it is fully compatible with Christian belief and with the character of the Bible as the Word of God.' Marshall, *op. cit.*, p. 86.

12. This view, that both the form and meaning of the Scriptures are inspired, has long been held. Preus summarizes the view of the seventeenth century Lutheran theologians as follows: 'Content cannot be expressed without words: the very purpose of words is to convey thoughts or contents. In the case of something already written, meaning cannot be known except from the words which express the meaning.' John Beekman and John Callow, *Translating the Word of God*, Grand Rapids: Zondervan Pub. House, 1974, p. 345.

13. Cf. Hays and Holladay, *op. cit.*, p. 17.

14. Some of the helpful guide-books in recent years are: Gordon D. Fee, *New Testament Exegesis. A Handbook for Students and Pastors*, Philadelphia: Westminster Press, 1983; J. Harold Greenlee, *A Concise Exegetical Grammar of New Testament*, Grand Rapids: Wm. B. Eerdmans Pub. Co., 1953; Walter C. Kaiser, Jr., *Toward an Exegetical Theology, Biblical Exegesis for Preaching and Teaching*, Grand Rapids: Baker Book House, 1981; Douglas Stuart, *Old Testament Exegesis. A Primer for Students and Pastors*, Philadelphia: Westminster Press, 1980; Yoshiaki Hattori, *Practical Steps in O.T. Exegesis*, Taichung, Taiwan: Asia Theological Association, 1989; etc.

15. In *Theological News* (July–Sept. 1991), Dr. Bong Rin Ro, says in the editorial, 'Both liberal and conservative theologians use the Scripture to prove their theologies; however, the question as to whether or not a theologian correctly interprets passages to support his theology has become an increasingly important issue. In other words, hermeneutics become the main issue in our theological discussions today.'

16. Marshall writes of this sort of approach, 'The difference between the two activities has been put in terms of finding out what the Bible "said" and what the Bible "says".' Marshall, *op. cit.*, p. 96, cf. also p. 95.

17. Hans Walter Wolff, 'The Hermeneutics of the O.T.,' trans. by Keith Crim, ed. by Claus Westermann, *Essays on the Old Testament Interpretation* (English trans. and ed. by J.L. Mays), London: SCM Press, 1963, p. 163.

8

C. René Padilla

In two theses Dr. René Padilla gives us a penetrating analysis of the nature of modernity and its consequent privatising of religion and the secularization of life. In two further theses on the uniqueness of Christ he shows the failure of liberal theology to disentangle Christianity from the ideology of Western colonialism and the challenge to evangelicals to restate and relive the gospel as public truth. He calls the Church to live out the confession of Jesus Christ in the whole of life, adopting a servant life-style.

In their classic analysis of modernization and consciousness from the perspective of the sociology of knowledge, Peter and Brigitte Berger and Hansfried Kellner claim that there are at least two assumptions that give modernity a peculiar place in the minds of many people today: that modernity is superior to whatever preceded it, and that they know authoritatively what modernity is all about.[1] Neither of these assumptions can be accepted. On the contrary, they are called into question as expressions of the modern mind conditioned by the myth of progress and 'the deceptions of familiarity'.

DEFINITION

In the interest of a working definition, modernity may be regarded as the complex of elements characteristic of modern societies, especially technological production and bureaucracy. It is not restricted, however, to objective realities: it includes a mind-set, a pre-theoretical consciousness that results from living in these societies with their technological development and their bureaucratic institutions. It is the fruit of the economic revolution produced by capitalism beginning in the thirteenth century, the industrial revolution initiated in the eighteenth century, and the political revolution fostered by the ideological movements in the nineteenth and twentieth centuries. Modernity has its own history. It now dominates human life in varying degrees around the world. It is the worldview that gives meaning to

Dr. C. René Padilla is an editor, writer and pastor, Buenos Aires, Argentina.

ordinary human existence in the advanced industrial societies and, increasingly, because of the process of modernization, in the so-called 'Third World'.

The purpose of this chapter is to show the implications of modernity for the proclamation of Jesus Christ as the Lord and Saviour of humankind and the whole universe according to the Christian confession which traces its origin to the New Testament. For the sake of brevity, I shall propose two theses regarding modernity and two theses regarding the uniqueness of Jesus Christ in a pluralistic world.

THESES CONCERNING MODERNITY

One. An Outstanding Characteristic of Modern Society is the Pluralization of Social Life-Worlds and Religious Pluralism, with the Consequent Privatization of Religion and Secularization of Life

The Pluralization of Social Worlds

All of us could provide plenty of examples to illustrate the extent to which lifestyles and ways of thinking today are conditioned by a technocratic and bureaucratic society governed by values such as productivity and maximization, orderliness and efficiency, competence and expertise, economic growth and individual success. This is not the place, however, to discuss these concomitants of technological production and bureaucracy on the level of consciousness. Far more relevant to our subject is another aspect of modernity closely connected with what the Bergers and Kellner have described as 'the *pluralization of social life-worlds*': religious pluralism, according to which the different religions are due to different perceptions of spiritual reality, but in no way are they a matter of truth and falsehood.

From the perspective of the sociology of knowledge, life-world is a way in which reality is collectively ordered so as to give meaning to human life. It is socially structured and maintained. According to our authors, a characteristic of modernity is the multiplicity of life-worlds. No longer is there a unified way to understand reality, an integrated order which includes all aspects of social life. In the past, work and family and government belonged to a single, coherent world. Today reality is fragmented into different social sectors, and this fragmentation is not limited to observable social conduct but extends to consciousness. As a result, life is divided into the private and the public spheres, both of which may in turn be also split in terms of the plurality of social experience.

The Privatization of Religion and the Secularization of Life

The pluralization of life-worlds has very important effects with regard to religion. In former times, the whole of life was held together by religious meanings and values and beliefs which made it possible for people to feel 'at home' in the world. With the fragmentation of life, no longer can the overarching religious symbols of the past be taken for granted. The individual is placed before a whole gamut of different, and even contradictory, meanings and values and beliefs. Religion becomes a matter of choice, far more related to personal preference than to the question of truth. The net result of pluralization, therefore, is the privatization of religion; life is dichotomized into a public and a private sector, and religion is regarded as irrelevant to the former and restricted to the latter. Furthermore, even in private life religious convictions, in the absence of social confirmation, become less certain and more open to revision.

The privatization of religion fits well not only with pluralism but also with what Robert Bellah has called 'the culture of separation' – a culture that, for the sake of the self-realization of the individual, has virtually made of personal freedom the predominant ideology and has elevated tolerance to the position of the highest value. In the consumer society each person is as free to choose religion as he or she is free to select the brand of a product in a supermarket. The only thing that cannot be tolerated is the intolerance perceived in any attempt to persuade others to adopt one's point of view.

The effect of the pluralization of life-worlds on a societal level is secularization – the progressive removal of religious ideas and institutions from all sectors of society and culture, one after another. Under the impact of secularization, religion is slowly banned from those areas of modern society and culture where very important decisions affecting human life are made, such as science and technology, politics, and economics. Closely connected with the privatization of religion, secularization represents a death blow against every attempt to organize society under an integrated world-and-life view, be it Christian, Jewish or Islamic.

Two. Christianity in the Past was Closely Associated with what may be Described as a 'Universal Colonialism' Centred in the West: in the Post-Constantinian Era, It Shares in the Crisis of the West and is Deeply Affected by the Privatization of Religion and Religious Pluralism

For several centuries Christianity in the West was not merely a private religion but was also a faith and a worldview regarded as relevant to public life and as of decisive importance for all the nations of the earth. In line with the New Testament, it was assumed that the life, death, and resurrection of Jesus Christ provided the clue to the understanding of the whole of human history. This conviction was at the beginning of the history of the Church. Long before Christianity became a world religion, Christians believed in the uniqueness of Jesus Christ and proclaimed him as the Lord and Saviour of the world.

On the other hand, however we may evaluate the fact today, it is now also beyond question that during the world expansion of the West, beginning in the fifteenth century, Christianity was used as the ideology of successive European empires to legitimize conquest and colonialism on a global scale. Born in a Roman province of secondary importance and initially persecuted as a Jewish sect, Christianity had become the official religion of monarchs and nations dedicated to aggressive imperialism. As a result, the 'rule of Christ' was indistinguishable from the rule of earthly kings and queens. The spread of Christianity was a joint effort of Church and State, and the 'orbis christianum' was the motto for the conquest of the world.

Christianity as the Ideology of Colonialism

A case in point is that of Latin America, where the Roman Catholic Church is presently celebrating 'five hundred years of evangelization'. During the colonial period, however, evangelization was so inextricably associated with the establishment of the imperial power of Spain and Portugal that, as Samuel

N. Rivera-Pagan has recently demonstrated,[2] the Iberian ideological debates regarding the conquest in the sixteenth century were predominantly expressed in theological language. The reason is clear: both defenders and opposers of what Leandro Tormo has called 'the military method of mission' recognized that the Christian mission and the military action were so intermingled in practice that they could not avoid debating their ideological positions in theological terms.

From this perspective, it is not surprising that the secularization of the West has resulted in the denial of the affirmation that the Christian gospel ought to be taken as truth in the public realm, as well as in the denial of the uniqueness of Jesus Christ and the relevance of his life and ministry to human history as a whole. At least part of the reason why the gospel claims regarding Jesus Christ are rejected is that for too long those claims were entangled with imperial power, violence and coercion. The affirmation of the gospel as universal truth is placed in the same category as the affirmation of Western imperialism, and both are discarded as expressions of an arrogance that belongs to the past.

THESES CONCERNING THE UNIQUENESS OF CHRIST

The Contemporary Liberal Interpretations of Christianity from the Perspective of Modern Religious Pluralism are a Misguided Attempt to Disentangle Christianity from Every Form of Western Imperialism for the Sake of Human Unity on a Global Scale

There is plenty of evidence to show that Western imperialism is not totally a thing of the past; that in this last decade of the twentieth century it continues to exercise its influence through structures and mechanisms that foster economic oppression on a global scale. This is not the place to substantiate this affirmation. Suffice it to say that today, as in the past, the same West that generates oppression also calls into being a shrewd, penetrating critique of imperialism and its inherent injustice.

The recognition of this phenomenon is essential to the understanding of contemporary liberal theologians who in the last few years have openly opted for pluralism and moved, in Paul F. Knitter's words, 'away from the insistence on the superiority or finality of Christ and Christianity toward a recognition of the independent validity of other ways' (Hick and Knitter[3]). We may not agree with them in the way they go about accomplishing their task, but that should not prevent us from recognizing the validity of their aim to disentangle Christianity from every form of Western imperialism.

That this is in fact their purpose is made clear by their frequent reference to the close association of Christianity with the expansion of the West during the colonial era. In anlayzing the recent developments of Christian theology that have led to the affirmation of 'the co-validity and the co-efficacy of other religions', Langdon Gilkey,[4] for instance, claims that the most important elements are the following:

(1)   A shift from an emphasis on faith to an emphasis on love. Before, 'defending the faith' against other religions was a Christian duty which outranked the obligation to love. Today, love is the major obligation. Correspondingly, 'the doctrines of faith – creeds, confessions and even the words of scripture itself – began to be seen as human, and therefore historical

and hence relative expressions of a truth that transcended any single expression.'[5]

(2) The Neo-orthodox emphasis on the relativity of doctrines and creeds and the priority of love over doctrinal orthodoxy.

(3) The cultural changes that have taken place in the West during this century – a massive shift from a position of superiority to a position of parity as a result of the collapse of the West on all levels, military, political, moral and religious, after World War II. 'The West no longer ruled the world,' said Gilkey. 'Western ways were no longer unassailable; Western religion became one among other religions; and (not insignificantly) the Christian faith became the one now most morally culpable, the chief imperialistic, non-spiritual, and in fact, barely moral faith!' When people in the West came to realize this fact, many of them converted to other religions.[6] According to our author, it is this dramatic situation, more than anything else, that has forced a new understanding of other religions, 'a new balance of spiritual power' (ibid.).

In a similar vein John Hick claims that what has led many 'thinking Christians' (sic) to abandon the 'absolutist position' regarding Christianity is, firstly, the better knowledge in the West concerning other religions, and, secondly, the realization that, because of human nature, Christian absolutism has lent itself to 'the validation and encouragement of political and economic evil'. 'The picture would be very different,' adds Hick, 'if Christianity, commensurate with its claim to absolute truth and unique validity, had shown a unique capacity to transform human nature for the better' (ibid.).

The reasoning of the pluralists seems quite logical: absolutist Christianity has been used as a means to legitimize Western imperialism with all its violence and intolerance, exploitation and oppression. For the sake of Christian unity, such absolutist claims should be abandoned; the way of the future is pluralism. In Tom F. Driver's words, this adoption of pluralism is 'a step that is ethically, and therefore theologically, necessary for Western Christianity to take . . . a demand laid upon us Christians, brought upon us by our own history, which has been largely one of "universal colonialism"'. Whatever our response to this kind of reasoning may be, it must begin with the recognition that at the heart of the pluralist approach to Christianity lies an ethical concern related to the need for justice and peace on a global scale.

For all its merits, however, the liberal attempt to disentangle Christianity from Western imperialism is sadly misguided. Although it rightly rejects the arrogant attitude toward other religions shaped by a colonial mentality, it throws out the baby with the bath water when it also rejects the uniqueness of Jesus Christ and Christianity. The answer to a distorted Christianity entangled with Western imperialism is not the privatization of faith. The answer is, rather, the New Testament confession of Jesus Christ as the Lord and Saviour of the world. And this, as Lesslie Newbigin has well put it in 'Truth to tell', is public truth.[9]

The Greatest Missiological Challenge We Face Today is the Recovery of the Gospel as a Message Centred in Jesus Christ, the Clue to Human History and the Only Basis for Hope of Human Unity in a Pluralistic World

Time does not allow me to offer a detailed response to the advocates of absolute religious pluralism. Moreover, Lesslie Newbigin has already done a very commendable work in this respect in *The Gospel in a Pluralist Society*.[10] I will therefore restrict myself to a few observations concerning the greatest missiological challenge we face today in the face of modernity.

In what many people regarded as the most provocative paper read at the second Lausanne Congress on evangelization, held in Manila in July of 1989, Os Guinness warned evangelical Christians against the dangers of modernity. In his view, modernity is a challenge to the Church because it affects not only how we communicate the gospel but also the gospel that we communicate and the very character of the Church that communicates the gospel.

The importance of Guinness' warning can hardly be exaggerated. Today, on the one hand, many people around the world, not only of the deprived but also of the most privileged, are suffering the effects of increasing modernization. On the other hand, many Christians have fallen into the trap of privatized religion and fail to see the relevance of their faith to public life. As a result, Christianity is all too often turned into a means for the maximization of self-interest, with no effective link to questions of justice and peace in modern society. The gospel becomes a powerless gospel which does not produce a spiritual and ethical transformation in people.

First of all we have to face modernity in ourselves. Thus, for instance, what difference does the confession of Jesus Christ as the Lord and Saviour of the world make if we allow modern fragmentation in terms of racism, classism, or sexism so to condition our thinking and our conduct that God's purpose to bring us together under his Son is frustrated by these social evils? Or if we allow the modern ideology of individual freedom – 'a false and idolatrous conception of freedom which equates it with the freedom of each individual to do as he or she wishes' – to become the major factor controlling our relationships in the field of economics? Or if we let modern technological production or bureaucracy determine our missionary strategy? In view of the many ways we may allow ourselves and our message to be moulded by modernity we would do well to remember Jesus' words: 'Not everyone who says to me, "Lord, Lord," will enter the kingdom of heaven, but only he who does the will of my Father who is in heaven' (Matt. 7:21).

In the second place modernity challenges us to live out our confession of Jesus Christ as the Lord of the whole of life. Over against the utilitarian emphasis on the maximization of self-interest so characteristic of modern society, we believe that God has not called us to be rich, powerful, and successful, but to be made into the likeness of his Son, who 'did not come to be served, but to serve, and to give his life as a ransom for many' (Mk. 10:45). Servanthood is at the very heart of Christian discipleship, and servanthood is at odds with every attempt to impose one's will on others and every form of imperialism. The hope for the unity of the human race, therefore, does not lie in a pluralism that exacerbates the affirmation of individual freedom and competing programmes to bring about unity, but in the gospel as a message centred in the Servant-King in whose presence every imperial power is disarmed.

Thirdly, lest the unity of the human race under the lordship of Jesus Christ be nothing more than an abstract ideal, the Church is called to be a reconciling community where men and women are accepted as equal regardless of all their differences. Over against the instrumental use of social relationships so characteristic of modern society, we affirm the fact that in his death Jesus Christ destroyed the barriers that separate people on the basis of nationality, culture, social class, or race. God has not called us to be more productive by manipulating our neighbour, but to be agents of reconciliation and love. The Christian witness in a pluralistic society requires of us the willingness to proclaim and to live out the gospel as public truth. Over against the rationalization of means and the privatization of faith inherent in modernity, we confess that ultimate truth has been revealed in Jesus Christ and that everything in society is to be evaluated in light of that truth. God has not called us to effective organization and technical inventiveness, but to a prophetic lifestyle which points towards the consummation of God's purpose 'to bring all things in heaven and on earth together under one head, even Jesus Christ' (Eph. 1:10).

NOTES

1. Berger, Peter & Brigitte, and Hansfried Kellner, *The Homeless Mind: Modernization and Consciousness* (New York: Vintage Books, 1973), p. 3.

2. Rivera-Pagán, Luis N., *Evangelización y violencia: la Conquista de América* (San Juan, Puerto Rico: Editorial CEMI, 1990).

3. Hick, John, and Knitter, Paul F., *The Myth of Christian Uniqueness: Toward a Pluralistic Theology of Religions* (Maryknoll, N.Y.: Orbis Books, 1987), p. viii.

4. *Ibid.*

5. *ibid.* p. 38.

6. *ibid.* p. 40.

7. *ibid.* p. 17.

8. *ibid.* p. 207.

9. Newbigin, Lesslie, *Truth to Tell: The Gospel as Public Truth* (Grand Rapids: Wm. B. Eerdmans Publishing Co., 1991).

10. Newbigin, Lesslie, *The Gospel in a Pluralist Society* (Grand Rapids: Wm. B. Eerdmans Publishing Co., 1989).

11. Newbigin, *Truth to Tell, op. cit.* p. 75.

9

Miroslav Volf

This chapter is an exercise in philosophic theology. Dr. Miroslav Volf wrestles with the question of how to speak about the truth of the uniqueness of Christ to people who either believe in the unitary truth of science and rational philosophy or in pluralistic and relative truth. Dr. Volf traces the shift from the foundationalism of the Enlightenment to the holism of more recent Modernity. He critiques the Fundamentalist response to Modernity. His own search for a provisional certitude in philosophy and theology suggests that he is a pilgrim towards the certainty and finality of life in Christ.

A STUDY IN PROVISIONAL CERTITUDE

Modernity denotes a particular way of living and reflecting that began to emerge in the West in the 17th century in the wake of the slow disintegration of medieval culture. Modernity has as much to do with technology, economy and politics as with philosophy and science. A proper answer to the question behind the title of my paper, 'How does the unique Christ relate to modernity?' would therefore involve sketching the contours of a Christian life and world view. I intend, of course, to do nothing of the kind in this short chapter. I will approach the issue by looking at the challenge of *modern epistemology* and discussing the problem, 'How does our Lord's claim to be "the way, the truth, and the life" relate to what modernity tells us about the nature of truth?' So I will discuss only one narrow aspect of the challenge of modernity, the one, however, which is at the very basis of the (largely Western) debate about the rationality of Christian faith and of the (now global) debate about the relation of Christian faith to other faiths and world views.

The primary horizon for my discussion are the questions, 'How do we speak about God to people who believe only in the one truth of science (or philosophy)?' and 'How do we speak about the one God, the Father of our Lord Jesus Christ, to the people who believe in Allah, Shiva, Vishnu or some impersonal form of "the Real"?' The fact that I am dealing only with this aspect of modernity does not of course mean that other aspects are

Dr. Miroslav Volf teaches theology at the Evangelical Theological Faculty, Osijek, Croatia and at Fuller Theological Seminary, Pasadena, USA.

unimportant. For as Liberation Theologians have reminded us, there is another horizon that we must always keep at the *forefront* of our attention. It is the question: 'How do we speak of a loving God in a dehumanized and suffering world?' This is the burning question of the peoples in the Third World. Their most prominent experience of modernity is the marginalization and oppression of the poor through modern industrialism. They (and increasingly the citizens of Eastern Europe) are faced more with the challenges of modern economy, technology and social theory than with the challenge of modern epistemology. But that is not only their problem. The forces of modernity have broken down self-enclosed cultures and made us all live in the one world, interrelated with one another and dependent on one another. Whether people in the First World are aware of it or not, a challenge to people in the Third World *is* a challenge to them, and vice versa. As Christians we have an additional reason to feel the pain of our brothers and sisters in other parts of the world. We are all members of the one body of Christ and when one member of the body suffers, all suffer with it (1 Cor. 12:26).

I hope that what I have to say here will be a small contribution toward our common project of learning how to speak and act in our interdependent and yet so fragmented world in the light of God's new creation. Contributions from other perspectives – especially from the Third World – and on other dimensions of the challenge of modernity need to supplement and enrich my reflection here.

I. THE CHALLENGE OF MODERN UNITARY EPISTEMOLOGY

Foundationalism and the Rational Method

Much of Descartes' *Discourse on Method*, one of the founding documents of modern thought, is an account of his search for 'the first principle' of philosophy that was 'so certain and so evident that all the most extravagant suppositions of the sceptics were not capable of shaking it' and for the 'true method of arriving at knowledge of everything [the] mind was capable of grasping'.[1] Descartes' stress on the unshakable foundation and the true method became paradigmatic for modern thinkers. As Alasdair MacIntyre explains, they insisted that 'truth is guaranteed by rational method and rational method appeals to principles undeniable by any fully reflective rational person . . .'[2] The belief that there can be only *one* set of (indubitable) principles and one rational method of proceeding on their basis lies at the very core of modernity.

A necessary consequence of the modern view of rationality is the unity of truth: there can be, strictly speaking, only one truth on any given matter – all other views are mere opinions that rest on wrong principles, erroneous method, or both. A correlate of the unity of truths is its universality: the one truth encompasses the whole of reality. Descartes hoped that, given his method, there will be 'nothing so distant that one does not reach it eventually, or so hidden that one cannot discover it' and he expected to be able to show that 'everything which can be encompassed by man's knowledge is linked' in the way mathematical demonstrations are.[3]

The challenge of modern epistemology at this stage to Christian theologians was to relate the one truth of the gospel to the one universal truth of philosophy and science. Can the claim of Jesus Christ to be 'the way, and the truth, and the life' (Jn. 14:6) stand as reliable truth or must it be discarded as the mere opinion of a more or less influential social group? In order to show that it stands, Christian theologians either had to demonstrate that Christ is the truth when judged according to the canons of modern rationality or to contend that these canons of rationality have to be rejected. Because you can have only one truth, the option was either to make peace with modernity on modernity's terms or to wage war against it. The alternative was the inevitable consequence of the fact that both Christianity and modernity made claim to one truth.

The Unity of Truth and the Plurality of Cultures

The belief in the unity of truth corresponded to the social experience of living in a single dominant culture. The one culture was a mechanism that generated and maintained plausibility for the claim to the one truth. But the modern way of life – modern science, modern way of production and modern means of communication – have undermined the dominance of the one culture. First, modern historical and sociological inquiry have made it clear that a culture is not simply given but that it develops from previous forms of culture. Second, industrialism has made modern societies highly differentiated and segmented so that an individual 'exists in a plurality of worlds, migrating back and forth between competing and often contradictory plausibility structures'.[4] Thirdly, capitalism and modern technology created a 'world culture' in which people of many ethnic origins and many different religious commitments live together. So modernity itself created a pluralistic situation which 'multiplied the number of plausibility structures competing with each other'[5] and thus undermined the belief in the unity of truth.

The more modernity was successful at eating away at the one dominant culture, the more relativist thinkers gained a hearing. For quite some time, of course, philosophers have been expressing doubts about modern foundationalism – the belief that we need an indubitable foundation if our reasoning is neither to be circular nor result in an infinite regress. It has become increasingly clear that there can be no foundational elements of knowledge that are independent of theories. So foundationalism was replaced by holism, which stresses not so much correspondence of beliefs to facts but the 'goodness of fit' of various components of an explanatory account.[6]

Relativism as the Heir of the Enlightenment

Holism as such does not imply relativism. One can develop criteria for the 'goodness of fit' which would serve as criteria of what is rational. Relativism – an epistemological position which holds that the correctness or incorrectness of judgments about matters of truth or value varies with individuals (or social groups) making the judgment[7] – surfaces, however, as soon as one calls into question the universal criteria of rationality. Paul Feyerabend attempted to develop a relativistic theory of knowledge by suggesting an anarchistic meta-methodology: 'The only principle which does not inhibit progress is: anything goes.'[8] The idea of 'a fixed method, or of a fixed theory of rationality, rests on too naive a view of man and of his social surroundings'.[9] Feyerabend's relativistic theory of knowledge was part and parcel of his interest in human liberation. Every theory, he claimed, which destroys the domination under which one system of thought holds the minds of people, contributes to the liberation of human beings. The one truth is a tyrant which needs to be deposed.[10] The early modern stress on the unity of truth has been replaced here by the multiplicity of traditions with their own internal truths.

I do not need to go here into a critique of relativism – either of 'total relativism' which claims that 'every belief is as good as every other' (and which 'no one holds'!)[11] nor of some other more reasonable forms of relativism. For my purposes here it suffices simply to add that relativists are not enemies of the Enlightenment but are, as Alasdair MacIntyre pointed out, 'to a large and unacknowledged degree its heirs'. Relativism, he writes, is 'the negative counterpart of the Enlightenment, its inverted mirror image'.[12] I will call (early?) modernity's belief in the unity of truth 'epistemological absolutism' and its counterpart stress on multiplicity of truths in the later stages of modernity 'epistemological pluralism'.

The Pluralistic Challenge to Christ as the Truth

Modern epistemological absolutism presents a challenge to the *context* of the Christian claim that Christ is the way, the truth and the life; the struggle here is between competing claims to possess the truth which both parties claim to be one. The alternative here is: surrender or perish. Epistemological pluralism presents a challenge to the *nature* of the Christian claim that Christ is the way, the truth and life; the struggle here is between the claim that the truth is one and the persuasion that such a claim is not only mistaken but oppressive. The alternative here is: join the company of pluralists or get lost. In one respect the second alternative is more civilized: and ultimatum ('surrender') has been replaced by an invitation ('join in'). Yet the threat is still there ('get in'): although all are invited to be friends, 'true believers' are excluded as enemies. Traditionally, the stress that the truth is one ('Christ is *the* truth') was as important to Christian piety and theology as was the claim that Christian beliefs are true ('Christ is the *truth*'). So the 'invitation' to be one among many touched the very heart of how Christian identity was perceived and experienced. And the challenge drew strength from the multiplication of plausibility structures which deprived Christian religion in the West of its status as 'taken-for-granted'.[13]

II. THE FUNDAMENTALIST RESPONSE TO MODERNITY

One of the most significant conservative Protestant responses to modernity was fundamentalism, a dominant force that shaped and is still shaping modern evangelicalism. Historically and sociologically fundamentalism can be understood as a belated religious reaction to modernity. More precisely: it was a reaction to the reaction of liberal Christianity to modernity. A book by Princeton New Testament scholar, J. Gresham Machen, which is probably the best expression of the fundamentalist theological agenda, suggests this by its title – *Christianity and Liberalism* (1923).[14]

'Modern inventions and the industrialism that has been built upon them,' claims Machen, 'have given us in many respects a new world to live in.' The new world, however, would be unthinkable without a new science. One of the crucial features of the modern scientific method is presumption against tradition: 'every inheritance from the past must be subject to searching criticism.' Since Christian faith is by definition based 'upon the authority of a by-gone age' the question arises 'whether first-century religion can ever stand in company with twentieth-century science'. For theological liberals the implicit or explicit answer was 'no'. The liberal theological project was to recast the whole of the Christian faith by searching within the early Christian expressions of faith for the trans-historical 'principles of religion' that contained 'the essence of Christianity'.[15]

In Machen's view the liberal strategy for fending off the onslaught of modern culture was doubly flawed. First, to abandon the 'outer defences' (biblical doctrines) to the enemy and withdraw 'into some inner citadel' (essence of Christianity) is useless, because the enemy will pursue one even there. Modern secular science recognizes no gaps in which Christians can safely hide their belief in God. In the intellectual conflict with modern science nothing can be gained by making concessions.[16] Second, the concessions liberal theologians were willing to make to save the Christian faith amounted to its all-out denial. Liberalism is no longer that 'great redemptive religion which has always been known as Christianity' but 'a totally diverse type of religious belief'.[17]

Machen's response to the challenge of modernity was a call back to the 'fundamentals of the Christian faith'[18] – to the rediscovery of 'the awful transcendence of God' [19] and of God's salvific action on behalf of sinful humanity. The stress on the Bible as the Word of God was at the core of this rediscovery. He denied the 'presence of error in the Bible' and this became the central tenet of the fundamentalist belief system, the foundation of the fundamentals. Liberalism, Machen argued, is based upon the 'shifting emotions of sinful men';[20] authentic Christianity rests on the rock-solid foundation of the completely inerrant Word of God.

A Critique of Fundamentalism

What is right with fundamentalism, I suggest, is the stress that the God of the Bible is the 'rock of ages' – God who saves humanity from their sin and its consequences through the sacrificial death of the Lamb of God and the resurrection of our Lord. What is wrong with it is the *way* it has formulated and communicated this message – its militant exclusivism. Militancy belongs to the very definition of fundamentalism. George Marsden, a leading authority on American fundamentalist, defined a 'fundamentalist' as 'an evangelical who is militant in opposition to liberal theology in the churches or to the changes in cultural values or mores, such as those associated with "secular humanism"'.[21] Fundamentalists' belligerence rests on a thoroughgoing dualism (which manifests itself in phenomena such as the tacit denial of the human element in Scripture, separatist ecclesiology and a blanket rejection of the Ecumenical Movement, and blindness to the social implications of the gospel[22]). Their world is a simple one: they are the angels of light; their enemies are demons of darkness; and there is nothing in between.

There is no need to waste words here explaining that between black and white there are various shades of gray. What might be less obvious than the fundamentalist 'dualistic fallacy' is the extent of the fundamentalists' debt to modernity. I will mention only two of its modern features directly related to the epistemological challenge of modernity. The first is acceptance of (inductive) *scientific rationalism*. Its penchant for over-simplifications notwithstanding, fundamentalism is not anti-intellectualistic and anti-scientific. John Dewey was certainly wrong when he claimed that 'the fundamentalist in religion is one whose beliefs in intellectual content have hardly been touched by scientific developments'.[23] When they polemicize against some scientific theories (like the theory of evolution), fundamentalists do it *in the name of science*. But it is a science of early modernity – a Baconian model of science based on common sense.[24] The fundamentalist interest in scientific 'truth' is intimately related to the persuasion that Christian faith, as Machen put it, is based 'not upon mere feeling, not upon a mere programme of work, but upon an account of facts'.[25] Christian faith has a definite cognitive content which science can either confirm or contest.

Is Epistemological Absolutism the Only Way?

The second and related modernist feature of Protestant fundamentalism is epistemological *foundationalism*. Unlike Descartes, fundamentalists, of course, did not claim to have a foundation that one cannot fail to believe in. The Bible – 'the foundation of the fundamentals' – *can* be doubted, as the fundamentalists' attempts to prove its divine character and truthfulness attest. But the sum of biblical propositions (all of which are true, because they are the inerrant Word of God) function much like the indubitable beliefs of the early modern epistemologies: The biblical 'basic propositions' are the cornerstone upon which the whole theological edifice of fundamentalism rests; fundamentalists believe either biblical propositions or proper deductions from biblical propositions, nothing more and nothing less – that is at least what the fundamentalist theory claims.

But must Christian beliefs be *either* 'indubitable' *or* 'unreliable' as fundamentalists would want it? Fundamentalists insist on the alternative because they operate with what I have called epistemological absolutism: foundational principle and proper method combined will give us the one absolutely certain truth. We can either choose to rest our lives on it or sink in the mire of this world's opinions. If we accept the fundamentalist alternative, religious exclusivism follows naturally with dualism not far away. The choice is then between being an irenic or a militant exclusivist. But are these the only real options for those who believe in Jesus Christ who died for the whole of humanity and is the Lord of the whole of reality? This is the question to which we must turn as we look for a fresh evangelical response to the epistemological challenge of modernity that is not merely a religious copy of modern epistemological absolutism.

III.   TOWARDS A PROVISIONAL CERTITUDE OF TRUTH

The Failure of Religious Relativism

If fundamentalism is *not* the answer to the epistemological challenge of modernity, neither is some form of religious relativism. As Langdon Gilkey – by no means a friend of fundamentalists! – writes,

. . . if they are relativized, God, Christ, grace and salvation, higher consciousness, *dharma*, nirvana, and *mukti* alike begin to recede in authority, to take on the aspect of mere projections relative to the cultural and individual subjectivity of the projectors, and so in the end they vanish like bloodless ghosts. We have no grounds for speaking of salvation at all, a situation of relativity far beyond asking about salvation of *all* . . . Ecumenical tolerance represents an impressive moral and religious gain, a step toward love and understanding. But it has its own deep risks, and one of them is this spectre of relativity, this loss of any place to stand, this elimination of the very heart of the religious as ultimate concern.[26]

Within the plurality of religions, Gilkey continues, 'are forms of the religious that are intolerable, and intolerable because they are demonic'. In order to resist them 'we must ourselves stand somewhere. That is, we must assert some sort of ultimate values.'[27] So, while bigoted fundamentalism contributes to oppression, relativism is unable to resist it; it is forced to tolerate the intolerable. Is there a way out of this impasse? Can we affirm both relativism and absoluteness?

Building on practical American tradition Gilkey suggests that we can do what we must do: we can affirm what he calls *a relative absoluteness*.

We do not relinquish our own standpoint or starting point: What is dialogue if our Buddhist partner ceases to be Buddhist or we cease to be Christian? Nor on the other hand do we absolutize our own standpoint – lest no interchange take place at all. On the contrary, we relativize it radically: truth and grace are *also* with the other, so that now ours is only one way. And yet we remain *there*: embodying stubbornly but relatively our unconditional affirmations.[28]

But how do we *know* that we are not just being stubborn? How do we *know* that truth and grace are also with the other (apart from us wanting it to be so)? Recourse to praxis will not solve the problem as Gilkey suggests. He claims that whereas the statements 'truth and grace are with me' and 'truth and grace are *also* with the other when she differs from me' are to reflection a contradiction 'to praxis [they are] a workable dialectic'. Such a claim implies that 'reflection must not, because it cannot, precede praxis . . . what is necessary to praxis is also necessary for reflection and theory – though the reverse is not true'.[29] It is, however, not at all clear to me that praxis can be pre-reflective; that liberative praxis does not presuppose at least an implicit decision as to whether the truth is with me or with the other. What is much clearer to me is that *Christian* praxis, being based on revelation of God, must not be pre-reflective.[30] Moreover, if the truth *is* with Hitler (to use Gilkey's example) what right do we have to fight him? Simply the fact that truth and grace are *also* with us no less than with him?

Truth From a Personal Standpoint

The only way we can know whether truth and grace is with the other is if we judge her views *from our own standpoint*, in the light of what we understand truth and grace to be. And this is the only standpoint we can take; for there is no absolute standpoint. One cannot begin with unassailable evident truths because there are no such truths. Jesus Christ is the way, the truth and the life. As Christians we will assert this as the truth. But we cannot assert it as *absolute knowledge*, we cannot assert it *as* the *final* truth. Short of becoming God, humans cannot possess the final truth, for, as Alasdair MacIntyre observed, 'no one at any stage can ever rule out the future possibility of their present beliefs and judgments being shown to be inadequate in a variety of ways'.[32] All Christian beliefs are *our* beliefs, *human* beliefs and as such always *provisional beliefs*. We assert that they are true; but we make this assertion provisionally. I call this *provisional certitude*. There is, if you want, an absoluteness about our beliefs: we cannot relinquish our standpoint but rather assert it as true. So the ground on which we stand as we act and reflect is firm. Yet we assert our standpoint as true in a provisional way: *we believe* our beliefs to be true. This hinders us from becoming arrogant and oppressive.

It we understand our views as provisionally true we will have to understand the views of others as *possibly* true. For if we are not entitled to assert absolutely that truth and grace are with us (though we believe that to be the case), we are not entitled to say that truth and grace *are not* with the other. Of course, neither will we be able to assert that truth and grace *are* with the other who disagrees with us. If we did, why would it not be irrelevant which standpoint we take? The provisionality of our own beliefs implies that truth and grace *may be* with the other. So there is nothing stubborn about our not moving to the position of the other, for we believe our position to be true. And there is nothing oppressive about believing that our position is true, for we grant that the positions of others *may* be true.[33]

The notion of provisional certitude might make sense philosophically, but is it persuasive theologically? The first question to clear is whether it is at all *possible* to talk about ultimate reality and its claims on the world in a provisional way. The problem is real. It is not difficult to see why a religious person would want to talk about the 'rock of ages' with absolute certainty: If the 'solid rock' is not to be just 'sinking sand' in the end, then my beliefs about the 'rock' *is* what I believe about it, because it is accessible to me only through my beliefs. Yet many Christians live with uncertainties that reach even to the very core of their faith; their faith is surrounded by doubt and their doubts are fed by faith. This lends credibility to Philip Clayton's claim that 'nothing inherent in the nature of religious belief requires us to disallow an interim component to religious assent'.[34] But the question is not simply whether it is possible to believe provisionally but whether it is *desirable* to do so. For I am arguing that provisional certitude describes the way *we should* make our religious affirmations. So we need to look first at the theological justification of provisional certitude and then discuss its implications for the quality of religious life.

Provisional Certitude as an Authentic Christian Way

I suggest that 'provisional certitude' not only transcends the false alternatives 'indubitable – unreliable' but is also *an authentically Christian way* of talking about the ultimate reality rooted in the very nature of Christian existence. To be a Christian means to experience God as revealed in Jesus Christ and live in the world through the power of the Spirit of the new creation. Yet this very real experience of God and this concrete new life are provisional: they are what Paul calls 'a first instalment' (2 Cor. 1:22) given under the conditions of the old world that is passing away. Within that old world there is no 'sacred space' in which Christians can have an absolutely pure encounter with God or live absolutely true lives. The only such 'sacred space' is the future new creation of God toward which they, the pilgrim people of God, are travelling.

The peregrine nature of Christian existence implies the provisional nature of Christian knowledge. Because Christians are a people on the way to the final destiny, their knowledge cannot be a knowledge of those who have already arrived. To treat beliefs about ultimate reality as ultimate themselves would be to confuse being-on-the-way with reaching-the-goal, i.e. to espouse an epistemological form of over-realized eschatology. Until we come to see the triune God face to face, we will have to carry our religious treasure in clay jars – in provisional beliefs no less than in transient bodies (cf. 2 Cor. 4:7). Our certitude is not that of seeing but of hoping; 'in hope we are saved' (Rom. 8:24) and it is therefore *in hope that we know*.[35] Our unsuppressable urge for the final truth must be tempered with the same patience as our eager longing for the final liberation (Rom. 8:25) – patience to accept the provisional nature of our own knowledge and patience to be open to the truth claims of others.

Of course, there is a patience of a hungry person who is only dreaming about food, and there is a patience of a person who has enjoyed the appetizer and is waiting for the main course. Christian patience is of the second kind. We are saved in hope, but we *are saved*; our jars are of clay, but we carry *a treasure* in them – the unique Jesus Christ (2 Cor. 4:5). And it is precisely the 'great value' of this pearl (see Matt. 13:45f.) that makes us uneasy about our clay jars. Instincts tell us that a pearl should not be carried in such fragile vessels. Jar breaks and pearl is lost! It seems wiser to keep it secured in a cast iron safe. But our instincts were acquired from encountering jewels that have much beauty but no life and no power. Jesus Christ, however, is the Lord of all reality. Half cracked jars of our evangelistic and pastoral sermons and of our theological reflection are no danger to *this* treasure! If anything endangers it, then it might be our cast iron safes! Paul writes: 'But we have this treasure in clay jars, so that it may be made clear that this extraordinary power belongs to God and does not come from us. We are afflicted in every way, but not crushed; perplexed, but not driven to despair; persecuted but not forsaken; struck down, but not destroyed; always carrying in the body the death of Jesus, so that the life of Jesus may also be made visible in our bodies' (2 Cor. 4:7–10). Our own power and success as messengers of the gospel, Paul suggests, would obscure the power of God. Might not the iron logic of our proofs that we are absolutely right and others absolutely wrong do the same? My point is not that God and reason do not go together, but the rationality understood as building on unshakable foundations with arguments that have the necessity of geometrical proofs has much to do with *our* desire for power and control. To renounce the contrived power of the indubitable might be an important step toward 'making visible' the 'extraordinary power that belongs to God', a power that is nothing else but the 'life' of the crucified and resurrected Jesus Christ.

NOTES

1. Descartes, *Discourse on the Method and The Meditations* (tr. E.F. Sutcliffe; Harmondsworth: Penguin Books, 1968), 53f, 40.

2. Alasdair MacIntyre, *Whose Justice? Which Rationality?* (Notre Dame: University of Notre Dame Press, 1988), 353.

3. Descartes, *Discourse*, 41.

4. Peter L. Berger, *A Rumor of Angels. Modern Society and the Rediscovery of the Supernatural* (Garden City: Doubleday, 1970), 42.

5. Peter L. Berger, *The Sacred Canopy: Elements of a Sociological Theory of Religion* (Garden City: Doubleday, 1967), 151.

6. On this development see Philip Clayton, *Explanation from Physics to Theology. An Essay in Rationality and Religion* (New Haven: Yale UP, 1989), 18ff; Nancey Murphy, *Theology in the Age of Scientific Reasoning* (Ithaca: Cornel UP, 1990), 3–9.

7. For a sympathetic discussion of relativism as it relates to theology see Joseph Runzo, *Reason, Relativism and God* (New York: St. Martin's Press, 1986).

8. Paul Feyerabend, *Against Method. Outline of an Anarchistic Theory of Knowledge* (London: NLB, 1975), 21.

9. Feyerabend, *Against Method*, 27.

10. Paul Feyerabend, 'How to Defend Society Against Science,' *Radical Philosophy* 2 (1975).

11. Richard Rorty, *Consequences of Pragmatism* (Minneapolis: University of Minesota Press, 1982).

12. MacIntyre, *Justice*, 353.

13. Berger, *Sacred Canopy*, 151.

14. Grand Rapids: Eerdmans, 1968. Though Machen disliked being termed a 'fundamentalist,' he came to be considered 'the foremost spokesperson for the fundamentalist coalition' (George Marsden, *Understanding Fundamentalism and Evangelicalism* (Grand Rapids: Eerdmans, 1991), 182.

15. Machen, *Christianity*, 3, 4, 6.

16. Machen, *Christianity*, 6.

17. Machen, *Christianity*, 2.

18. Machen, *Christianity*, 18.

19. Machen, *Christianity*, 62.

20. Machen, *Christianity*, 79.

21. Marsden, *Understanding*, 1.

22. For a critique of some of these and other features of fundamentalism see John Stott's comments in David L. Edwards and John Stott, *Evangelical Essentials. A Liberal-Evangelical Dialogue* (Downers Grove: Inter Varsity Press, 1988), 89ff.

23. John Dewey, *A Common Faith* [1934] (New Haven: Yale UP, 1969), 63.

24. See George Marsden, *Fundamentalism and American Culture. The Shaping of Twentieth-Century Evangelicalism: 1870–1925* (New York: Oxford UP, 1980), 212–221.

25. Machen, *Christianity*, 21.

26. Langdon Gilkey, 'Plurality and Its Theological Implications', *'The Myth of Christian Uniqueness.' Toward a Pluralistic Theology of Religions* (ed. J. Hick/P. F. Knitter; Maryknoll: Orbis Books, 1987), 37–50, 43f.

27. Gilkey, 'Plurality,' 44f.

28. Gilkey, 'Plurality,' 47.

29. Gilkey, 'Plurality,' 47.

30. See Miroslav Volf, 'Doing and Interpreting: An Examination of the Relationship Between Theory and Practice in Latin American Liberation Theology,' *Themelios* 8 [1983], no. 3, 11–19, 17.

31. MacIntyre, *Justice*, 361.

32. Shubert Ogden recently formulated a fourth option in answering the question whether there is only one true religion (in addition to exclusivism, inclusivism and pluralism). He states it most succinctly in the following way: '. . . if the Christian religion is itself true, then any and all other religions can also be true in the very same sense, because or insofar as they give expression to substantially the same religious

truth' (Shubert M. Ogden, *Is There only One True Religion or Are there Many?* [Dallas: SMU, 1992], 103). His position is formally similar to mine in that he (a) asserts that every religion at least implicitly claims 'to be *the* true religion' (12), (b) allows a priori only for the *possibility* that other religions are true, and (c) that he proposes to judge whether they indeed are true on the basis of *one particular religion*, in his case, Christianity. He goes on, however, to argue that there can be *more than one* true religion (rather than saying merely that other religions *may* be true). Whether this is in fact the case can be determined only by abandoning the terrain of epistemology (which is my sole concern here) and looking at some substantive theological issues. For Ogden's claim that there can be more than one true religion rests not only on the belief that 'substantially the same religious truth' can be expressed through differing concepts and symbols that belong to different cultures (103), but also on the christological persuasion that the 'saving event of Jesus Christ' does not *constitute* the possibility of salvation but 'only *represents* it' (84); salvation 'that is decisively re-presented through Jesus Christ is always already constituted for each and every sinner by God's very being as love' (99).

33. Clayton, *Explanation*, 140. See pp. 140ff for arguments for the viability of the notion of 'interim assent'.

34. In his own way Wolfhart Pannenberg stressed the relation between eschatology and the provisional character of theological affirmations (see Wolfhart Pannenberg. *Theology and the Philosophy of Science* [tr. F. McDonagh; Philadelphia: The Westminster Press, 1976], 310ff).

Part Three

The Unique Christ and Political Ideologies

10

Valdir R. Steuernagel

In this chapter Dr. Valdir Steuernagel addresses issues of how the Church and the Missionary movement in the past and at present relate the uniqueness of Christ to the rise and fall of political ideologies. He gives special focus to the 500 years of political and Christian domination of Latin America. He searches for answers as to how we address the uniqueness of Christ in the context of the failure of socialist ideology and the oppression of capitalism in the Third World. He argues the impossibility of the Christian movement being ideologically neutral in the light of the emerging 'culture of survival' of empty stomachs. Again and again, the author affirms that Jesus Christ is Lord of history, of all of life and of the Church. Effort put into the reading of this chapter is well rewarded.

But Peter and John replied, 'Judge for yourselves whether it is right in God's sight to obey you rather than God. For we cannot help speaking about what we have seen and heard'. (Acts 4:19–20).

THE BREAKDOWN OF THE WALLS OF IDEOLOGY

In the seventies and eighties, especially in Latin America, 'ideology' became a kind of catchword in many theological circles. If there was a theological conversation it had to be brought in. In a superficial statement, the word became a tool to denounce Western theology and Western capitalism and to feed the utopia of a socialist society.

During the nineties, there were signs that people were becoming tired of this subject. But, more than this, there were major historical developments, especially in Eastern Europe but also in China and Nicaragua. It became impossible to continue to denounce the conservative ideologies from the North and to dream of revolution within a socialist framework. Almost all of the self-entitled 'socialist regimes' had broken down and no longer entered into the dreams of any utopia.

Hence, a remaining and very important question is, how to interpret the recent historical developments and how to relate them to the discussion about

Dr. Valdir Steuernagel is a Lutheran pastor and a theological teacher at Curitiba, Brazil.

ideology? However, let me be very clear by saying that I do not share Francis Fukuyama's 'illusion' when he speaks about 'the end of history'.[1] Neither do I think that theologians or Christians in general can conclude that it is time to retire from the discussion about ideology and to concentrate completely on in-house issues. Nor would it be possible for me to join in chorus with those who triumphantly proclaim the victory of capitalism, proclaiming Adam Smith as a king and 'the free market myth' as the royal sceptre.[2]

In spite of the danger of radicalization, perceived in the seventies and eighties, where everything at all times and in any place became ideological – an argument for every occasion – there was a richness to the discussion that should not be put aside.

Let us step back and ask two basic questions: (1) What were the basic motives that led so many theologians and church practitioners to incorporate the ideological dimension into their theological discourse and Christian practice? (2) What were the main contributions that this discussion brought to that discourse and practice?

Searching for Motives – Why Talk About Ideology?

In a very simple way it could be said that, in Latin America, the discussion about ideology was related to the conclusion, reached by sectors of the Roman Catholic Church, that they could no longer maintain their traditional alliances with the conservative forces in power, while increasing numbers of the population were becoming not only poor but miserable and many young people and organized workers' associations were embracing revolutionary options of socio-political and economic changes.

The economic and political alternatives officially at hand in the continent were not working but instead produced deep scars of injustice. In spite of the 'Alliance for Progress' slogan, the development model was being recognized as a social failure and the military dictatorships, which were spread all over the continent, had their dirty hands full of blood.

By analyzing this situation the traditional way of understanding the Christian faith and of doing theology was put under suspicion. A new way of reading the Bible and relating to the struggles of everyday life was asked for, as well as a new way of doing theology. The traditional mediation of philosophy, in the process of doing theology, was recognized as being inadequate. It did not help to uncover and change reality and to establish the necessary bridge between faith and life. Social Sciences, and their tool of analysis, would be much more helpful for the Church to understand its task in the context of the specific reality of poverty, injustice and oppression in Latin America.

Furthermore, by using those tools of interpretation, it was concluded that much of local poverty and many of the patterns of injustice in the Third World had transnational roots. Those roots had not only to be denounced but also eradicated. It is within this context that the Dependency theory was brought into the theological discourse. In David Bosch's words:

> Since the 1950s, however, the mood had been changing in Third World countries themselves, particularly in Latin America. Socio-politically, development was replaced by revolution; ecclesiastically and theologically by liberation theology . . .

Soon 'liberation' was cropping up everywhere in the ecclesiastical landscape. The opposites we were dealing with were not development and underdevelopment, but domination and dependence, rich and poor, Capitalism and Socialism, oppression and oppressed.[3]

Looking for Contributions – Was the Discussion About 'Ideology' Helpful?

To bring the discussion about ideology into the theological field was helpful and not only presented the theologians with new challenges but also enriched the understanding of Christian faith and practice. Let's look into some aspects of such contributions:

a. We are all part of what Guillermo Cook calls 'the ideological game'.[4] While the Christian faith, as an affirmation of the 'Lordship of Christ', is not an ideological statement, the public witness of that faith, in word and deed, does have an ideological flavour. 'To be sure,' says Costas, 'the confession of the lordship of Christ is not an ideological affirmation . . . it is acceptance of God's free gift of forgiveness, obedience to Christ's will through the help of the Holy Spirit, and hope in the future revelation of God's kingdom.' However, Costas continues, 'just as it is impossible to talk about our God experiences without religious language, so there cannot be a public confession of Christ without an ideological mediation.'[5]

This ideological mediation occurs not only because the Christian faith is embraced and witnessed about by people and communities with their roots in history, carrying their historical baggage, but also because the Christian commitment to ethical imperatives such as justice, peace and love, demand an ideological mediation in order to be coherent and to become concrete in each and every historical context.[6]

b. To become aware of the impossibility of absolute ideological neutrality is necessary and important. All of us are, consciously or unconsciously, exposed to ideological influence. If we recognize this fact we should, as Cook says, 'critically revise our own ideological presuppositions', practising, on a personal and collective level, what has been called the 'sospecha ideologica'.[7]

c. By applying the criteria of the 'sospecha ideologica' to the life and historical activity of the Church, many Christians in the Third World have become aware of the ideological background and influence which has been determining the public witness of the Christian faith; Latin America being an example, as expressed and articulated by the modern missionary movement. Costas says:

> For one thing, third world Christians have become much too aware of the ideological ties between the modern missionary movement and the colonization and exploitation of their countries. For another, they have uncovered the historic economic and ideological ties between Western missionary expansion and the economic interests and military aggression of the United States and its European allies. This has led to a growing suspicion not only of the hidden motives behind a lot of present-day foreign missionary activity and development projects, but especially of the ideological presuppositions in Western theological thought.[8]

FROM IDEOLOGICAL ABSOLUTISM TO VULNERABILITY

There are different ways of defining ideology. Referring to political ideologies, Orlando Costas says that 'a political ideology involves a vision of the future, a

coherent interpretation of reality, and a programmatic line of action con-
ductive to the organization of society'.[9] By involving a vision of the future and
proceeding towards an interpretation of reality every and each ideological
proposition has the virus of relativism and myopia which is inherent to any
human production. In other words, the criteria of 'sospecha ideologica' must
be applied to any and every ideology.

François Chatelet even says that ideology is a cultural production which
expresses the viewpoint of a social class or caste. According to this definition,
as Cook concludes, ideologies do not have the primordial function of
communicating the truth. Ideologies interpret and sustain specific perceptions
of reality.[10] As such, they are very important but their importance is relative.

Only a few days ago, the anchorman of a Brazilian nationwide television
network said that Fidel Castro is reinstituting in Cuba the practice of the
death penalty – the *pared-āo* – which characterized the revolution in its early
years. A desperate political act to keep together an old revolution. Furthermore, in this month of February, a group of Brazilian artists, politicians,
writers and intellectuals spent a week in Cuba on a solidarity trip. They
wanted to make their support of the Cuban revolution very clear – quite a
difficult task. The shadow of the *pared-āo* made this act of solidarity very
difficult. And there was more. As an act of solidarity each one of the voyagers
had to take along thirty-five kilos of medicine. A public mirror of the state of
despair of an aging revolution.

Would this short concentration on Cuba mean that the long-standing North
American boycott of the small Caribbean island should be supported? Not at
all. I'm against the boycott. What I'm trying to say is that the vulnerability of
the old revolution can no longer be hidden . . . and this is very hard to
recognize. The old Christian principle of human relativity and sinfulness is
again on the agenda. There is a human tendency to elaborate and implement
plans and projects and then be unable to recognize mistakes, exercise the
practice of a healthy self-criticism and be open to changes. Ideological options
and historical projects do get old and tired and carry with them the virus of
death.

The reference to Cuba is just one example of a worldwide ideological crisis.
More than an ideological crisis, we face a crisis of hope. The dreams of our
youth do not go beyond their effort to get some money, buy a new shirt and
go dancing on Saturday night, after having a sandwich at a new local shopping
centre. The intelligentsia of our societies are lost and while some of them
decide to make money others still travel to Cuba with thirty-five kilograms of
medicine.

While this ideological crisis indicates that the emerging generations are
frustrated with the proposals of their parents, it also demonstrates a crisis of
the modern state. In this sense it must almost be questioned if what we are
facing is not both a crisis of utopia and a financial crisis where the state is
unable to finance not only the dreams of changes but also the most
elementary necessities of human life such as health and housing, transpor-
tation and work.

Where are we heading to? Is there such a thing as a post-ideological
society? While this question is too complex to be answered, the emergence of
a new, global and enchanting ideological articulation cannot be detected on
the horizon. What can be detected is a kind of culture of survival, determined

by increasing levels of poverty, on the one hand, and a struggle for room to be free and to be yourself, on the other hand.

The culture of survival could also be identified as the revolution of the empty stomachs, which expresses itself in an anarchical adventure of crossing the frontiers between rich and poor; between those who have, and those who do not have and do not even have the perspective to have. Yesterday, thousands of poor Brazilians migrated from the Northeast to São Paulo searching for a better life. Today, the quality and perspectives of life in São Paulo might not be, to those people, much better than in their former homeland. Furthermore, many Brazilians are looking for some other place in order to 'make some money'. One of the key challenges of the nineties will be named MIGRATIONS. Voluntary, desperate, uncontrollable waves of migrants will invade Europe and North America in search of work and in order to survive. The mobilization of those waves of migrants does not respond to any ideological proposal. Their utopia goes as far as their stomachs and the network of their families.

Motivated, among others, by economic problems the struggle for room to be free and to be yourself can be seen in a frightening dimension in the increasing numbers of nations which are emerging in Eastern Europe. The re-emergence of ethnic, racial and religious identities and the upheaval of minority groups will put its mark especially on the future of Europe and will become even more explosive as it faces the waves of migrants invading that old continent.

Looking at the blank screen created by the absence of collective and motivating dreams, I also perceive, in the context of my country and culture, decline in values, on the one hand, and a desire to participate, mainly on a micro level, on the other hand. The decline in values can best be seen on the national political scene where corruption, involvement with drugs traffic, family breakdown and sexual involvements are part of everyday life . . . without constraint. The desire to participate, on the other hand, occurs mostly at the grassroots level, establishing a political culture that stresses micro organization and participation on decision-making processes.

The second major question of this paper is, How to address the uniqueness of Christ within the context of this hour without talking only to yourself, or within the walls of 'closed' church buildings?

JESUS CHRIST IS LORD OF HISTORY

That Jesus Christ is Lord is one of the oldest confessions of the Christian faith. And from its beginning it was a confrontationally exclusive, universal but contextual affirmation. In answer to the demand for silence from the established religious system in Jerusalem, Peter declared his absolute dependency on God and the impossibility of keeping silent. His calling to tell the story of Jesus was so intense and radical and his experience with Jesus so life-changing that there was no other way than to keep telling the story further and further. Over against the petulant confession that Caesar is Lord, the Christian family declared, from its early hour and for the whole Roman Empire to hear, that Jesus Christ was Lord . . . Lord of the whole Empire, Lord of history, Lord of the universe.

The affirmation that Jesus Christ is Lord of history is a life-changing, a contextual and a universal statement. If those different but integrated dimensions of the confession of the Lordship of Jesus Christ do not keep together, the confession runs the risk of becoming either parochial or abstract. There are examples of both to be told. It may be an inhouse confession of the Lordship of Jesus that is unable or unwilling to relate such confession to the surrounding reality, or it may be an abstract construction of the uniqueness of Jesus that is unable to dialogue with the real challenges of life, either at a personal or a global level.

To affirm that Jesus Christ is Lord is always an invitation to life, a denunciation of death and a relativization of the powers and systems of the day. By inviting people to surrender their lives to Jesus and to belong to a worshipping, witnessing and serving community, the Christian faith is promoting life: 'When they came to Jesus, they saw the man who had been possessed by the legion of demons, sitting there dressed and in his right mind . . .' (Mk. 5:15). And, as the passage continues, this experience of life has a contagious nature: 'As Jesus was getting into the boat, the man who had been demon-possessed begged to go with him. Jesus did not let him, but said, "Go home to your family and tell them how much the Lord has done for you, and how he has had mercy on you."' (Mk. 5:18–19).

To affirm the Lordship of Jesus implies a denunciation of forces of death, be it the demons who possessed and violated the humanity, dignity and identity of the Gerasene man; be it all and every 'Caesar's system' that believes itself to be absolute, behaves as if exclusive, oppresses those who do not agree with it and exploits those who are unable or unwilling to react against it. Not least, it relativizes powers and systems that are unable and unwilling to perceive that they are only powers and systems of the day, waiting to be replaced tomorrow. But we have not yet addressed the question of how to relate the uniqueness of Christ to the challenges of this hour or, how to confess that Jesus Christ is Lord today. I would start by suggesting what we should not do.

Lessons from 500 years of Christian History in Latin America

In this hour of ideological crisis and the absence of any utopia we should avoid, at any price, singing a naive chorus of victory, by arrogantly and simply saying that we knew it all along and were only waiting for the whole ideological apparatus and revolutionary proposals of the last decades to fall down.

Why should we avoid singing such a chorus? First, because this would only show our ideological bias. Second, because we should remember that we live under a glass roof. Third, because the ideological crisis is ours too.

First. One of the side effects of the breakdown of the Berlin Wall is the danger of romantically raising up a monument of victory to the capitalist ideology, celebrating the belief that some day the whole world will submit to the law of privatization and the free-market economy. From the perspective of the Third World it could be said that such a monument does already exist, except that it has been erected in the world's backyard and it does not look nice at all. We, in Latin America, have been exposed to the capitalist ideology for a long time and it has not worked well. Hence, when Miraslov

Volf says that 'Eastern European countries are more and more facing problems similar to those that plague the countries of the Two-Thirds World',[12] many of us from the Third World have to say that we are already moving on to the Fourth World. There are no illusions, and we know that while capitalism has been able to provide an opulent table to many in the First World and to a few in the Third World, there is an increasing number of empty tables in our villages and communities, while unjust structures and exploitative working relations continue to provide delicacies, mostly to those tables that are already opulent.

As Walter Altmann has shown, one of the consequences of the easing of the tension in the East–West relations is that the North–South conflict will emerge much more strongly as the world's open wound. Since the economies of the North are becoming more self-sufficient and no longer need the South in the same proportion, the weakness and abandonment of the South will be seen as never before. As Altmann says:

> The masses of the Third World, transformed into Fourth World, are becoming superfluous. We have to count more and more with the 'lumpen' reality: poor masses thrown to the margin without any perspective of a dignifying life, deprived from everything that is essential and even from the ability of taking initiatives and from hoping.[13]

And, not last, there is the danger of celebrating the defeat of the materialistic socialist dream, while proclaiming, in the name of a free Christian world, the victory of the capitalist ideology.[14] We should view the capitalist world (which is also essentially and programmatically materialistic), with the same suspicion with which many of us viewed the state-socialist experiment. By so doing we would become less bound by ideology and render a better service to the Kingdom of God.

Second. What about our 'glass roof'?

It is somehow easy to proclaim the ideological captivity of others and to condemn the ideological options of those who are far away. In 1992, in Latin America, we are searching for a language that better expresses the meaning of the 500 years of Christian presence in the Continent. And as we move from 'celebration' to 'invasion' and vice versa we are impelled to conclude that the gospel has been captive to and impoverished by different ideological expressions, responding to the political apparatus and economic needs of those who, in power, had their tables well set. While we rejoice in the fact that God has been with us and speaking to us, throughout all this time, we also have to recognize that much harm has been done to the gospel and many lives have been cut down – literally and figuratively speaking – in the name of that faith that should bring life . . . abundant life.

However, from an evangelical perspective, it might be tempting to denounce the negative effects of the presence and ministry of the Roman Catholic Church in the Continent for so long, without recognizing that we built on the basis established by them. And, in many cases, we are not aware – or do not want to be aware – of our own ideological captivity. After all, the historical presence of evangelicalism in Latin America also responds to ideological presuppositions which are foreign to the gospel. Furthermore, there is the temptation to say naively that we will do everything right and that

Latin America will be changing its social picture as it becomes evangelical. The hour has come to say 'NO' to this temptation. While the church is growing, and evangelicals are entering their first major experience of national politics in this continent, there are many signs that we are not only being blind but also captive to dreams of change that resist a solid biblical hermeneutic, that do not have a good economic and socio-political basis, and to which history has already said 'NO'. The challenge to exercise the Lordship of Jesus Christ, in the political arena, vis-à-vis the discussion of political ideologies, is very much needed in Latin America today, even if the desire to face such a challenge is evaporaring.

Third. Are Evangelicals facing an ideological crisis too?

It is usually very difficult for us, as evangelicals, to recognize that we are in crisis. We work with the assumption that we have answers while others have questions. Alongside this way of perceiving the crisis of others and our own sense of security there is even a tendency to hold a party around the empty table of utopias, a characteristic of the end of this century and of today's younger generations. I would suggest that there is no longer room for this kind of apologetic posture that always waits for the worse scenario to emerge in order to proclaim the rescuing message of Jesus Christ.

While we cannot and do not want to give up the privilege of experiencing hope in Christ Jesus as well as of sharing this hope with others, we should be humble in order to experience the agony of emptiness and hopelessness that characterize this hour. If our Christian witness is not marked by a humble attitude of openness which is willing to suffer the pain of the world we will not be able to understand the lack of commitment of our youth, the despair of mothers concerning their children, the abandonment of the elderly, the increasing levels of drugs consumption, the proliferation of AIDS, the acceptance of corrupt practice as a normal procedure and the complete breakdown of the morality which gave some sense of coherence to former generations.

We should recognize that the crisis of utopia of our days is our crisis too. We are not only a part of this historical moment but are much more contaminated by the virus of hopelessness than we think. I myself have been experiencing the pastoral challenge to share about hope in Christ in a context where the axe of unemployment is over almost everyone's head from Sunday to Sunday, and where the younger generation seems to be suffering from an unshakable commitment to a hedonist lifestyle that produces a scaring sense of immunity in the midst of a world in flames. Yes, the ideological crisis is our crisis too.

JESUS CHRIST IS LORD OF THE CHURCH

As Christians we experience the hopelessness of this hour by identifying with the weeping of Jesus over Jerusalem, by committing ourselves to the witnessing community of Christ, and by rooting our faith in the promise that 'we are looking forward to a new heaven and a new earth, the home of righteousness' (2 Pet. 3:13).

Are we able to weep over 'Jerusalem'? In the last decades the contextual theology that has been erupting from the Third World has said that

INCARNATION is a key missiological concept in the search of understanding the missionary task of the church today.

Applying this emphasis to the discussion about the uniqueness of Christ it must be said that there is not much room for a kind of theoretical discourse which, using philosophical categories, wants to 'prove' how unique Christ is over against other philosophical statements, political proposals or religious alternatives. While the Christian faith has a discursive dimension – proclamation, dialogue-attached to it, it must be able to relate to people within the context of their everyday life experience. The Christian faith becomes contextually unique when the Church follows the steps of the Lord. To put it in another way: there is little room for systematic discourses about the uniqueness of Christ when and if the Lordship of Jesus does not become a touchable reality within the context of the living Christian community . . . down there at the village. There is no place for victorious discourses about the superiority of the Christian faith if the streets of 'Galilee' are empty of acts of love in the name of Jesus. The universality of the statement about the uniqueness of Christ is best seen and becomes authoritative when the Lordship of Jesus becomes reality at the contextual level of individual and contextual life.

We are not talking of a local context only. We need the ability to relate to reality and to interpret historical developments and challenges. In this sense we as Christians not only experience the pain of this hour but also engage in dialogue which we perceive as being in favour of life. Hence, while old and new political ideologies are put under the scrutiny of a Christian analysis they should also come under Christian influence while in the process of articulation and/or implementation.

A Unique Community. While the Christian faith is essentially a communal faith, the community of faith is essentially missiological. Hence, the commitment to the Lordship of Jesus Christ and the assertion concerning the uniqueness of Jesus is, by its very nature, missiological. The way in which the Lordship of Jesus becomes reality in the everyday life of the Church and the means through which the Church relates to and engages in favour of life, with other living forces in society, sets the tone about the acceptance and experience of Christ as being unique.

In the Latin American context this points to the fact that both Church and poverty are growing and ideological discourses and options are out of fashion. But how do Church, poverty and ideologies relate to each other? According to the gospel, the Church cannot ignore the poor and the levels of poverty will not diminish without a political action that responds somehow to an ideological option. Without ideologizing the Christian faith, the Church in Latin America today has the responsibility of participating in the different national dialogues which search for an economic and socio-political option for today. This is a consequence both of the demand of the gospel and of the growth of the Church. There is no way for the Church to say that saving souls is its business without betraying the gospel and the poor. And there is no room for strategies on world evangelization toward the year 2000 without asking the question about the contextuality of those same strategies.

An Expectant Community. In times of crisis there is always the tendency to embrace a kind of escapist eschatology. While the hope of the ultimate return of Christ and the installation of the Kingdom of God is a very important source of endurance and witness in our days, any eschatology that diverts the Christian community from its healthy and necessary involvement in present history is harmful to the Christian community as well as to the human communities that need to know the Lord.

While waiting for the Kingdom of God to erupt in plenitude the Christian community is committed to signalize this Kingdom by preaching the gospel, healing the sick and reproving the evil spirits. By doing so, the Church will not and cannot abandon present history to the devil. Furthermore, it cannot avoid taking ecological co-responsibility for the earth, being consistent to the proclamation of faith that claims that 'the earth is the Lord's' (Psalm 24:1). A healthy eschatology waits eagerly for the Lord to come; but while waiting it plants a tree. This we should have learned from Martin Luther.

NOTES

1. See Strobe Talbott, 'Terminator 2: Gloom on the Right', in *Time*, January 27, 1992, p. 28.

2. Miroslav Volf's paper, 'When the Unclean Spirit Leaves', describes 'the recent Eastern European revolution' as a 'revolution of return': 'The only option was to shift into reverse. So the revolution acquired the character of a restoration. Smith, the realist, was proven right; Marx, the adventurist, had failed. The socialist prodigal son returned in rags, as his older capitalist brother had predicted all along' (p. 3).

3. David J. Bosch. *Transforming Mission. Paradigm Shift in Theology of Mission* (Orbis Books: New York, 1991), p. 434.

4. Guillermo Cook, 'Ideologia y Comunicación Cristiana: Imagenes Bíblicas', p. 14.

5. Orlando Costas, *Christ Outside the Gate. Mission Beyond Christendom* (Orbis Books: New York, 1982), p. 121.

6. See Costas, p. 121, p. 122.

7. See Cook, p. 14.

8. Costas, p. 122, p. 123.

9. Costas, p. 121.

10. Cook, p. 15.

11. Costas refers to this absolutist tendency as follows: 'Ideologies, however, can be potentially explosive for Christians, since they tend toward absolutism when they demand complete loyalty from their adherents to a coherent (and inflexible) system of political thought and action. Insofar as Christians are motivated by vision of God's eschatological kingdom, they will always find themselves uneasy with any ideology, even with those that come close to their ethical concerns.' (p. 122).

11

Frances Adeney

Using the socio-economic approach, Dr. Adeney analyzes several different attempts to find an ideological framework for knowledge and shows the inadequacy of each. She argues that only a biblical framework can provide a coherent basis for relating social theory and political ideology. She then shows the disastrous results when Marxism rejected the biblical source of its own ethic and the dangers of the 'politically correct' stance on ethics among current American college students cut off from its biblical source and moving towards a new authoritarianism. Having outlined some unrealized visions of a just society she points to the vision of the Kingdom of God as the hope for a stable socio-economic and moral future for humankind.

A FRAMEWORK FOR KNOWLEDGE, A SOURCE FOR ETHICS AND A VISION OF JUSTICE

INTRODUCTION

Today we live in a world without a Berlin Wall or a Soviet Union, a world which is experiencing a de-escalating arms race and an end to apartheid. Yet it is a world still struggling with totalitarianism, terrorism, environmental pollution, and widespread poverty. In such a world evangelical Christians must ask what the unique Christ has to do with political ideologies.

The World Evangelical Fellowship has not been silent on this topic. Much work has been done on seeking justice in global political and economic spheres. A theology for social action, jointly developed with the Lausanne Committee in 1982, clearly articulates a Christian evangelical call to a new life, a new community, and a new world.[1] W.E.F. has consistently directed evangelicals to committed political action to change unjust systems.[2] It is therefore appropriate that we analyze current political ideologies and contribute to future political visions thus helping to shape the political landscape of the twenty-first century.

Dr. Frances Adeney has taught for several years in Indonesia.

Political theory faces many challenges in today's world. Economic viability and the demands of practical implementation are ever-present in developing public philosophy. But today, questions about the basis of truth itself, the moral sources for political ethics, and the need for visions of justice must also be addressed. We will argue that evangelical Christian theologies, centred on belief in the unique Christ, can address each of these issues:

Framework for Knowledge: Increasing realization of the situated and historical dimensions of human knowledge establishes parity between Christian and secular theories of truth. The study of ideology has shown that science itself is based upon beliefs, is centred in communal understandings, and is infused with values. Evaluations of social and political theory from a Christian perspective may be no more or less ideological than evaluation from a 'scientific' vantage point.

Moral sources for political ethics: The loss of connection between political ethics and the moral sources undergirding those values demands that we rethink the foundations of political ideologies. Evangelical theology can delineate a biblical basis for a political ethic of justice and benevolence, equality and freedom.

Vision of a just society: Drastic and rapid changes in world political systems call for reevaluation of political ideologies and creative restructuring of political systems. Christian theologians can outline a vision of a just society that can provide a standard by which to judge current policies, give shape to future political commitment, and generate energy for social action.

I.   AN ANALYSIS OF IDEOLOGY AND THE SEARCH FOR KNOWLEDGE

In order to understand how Christian theology can make these contributions, we begin with an analysis of ideology itself. What is ideology and why should we want to contribute to it? The answer lies in the historical changes in the notion of ideology, the ideological dilemma of modern social theory, and the possibility of positive contributions of ideology to social life.

Before Karl Marx made his definitive statements about ideology as false consciousness, the term was used in a more positive way. Coined in 18th century France by DeStutt de Tracy, the word 'ideology' was used to express a new 'science of ideas' whose empirical findings would forever lay aside the need for the authority of state or religion.[3]

But the term acquired negative connotations during Napoleon's reign. Needing the structures of authority already in place in France to bolster his power, Napoleon had little time for the enlightened notion of authoritative truth discovered through science. He applauded traditional religion and labelled the intellectuals as 'ideologues', irresponsible speculators who were subverting morality and patriotism.[4]

Marx followed Napoleon, stressing not the convergence but the difference between science and ideology. Ideology veiled the truth about reality while science revealed that truth. Religion, in Marx's view, presented the most destructive ideology, preventing the oppressed from realizing their true situation. Marx never dreamed that his own 'science' would lead to the simplistic quasi-religious ideological catastrophe of Marxist/Leninist political theory.

Since the time of Marx, the word ideology is most often used to denote a rather simplistic system of thought, centred in moral commitment, and spread with impassioned rhetoric. Its focus may be religious, political, social, or even personal. An ideologue may support the status quo, or argue for a utopian future. In either case, ideology usually denotes the position of 'the other' the unwarranted ideals of the opposition, not one's own thought.[5]

The critique of ideology became a project of social science, especially the critical theorists of the Frankfurt school. But when Karl Mannheim asked on what basis science could critique ideology, he came to the disturbing conclusion that no thought system is free from ideological posturing.[6] Science itself, it appeared, was ideologically conditioned, based on a set of beliefs, without which it could discover nothing.

In 'Mannheim's Paradox' we confront the irony of the perspectival nature of all our knowledge: it is communal, committed, limited, and probably distorted.[7] No one can escape the ideological dimension of knowledge. The 'objectivity' of the human sciences was being questioned on many fronts. The objectivity of the social scientific study of ideology was no exemption.

Realizing the perspectival, limited viewpoint of any search for knowledge, Clifford Geertz set out to delineate a non-perjorative view of ideology. He wanted to examine ideologies 'as systems of interacting symbols, as patterns of interworking meanings'. Using symbolic action theory and literary criticism, Geertz sketched the rise of ideology as a response to social instability, an enabler in the transition to an autonomous polity.[8]

Without conflating social theory and ideology, we see that both assume a framework for knowledge as understood by their historical context and present community. Both participate in ethical commitment and reflection that grows out of moral sources. Both are committed to social change. Ideologies contain theories of how the world operates. Social theories contain elements of commitment and visions of the good society.

The study of ideology shows that social science itself is based on a contextual, limited framework of knowledge. Christian theology can also contribute to the search for knowledge about society. A theological framework for knowledge emphasizes the revelation of God through God's acts in history, through the incarnation and death of Christ, and through the revelation of the Word of God. The international community of Christians exhibits the presence of God's Holy Spirit in the world. The Church's commitment to the poor incarnates, in the present day, the truth of God's love for the world. The spread of the Good News exhibits God's power to change lives and social structures. These theological convictions can help frame social theories and political ideologies that correspond with reality in the world.

In these contributions, is Christian theology acting as truth-telling science or commitment-engendering ideology? Geertz maintains the distinction between science and ideology by claiming that although both are symbolic structures, science is diagnostic and critical, whereas ideology is justificatory and apologetic.[9] Perhaps the distinction is a matter of degree. Social theory strives for objectivity, political ideology strives for committed action. Christian theology participates in both.

II. IDEOLOGY AND MORAL SOURCES FOR IDEOLOGICAL AND POLITICAL ETHICS

A social theory does posit a view of the good society; it does strive for understanding that can generate action. When a social theory loses touch with the sources of its values, it easily degenerates into an unthinking ideology. Usually political ideologies, understood in the perjorative sense, begin as social theories.

Understanding social theory and political ideology on a continuum, one can see that Marxist social theory generated Marxist political ideology. Marx postulated a materialist framework for knowledge and a dialectical process of social change. Basic ethical convictions undergirded Marx's social theory. A vision of a just society informed his theory and generated commitment for action. Marx's moral commitments and vision of justice were rooted in Christian values and humanistic visions. With the rejection of Christianity, Marxist theory lost touch with an important source of its own ethics, with disastrous consequences for the implementation of Marx's vision.

A current example of the importance of moral sources for political ideology is the furore over 'politically correct' values in American universities.[10]

When my eldest daughter, a student at the University of California at Santa Cruz came home for the holidays a bit more than a year ago, she announced, 'I am NOT politically correct'. Then in a more tentative voice, she added, 'although I agree with most of what they're saying'. A few days later the often irrational and even violent political correctness debate hit the cover of *Newsweek* with the headline, 'Thought Police: Watch What You Say' (Dec. 24, 1990). Jenny does agree with the values of equality, ecological and multicultural awareness, and an end to hunger and oppression in evidence in current attitudes on campus. But the pressure to be 'politically correct' seems to contradict the ethic of self-chosen values and tolerance that is so much a part of her Berkeley milieu. The contradiction confuses Jenny. Somehow it feels wrong to be pressured into touting values she thinks are right.

The university now educates (indoctrinates?) students in university housing to abhor racism, sexism, heterosexism and other 'isms' chosen by the university to be the 'bad values'. But in a society that has told young people for decades that values are privately and freely chosen, the authoritarian approach appears coercive and unthinking. Why these values and not others? What are they based on, i.e. what moral sources do they spring from? Why is freedom of speech curtailed and consensus insisted upon? Who decides what values are 'politically correct' and why?

The moral sources underlying many 'politically correct' values remain hidden to many holding those values. Disparate values are linked together, conflicts among goods are concealed, moral sources that could aid evaluation of those goods remain unexplored. The pressure to conform without analysis undercuts the very goods purported, thus presenting a new authoritarianism.

The moral sources of Christianity can undergird an adequate social ethic, providing not only critical analysis but a base in reality as revealed by God. The Lausanne Covenant articulates some of the basic biblical affirmations that can provide a foundation for political values: God as creator and judge, God's concern for reconciliation, God's transforming action in humans and in the world. Most of all, the Bible reveals a God who loves the world so much that God was incarnated as a person, the unique Christ who died and rose for every person, race, and nation. As moral sources, these doctrines result in an ethic that stresses human dignity and responsibility, freedom from oppression and the work of reconciliation.

The ideology of political correctness in American universities is based in part on those Christian moral sources. But for many, those sources have been lost, their language forgotten. Moral values derived from them become a new ideology, asserted ever more adamantly because their sources have been rejected. The dangers of decoupling this political ethic from its moral roots are serious.

These dangers are presently being realized by philosophers and social scientists in North America. Charles Taylor in *Sources of the Self: The Making of the Modern Identity*, outlines a modern, Western political ethic based on values of universal human rights, the demand to reduce suffering, the ideals of freedom, quality, and self-determination.[11] He describes a consensus on morals but a poverty of moral sources. Having jettisoned traditional theism as a moral source, moderns are left with disengaged reason or expressivism as sources for a framework for ethics.[12]

Taylor claims that these moral sources are not strong enough to undergird the modern ethic of justice and benevolence that has become 'politically correct'. Disengaged reason leads to an ethic of calculation of personal interests, while expressivism leads to total subjectivism. Both, according to Taylor, stifle the human spirit and neither is substantive enough to undergird the high demands of benevolence expected by the ethic itself. The original model for universal benevolence in the West is the Christian notion of *agapé*. Can *agapé* survive the demise of the Christian religion?[13]

Robert N. Bellah, in *Habits of the Heart*, describes a loss, in the United States, of moral language that can describe Christian and republican moral sources of societal values. As a result, the languages of individualistic utilitarian or expressive values increasingly define mores in that society.[14] But a modern ethic based on expressive individualistic or utilitarian calculation proves an insufficient base for the humanistic ethic that Jenny encountered at the university. The ethic is alive, but without an understanding of its moral sources, it becomes a narrow political ideology, requiring authoritarian education and enforcement.

Bellah advocates a return to biblical moral language to support the ethic of care and justice many United States citizens still hold but cannot articulate. The time is right for evangelical Christians to reassert biblical moral sources for political ideologies, moral sources that can support a consensus on values of benevolence, freedom, equality, and justice. Christian theology can provide reasons to support that ethic; thus avoiding the need for indoctrination and the dangers that accompany it.

III. A VISION OF A JUST SOCIETY

Evangelical Christian theology can also provide a vision of justice for a good society. Taylor claims that, 'In order to make minimal sense of our lives . . . we need an orientation to the good, which means some sense of qualitative discrimination, of the incomparably higher.'[15] Christians can articulate an understanding of justice that is more complete than anything that now exists in the world.

Political ideologies, whether philosophical liberalism, South American liberation theology, Indonesian Pancasila, or democratic socialism, each articulate an unrealized vision of a just society. But utopian visions have been maligned, along with ideologies, for their air of unreality. They are criticized because of their unsuitability for implementation in society. Mannheim paired utopias with ideologies, deeming them both unscientific and uncredible.

Because of this assessment, utopian visions are often ignored and their influence goes unnoticed. Although not implemented in society, utopian visions do play an important role in both social theories and the development of public philosophy. The resulting political ideologies do contain visions of the good and just society.

Ricoeur notes that both ideologies and utopias are symbolic constructs that organize meaning in society. According to him, the utopian vision provides a critical standard by which to evaluate present systems and ideologies. The vision of a good society exposes the gap between claims of present authorities and a citizenry's beliefs in the higher system claiming legitimacy.[16] The utopian vision acts as a higher authority than the state, enabling citizens to call leaders to accountability to an ethical standard not created by the state itself.

Christianity has always claimed a higher authority for its vision of justice. In our own context, Orlando Costas, who we remember as both a fine friend and an excellent scholar, outlined such a vision in his paper, 'A Strategy for World Missions' in 1979.[17] The kingdom of God points to a redemption of creation and an abrogation of evil and chaos by Jesus Christ. It is through this vision that we commit ourselves to work in the world and critique not only our political systems but the Church itself. The vision of the kingdom of God gives us a standard by which to judge current political ideologies and social action.

A utopian vision need not be religious. Social theorist Juergen Habermas builds his theory of communicative action on a vision of justice lodged in speech acts themselves. The anticipated moment of emancipated free and equal communication provides a standard by which to judge the goodness of actual communication.[18] Political ideologies that do not encourage free and equal processes of decision-making are deemed lacking by this vision of emancipated communication. Ideologies that foster free and equal communication geared to understanding are judged to be good.[19]

A utopian vision as a measure of goodness for political ideologies seems to be inherent in the political project itself: creating a world where people live in ordered harmony, without oppression or chaos. A strong vision of justice can be provided by a Christian vision of the kingdom of God.

We believe that vision is rooted in God as Creator, in the nature of reality itself, and in the work of the unique Christ in history. Our construction of a just society is not untouched by distortions and historical interpretations. Our vision is limited. But a Christian vision of a just world is related to a reality we believe to be true. The vision is supported by the revelation of Scripture, the life and death of Jesus, and the witness of the Church in history.

A Christian vision of justice provides a standard by which to evaluate present realities. It also engenders the commitment to work toward a vision of justice that resonates in humans whatever beliefs they hold. Habermas' vision of open communication, the political ideology of Indonesia that stresses harmony in all of life, the Marxist concepts of equality and community – each of these visions can be articulated in Christian ways, framed by a Christian view of knowledge, and related to the moral sources of biblical faith.

The commitment to a vision of community and quality motivated many to work for justice in a Marxist frame of reference. But the moral sources for that vision were cut out from under it by Marxism's founding political ethics and visions of justice in the state itself. The Marxist vision became distorted, and the energy for implementing it drained away. The dismantling of the Soviet Union cannot be explained on the basis of this lack of moral sources and corruption of vision alone. But these factors played a definitive role in the recent decline of communist systems.

The fall of the Berlin Wall and the mass exodus to West Germany in the final months of 1989 also mark a *kairos* moment in world history. The fall of bricks and mortar symbolized the end of a political ideology that had sparked hope or struck terror in millions during this century.

The world looks for political visions that can be realized in reality. With the demise of communism in Europe and the Soviet Union, Marxism as a political ideology is called into question. Many today, in Eastern Europe and in the two-thirds world, now look to capitalism and to economic and political freedom as the source of a utopia, a land flowing with milk and honey. But the materialism and greed of unfettered capitalism provides no more firm a base for a just society than does the materialism of Marxism. The weaknesses of capitalism are ever more apparent as national debt levels rise, increased production of nonessential items destroys the environment, and the gap between rich and poor widens.

From where will a vision of justice arise that captures the imagination, motivates the will, and evaluates the goodness and rightness of political decisions? The Christian vision of the kingdom of God provides such a vision. It ties the political imagination to a Christian understanding of a political order characterized by righteousness and peace. Its dream of the good society connects memory and hope, linking future visions of justice to the memory of God's past saving acts in history.

CONCLUSION

We stand at a unique point in history. It is clear that all apprehensions of truth are historically situated and hermeneutically mediated by culture and tradition. Assumptions and beliefs are inherent in any articulation of knowledge, be it political, social scientific, or religious.

The value-oriented 'bias' that separated ideology from science has now been seen by scholars to be a bias that is true not only of ideologies but of science itself. Sources for the beliefs and assumptions of both ideological and scientific analyses must, therefore, be clearly articulated. Truth mediated symbolically can be found in both ideological and scientific analyses.

Only recently has the academic establishment to which society has granted so much authority to define meanings, realized the situated, partial, and valuing dimensions of scientific investigations and the positive contributions of ideologies. Mannheim disclosed the ideological component of social science. Geertz documented an integrative role for ideology in society. Ricoeur brought ideology and utopia together as complementary aspects of the development of social meanings in times of historical transition.

It is the failure of reason and science to provide a foundation for knowledge that spawned investigations into the nature of science and ideology. Evangelical theology offers a cogent framework for knowledge. Social science has always had a normative dimension, although repeatedly denied.[20] Evangelical theology offers moral sources that can undergird the normative dimension of social and political theories. Visions of a just society are crucial for directing and motivating action recommended by political ideologies. Evangelical theology can offer a vision of justice and peace realizable through human effort and divine action.

Without a framework for knowledge, truth becomes not merely perspectival but relative and ultimately meaningless.[21] Without adequate moral sources, rooted in an understanding of what is true, and good, and beautiful, political visions degenerate into destructive ideologies, and leaders resort to authoritarian means to support their values. Without a vision of justice, a critical standard by which to evaluate present realities disappears, leaving the state as the final arbiter of the good society.

Christian theology can aid the developments of social theories and political ideologies. Evangelical theology offers a cogent framework for knowledge, a source for ethics that foster benevolence and justice, and a vision of justice that can critique present political ideologies and motivate and direct social action. Without returning to a mythical medieval synethsis, Christian visions of truth and justice can help build viable political ideologies that can lead to a better world.

And Jesus said, 'To what should I compare the kingdom of God? It is like yeast that a woman took and mixed in with three measure of flour until all of it was leavened' (Luke 13:20).

NOTES

1. 'Evangelicalism and Social Responsibility: An Evangelical Commitment,' a joint publication of the Lausanne Committee for World Evangelization and the World Evangelical Fellowship, Wheaton, IL: W.E.F., P.O. Box W.E.F., 1982, p. 30. Quoted by Robert E. Webber in *The Church in the World: Opposition, Tension, or Transformation?* (Grand Rapids MI: Academie Books, Zondervan Publishing House, 1986), p. 252.

2. See Robert E. Webber, *The Church in the World* (op. cit.) Chapter 16 for an account of those activities.

3. Daniel Bell, *The End of Ideology: On the Exhaustion of Political Ideas in the Fifties* (NY: Collier Books, Revised Edition, 1962), p. 395.

4. Ibid.

5. There are exceptions to this perjorative view of ideology, for example, in Indonesia, national identity is based on 'Pancasila', a list of five values. These basic beliefs are called the national ideology.

6. Karl Mannheim, *Ideology and Utopia: An Introduction to the Sociology of Knowledge*, Trans. Louis Wirth and Edward Shils (NY: Harcourt, Brace & World, Inc., 1936), p. 74.

7. See Michael Polanyi, *Personal Knowledge: Towards a Post-Critical Philosophy*

(Chicago: University of Chicago Press, 1958), and Thomas Kuhn, *The Structure of Scientific Revolutions*, 2nd ed. (Chicago: University of Chicago Press, 1970).

8. Clifford Geertz, 'Ideology as a Cultural System' in *Interpretation of Cultures* (NY: Basic Books, 1973), pp. 193–233. Quote, p. 207.

9. Clifford Geertz 'Ideology as a cultural system' in *Interpretation of Cultures* (NY: Basic Books, 1973), p. 231.

10. The following description is taken from my book review of Charles Taylor's book *Sources of the Self: The Making of the Modern Identity*, in *Theology Today*, Vol. 48, No. 2, July, 1991, pp. 204–210.

11. Charles Taylor, *Sources of the Self: The Making of the Modern Identity* (Cambridge, MA: Harvard University Press, 1989), p. 495.

12. Taylor defines disengaged reason as a new notion of procedural reason. 'Knowledge comes not from connecting the mind to the order of things we find but in framing a representation of reality according to the right canons.' (p. 197) He contrasts this with substantive reason: '. . . rationality is the power to grasp the order of things, itself a reflection of reason.' (p. 255). Use of disengaged reason can lead to instrumental or utilitarian ethics, in which the good is decided on the basis of what works or benefits the actor. The notion of substantive good is relinquished in order to obtain freely chosen ends of action. Taylor argues that the modern loss of moral sources stems, in part, from the loss of the notion of substantive reason, reason that is related to the good that is inherent in the order of things.

13. See Taylor, *Sources on the Self*, 'The Conflicts of Modernity,' Chapter 25, especially pp. 516f.

14. Robert N. Bellah, *Habits of the Heart: Individualism and Commitment in American Life* (Berkeley and Los Angeles: University of California Press, 1985).

15. Taylor, *Sources of the Self*, p. 47.

16. George H. Taylor, ed., Paul Ricoeur: *Lectures on Ideology and Utopia*, (NY: Columbia University Press, 1986), p. xxii. See also Lecture 17, p. 298.

17. In Theodore Williams, ed., *Building Bridges or Barriers* (Bangalore, India: Evangelical Literature Service, 1979).

18. Juergen Habermas, *A Theory of Communicative Action: Reason and Rationalization of Society*, Vol. 1, trans. Thomas McCarthy (Boston: Beacon press, 1984), p. 25.

19. For further explanation of how the ideal speech situation, located in human reason, functions as a critical standard, see Frances S. Adeney, *Citizenship Ethics: Contributions of Classical Virtue Theory and Responsibility Ethics* (Ann Arbor, MI: University Microfilms International, 1988), pp. 35–38.

20. Unless this normative element is articulated, and its sources documented, social science unwittingly mimics the values of prediction and control set out by the natural science model. Its values of improving societal life, set out by classical theorists, e.g. Marx, Weber, and Durkheim, are lost.

21. For a cogent explanation of the trend toward relativism in social anthropology, see Paul Rabinow, 'Humanism as Nihilism' in *Social Science as Moral Inquiry*, eds, Norma Haan, Robert N. Bellah, Paul Rabinow, and William M. Sullivan (NY: Columbia University Press, 1983), pp. 52–75.

12

Jonathan Chao

The central concern of modern China is how to go beyond revolutions that overthrow political powers to the building of a just society and to developing human character. Dr. Jonathan Chao traces this search through the several attempts to modernize China from the Self-Strengthening movement following the humiliating defeat in the Opium War of 1839–42 at the hand of the British to the present post-Mao Reform Movement of Deng Xiaoping. He discusses the ideological goals of freedom from foreign aggression, acquiring Western technology and education, and political institutional reform through the successive revolutions of Sun Yat-sen, Chiang Kai-shek, Mao Zedong and Deng Xiaoping. The author traces the growth of the Church from its early identity with imperialistic aggression to the present indigenous church movement. He concludes that the Chinese people are discovering the uniqueness of the risen Christ in the lives of Christians and their suffering for Christ's sake.

A CASE STUDY

After the June 4th event in 1989, there arose a new quest among Chinese intellectuals and students: how can we know God? More than ever before the Chinese people today feel an intense need for God. Though they have been indoctrinated with faith in materialism, they are asking questions concerning transcendental realities. They are in search of a new structure of meaning for their individual lives and for China as a whole. That is why religion has been on the rise in China during the last ten years, but especially during the last three years. One of the articles published in a regional magazine published in Nanchang, Jiangxi, called Xinsheyish (New Vision) reported that in one of the counties called Chinxien, there were only 20 Christians in 1984, but by 1991 there were 6,000 plus believers. Furthermore, among the believers a good proportion are male, educated and elite intellectuals. Similar reports are numerous both from published sources and from the house church movement. To understand this welcome phenomenon of Chinese readiness for the

Dr. Jonathan Chao works with the Chinese Church Research Centre in Hong Kong.

gospel and their eagerness to believe in Christ, we need to analyze how Christ was perceived within the context of successive dominant ideologies and within the larger context of the Chinese search for personal and national salvation.

CHINESE QUEST FOR MODERNIZATION

In 1978 I met a Chinese physicist in London who had just come back from China after serving her in a painful way for twenty years. In 1958, soon after he had received his Ph.D. degree in laser physics from one of the major universities in Britain, he returned to China at the invitation of Chou En-lai, the former Premier. He worked very hard in the Academy of Sciences in Beijing. During the Cultural Revolution, he suffered much under the Red Guards. After having survived the difficult days of the Gang of Four, he was thankful that he came out alive. He concluded our conversation by saying that China has been plagued with three basic problems: poverty, backwardness, and a huge population.

His analysis left a strong impression in my mind, causing me to ponder over a most fundamental question: What have the Chinese people been striving for during the last 150 years since China was defeated by Britain in the Opium War (1839–1842)? Was Christ perceived as relevant to that Chinese quest?

It is true, as the Chinese physicist had analyzed, that China has been trying to overcome the problems of poverty, backwardness, and a huge population for the past hundred years or so. However, I submit that in addition to the above search to solve her economic problems, China has been in search of freedom from foreign aggression and of a place among the nations in the modern world.

The way to both economic and political freedom was perceived as modernization by way of Westernization. From the Self-strengthening Movement (1860–95) under the Ch'ing Dynasty to the present Reform Movement advocated by Deng Xiaoping China has been trying to overcome the problem of poverty, backwardness, and the threat of foreign aggression by way of modernization.

The history of modern China can, in a way, be interpreted as a sustained quest for modernization. However, this has been pursued under different changing political ideologies. Or, it may be said that successive political leaders have introduced different cultural ideologies through which they sought to pursue modernization and which have also subsequently affected the way Chinese people perceived Christ as presented by foreign missionaries and the Chinese church.

THE SELF-STRENGTHENING MOVEMENT

During the first three decades after the Opium War (1839–1842), in which she was defeated by Britain and suffered national humiliation, China sought to strengthen herself by acquiring Western technology in warfare and by the development of her natural resources in order to become 'rich and strong' (fu-chiang) in order to regain her freedom from foreign aggression. This was the Self-strengthening Movement launched by Chinese official-literati of the

Ch'ing Dynasty from 1860 to 1895. The idea was to learn from the foreigners in order to defeat them. The Self-strengthening Movement sought to modernize China by borrowing Western science and technology, while preserving the spirit of Chinese Confucian culture.

This was the period of initial Protestant mission work inside China. Although sacrificial missionaries sought to preach an evangelical gospel of sin, condemnation, and hell, Chinese official literati and the gentry perceived Christianity as a religion of white conquerors and missionaries as an integral part of foreign aggression. In fact, Christianity gained the right of propagation through a 'toleration clause' written in the Treaty of Teinjin (1858), thereby ending a hundred years of cruel persecution against the Catholics (1724–1842). The Chinese official-gentry instigated anti-Christian riots by stimulating the ignorant peasants.[2] While the upper class avoided missionaries for fear of being implicated, the poor and the socially marginal people responded to the kind overtures of the missionaries who offered them employment, free education for their children, modern medical care, and protection from the oppressive bureaucracy. Christ was not seen as relevant to China, and Christianity was relegated to the fringe of Chinese society as a religion to take care of the poor and the needy in the same way that Buddhism was consigned for centuries.

THE REFORM MOVEMENT

Although the self-strengthening movement brought in Western arms, gunboats, navigation, minings, railroads, telegram and other modern technologies, it proved to be inadequate for national defence. In 1895 China suffered a humiliating defeat at the hand of the Japanese in Korea. This made her intellectuals realize that technical modernization by acquiring foreign military hardware, and by developing her own natural resources was not enough to enable China to survive in this modern world. This realization led the young intellectuals to see that they must go beyond technical and economic reform to political institutional reform if they were to create a modern China. So leaders like K'ang Yu-wei, Liang Ch'i-ch'ao and others launched out a Reform Movement (1898) in which they sought to bring in Western political institutions like the British Parliament under a monarchy.[3] Unfortunately the Reform Movement lasted only a hundred days, and then it was crushed by the Empress Dowager and her conservative Confucianists, more or less a precursor of the Tienanmen Square event.

The Reformers sought help from missionaries in their search for a better understanding of the Western world in general and of Western political institutions in particular. Chief among these was Timothy Richards of the English Baptist Mission who served as an adviser to the Reformers and later as President of Peking University, as Western education was perceived to be an essential foundation for modernization. During this period Western culture was presented by missionaries as superior to Chinese culture by demonstrating the superiority of Western science and medicine. Within this larger context of Western culture, the Christian religion was presented as superior to Chinese religions. It was not so much the uniqueness of Christ that was presented as a comparative Western Christian religion. After the fiasco of the Boxer Rebellion, the Chinese people became more open to Western learning, and also to Christianity. The period from 1901 to 1911 witnessed a season of Chinese openness to the gospel.

REVOLUTIONARY MOVEMENTS

After the failure of the Reform Movement, Chinese youths like Sun Yat-sen and his friends adopted a revolutionary approach to creating a strong China by overthrowing the backward Ch'ing dynasty of of Manchu rule and by creating a new republic patterned after the West. However, after the overthrow of the old empire, China remained poor and backward, and foreigners continued to exercise their special privileges on Chinese soil. Sun failed to create a strong, democratic, modern China. In fact Sun lost control of the new republican government, and the warlords took over China, making it worse than it had been under the monarchy. In his frustration, Sun turned to socialist Russia for help. Concurrently a few Chinese intellectuals and youths began to form a Marxist study group in 1919 and two years later established the Chinese Communist Party. They saw Lenin's revolutionary theories and tactics as ideologies which could lead to political action in overcoming foreign colonialism (imperialism), feudalism, and as a means of creating a new China.

In 1924 Sun reorganized his Kuomintang party after the pattern of the Soviet Bolshevik model and, together with the Communist International, created a collaboration between the Chinese Communist Party and the Kuomintang. Sun adopted a new goal of accepting the Chinese Communists, of uniting with the Soviet Union, and supporting workers' and farmers' movements. Sun died in 1925 before he could see the success of the revolution. In June 1926 Chiang Kai-shek launched out his Northern Expedition with Russian arms and military aids, but as soon as he had captured the territories south of the Yangtze, he purged the Communists in April 1927, and drove the Russian advisers away.

Sun and his followers had adopted a revolutionary approach because of the failure of the Reform Movement. Actually it was not so much the failure of the Reformers as the continuing strength of the conservative Confucianists. The problem was not the lack of new ideas or men for modernization, the problem was one of old ideology exercising control via political institutions, and hence the revolutionaries realized that in order to change the controlling ideology, they must deprive it of its political institutional power.

During the initial phase of the revolution Sun Yat-sen borrowed the American model of a democratic political institution only to find that neither Chinese leaders nor the people had any idea of how democracy works. What Sun succeeded in was to overthrow the monarchy of the Ch'ing Dynasty, or to bring it to a quicker demise. In his second revolutionary attempt, Sun used the Russian Bolshevik model of 'dictatorship of the people' based on a singular Leninist ideology which was a powerful tool against Western colonialism. A part of Lenin's anti-imperialist campaign was the anti-Christian movement which was propagated by the Chinese Communist Party and the Kuomintang Party together with their youth organizations during 1922–1927.

During this latter part of the revolutionary movement, Chinese intellectuals and youths perceived Christianity as an integral part of Western imperialism. Christianity was first rejected on scientific grounds as outdated during the New Culture Movement, and later rejected as the cultural wing of the imperialists, and hence as unpatriotic during the Anti-imperialist Movement.[4] In response to these accusations, Chinese church leaders sought to present Christ as a 'revolutionary' who was one of the proletariats and who took the side of the oppressed. In order to distance themselves from foreign imperialism, Chinese church leaders sought to develop independent indigenous churches that were free from foreign missionary control. In this indigenous movement, Chinese church leaders sought to make Christianity more Chinese by integrating it with Chinese culture, and they were united in a determination to sinize it and thereby create a 'Chinese Christianity'. In the process Christ began to take on a Chinese face, and there are paintings which show Christ wearing a Chinese garment. Within this context Christ was not presented as unique, but as very much like one of the indigenized religious leaders.

IDEOLOGICAL PLURALISM UNDER POLITICAL TUTELAGE OF THE KUOMINTANG

After Chiang Kai-shek had driven the Communists out of his Kuomintang Party in 1927 and after he had completed his 'Northern Expedition' in 1928, he changed his national official ideology to Sun's Three-principles. Under Kuomintang's 'political tutelage', Chiang tolerated a wide range of ideological and religious pluralism, such as Confucianism, Taoism, Islam, Buddhism, Christianity, and Western liberalism of all sorts – so long as they did not challenge his political authority. This was the state of affairs under Kuomintang even after Chiang came to Taiwan in 1949 and the R.O.C. government continued with this kind of pluralism until it was further opened up in 1987. One may say that from 1928 Chiang Kai-shek sought to overcome the problems of foreign aggression, poverty, and backwardness through military and economic self-strengthening under an official political ideology of Sun Yat-san's three principles. The Nanking government showed some favour towards Confucianism, and Christianity from time to time enjoyed a special favour due to the Generalissimo and Madame Chiang Kai-shek's affiliation with the Christian faith. Under these circumstances Christianity was allowed to be preached and practised, but not to exert an influence over the area of education and politics. Christianity continued to be perceived as a Western religion, and Christ was seen as one among many religious founders.

MARXISM, LENINISM, AND THE THOUGHT OF MAO

In 1949 Chiang Kai-shek was driven to Taiwan by the Chinese Communists, who took pride in driving out the foreign imperialists. As Mao declared on October 1, 1949: 'We have stood up!' Finally, China became free from foreign aggression. Missionaries were driven out by March 1951, soon after the outbreak of the Korean War. The KMT was defeated, the foreigners driven out, yet China was still poor and backward, and her population continued to grow.

In the 1950s Mao and the Chinese Communist Party wanted to build 'a new China' that was strong and prosperous. They adopted the Russian model of modernization through industrialization. They believed that by nationalizing natural resources and the means of production, and by building a new, proletarian society, China would become rich and strong. After nearly a decade's attempt at implementing the Russian model, China remained poor and backward. Her backwardness bothered Mao Zedong greatly. For, according to Communist theory, when the means of production has been changed, the people's thinking would also be changed. Yet in the Chinese case, the Chinese people remained 'feudalistic', that is, backward and set in their traditional Confucian ways. So in 1957 Mao launched his Socialist Education Movement, and in 1958 he launched the Great Leap Forward Movement, hoping to bring about an ideological change in the thinking of the people through a programme of rural farm labour. But the Great Leap Forward Movement turned out to be a great fiasco, and he lost his leadership in the government to Liu Shao-chi, though still retaining his chairmanship and command over the military. Mao continued to push his Socialist Education Movement from 1959 which culminated in the outbreak of the Great Proletarian Cultural Revolution in 1966. He wanted to create 'new men' as the way to create a 'new society', that is, modernization through ideological transformation. The Cultural Revolution was essentially Mao's attempt to achieve this objective through regaining political leadership. But in the end he plunged China into deeper misery. His failure proved that if changing the means of production cannot change human nature (the traditional Marxist view), neither can the 'return to the countryside' process through manual labour plus ideological indoctrination change human nature. The Communist experiment failed precisely because the Communist entertained an erroneous doctrine of man: that there is no such thing as universal human nature, but only class nature, which is determined by labour or his relationship to property ownership. What the Communists failed to understand is the theological definition of man as fallen man, whose nature is characterized by sin, and sin is most clearly manifested in self-centredness and selfishness.

After Mao died, China began a process of de-Maoification under the leadership of Deng Xiaoping. He replaced Mao's attempt to modernize China through ideological transformation with economic pragmatism under the rubric of 'Four Modernizations'. Deng's reform programme, marked by his open door policy, marks a return to the Party's attempt during the early 1950s: modernization through economic development, which in turn goes back to the self-strengthening movement in the 19th century. More than a decade has passed since Deng inaugurated his reform programme in 1979, and China has made some progress, but not significant enough to satisfy the demands of the people, nor fast enough to please the intellectuals who want more than economic progress. Today China is still backward and poor.

During the three decades of Mao's rule, traditional Christianity in all its Western institutional forms was destroyed. Christians had to undergo repeated stages of humiliation and suffering just because of their identity with Christ. The Christian faith could not be publicly preached or confessed. The Marxist and Leninist view of religion were inn the ascendancy. The only difference was between the approaches of the hardliners who advocated extinction, and the softliners who preferred limited tolerance under government control. It was such circumstances of persecution that the Chinese Church rose again from the ashes of institutional imported Christianity. All former privileges derived from the treaties or from affiliation with Chiang Kai-shek were removed. House church Christianity was built on the foundation of being crucified, buried, and risen again with Christ through suffering. Finally Christianity has become indigenized, not by becoming more Chinese, but through participating with Christ in his experience of death and resurrection and the gift of the Holy Spirit. Today the Church in China has grown from less than one million in 1949 to over 60 million precisely because believers discovered the power of the resurrection in their lives. That is the uniqueness of Christ which is lacking in all Chinese religions, ideologies, or cultural traditions.

MODERNIZATION CANNOT BE LIMITED TO ECONOMICS

The modernization programme under Deng Xiaoping ran into trouble by late 1986. Hu Yaobang and his fellow reformers came to realize that economic reform requires changes in the area of politics. In other words, economic structural reform requires corresponding political structural reform. The reformers realized that the market economy requires a politically pluralistic society which can provide adequate room for competition in supply and demands. So they demanded political structural reform in the summer of 1986. Hu Yaobang's accelerated reform movement also resulted in his dismissal, and an 'Anti-bourgeois Liberalization Movement' was launched and continued until 1988. In 1989 the voices for further ideological reform became louder and louder until they were crushed by the hardliners on June 4th 1989. Since January 1992 Deng Xiaoping has been advocating a return to his economic reform movement with an accelerated pace. Furthermore, he is even advocating that China learn from the capitalists, just as the self-strengthening movement had advocated learning from the foreigners.

CONCLUSION

China is going to move much faster from now on towards a greater openness along lines of economic reform, which will eventually lead to ideological reform, resulting in the natural rejection of Marxism, Leninism, and the thoughts of Mao in the interests of the economy. The intellectuals have already pushed these ideologies aside. They have been rejected not because they were of no value as ideas or theories, but having tried them for more than seventy years, the intellectuals have come to see that these ideologies are capable of overthrowing other political powers, such as Kuomintang or colonial powers, but they are not able to build a nation and society, let alone build up human character. They have come to see that neither traditional Confucianism, nor Western liberal democratic thinking, nor Communism, are able to satisfy their personal quest for salvation, nor are they able to provide adequate basis for building a just society. Gradually they are learning from the Chinese Christians who have gone through the crucibles of suffering that there is something extraordinary in the person of Jesus Christ who through his self-giving death and his resurrection is able to give life to a person and that that life can not only generate hope for the individual, but also lay the foundation for a better society and for a world to come. Finally the uniqueness of Christ has been discovered by the Chinese people after 150 years of suffering!

NOTES

1. Hu Yuchin and Yu Haoron, 'New Trends of Development in Christianity,' *Xinshiyieh (Nanchang)*, March 1991, pages 21–23; reprinted by Wushenlun and Zhongjian [*Atheism and Religion*], March, 1991, pp. 62–63.

2. See Paul Cohen, *China and Christianity: anti-foreignism in China*, 1860–1870 (Cambridge: Harvard University Press, 1961).

3. See Immanuel C.Y. Hsu, *The Rise of Modern China* (New York: Oxford University Press, 1970), pp. 423–440.

4. For fuller details, see my Ph.D. thesis, 'The Chinese Indigenous Church Movement: a Protestant Response to the Anti-religious and Anti-Christian Movement in Modern China, 1919–1927', University of Pennsylvania, 1986.

Part Four

The Unique Christ in the Church's Diversity and Unity

13

John A. Vessers

The focus of this chapter is on the Incarnation and on a Christological understanding of the Church with only secondary reference to the uniqueness of the Cross and the Resurrection. Dr. Vessers takes us through the Christological issues in the early Church culminating in the formulae of Nicea and Chalcedon. Unity in the Church was a Christological one. He then surveys seven images of Christ in the contemporary North American Church which though contextual, conflict with classical Christology. The author discusses what the Lordship of Christ should mean in our post-modern Church and calls upon evangelicals to restate the classical view, freed from the intellectual chains of the Enlightenment. He believes evangelical Christology must transcend the dichotomy of 'Christology from below' from 'Christology from above' and discover its implications for the unity and diversity of the Church.

INTRODUCTION

'You are the Christ, the Son of Living God.'[1] This is the remarkable confession made by Peter in response to the question of Jesus to his disciples: 'who do you say that I am?' This same question has been before the Church throughout its history and continues to confront it today. The Church's life depends upon giving a faithful answer to this question. Whenever and wherever the Church is in decline its cause can usually be traced back to the fact that it gets the answer to this basic question wrong.[2] The fact that the uniqueness of Jesus as the Christ, the Son of the living God, is not always everywhere acknowledged today in the Christian Church is in itself sufficient reason for maintaining a distinctly evangelical witness in the global Christian community.[3] In our day it is not too much to say that this article of faith is the 'articulus stantis et cadentis ecclesiae' (the article by which the Church stands or falls).[4]

Jesus first asked his disciples, 'Who do people say the Son of Man is?' As important as this question is, the Church cannot be content simply with rehearsing the diverse answers and opinions which exist in the Church and the

Dr. John A. Vessers teaches theology at the Ontario Theological Seminary, Canada.

world concerning the identity of Jesus. While it is always interested in how others look at Jesus, its own confession of Jesus is what constitutes its faith and life. Like the disciples the Church must answer for itself the question: 'But what about you? . . . Who do YOU say that I am?' While such a confession is made within the context of a plurality of understandings of the person and ministry of Jesus of Nazareth, it is always concerned to set forth faithfully the identity of Jesus Christ as Jesus revealed himself to be.

Almost all Christians would agree that the confession of Christ as Messiah, the Son of the living God is central to the Church's life.[5] But the shape of this confession is very different within the diversity of the worldwide Church. It is a matter of fact that Christians live not only in a pluralistic world but also within a pluralistic Church. The diversity of the Christian community is reflected in denominational distinctives, geographical and national boundaries, social, economic and political divisions, and the diversity of racial, ethnic, and people groups, all of which make the unity and catholicity of the Church a complicated matter. What does it mean today, then, to acknowledge the unique Christ in our pluralistic Church? How is the uniqueness of Christ understood within the diversity and unity of church understanding? Does pluralism within the Church mean a plurality of Christs? Is there a common confession of Christ to which we must all adhere? What constitutes the uniqueness of Christ in our faith today? What are the implications of our Christology for the unity of the Church in the world today?

These are the questions taken up in this paper. The first part of the paper sets out the incarnational Christology of the early Church and notes the reasons for the abandonment of Nicea and Chalcedon in contemporary Church and theology. Here the focus is upon what the answer in the Church has been to Jesus' question about his identity. In the second part of the paper I explore some diverse images of Christ in contemporary theology and try to show how Christology has been captured by the ideologies of Enlightenment thinking in the Western world. Here the focus is upon Jesus' question, 'Who do people say that I am?' in our own day. Thirdly, I discuss the implications for Christology and ecclesiology of the new so-called postmodern worldview in the west and argue that it may provide an opportunity to recover a biblical and classical confession of Christ for the churches. Here I propose what the answer to Jesus' question ought to be for the Church today.

The argument may be summarized as follows: the classical Christology of the Church, rather than providing an obscure and irrelevant portrait of Jesus, in method and substance provides a Christology both appropriate to the biblical witness and, insofar as it is biblical, a Christology adequate to the needs of religious pluralism and human experience today since these questions too confronted the Church as it sought to confess Christ as Lord.[6] The Christologies of the churches in the last two centuries have been captivated by the ideologies of a Western Enlightenment worldview now in decline, thereby providing a new opportunity for the Church to return to its biblical faith in Christ. Such a return can provide the substantial basis for the unity of the Church in today's world. The reader will soon discover that while I have included some discussion of two thirds world theologies I write primarily with an eye on developments in western theology, and specifically North America. When I discuss developments outside of this context it is with the intention of understanding how these theologies have affected the contemporary Church in North America.

I. THE INCARNATIONAL CHRISTOLOGY OF THE CLASSICAL CHURCH

The Shape of the Church's Incarnational Christology

When confronted with competing claims concerning the identity of Jesus of Nazareth the ancient Church decisively affirmed the absolute deity and the absolute humanity (two natures) of Jesus as the Christ, the Son of the living God (one person). The Church understood its affirmation as consistent with the Old Testament tradition of radical monetheism and the New Testament revelation of Jesus as Saviour and Lord. It took this decisive stand against competing religious and theological claims within and outside of the Church. And in making the claim it utilized the philosophical language of the culture in order to articulate with clarity the identity of Jesus in a world shaped by Greek philosophical constructs. The confession that Jesus is both God and man emerged within a Church which was struggling to understand and assess a number of competing Christological developments.[7]

First, in the face of Ebionism and Arianism the Church affirmed the absolute deity of Jesus. Neither the Ebionites nor Arius and his followers could reconcile the deity of Jesus as the Christ with the strict monotheism (Deut. 6:4) of the Jewish tradition. The Ebionites therefore saw Jesus as the human son of Mary and Joseph who so fulfilled the Mosaic law that God chose him to be the Messiah. Utilizing an adoptionist Christology they argued that only this view of Christ could be reconciled with faith in one God. Later Arius proposed a Christology based upon similar presuppositions. If God is one, perfect, eternal, infinite, unbegotten, undifferentiated and unoriginated being then God must be timeless, immutable, and impassible. Since Christ is subject to the limitations of space-time in the world these attributes of the divine being cannot be applied to Christ in the same manner. The Son, therefore, is not co-eternal with the Father and is not God in the same way that the Father is God. There was a time when the Son of God did not exist, Arius concluded. While it may be said that he is homiousios with the Father (of a similar substance) it may not be said that Christ is of the same substance (homoousios). Jesus as the Christ is Godlike but he is not God. In response to the Arian party Nicea and Athanasius demanded an absolute reaffirmation of the deity of Jesus. For them the Church's identity was not rooted in a general affirmation about God but in a particular confession of faith in Jesus as the Christ, the Son of the living God. The deity of Christ was for them the starting-point of all talk about God. When forced to choose, the early Church opted for the logic of incarnation rather than the logic of monotheism.[8]

Secondly, when confronted by Docetism and Apollinarianism the Church affirmed the absolute humanity of Jesus. Docetist Christology emerged under the influence of gnosticism with its metaphysical dualism (the material or physical is inherently evil while the spiritual alone is good), its attribution of creation to a semi-divine being, and its depreciation of the process of human generation and birth.[9] While Jesus as the Christ certainly appeared to be human he was not in reality a human being since such a human nature, in its very essence evil, would by its very existence compromise the deity of Jesus. Apollinaris, bishop of Laodicea in the fourth century, reconstructed the image of Christ on the basis of a Greek anthropology with a similar result. In an effort to emphasize a Word-flesh Christology he argued that in Jesus is united the divine logos with human flesh. The humanity of Christ was reduced to his fleshly or bodily existence while the mind-soul dimension was divine. This view, because it seemed to deny the reality of a full human nature, was rejected at Constantinople in 381 and again at Chalcedon in 451.

Thirdly, when confronted by the followers of Nestorius and Eutyches the Church affirmed the integrity of the two natures in the one person. Nestorianism is usually understood as a Christological formulation in which the real union of the human and the divine natures of Christ is denied. While there is a moral or acting union there is no real union of these natures in one person. Recent scholarship has demonstrated that Nestorius himself never actually taught this. Furthermore, his view is to be understood within the context of his rejection of the phrase theotokos. Nevertheless, this view was interpreted at Ephesus (431) and Chalcedon (451) as opening up a Christology which allowed for two persons as well as two natures. Eutyches, on the other hand, sought to solve the same problem by arguing that the language of two natures itself was inadequate. Rather, in Christ exists one human-divine nature co-mingled in one theanthropic person. In response to Nestorius and Eutyches the council at Chalcedon declared that in Christ existed a fully human nature and a fully divine nature in one person 'without confusion, without change, without division, without separation'.

Fourthly, in making these affirmations concerning the uniqueness of Christ the saving work of Christ was always in view. It is sometimes suggested that the Christological formulations of the early Church are deficient in that they focus on the person of Christ apart from his work. To put it slightly differently, the creeds develop an ontological Christology in distinction from the functional Christology of the New Testament. Aside from the question of whether there is such a neat division within the New Testament itself, this view overlooks the fact that for many of the church fathers what was at stake in these discussions was the efficacy of the saving work of Christ. Certainly this was the case for Athanasius. In his writings Athanasius made clear that since only God can save it is essential to affirm the deity of Christ if redemption is to be a reality. Likewise, other church fathers developed understandings of salvation (recapitulation, ransom, deification, illumination) which depended upon a high Christology. The uniqueness of Christ is not an abstract discussion about his person only, then, but a very real discussion about the nature and efficacy of the salvation effected by God in and through Christ alone for humanity.

Fifthly, these affirmations concerning the uniqueness of Christ provided the basis of the unity of the ancient Church. The early Church's unity was a Christological unity. The battle over the uniqueness of Christ in a very real sense created the Church. Thus, there is a relationship between Christology and ecclesiology which has implications for our confession of Christ and for our understanding of the nature of the Church. On the one hand this meant for the early Church there could have been neither a plurality of churches nor a plurality of images of Christ which were mutually exclusive. Yet it is also true to say that within the Christological parameters of the one holy catholic Church there was a diversity of faith and practice. Consequently, an evangelical Christology today must be developed within the context of a commitment to the unity of the Church while at the same time acknowledging the diversity which can legitimately exist within this unity.

The Challenge to the Church's Incarnational Christology

In its basic form this Christology provided the basis of faith in the eastern and western churches, in the Roman Catholic and Protestant churches, and in the various branches (Reformed, Lutheran, Anabaptist) of Protestantism until at least the nineteenth century. To be sure, there were variations in emphasis (e.g. the debate between Lutherans and Reformed over whether the divine logos was completely encompassed within the human Jesus) and direct challenges to this view (e.g. the rejection of the deity of Christ by Socinus and Unitarianism). Nevertheless, it has only recently been the case that within the Church more diverse understandings of Jesus have begun to emerge. During the last two centuries the incarnational Christology of the Church has been challenged for a number of reasons.

The first challenge came from the rise of historical consciousness and the application of the historical-critical method to the Bible, especially the Gospels.[10] Does the traditional Christology of the Church truly reflect the Christology of the New Testament? The so-called biblical objection encompasses a number of questions. Is there not a real historical Jesus behind the Church's faith-shaped portrait of him in the texts of the New Testament which is not accounted for in the Christology of the early Church? Is there not a plurality of Christologies in the New Testament which make it difficult to say that one particular Christology, i.e. the high incarnational Christology of the creeds is the biblical Christology? Is it not the case that the Christology of the New Testament utilizes functional categories rather than the ontological language of Greek philosophy which is found in the creeds?

A second question concerns the intelligibility of the Greek philosophical language of the ancient Christological creeds.[11] Since the language of 'one substance' (homoousion), 'two natures united in one person'; (hypostasis), etc. no longer obtains in our culture, it is argued that the creeds themselves can be interpreted only as historically conditioned statements which have no real value for the Church today.

Thirdly, there is the problem of the exclusive claim made in the traditional incarnational Christology of the Church. Christians have claimed that in this Jesus of Nazareth, the Son of the living God, and in no other, has God become incarnate and chosen to reveal and to effect the work of salvation. This is what Kittel called the scandal of particularity. Can this particular one be the saviour of all? Feminist theologians ask whether a male saviour can save women? Black theologians wonder whether a Jewish male can save black people? Is there any ontological necessity for Jesus' maleness or his Jewishness? Advocates of cooperation among religions argue that exclusive and particular claims violate the inclusive and universal faith required in an age of religious pluralism.[12]

In sum, these critical challenges to the incarnational Christology of the

Church resulted in portraits of Christ which either moved beyond Nicea and Chalcedon or abandoned them altogether. It is to these images of Christ in contemporary Church and theology that we now turn.

II. IMAGES OF CHRIST IN THE CONTEMPORARY NORTH AMERICAN CHURCH

When confronted with the combined challenges of critical biblical and historical scholarship, cultural relevancy, and competing religious claims the modern churches in the west frequently reconstructed their portraits of Christ in ways which seemed to them to be both adequate and appropriate. It is to some of these reconstructed images that we now turn our attention. In each case our concern is to identify what constitutes the uniqueness of Christ in the view presented.

Revisionist Christology

First, an important image of Christ emerging in the churches of North America is the Christ of religious and cultural pluralism being advocated by revisionist theologians. While many theologians are working at this question specifically in terms of the relationship of Christianity to other world religions (e.g. John Hick, Paul Knitter) others are addressing it from the perspective of a theology of culture. The work of University of Chicago theologian David Tracy, for example, represents perhaps one of the most comprehensive and sophisticated attempts by a contemporary Roman Catholic theologian to set forth a way of understanding the person of Christ within the cultural pluralism of modernity.[13] In his books *Blessed Rage for Order* and *The Analogical Imagination* Tracy seeks to meet the challenges of contemporary cultural pluralism in the west in order to maintain a public role for theology. Tracy's theological method is developed around the concept of 'the classic'. The classics are by definition public. Religious traditions and symbols, insofar as they fulfil the criteria of the public classic, also make a genuine contribution to human understanding. Christians may participate in the public discussion insofar as their classic is a genuine expression of a cultural and religious classic. For the Christian the classic is the Christ-event-person, and the theologian, utilizing a theological analogical imagination, may render an interpretation of the whole of reality based upon Christ and enter this interpretation into the public arena. For Tracy, this Jesus is 'the Jesus remembered by the tradition which mediates the event in the present through word, sacrament, and action; the Jesus remembered as the Christ, the presence among us of God's own self'.[14] The image of Christ which emerges, however, is of a Christ whose particularity is reinterpreted in terms of universal criteria of culture and religion. The classic Christ is symbolic of a greater reality and is not himself that reality. Furthermore, while Tracy assigns that Christ-event-person classic status, he admits a plurality of Christs in the New Testament and the pluralism of interpretations. Without any normative image of Christ, it would appear, we are left with a series of mutually exclusive Christological portraits which relativise each other.

Process Christology

Secondly, a process Christology develops an image of Christ in terms of a new metaphysic. It is argued that the classical incarnational Christology of the Church utilized a Greek metaphysic in which permanence, substance, being, and nature were primary categories. This view of reality no longer obtains in our world and the basic units of reality are processes and events. Reality is not a static and substantive being but rather a dynamic process of becoming. Process theologians recast the image of Christ within this framework. John Cobb, for example, argues that the humanity of Christ's person does not refer to a fixed mode of being. A person is not a static being but a dynamic, changing set of relationships centred around the past, present, and future.[15] A process Christology also emphasizes the historical reality of Jesus's existence and speaks of God's work in the life of Jesus. This divine reality (process) at work in the life of Jesus in no way diminishes his humanity. It is appropriate to speak of the divinity and uniqueness of Christ in these terms. Jesus represents a greater degree of the activity of God in his life than any other human being. Put slightly differently, the difference between Jesus and other human beings (his uniqueness) is one of degree rather than kind.[16]

Liberation Christology

Thirdly, an important and influential image of Christ emerging in the Church today is that of Jesus Christ the liberator.[17] The Christology of liberation theology, especially in its Latin American expression, is reshaping our understanding of Christ not only in the two thirds world but also in North America. Defining theology as critical reflection on praxis and utilizing a sociological hermenuetic to interpret the context as well as the biblical text, liberation theologians argue that the unique Christ of the Gospels can be truly apprehended only from the perspective of the poor and the oppressed. Leonardo Boff and Job Sobrino argue that Christological investigation must begin 'from below', that is with a study of the historical Jesus. Christology begins with 'the person, teaching, attitudes, and deeds of Jesus of Nazareth insofar as they are accessible, in a more or less general way, to historical and exegetical investigation'[18] rather than with 'the Christ, the only begotten and eternal Son of God, sent as man to liberate us from our sins'[19]. While liberation theologians do not set aside Chalcedon altogether, they argue that it presupposes a Christology of descent in which 'it starts off with God and then goes on to affirm how the eternal Son became man' rather than the biblical approach 'which starts off with the man Jesus and then goes on to reflect upon his divinity'[20]. Furthermore, it does this using Greek philosophical concepts rather than biblical language. Boff's conclusions concerning the two natures in the one person of Christ are in continuity with Chalcedon, however. He affirms that if we accept in faith that Jesus was both a human being who could relate to God in a unique way, and the reality of God becoming human in a unique way, then we accept and profess this incarnation – the unconfounded, immutable, indivisible, and inseparable unity of God and humanity in one and the same Jesus Christ.[21] Sobrino's position, on the other hand, is somewhat less than classical when he advocates a developmental Christology in which the man Jesus became God. The problem here is that it is not always clear just whether Jesus' divinity is qualitatively different from the experience of an exalted and perfected humanity in right relation-ship to God.[22] Liberation Christology focuses less on these questions, however, and more on Jesus' message of the kingdom of God. Jesus did not preach about himself or even simply about God, but rather about the kingdom of God.[23] As such, Jesus announced good news to the poor and oppressed, and he proclaimed release to the captives, recovery of sight to the blind, and the year of the Lord's favour (Lk. 4:18, 19). The kingdom of God is a kingdom of personal conversion and social transformation. It is a kingdom of discipleship in which the believer follows Jesus in this praxis. In sum, the unique Christ is the true liberator who announces God's kingdom, who calls men and women to follow him in this kingdom, and who, in his humanity and divinity, himself embodies the liberating and eschatological activity of God in the world.

Feminist Christology

Another image of Christ emerging in the churches of North America is that set forth in feminist theology. Utilizing the method of liberation theology, feminists argue that the starting point of theology is the experience of women's oppression under the patriarchal structures of a male-dominated society.[24] Such a starting point renders a rather different interpretation of the Bible and the Christian tradition from those interpretations given by male theologians, particularly in regard to the doctrine of God and Christology. Feminists object to the traditional Christian concept of God in which the supreme being is understood as male and as father.[25] They further object to a traditional Christology because they believe that the doctrine of the deity of Jesus Christ (and the doctrine of the two natures in one person) – that God became uniquely incarnate in one particular male being – contributes to and supports patriarchalism.[26] Canadian feminist theologian Pamela Dickey Young, for example, argues that the divinity of Jesus is better understood as a re-presentation of God, and that Jesus should not be seen as the one in whom we find a human nature and a divine nature as a combination of substances or natures.[27] The image of Christ which then emerges can vary greatly. Mary Daly represents the most radical option when she rejects as mythological and idolatrous the traditional view of Jesus as the unique and exclusive incar-nation of God. Since this view has reinforced male supremacy Jesus can no longer function as a saviour for women and his actions and teachings likewise must be abandoned.[28] Carter Heywood can argue that while Jesus is not uniquely divine he nevertheless, when rightly understood, can have value for all people, including women and feminists. She emphasizes the universality of the term Christ. Jesus is the Christ in the sense that he reveals what 'Christ' is, and makes it possible for all people to experience the reality of Christ in their lives.[29] One of the most prolific and articulate feminist theologians, Rosemary Reuther, sees Jesus as a champion of women. She too argues that the orthodox 'Christology has been the doctrine of the Christian tradition that has been most frequently used against women'.[30] In addressing the question of whether a male saviour can save women, she proposes a Christology in which Jesus is seen as the prophetic iconoclastic Christ who stands against all forms of hypocrisy, oppression, and hierarchy and advocates for the poor, the outcast, the downtrodden – including women. Princeton Seminary theologian

Mark Kline Taylor proposes the image *Christus Mater* (Christ as Mother) as a metaphor that 'conjoins the maternal powers of women (whether these are actualized or not) with the Christ taken by the traditions as the locus of divinity and of salvific efficacy'. It is an image which allows for a convergence between christic ultimacy and womanform while overcoming the oppression of sexism, heterosexism, classism, and racism which pervades North Atlantic culture.[31] And finally, Leonard Swidler portrays Jesus as a feminist who in the Gospels favoured, promoted, and advocated the equality of women and men in a male-dominated culture where it was considered woman had no place.[32] In sum, in each of these views Jesus is refigured in such a manner as to resonate with the experience of women's structural and systemic oppression in a patriarchal culture.[33]

Black Christology

Fifthly, another important image of Christ which has emerged in the North America churches during the last twenty years is that of Jesus as the black Christ. The term black theology may be applied to North American black theology (Afro-American), African theology (theologia Africana), and South African black theology,[34] but our focus in this discussion is upon developments in North America. Black theologians such as James Cone and J. Deotis Roberts emphasize the uniqueness of the black experience of oppression within a white racist society as the starting-point and the context for theology.[35] In common with liberation theologians they note that most of the Church's theology has been done from a white, male, western perspective. By definition, Cone argues, Christian theology is liberation theology.[36] The hermenutical principle which guides black theology in its interpretation of the meaning of contemporary Christianity is the black Christ: 'the norm of all God-talk which seeks to be black-talk is the manifestation of Jesus as the black Christ who provides the necessary soul for black liberation'.[37] In describing Jesus as the black Christ Cone identifies the uniqueness of Jesus in terms of his identification with the oppressed. As the oppressed one, Jesus is the black Christ.[38] In affirming the importance of the historical Jesus as the basis of Christology Cone says that the incarnation means that in Christ God becomes oppressed (black) humanity and thus demonstrates that the achievement of full humanity is not inconsistent with divine being.[39] At the same time, a basically orthodox view of the deity of Christ, the incarnation, and the resurrection shapes much of black Christology.[40] Black theologians emphasize, however, the retrieval of an image of Jesus from the tradition appropriate to black experience, culture, and history over against the images of Christ dominant in the white suburban churches of North America which they argue frequently use Christianity as an instrument of oppression.[41]

Postliberal Christology

Sixthly, another interesting development for North American Christology is the emergence of the postliberal school. Centred around the work of Yale theologians George Lindbeck and the late Hans Frei, 'postliberal theology attends to the biblical narratives as narratives rather than simply as historical sources or as symbolic expressions of truth which could be expressed non-narratively'.[42] Postliberals, however, unlike narrative theologians, do not let the stories of our lives set the agenda for theology.[43] The biblical narratives 'provide the framework within which Christians understand the world'.[44] In his book *The Identity of Jesus Christ*, Hans Frei sets out his understanding of New Testament Christology. In considering the concepts of Jesus' identity and presence Frei maintains, 'that the logic of Christian faith requires that we begin with identity, not presence'.[45] If we begin with the presence of Christ we inevitably allow our experience to set the agenda for Christology. This leads us, then, to establish Christology on purely historical evidence or to reconfigure Christ as an eternal symbol of universal human concerns. The focus of Christology, Frei contends, should be upon the unsubstitutable identity of Jesus Christ given to us in the biblical narratives. It is there that we find the identity of Jesus in what he says and does, not in some mysterious abstract description of his being. The task of theology, and specifically Christology, is to lay out the logic of Christian faith centred in the identity of Jesus Christ. The uniqueness of Christ is defined by the identity of Christ. Christ defines his own uniqueness rather than fitting into some preconceived concept of uniqueness. The problem with this approach to christology, some have argued, is that it tends toward a fideism which makes Christ culturally and philosophically inaccessible, and therefore not truly universal.

Deconstruction Christology

Seventhly and finally, perhaps the most radical reshaping of Christology in North America today is found in the theology of deconstructionism. Having concluded that the modern worldview along with all other worldviews is in decline, deconstructionist theologians argue that an objective approach to truth is no longer possible. Relying on the work of philosophers such as Jacques Derrida they believe that paradox, relativism, and subjectivity reign in a postmodern world. In his books *Erring* and *Altarity* Mark C. Taylor sets forth his approach to a deconstructionist Christology. In the incarnation God is embodied in the world so that God is now dead. The divine is forever inscribed in the world as a continual process. Jesus as the Christ is not a once-and-for-all event in which the word became flesh but rather is the point at which the divine is united with the world, signifying the death of the transcendent God for human understanding. The implications of the death of this understanding of God have been making themselves felt on human existence for the past two thousand years to the point where we are now confronted with the death of self. Thus, we now live in a postmodern age of despair and paradox. It is difficult to evaluate this view using the criteria of classical Christology. It is enough to say that in Taylor's Christology even any vestige of a Christian understanding of Jesus Christ has been set aside. Neither Scripture nor Chalcedon finds any place in his Christology. With this view we come to the farthest point possible from Chalcedon.[46]

In sum, the Christologies set forth above represent some of the major currents in contemporary North American theology. Others such as existentialist Christology, critical Christology, functional Christology, mythological Christology, and narrative Christology may also be mentioned. I have also deliberately not mentioned the developments in Europe in the work of theologians such as Wolfhart Pannenberg, Jurgen Moltmann, Walter Kasper, and Edward Schillebeeckx. While these Christologies are all significant, those identified above generally are unique to North America and are making an impact on the churches there.

III.   THE LORDSHIP OF JESUS IN THE POSTMODERN CHURCH

What then shall we believe concerning the uniqueness of Jesus Christ in our day? In this section of the paper I wish to take up some of the main lines of the exposition of the first two parts in an effort to make some critical and constructive comments which might be used as a framework within which a contemporary evangelical Christology may be developed. What is sketched out below pretends to be nothing more than a few cursory remarks which might inform evangelical thinking in the future.

Christology Beyond Modernity

First, many of the recent Christologies in North America which move beyond or abandon Chalcedon tend to reflect the modern worldview. David Wells has perceptively observed that 'modernity vitiates any appeal to tradition or a transcendent order. Because we cannot look outward, backward, or upward, we look inward.'[47] In Christology this is everywhere evident. Historical critical methodologies and historical relativism have cut us off from the Jesus of the biblical and classical tradition. Christology 'from before' and 'from above' seem impossible so we do Christology 'from within', 'from below', and 'from the future'. Liberation, feminist, and black Christologies all take their starting-point from the human experience of oppression. Revisionist Christologies re-present Christ in terms of North American cultural pluralism. Process theology looks to the future and the Christ as a transforming force who is yet to become. Deconstructionist Christologies demonstrate the ultimate move inward: our understanding of Christ is Christ and so when our understanding changes so does Christ. No trace of a unique Christ remains. A contemporary evangelical Christology cannot be content to mimic this type of Christological method. The lesson is clear: questions of transcendence, tradition, and truth cannot be set aside in Christology without abandoning at the same time a distinctly Christian identity.

Secondly, the dominance of the modern worldview in North America and the Western world is waning and we are moving into what many cultural observers are describing as a postmodern world. Postmodernism is difficult to describe and define since it embraces widely divergent concepts and agendas. A common theme, however, is the widely felt dissatisfaction with the modern worldview. Princeton Seminary philosopher and theologian Diogenes Allen has argued that the assumptions of the modern mind – the idea that God is superfluous, that morality can be based upon secular reason alone, that progress is inevitable and that knowledge is inherently good – are crumbling under the weight of their own inconsistencies.[48] The Enlightenment values which found expression in the Scientific, Industrial, and French revolutions have simply failed to produce what they promised in terms of something akin to heaven on earth. The Christologies of the past two centuries have largely been attempts to rethink the person and work of Christ in terms of an

Enlightenment worldview. It would be ironic should evangelical theologians begin to develop a Christology in these terms at just the point the hegemony of this worldview no longer obtains.

Thirdly, the move towards this so-called postmodern world provides a unique opportunity for orthodox Christology. David Ray Griffin summarizes four theological responses to the postmodern world in his book *Varieties of Postmodern Theology*. Constructive or revisionary postmodern theology seeks to develop a public theology which is credible along the lines of self-consistency and relevant to matters of public policy. Some have argued that revisionist and process theologies are examples of this response to postmodernity.[49] A second type is deconstructive or eliminative postmodern theology. In this sense Mark C. Taylor's Christology represents a kind of postmodern relativism.[50] Thirdly, Griffin argues that liberationist postmodern theology emphasizes the need to transform society and be accountable to the human experience of oppression. Latin American, feminist, and black theologies fall into this category.[51] Finally, restorationist or conservative postmodern theology sees the postmodern context as an opportunity to retrieve the tradition of premodern Christianity, thereby providing an adequate and appropriate rendering of the Christian faith. Griffin notes that this is primarily being done in Roman Catholic theology.[52]

It is this fourth response to postmodernity which provides help for evangelical Christology today. In addition to the Roman Catholic theologians cited by Griffin I would add the postliberal school in Protestantism. The focus of the Yale school as discussed above is to retrieve the best of the classical tradition and move beyond the divided mind of modern theology. American Methodist theologian Thomas Oden speaks of the need for a postcritical orthodoxy in theology. His own work takes him back to the church fathers in an effort to render a faithful and meaningful interpretation of the Christian faith. It seems that evangelical Protestant theologians will find the most help from conservative Roman Catholic theologians and postliberal Protestant theologians who are working at setting forth a classical Christology in the postmodern world. While some differences will remain, a fundamental presupposition can be accepted: the intellectual chains of the Enlightenment which have held Christology in bondage in the modern period are being loosed so that Jesus may once again be declared to be who he is – the Christ, the Son of the living God!

Fourthly, it can only be the case, then, that evangelical Christology must continue to emphasize the uniqueness of Christ along the lines set out in scripture and the early creeds and confessions of the Church. If there is a new openness to the reality of the transcendent and the significance of tradition in the postmodern world, and if we do indeed live in a world of diverse religious, philosophical, and spiritual worldviews, then we find ourselves in a similar situation to that of the early Church. Their struggle is our struggle. Their questions are our questions. Their answers inform our answers. Do not misunderstand. Evangelical Christians cannot simply revert to a premodern worldview. Faithfulness entails more than repetition of well-worn formulae – even those as significant as Nicea and Chalcedon. But at the same time we must not fall into the trap of thinking that our situation is so different, with its global religious pluralism, that our confession of Christ must be radically different.

The Shape of a Postmodern Evangelical Incarnational Christology

The lines of a contemporary evangelical Christology which seeks to make plain the uniqueness of Christ are clear. *First*, the uniqueness of Christ must be defined by the identity of Christ as revealed in scripture. The unique Christ is the CHRIST who is unique rather than the Christ who is UNIQUE. Uniqueness cannot be utilized as an external category determined by human reason, culture, or experience into which Christ must fit. Christ must not conform to some ideal pattern of what we may think of as unique. For the Christian, Jesus Christ is the unique one as the way, the truth, and the life against which all reality is measured and interpreted. This is why Christology is so central to Christian identity. Without Christ there is no reality around which to develop a Christian knowledge of God. The beginning and the end of any Christian church's talk about God is Jesus Christ. This is the basic position of Nicea and Chalcedon as the early Church sought to be faithful to the Jesus Christ revealed in scripture.

Secondly, an evangelical Christology must emphasize the full deity (vere Deus) and full humanity (vere homo) of Christ. It must do so utilizing some form of the enhypostatic union if justice is to be done to the full range of New Testament teaching.[53] While the language of Nicea and Chalcedon might not always be adequate, the biblical affirmations which they make cannot be abandoned as has often happened in modern Christology. The humanity of Christ emphasizes his continuity with all humanity and the movement from below to above. The deity of Christ emphasizes the 'infinite qualitative difference' (Kierkegaard), and therefore discontinuity, between Christ and us, requiring a movement from above to below. Evangelical Christology, then, must transcend the dichotomy in modern Christology between a 'Christology from below' and a 'Christology from above' in an effort to maintain both the uniqueness and universality of Christ.

Thirdly, contemporary evangelical Christology must transcend the divide in modern Christology between the historical Jesus and the Christ of faith. The project to reconstruct a real historical Jesus behind the texts of the New Testament, based as it is upon certain modern critical historical assumptions, is doomed to failure. Throwing Christology over to the subjectivity of human experience, however, is likewise inadequate. Given an evangelical view of scripture, Christology can proceed only along biblical lines. But evangelical Christology cannot simply be based upon precritical interpretations of the Bible. The challenge is to utilize a critique of criticism and to develop a postcritical biblical Christology for a postmodern world.[54] Such a Christology will emphasize the biblical Christ as the one who is the same yesterday, today, and forever (Heb. 13:8). The Christ whom we meet in our lives in the present is the Christ revealed to us in the scriptures of the Old and New Testaments as the Lord who has come in the past and the Lord who is to come again in the future.

Fourthly, evangelical Christology must proceed from the particularity of the incarnation in Jesus of Nazareth as revealed in scripture to the universal implications of his work without transforming Christ into some eternal symbol of universal human concern. The scandal of the incarnation and the cross means that it is this particular Jesus with whom we have to do. He may not be interpreted as a symbol of some higher reality. The symbol of Christ cannot be divorced from the reality of Jesus. Jesus as the Christ, the Son of the living God, the way, the truth, and the life is in his own person and work the measure of all truth and reality. He interprets our world; we do not interpret him in terms of our world.

Fifthly, evangelical Christology must encompass both the person and work of Christ. The work of Jesus is meaningful because of who he is. It is possible only because he is the Son of the living God. The biblical doctrine of the incarnation avoids the dichotomy of separating the person of Christ from his work. The identity of Jesus is bound up with what he says and does but may never be reduced to it. While Athanasius and many other of the church fathers emphasized this it is sometimes lost in the discussions around Chalcedon. The uniqueness of Christ may never be divorced from the salvific work of God in Christ.

Sixthly, the confession of Jesus as the Christ, the Son of the living God, is the essence of Christian identity. Christian identity is centred in the identity of Jesus Christ. Without Christ there can be no church. There ought never to be a divide between our Christology and our ecclesiology. If in evangelical faith the uniqueness of Christ rests in his lordship as the eternally begotten Son of God, his being of the same substance as the Father, and his being sent by the Father in the power of the Spirit into the world for the work of redemption, then surely the very nature of the Church as Christ's body in the world is shaped by such a confession. The unity and diversity of the Church is itself Christologically determined. The pluralism of the Church can never mean a plurality of Christs. At the same time, Christ is never bound by our narrow and fallible formulations of the Church in the world. The uniqueness of Christ ought to give incentive to evangelical Christians to take ecclesiology seriously. This includes recovering the Church as an article of faith. It also requires that we acknowledge our fellowship with all those who confess Jesus as the unique Christ, the Son of the living God within the diversity of the Church.

Finally, an evangelical Christology in a postmodern world must be shaped by a commitment to the unique Christ who is the universal Christ. The uniqueness of Christ is centred in his universal lordship as the Son of the living God; the universal lordship of Christ which makes him accessible to all and captive to none. When Christ's uniqueness is reconstructed according to the needs of historical relativism, cultural relevancy, and human experience, that which is intended, a Christ who is relevant to men and women today, is actually lost. It is this connection between the uniqueness of Christ and the universality of Christ which, when kept in view, can help shape a Christology which is both appropriate to the Bible and adequate to the needs of religious pluralism in the world, and theological pluralism in the churches.

CONCLUSION

It is not enough for the Christian community to say that Christ is unique without saying at the same time what constitutes his uniqueness and to spell out the implications of such a confession for Christian faith and life. To call Christ unique in and of itself is of no real significance since it can be argued that every living person is unique. With Peter, the Church today must say that

Jesus is the Christ, the Son of the living God. We must confess his Lordship and be prepared to follow the pathway of discipleship, developing and applying our understanding of his Lordship to every area of our life together as the people of God. In acknowledging Jesus as Lord we acknowledge his person and his work as the crucified and risen Saviour from the perspective of faith. To do anything less is to abandon our Christian identity.

NOTES

1. Matthew 16:16; cf. Mark 8:29, Luke 9:20.
2. A.W. Tozer, *The Knowledge of the Holy*, pp. 9–12. Tozer makes a similar comment with reference to the doctrine of God. For the Christian, however, the question of God and the identity of Jesus Christ are inextricably bound together.
3. John R.W. Stott, *The Cross of Christ*, p. 7. While Stott makes a similar comment with reference to the substitutionary atonement, it is equally applicable to the person of Christ since, as we argue below, Christ's person and work must be kept together in Christological thinking.
4. Martin Luther argued that the doctrine of justification by faith was the article by which the Church stands or falls. Again, the work of Christ cannot be separated from the person of Christ. In a very real sense the confession of Christ as Lord in our day is bound together with this article.
5. Statements by the Greek Orthodox Churches, The Roman Catholic Church, The World Council of Churches, The World Evangelical Fellowship, and other church councils and alliances reflect this basic confession.
6. The criteria of adequacy and appropriateness are borrowed from David Tracy's *Analogical Imagination* to which further reference is made below.
7. For recent scholarly discussions of biblical and classical Christology see Aloys Grillmeier, *Christ in the Christian Tradition*, Volume 1; Gerald Bray, *Creeds, Councils, and Christ; Present-Day Christological Debate*; David Wells, *The Person of Christ*; Millard Erickson, *The Word Became Flesh*.
8. Millard Erickson, *The Word Became Flesh*, pp. 42–44; 47–58.
9. *Ibid*. pp. 45–46.
10. Daniel Migliore, *Faith Seeking Understanding*, p. 140.
11. *Ibid*. p. 140.
12. *Ibid*. pp. 141–142.
13. John A. Vissers, 'Interpreting the Classic: The Hermenuetical Character of David Tracy's Theology in The Analogical Imagination', *Calvin Theological Journal*, November, 1990, pp. 194–206.
14. David Tracy, *The Analogical Imagination*, p. 234.
15. John B. Cobb, *Christ in a Pluralistic Age*, p. 140.
16. Millard Erickson, *The Word Became Flesh*, pp. 243–273.
17. Leonardo Boff, *Jesus Christ Liberator*; Jon Sobrino, *Christology at the Crossroads*.
18. Sobrino, p. 3.
19. Boff, p. 2.
20. Sobrino, p. 4.
21. Boff, pp. 197–198.
22. Sobrino, pp. 339–340.
23. Sobrino, p. 60; Boff, p. 63.
24. Elisabeth Schussler Fiorenza, *Bread Not Stone.* p. xvi and *In Memory of Her*.
25. Millard Erickson, p. 194.
26. *Ibid*. p. 201.
27. Pamela Dickey Young, *Feminist Theology/Christian Theology*, p.101.

28. Mary Daly, *Beyond God the Father*, p. 13.

29. Carter Heywood, *Our Passion for Justice*, p. 13.

30. Rosemary Radford Ruether, *To Change the World: Christology and Cultural Criticism*, p. 45.

31. Mark Kline Taylor, *Remembering Esperanza*, p. 195.

32. Leonard Swidler, 'Jesus was a Feminist', *Catholic World*, 212, No. 1270 (January 1971), pp. 177–183.

33. Millard Erickson, pp. 187–214.

34. Patrick Kalilombe, 'Black Theology' in David Ford, *The Modern Theologians*, Volume II, pp. 193–216.

35. James Cone, *A Black Theology of Liberation*; J. Deotis Roberts, *Black Theology in Dialogue*.

36. James Cone, pp. 1–10.

37. *Ibid.*, p. 38.

38. Millard Erickson, p. 179.

39. *Ibid.*, p. 179; cf. Cone, pp. 121–123.

40. Millard Erickson, p. 182.

41. *Ibid.*, pp. 163–186.

42. William Placher, 'Postliberal Theology' in David Ford, *The Modern Theologians*, Volume II, p. 118.

43. *Ibid.*, p. 117.

44. *Ibid.*, p. 117.

45. *Ibid.*, p. 118.

46. Millard Erickson, pp. 305–331.

47. David Wells, 'Evangelical Megashift: Assaulted by Modernity', *Christianity Today*, February 19, 1990, p. 16.

48. Diogenes Allen, *Christian Belief in a Postmodern World*. pp. 1–19; See also John A. Vissers, 'Presbyterian Faith and Life in the Postmodern Nineties', *Presbyterian Record*, January 1991, pp. 12–14; Millard Erickson, pp. 305–331.

49. David Ray Griffin, *Varieties of Postmodern Theology*, p. 3.

50. *Ibid.*, pp. 3–4.

51. *Ibid.*, pp. 4–5.

52. *Ibid.*, pp. 5–6.

53. David Wells, *The Person of Christ*, pp. 177–178.

54. Thomas C. Oden, *After Modernity . . . What?* pp. 103ff.

14

Rolfe Hille

This chapter concerns the tension between the uniqueness of Christ and the pluralism of the world as theologically rooted in the dialectic of unity and diversity. In the context of God's unity and diversity as a Trinity and in his salvation history, Dr. Hills discusses this dialectic in creation in which he declares the harmonious polarity to be good. The entrance of sin overturned this harmony which is restored in the new creation. The unity and diversity of the Church is grounded in the correlation between nature and the new creation, now incomplete but as a sign of the eschatological consummation of the Kingdom. Thus the Church is a dialectical polarity of a higher order. Dr. Hille concludes by discussing the criteria of the unity and diversity of the Church in aspects of its individual, spiritual, theological and structural life. The author's attempt to 'baptize' the rational-philosophical way of thinking of the West on urgent missiological issues deserves careful study.

THE NEW GLOBAL AWARENESS OF PLURALISM

'The Unique Christ in our Pluralistic World' is the main theme under which we are meeting as the Theological Commission of the World Evangelical Alliance in Manila in June, 1992. Nevertheless, for everyone living at the end of the Second Millenium (AD) it is not so much Jesus Christ as the fact of our pluralistic world which can be considered to be unique. Although the world, with its various cultures, political systems and ethnological and anthropological realities, has been pluralistic throughout all of Church history since the days of the early Church, the Church has not been aware of this pluralism and, therefore, did not take it into consideration. The unique philosophical and historical challenge that our generation presents to the Church is the new global awareness of pluralism. This awareness has been produced by an international information and cultural exchange at a level never before experienced. This awareness of pluralism has resulted in all convictions and commitments being relativized and competing with each other. Is it still possible in this situation to talk about a Jesus Christ who appeared once in

Dr. Rolf Hille is Dean of Albrecht Bengal Haus, Teubingen, Germany.

history, unique and unrivalled, the universal Lord and Saviour in the way the Christological creeds speak of him? Within the framework of the Manila Consultation on the Church and Missions, of which we are a part in the World Evangelical Alliance, we must find answers to this burning theological problem. These answers must be helpful, serve to advance our understanding, and convincing.

The fact that delegates from all parts of the world are included in this Theological Commission or, to put it in other words, that we ourselves as a group incorporate an international pluralism of cultural traditions represents an exceptional opportunity to live up to our main theme and to meet its challenge. The following paper is concerned with the sub-theme. 'The Unique Christ and the Diversity and Unity of the Church's Understanding of itself'. The brethren who are concerned along with me with the same question come from Africa, North America and Asia.

I would, therefore, like to approach the ecclesiastical topic assigned to us from my perspective as a European, or more specifically as a German. This should help to make clear the uniqueness of a theological way of thinking which has been derived from the intellectualism of the Latin-Western tradition. Thus my discussion will be basically philosophical in orientation and will deal with only one aspect of our theme. In the second part of my paper the discussion of practical problems and their solutions will be only roughly sketched. I am assuming that the other speakers, based on their theological insights and experience with the Church, will supplement and elaborate other aspects. The philosophical-rational approach is one which demands that the question of the uniqueness of Jesus Christ in our pluralistic world has to be dealt with in the framework of apologetics or the defence of the faith. In approaching this discussion from a fundamental-theological angle, I hope to make clear that the tension between the uniqueness of Christ and the pluralism of the world is theologically rooted in the dialectic of unity and diversity. Only when we grasp the relationship between unity and diversity in the context of God's unity and diversity as a Trinity and in the context of his salvation history can the special nature of the biblical revelation be properly recognized, and along with it the actual contour of the Christian faith. A comparison of the leading world views or Weltanschauungen of our era can show how useful this kind of fundamental-theological consideration can really be for the solution of the practical problems that arise out of the pluralistic cultures in which we live and the factual plurality of our churches.

Islamic and Orthodox Jewish fundamentalism both deny, or attempt to combat, the pluralistic challenge of the modern era.

One of the theological reasons for this lies in a rigorous monotheism which is not able to contemplate any diversity in God.

A secularized variant of such monolithic monotheism is the ideology of Marxism, a political ideology which has disintegrated in the last few years. As opposed to this we meet in Hinduism and Buddhism an unusual relativization of all forms of reality up to and including totally diverse images and concepts of the gods.

No disparate physical being is truly real, but is simply 'Maya', a deceptive appearance and delusion. Thus, for the religious monism of the advanced cultures of East-Asia, all controversies about the truth of particular world views seem to be irrelevant and therefore superfluous. The secularized person in Europe and North America finds a great deal of sympathy for this position of easygoing tolerance because it fits in nicely with his or her relativistic and agnostic world view.

I. A BIBLICAL APPROACH TO THE RELATIONSHIP BETWEEN UNITY AND DIVERSITY

With this background in mind, we must ask what a biblically responsible understanding of the relationship between unity and diversity would look like in light of the conflict with the pluralism of the modern world. If we can arrive at a perspective which makes it possible for us to find our way in our multiform world in a positive sense, and on the other hand, able to develop criteria for entering into a critical discussion with every unbiblical form of pluralism, then we will have made significant progress toward the solution of our main theme, 'The Unique Christ in our Pluralistic World'. I would like to contribute to such an advance in understanding through this study on 'The Unique Christ in the Unity and Diversity of the Church's Understanding of Itself'. It represents an effort to biblically 'baptize' the rational-philosophical way of thinking of the West. This way of thinking has caused much damage to theology and to the Church through its Liberalism and Modernism. By taking this approach, I hope to lay out a fruitful approach for our joint endeavour that is truly 'contextual' in the best sense of the word.

The Tension Between Diversity and Unity of the Church

'Even a seven year old child knows what the holy Christian Church is, namely the sheep of our Lord Jesus Christ – those who hear the voice of the Good Shepherd.' With this simple explanation Martin Luther describes the essence and the unity of the Christian Church in the Formula of Concord (1577), one of the most fundamental creeds of the Reformation. Because of the contradictions and contrasts in the modern world at the end of the 20th century, people are longing for security. They are searching for security in light of the unimaginable variety of opinions in an increasingly complex industrial society. When our contemporaries and even Christians who are uncertain about their convictions, look to the Church, do they find there that security and sheltering unity which Martin Luther so clearly and simply describes with his biblical picture of the one shepherd and the one flock?

The Practical Task of Unity in the Church

In the early 1970s John Stott wrote a defence against all false polarizations, with the title 'Balanced Christianity'. Stott argued for a balance between the cognitive and the emotional in the expression of Christian life and for a balance between the tendencies to conserve and the tendency to change when faced with new challenges. He also pleaded for a balance between social action and evangelism in the work of the Church. In this way extremes are to be avoided and/or overcome. The points which John Stott makes here are of extremely practical significance and relevance. We dare not lose sight of these things in our theological reflection if we are to appropriately address the concrete challenges facing the Christian Church. However, when we search for the source of the tension between unity and diversity within the Church we are not merely dealing with a modern problem that Christians in this ecumenical age find particularly distressing. With the question of unity and diversity we also touch upon some fundamental theological factors which are rooted in the very nature of biblical salvation history.

II. FUNDAMENTAL THEOLOGICAL CONSIDERATIONS IN UNITY AND DIVERSITY IN THE DIALECTIC OF SALVATION HISTORY

First of all, it is important to hold fast to the fundamental truth: God is the one and unique God. All unity has its roots in him. True unity cannot be found or experienced apart from God. But this one God is at the same time the creator of the seen and the unseen world and this creation of God is characterized by infinite diversity. Thus, God intended for there to be a polarity between unity and diversity in all created reality. This is clear because of the fact that all created beings originate with God as their basis and source, and at the same time reflect the diversity of his creative power.

The Harmonious Polarity of Creation and the Diametrical Contradiction of Sin

The statement, 'it was very good' (Gen. 1:21) stands out in the biblical account of creation. This account attributes all the manifold works of creation to the one creative word of the one true God. The polarity of unity and diversity thus corresponds to the good intentions of God. The tension between unity and diversity as protological, that is polarity beginning with the original creative source, is very good. It demonstrates itself to be a fruitful, constructive and in itself a creative tension: because this tension is rooted in the unity and diversity of the one true God. The protological polarity of creation may be described as the unlimited depth and immeasurable riches of life given by the one true God. Unity means security and peace for all creatures in the one and only God. Diversity opens the way to participation in God's trinitary joy of life and eternal love.

But this constructively fruitful and creative polarity in a harmonious world does not correspond to the empirical reality of our experience. Instead, diversity is characterized by an irreconcilable conflict. There is a conflict not only between humans and animals, but also between individual people, cultures and societies. 'Mankind is his own wolf', as Thomas Hobbes correctly observed. And since a war is raging in which everyone is against everyone else – even in the nonhuman realm of nature – war is the father of all things. (Heraklit). The harmonious polarity of creation has reversed itself, namely into the self-contradiction of the world itself. Unity and diversity diverge as irreconcilable antitheses and the individual members are torn asunder in crass contradiction. The cause of this overturning of the harmonious polarity of creation into the empirical antagonism of world's polarity lies in the sinfulness of man.

The shattering of our relationship to God leads with intrinsic necessity to all other concrete disintegration and dissension which characterize our present world and its history.

Now it is important that both polarities, namely that of creation and that of the empirical world, mutually permeate and overlap one another. This results in the ambivalence which is so characteristic of our experience of reality. On the one hand we experience the unity and diversity in our life as productive tensions. On the other, we encounter diametrical contradictions in our world which shatter us because we cannot reconcile unity and diversity. The problem in which the natural person finds him or herself is therefore determined by two contrasting polarities that stand in a dialectical relationship of tension to one another. On one hand we are, as God's creatures, within the sustaining grace of the Creator. On the other hand, the fallen world is sinful and therefore under the curse of transitoriness and death. Both, preservation of the original harmonies and at the same time the destruction of life through sin and death determine our existence. The dialectic relationship between the harmonious polarity of creation and the disharmonious polarity of the world gives our life its characteristically ambivalent character. It is through this that unity and diversity becomes a problem, that is, an obstacle which is thrown in our path.

The Church in the Tension Between Creation and Recreation as a Dialectical Polarity of a Higher Order

How then are we to view the unity and diversity of the Church in light of this complex and conflicting dialectic of these two overlapping polarities? First, the Church is indebted to the working of the Holy Spirit. But this is the creator spiritus, the creative Spirit of God, who calls into being an earthly visible expression of the eternal and invisible secret of the trinity through the Word. The Spirit is the creative author of the material world, which we encounter in the diversity and unity of our lives – that is the polarity of creation. But the Holy Spirit is also the New-creator, who in the midst of the temporal world – that is in the polarity of the world – creates a new creature in Christ. That is to say, he creates the Church and will someday consummate it. The diversity and unity of the material world correspond with intrinsic necessity with the diversity and unity of the realm of spiritual reality because they have their source in the one creator spiritus. The correlation between creation and new-creation which are both grounded in the Spirit of God, becomes visible in the nature of the Church. For, on one hand, the Church belongs as a spiritual reality totally to God's new world, but at the same time it is a completely human fellowship, subject to all the structural constraints of communication and socialization which are part of this world. This means for example: the diversity represented within a single human species corresponds typologically to the diversity of individual Christians, which all have their mutual essence in the one new creation. See 2 Cor. 5:17. The diversity of human societies with their various cultures corresponds typologically to the diversity of various distinctive types of churches, which all participate in the essence of the ecclesia invisibilis (invisible Church).

So when we speak about the Church in light of the dialectic of diversity and unity, this takes place within the boundaries of a dynamic movement of salvation history. These situations stand in turn in an extreme dialectic relationship to one another: first of all, there is the protological polarity of diversity and unity as harmony in original creation. However the historical polarity of diversity and unity is in irreconcilable and contradictory opposition to this harmony, for, in a sinful and transitory world, either diversity destroys unity or unity violates diversity. In the 'progress' from creation to the sinful world there comes into force a negative dialectic, which perverts the original harmony into a radical contradiction. In the midst of a self-contradictory world – contradictory because of sin –, the creative Spirit can nevertheless create as a new creation the healing fellowship of the Church. Because the Church is a spiritual reality in earthly form, she is characterized in turn by a dynamic dialectic. The polarities which were there when she came into being are present in her. The Church embraces the tension of the original polarity of diversity and unity in creation, because she incarnates in herself the Spirit of the new creation within the existing structure of the created world. She strives, nevertheless, to overcome the sinful contradiction between the sinful creature and the creator, because she is called to overcome the sinful world as it actually is. In this calling the nature of the Church expresses itself as the beginning and vanguard of the new creation. Finally, the Church points beyond itself toward the completion of the kingdom of God yet to come, in that it overcomes the disharmony between diversity and unity only in an incomplete way. Not until the kingdom is the eschatological goal of salvation history present. Inasmuch as the Church recognizes the contrast between its present reality and her promised future and therein distinguishes between herself and the kingdom, does she recognize herself as a sign of this eschatological delay. And it is exactly this eschatological delay that describes the specific expression of the ecclesiological polarity of diversity and unity in contrast to the other polarities found in the process of salvation history: namely in contrast to the harmonious polarity of creation and the contradictory polarity of sin as well as in contrast to the completed polarity of the kingdom of God. The ecclesiological polarity of diversity and unity thus comprises the dialectical focus of salvation history as it dynamically unfolds. This ecclesiological polarity therefore reflects all of the basic polarities of diversity and unity. For each of the different stages of salvation history contain in themselves a polarity in terms of diversity and unity. In addition, the Church also stands in a dialectical relationship toward all these polarities. The specific ecclesiological polarity of diversity and unity is therefore to be seen as a dialectical polarity of a higher order.

The Church in Tension Between Salvation and Fulfilment

This dialectical polarity of a higher order will be suspended in the kingdom of God only via a fulfilled or eschatological polarity, in that it will be encompassed by it. For the participation of the churches in the framework of the sinful and therefore perishing world (i.e., in the contradictory world polarity) results in the Church being incomplete, even though she is the beginning of God's new creation. She therefore stands within the conflict of diversity and unity present in empirical reality. Here, from an ecclesiological point of view, the tension can be seen between 'already' and 'not yet' and this is the basic expression of the eschatological delay. In the eschatological polarity not only is the contradictory polarity of the sinful and therefore perishing world overcome, but even the original harmonious polarity of creation excelled in a movement toward an eternal fulfilment. The apostle Paul describes this eschatological polarity in Cor. 15: 28 with the words: 'When he has done all this, then the Son himself will be made subject to him who put everything under him, so that God may be all in all.' This does not in any way mean that in the kingdom of God only the triune God would be present without the creation, for this would mean that the confession of the resurrection would prove itself futile. The resurrection denotes rather the completion of creation in the eternal fellowship with the one Father, Son and Spirit.

The eschaton is the perfect fellowship between God, the Creator, Saviour and Perfector with the created, redeemed and perfected world. The Church, though, proclaims this fellowship already as an eschatological polarity through faith, hope and love.

The Unity and Diversity of the Church in the Relationship of the Immanent Trinity and the Trinity in the Economy of Redemption

When we reflect upon the unity and diversity of the Church we come upon a twofold theological reality. On the one hand we are dealing with God's working in the world, that is, with his creation and salvation history. This we just discussed. This aspect of theological reality is called the 'economic' trinity because the triune God acts in the unity and diversity of his persons. But this outwardly oriented economical trinity has a corresponding and different theological reality. That is the inner or immanent trinity, i.e., the side of the trinity directed toward us. Only as a result of the traces of the trinity in creation and history does the knowledge of the immanent trinity of God disclose itself to us. Nevertheless, ontologically speaking, the unity and diversity that we experience in creation and history is only the outward expression and reflection of the inner unity and diversity in God's own triune nature.

The Christological Unity of the Church

What consequences does the relationship between the economic and immanent trinity have for the relationship between the unity and diversity of the Church? The deepest and most thorough description of the unity and diversity of the Church is found in the picture of the Body of Christ. This is because the working of the triune God in his specific redemptive economical orientation is portrayed in this image. Christ is the head of the church, i.e., the personal, understanding and especially intentionally decisive centre of the church. The unity of the church is anchored in the one and only Christ, who himself reveals God himself and in whom God created and redeemed the world. In him God will judge and complete the world. In Christ all of the economical redeeming action of the trinity is concerned. Christ is the outwardly oriented reality of God, i.e., as God's word he is the absolute expression of God. The incarnation of the world, i.e., the permanent connection of the eternal immanent trinity with created, historical reality, is characteristic of the absolute uniqueness of Jesus Christ. In that the resurrected Christ is head – that is the mental integrating centre – of the earthly, concrete and historical Church. Thus, the Church participates in his uniqueness and divine unity.

Pneumatological Diversity of the Church in Triune Unity

Pneumatologically, the diversity of the members of this one body corresponds to this Christological unity. The one Christ through the one Spirit does not produce an empty uniformity, but rather unlimited diversity of fruits and gifts of the Spirit. Even the first creation, the natural human body, is made of an unfathomable differentiation of cells and organs in its harmonious functionality.

This applies all the more to the new creation. Creation and new creation derive their diversity out of the world of the creator spiritus, which is the Spirit of Jesus Christ: 'The Lord is the Spirit' and 'where the Spirit of the Lord is, there is freedom' (2 Cor. 3:17). The diversity of the triune God – who expresses himself as the word in the person of Christ in the economy of redemption, and even incarnates himself in the world – this diversity of God continually creates diversity in the Church through the presence of the Spirit. As the multifaceted body of Christ, it manifests the unfathomable riches of God. In her Christological unity and pneumatological diversity the Church is representative of the unity and diversity of the triune God. The unity of the Church is a testimony of the unity and uniqueness of Jesus Christ in contrast to the sinful disunion of the sinful and perishing world. In her Spirit-caused diversity the Church is a protest against all demonic standardization originating in the worldly powers of this perishing eon. The Church testifies here and now in her christocentric unity and pneumatological diversity both the eschatological unity and diversity of the kingdom of God.

Unity and Diversity of the Church as a Hermenuetical Problem

However, the question we have posed does not simply concern the unity and diversity of the Church as such, but rather 'the understanding of the unity and diversity of the church'. This touches upon an epistemological or hermeneutical problem. The starting-point for all theological knowledge is neither pure rational human speculation nor simply the facticity of the empirical human experience, but rather the self-revelation of God, which is grounded in the nature of the triune God.

We must consider this self-revelation of God, which leads to the biblical understanding of the unity and diversity of the Church, not only with regard to the immanent trinity (section 3) but also in regard to the redemption-economical trinity (section 2). The basic dimensions of the epistemological description of the understanding of unity and diversity of the Church arise from this.

Certainty of Knowledge in Protological and Eschatological Perspective

We emphasized, to begin with, that all true unity is grounded in the one true God and all true diversity is an expression of his triune fullness. Unity and diversity of creation and of new creation are therefore, as far as they are related to the triune creator, saviour and perfector, a reflection of his divine glory and love. The hermeneutical question as to where the transition from unity into diversity can be recognized thus shows itself – in light of this trinitarian consideration – to be evident with regard to this created world in both senses: protologically as well as eschatologically. For all creation or new-creation is per se diverse and its unity can be found in every one of its members. This is because every member of the fulness of creation points back directly to the creator (cf. Rom. 1:20). Protologically and eschatologically the triune God can and must be clearly distinguished from his creation, but the creation itself confronts us only in a diversity whose integrating unity lies in the fact of its createdness and thus in its connection with God. For this reason, knowledge of the inner unity in diversity of the proton and the eschaton is self-evident.

In this respect every hermeneutical problem resolves itself.

Knowledge in the original creation and in the ultimate kingdom of God is always pure, distinct and simple.

The Ambivalence of Knowledge in Harmatological Perspective

With the fact of sin an ambivalence has now not only ontologically, but also epistemologically entered in. In addition to the divine unity there exists also an intrinsically sinful anti-Christian and satanic pseudo-unity in the world. This pseudo-unity has infected every part of creation in its diversity.

It is this that confronts the Church with the hermeneutical task of the discernment of spirits. Thus, the epistemological difficulty, i.e., the transition from certainty to ambivalence of knowledge, accurately reflects the problem of the meta-level of perception. Knowledge after the Fall is difficult, indistinct and ambiguous.

Theological Criteria for Evaluating the Unity and Diversity of the Church

The systematic considerations concerning the salvation historical position of the Church discussed above must therefore be thought through in terms of the concrete constellations of unity and diversity in the Church. We have described the Church as a dialectical process of overlapping polar relationships and it is possible therefore to deduce a number of essential criteria for the evaluation of unity and diversity in the Church of Jesus Christ. Our task in the following section of our discussion is to apply the triune as well as the salvation-economical insights concretely.

In doing so we will have to clarify, on the one hand, how Christological unity and pneumatological diversity can be recognized in the Church (trinitarian theological aspect) and how, on the other hand, the dialectical process between the overlapping polarities occurs (redemptive economical aspect).

For the redemptive economical aspect we need to consider the following questions according to the basic structure of salvation history.

First in Respect of Theology of Creation: Where in the Diversity of the Church Do We Encounter the Diversity of the Originally Good Creation?

This question is, for example, missiologically relevant. For instance, in the Manila Manifesto of 1989 'Cooperation' is stated to mean 'finding unity in diversity. It involves people of different temperaments, gifts, callings and cultures, national churches and mission agencies, all ages and both sexes working together.' (Section 9) Therewith the unlimited diversity of human possibilities is integrated into the one Church: anthropologically, ethically, sociologically, etc.

Secondly Harmatologically:

Where is the Church threatened by a pseudo-unity of satanic origin, i.e., where do the differences in the Church cause separation and destruction? Examples of such deceptive diversity and unity which need to be recognized and rejected are heresies, sinful behaviour in the Church/of the Church. The temptation of the Church to embrace false teaching and sin challenges the local churches with the task of doctrinal and church disciplines. With the following words the Manila Manifesto describes the spiritual discernment necessary for this task. 'All evangelism involves spiritual warfare with the principalities and powers of evil, in which only spiritual weapons can prevail, especially the Word and the Spirit, with prayer. We, therefore, call on all Christ's people to be diligent in their prayers both for the renewal of the church and for the evangelization of the world. Every true conversion involves a power encounter, in which the superior authority of Jesus Christ is demonstrated. There is no greater miracle than this, in which the believer is set free from the bondage of Satan and sin, fear and futility, darkness and death.' The context of this statement deals with the relationship of the uniqueness of Jesus to the non-christian religions. This shows that the problem of the destruction of unity caused by sin is contagious in the religious and missiological context – namely outside as well as inside the Church. Any unity is destructive which does not arise out of fellowship with the one Head, Jesus Christ. Diversity which is not produced by the one Holy Spirit leads astray and results in destruction.

Thirdly Eschatologically:

Where does the bright light of the gospel shine in the diversity of the Church in such a way that in the midst of our sinful and perishing world something of the brilliance of the coming kingdom of God appears? Where do we get a glimpse of the unity and beauty of the body of Christ as an eschatological reality already present in the diverse forms of church worship, of theological understanding, of the various gifts and fruit of the Spirit and of evangelistic witness? With this hermeneutical question just discussed we have named the elementary areas in which we encounter unity and diversity of the Church. In the next section we will apply the above deduced systematic-theological criteria to these elementary areas.

III. THEOLOGICAL SPECIFICATIONS IN VIEW OF THE PRACTICAL REALITY OF THE CHURCH

In the following section we want to discuss briefly the criteria developed above for the evaluation of unity and diversity of the Church in four important ecclesiological aspects. These applications should be of assistance in dealing biblically and responsibly with the tension between unity and diversity in church practice.

The Unity of the Body of Christ in the Diversity of its Individual Members

The Biographical Aspect

The Christian faith emphasizes the unity and dignity of the individual person as no other religion or philosophy does. Not only the natural expression of individuality, but also the personal biographies of people are taken seriously in Christianity and are expected to be developed. Every human being is a testimony to the diversity of divine creation and no human being lives on the earth for whom God did not have a unique plan from the beginning of time. Nobody's personal history is exchangeable. This anthropological fact applies also in terms of the soteriological reality of a person's salvation through Christ and sanctification through the Holy Spirit. 'God has no grandchildren.' From this simple statement it follows that the conversion of each individual person is a one time encounter between him or her and the living Christ, out of which a new spiritual individual, a new creation, grows. And just as the natural person is characterized by a unique combination of gifts and abilities, so the Holy Spirit also produces a unique combination of lifestyles, gifts and spiritual fruits in every new born-again child of God. The gifts and fruits in their uniqueness constitute the wealth of the concrete local church and they also edify it. The gifts make possible a great number of ministries in the Church. The eschatological promise regarding the fruit of the Spirit is that they will remain in eternity. The individuality of salvation, i.e., the unique character of the new person is rooted in the individuality of the human being as created. The 'old man' is cleansed through repentance and conversion. The 'first man', that is the one who has become sinful, is in this way transformed into the image of the new second Adam, that is, into the image of Christ. The renewed person is the down-payment of individual salvation and model of diversity of life in the coming kingdom of God. In accordance with this, the anthropological, soteriological and eschatological uniqueness of every human being is grounded in the one human being Jesus Christ. On the one hand as the God-man he distinguishes himself in his uniqueness qualitatively from every created individual; on the other hand, because he is unique, the members of his body are in and of themselves also unique in their individual being and their individual history with God. In this way, then, it is the very uniqueness of Jesus Christ that affirms and advances the diversity among the members of his body.

Moreover, through the struggle with the sinful egotistical man, who turns his own particularity against that of his neighbour, it becomes clear how indispensable the development of the individual is for the Christian Church. The sinful misuse of individual existence and individual gifts does not nullify the diversity which God wanted and constituted in Christ and produced through the Holy Spirit. Rather, the Church must always, in each of its members, continue to struggle so that the danger of sinful, destructive individualism is overcome through Christ, the head of the body. The main point is that everyone should use his or her gifts as an opportunity for serving others and not misuse them as a means to exercise power over others. Our individuality, which is egotistical and has been warped by sin, must be integrated into the body of Christ in such a way that it is renewed and sanctified, in order that all diversity of gifts and power of the Spirit can become ecclesiologically and eschatologically fruitful.

The Unity of Spiritual Life in the Diversity of the Forms of Piety and Service of God

The Spiritual Aspect

'Corporeality is the goal of all God's ways' is how Friedrich Christoph Oetinger, a leading theologian of the German pietist movement, once put it. The indispensable individuality of our encounter with Christ does not imply lack of accountability in the form of a private 'protestant' religion. Personal faith rather takes on a concrete expression of spirituality: in prayer, in meditation, in Bible study and in confession of sin, etc. This variety of individual spirituality must have its centre in the services of the local church.

Even the New Testament accounts show that in the early Church the forms of the services were quite varied, depending on the cultural tradition and religious background of each congregation. The participation of the Jerusalem church in the Jewish temple services differed from that of the specific home Bible studies in Jerusalem. These again were very different from the church meetings in Corinth.

In view of this, we are prohibited from attempting to impose liturgical uniformity on spiritual life and service of God. The Holy Spirit should not be hand-cuffed in terms of his creative diversity. Nevertheless, we find in Christianity throughout all of church history that there are indispensable and fundamental elements, in which the unity of Christian spirituality and liturgy is expressed; such elements are described in Acts 2:42: 'And they were continually devoting themselves the apostles' teaching and to fellowship, to the breaking of bread and to prayer', and Col. 3:16 'Let the word of Christ richly dwell within you, with all wisdom, teaching and admonishing one another with psalms and hymns and spiritual songs, singing with thankfulness in your hearts to God.'

The material criteria of all spirituality is its connection with the unique Christ, who is present in his Church as the Resurrected One at all locations and at all times. Spirituality and service in their diversity enrich the Church only when they are in accordance with Christ. They are in accordance with Christ when they strengthen the fellowship of the individual with Christ, edify the Church as a whole, and lead non-christians into a life-renewing saving encounter with Christ. All efforts to contextualize which are in accordance with Christ in the above sense serve and vitalize the body of Christ in its diverse unity.

The Unity of Christian Confession in the Diversity of Theologies

The Theological Aspect

The profession, 'Jesus is Lord' characterizes the foundation of the Church and the unity of the universal congregation of Christ expresses itself in this confession. The confession that Jesus alone is the Christ, in whom God reveals himself and through whom God created, saved, sanctifies, and completes the world, was never disputed from the beginning of the Church until today. After a long period of wrestling with the issue, the pre-reformation church formulated the mystery of Jesus Christ in the language and thought of Greek philosophy in the creed concerning the two natures and the one person of Christ. Jesus is undivided and unmingled, truly God and truly human in the unity of his person. Since the 18th century, that is, since the European enlightenment, the divinity of Jesus and with that, his uniqueness, has been called into question by many theologians. For that reason the distinct profession of Christ is the virulent point of dissension not only outwardly, i.e., the inter-religious dialogue, but also inwardly in the ecumenical dialogue.

The Bible, a revelation given in history, is of central importance in view of the unity of the confession of Christ. The Bible reflects in the diversity of its testimony in turn the diversity of life-situations into which the Word of God was spoken. The complexity of the church situation in the history of missions corresponds to the complexity of salvation-history seen in the Bible. Hence it is the task of theology to arbitrate intellectually between the diversity of salvation history and church history in an appropriate and accurate fashion. Because salvation history and church history – especially in terms of world missions – present themselves as so complex and multifaceted, every theological analysis of them must also be in depth; only in this way can we adequately fulfil our task of contextualizing the gospel in each new situation.

The diversity of theology drifts into heresy whenever it loses its centre, its organizing focal point. This centre is the confession of the unique Christ, 'in whom are hidden all the treasures of wisdom and knowledge' (Col. 2:3). Freedom of thought and obedience of faith grow out of the freedom of the gospel in commitment to Christ.

It is important for the discernment between legitimate theology, and heretical pluralism, that evangelical theologians in particular emphasize the validity and authority of scripture as the norm for all theology. The testimony to the incarnate Word of God in the unique Christ cannot be separated from the unique book which proclaims this Christ. The Bible is the only written form of the Word of God (cf. 2. article of the Lausanne Covenant of 1974). The unity of the Church demands formal unity in reference to the Scriptures in view of the necessary diversity of theological reflection. The diversity of theology can be appropriately and objectively evaluated only on the basis of the profession of Christ. Only from scripture is it possible to discard heresy and to develop the healing doctrine of the gospel. Therefore the entire Scriptures and only the Scriptures are the binding canon; the ecumenical canon of the Church that unites the diversity of all theological reflection.

The Unity of the Universal Church of Jesus Christ in the Diversity of its Offices and Ministries

The Structural Aspect

Christ alone is Shepherd of Christ's sheep. It is from him that Christians receive their qualification and commission for ministry. All offices of ministry must prove themselves in humility, in the same way the Lord demonstrated that he was the servant of all (cf. the feet washing in John 13: 1–20 as the fundamental paradigm of the doctrine concerning offices of Christian ministry). In addition, the structural unity of church organization and institution can be appropriately evalued only from the perspective of the organic image of the body of Christ. The Church as an institution has no binding effect with regard to salvation either as a mediating or as a normative instance. This understanding of the Church is the deepest error of Roman Catholic ecclesiology and its hierarchy with the pope at the head. Neither the pope nor a bishop's teaching office nor a well-defined church tradition can guarantee unity in diversity in local and regional churches. Neither can these things guarantee the historical unity of the Church due to ever-changing ecclesiological and missiological conditions. Only a personal relationship to the unique resurrected Christ creates the unity that supports the 'semper ubique et ab omnibus' (always, everywhere and by everyone) of the many churches.

Unity in diversity allows, therefore, not only freedom in terms of the concrete expression of the different forms of liturgy, but also the creation of organizational structures of the Church. Moreover, we see very clearly as early as the New Testament not only in the travelling ministry of the apostles but also in the apostolic epistles, that over and above the unity of the local church of Christ there existed the structures of trans-regional unity in the universal Church of Christ. The Church of Jesus Christ is not only united world-wide inwardly in faith but also outwardly through the exchange of experience, knowledge, and mutual evangelistic responsibilities and social ministry. The form of this unity can be realized in many different ways. The Lausanne movement and the World Evangelical Fellowship demonstrate two concrete expressions of the unity of Christians and churches/para-church organizations which are denominationally and traditionally different from one another. The evangelical movement as such is an unmistakeable testimony of the unity of the Church in its diversity. It is a demonstration of the one flock under one Shepherd particularly in view of the minimal expenditure regarding external organization coupled with a maximum of internal unity of faith and ministry. The more all individuals in this fellowship cling to Jesus Christ with their words and deeds, the stronger and deeper becomes the fellowship with one another. To clarify and strengthen the understanding of this unity and diversity internally and to declare it outwardly to our pluralistic, torn and divided world is the humble but important commission of our theological consultation here in Manila – to the glory of the Lord Jesus Christ.

Part Five

The Unique Christ for Peace and Justice

15

Christopher Sugden

The carefully reasoned thesis of this chapter is that humanity is more than the aggregate of individuals; it is persons in community. God's activity in bringing salvation is seen in the Bible as God's action in creating a community of people belonging to him. Thus God's covenant with the community is the basis for the identity of the individual. Some divisions in society are due to nature, for example sex and race, but other divisions are the consequence of the Fall. Thus peace and justice in community begin with a new relation to God made possible in the unique death and resurrection of Jesus Christ. The author then works out his thesis in the context of the rich and poor, focusing on responsible stewardship.

What is the unique contribution Jesus makes to issues of peace and justice?

THE BASIS FOR CLAIMING THAT JESUS IS UNIQUE

Jesus' ministry was God's action in history. The basis for the unique claims of Jesus Christ is that he was the anointed one of God to bring God's kingdom in history. Were these claims true? The cross seemed to be the decisive evidence that they were not. How could a person who died under God's curse be the one anointed to bring his kingdom? The resurrection was the substantive evidence that Jesus was God's anointed; for before the end of the world, one person, who had claimed to bring the kingdom, had demonstrated the decisive blessing of the kingdom, resurrection from the dead.

The ministry of Jesus in bringing the kingdom into history, and in achieving and demonstrating the kingdom's victory over evil in his cross and resurrection brought justice between hostile groups according to Paul. For Paul the problem was how there could be justice between the Jews and the Gentiles. How was God's justice to be established between them?

To understand this we have to understand the Bible's perspective on humanity as persons in community.

Dr. Christopher Sugden is Director of the Oxford Centre for Mission Studies, England.

HUMANITY AS PERSONS IN COMMUNITY

The Bible understands problems of peace and justice in the categories of groups in conflict. It sees solutions to these problems in reconciliation between people in different groups. This is because the Bible sees humanity as persons-in-community, and sees God's activity in bringing salvation as action in creating a community of people belonging to him.

Thus Vinay Samuel and I wrote for the WEF/Lausanne consultation on the Relation between Evangelism and Social Responsibility in Grand Rapids in 1992.

'In calling people to join him and his community, Jesus established people's new identity as people of God. The emphasis in the New Testament on Christians' identity as children of God is on the community first. The "children of God" was a phrase for Israel. The children of God are a family and a community, not just an aggregate of the sons of God. Just as individuals gained their identity by belonging to the covenant community of Israel, so followers of Jesus gain their identity by allegiance to him and incorporation into his community.'[1]

'God's covenant with the community is the basis for the identity of the individual, and a vital community life in obedience to God requires members who are personally loyal to the community's Lord and to one another. Thus the very basis for personal change is the establishment of a new society which is in itself an element of social change.'[2]

Christopher Wright affirms this insight in the Bible:

'Westerners like myself have to undergo a certain reorientation in our habitual pattern of ethical thought in this matter if we are to see things from a biblical perspective. We tend to begin at the personal level and work outwards . . . However the Bible tends to place the emphasis the other way round: here is the kind of society that God wants . . . what kind of person must you be to be worthy of your inclusion within it, and what must be your contribution to the furthering of these overall social objectives?'[3]

Humanity is theologically divided. Humanity as affected by the fall and addressed by the gospel is divided into opposing groups: Jew and Gentiles, slave and free, male and female. These divisions are not contingent facts about humanity. They belong to the essential nature of fallen humanity.

The Bible asserts that humanity comes from one origin, one primal couple. It asserts that humanity has one goal, to bow the knee to Christ either in humble submission as Lord or in recognition of his ultimate judgement. Paul in Romans sums up this unity as in Adam and in Christ. The Bible takes seriously the division of humanity into groups. They are inherent in creation, (male, female; parent, child). But some divisions are infected by human sin so that divisions become barriers rather than complementarities. Thus men oppress women and children disobey parents. Other divisions are the product of principalities and powers of evil, producing the enmity that divides for example Jew and Gentiles (see e.g. Gal. 4:8–10).

Paul understands the gospel as the basis of the reconciliation between these groups. For him 'the secret (which God has revealed) is that by means of the gospel, the Gentiles have a part with the Jews in God's blessings; they are members of the same body and share in the promise that God made through Christ Jesus (Eph. 3:6). This reconcilation was made possible by the death of Jesus Christ: 'By his death on the cross Christ destroyed their enmity; by means of the cross he united both races into one body and brought them back to God' (Eph. 2:16).

For the New Testament a major sign of the gospel, and indeed its purpose, is to bring reconciliation. The unity of the human race is thus a goal to be achieved as the fulfilment of a common origin that has been spoilt by sin and division. But while the goal of unity is based on this origin, unity cannot be assumed now because the original unity has been shattered.

THE INADEQUACY OF INDIVIDUALISM IN THEOLOGY

Theological formulations which articulate the faith in terms that address the individual can address group behaviour in society only in terms that see groups as aggregates of individuals. A theology of reconciliation is then expressed in terms of being reconciled to Christ and therefore to each other.

When the work of God is located only in the individual, the only continuity between the work of God and the human community is through transformed individuals. The individual is described and addressed independently of the context, in religious categories as a creature of God and a sinner. Issues of the context are not seen as relevant either in describing sin or expressing salvation. Thus the context, and as part of that the social dimension, has no central place in either the plight of humanity nor the salvation of God.

Such individualistic theologies are inadequate both to the Bible and to the situations in the world today. Such formulations relate humanity-in-community to God only through the aggregation of individuals. Spiritual life is confined only to individuals. When people with these formulations discuss society, they either effectively leave God out and become reductionist, or emphasize the spiritual dimension in purely individual terms, reduce the problems of society to individual categories and spiritualize the problems. This leads to spiritualizing Jesus.

Such individualistic theologies are inadequate to the biblical focus on the poor. The focus on community puts the Bible's emphasis on the poor in its proper context. The Bible gives a role to the poor in evaluating a community's faith. In the Bible the poor refers to the physically and socially poor.[4] The poor are the biblical acid test for the health of a whole society. A society is to be judged by how the poor fare. An individualized approach to the Bible makes it seem unfair that a special position should be given to the poor, for the good news is also intended for the rich. So one interpretation common among evangelical Christians spiritualizes the meaning of poor in the Bible to mean either spiritually bankrupt or spiritually humble. But it can be argued that what is meant by 'Good news to the Poor' is that what the good news given in scripture means to poor people who receive it defines its meaning for everybody.

I have a very strong suspicion that the divisions between those who focus almost exclusively on verbal proclamation as the means of Christian witness, and those who want to include an integral relation between verbal proclamation and social ministry are not divisions over theology (though they may be expressed in those terms) but divisions over anthropology; between a view that sees people as essentially isolated individuals and a view that sees people as persons in community.

HOW JESUS ESTABLISHED PEACE AND JUSTICE BETWEEN HOSTILE GROUPS

The Jews believed that justice was established when the Torah was perfectly obeyed. Jesus took a distinctive stance both in terms of what constituted the justice which the law spoke of and in terms of how that justice was established.

Jesus brought a distinctive contribution to the definition of the justice which the law required. He defined love of the neighbour in terms of love for those of a hostile group. This is a distinctive feature of the Christian faith in the world of other religions. Many religions enjoin love and care for the brother, the fellow members of the religion, tribe or group. The distinctive feature of the Christian faith is the love of those who are not of our group. The model of love for the neighbour is Jesus' story of the Samaritan who helped a Jew.

Jesus affirmed that justice was established when God by grace accepted repentant sinners into his Kingdom. He reached across the barriers created by people against other groups to welcome people to his new people of God in the Kingdom. Thus he welcomed sinners, outcasts, the lost sheep of the house of Israel, Samaritans, Gentiles, tax-collectors, to membership of a community of the people of God which the Jewish leaders had endeavoured to ring fence by the law. No wonder the Jewish leaders wanted him removed and no wonder Paul persecuted those who followed Jesus. Paul's conversion came when by meeting the risen Jesus on the Damascus road, he realized that God had vindicated the way in which Jesus had sought to establish justice.[5]

For Paul the Christian, God established justice between the hostile groups of Jews and Gentiles by grace. Both groups had to realize they were alienated from God as well as from one another. Indeed their alienation from one another was an expression of their alienation from God. They had to realize that Jesus' death was the means by which humanity's alienation from God was overcome and God's wrath against humanity was fully propitiated. They had to realize that on the cross Christ disarmed the principalities and powers that created division and so broke down the dividing barriers between them (Eph. 3:9–10, Col. 1:15). The two groups had to realize that his love for those who were his enemies meant that to be sons of God they had to love their enemies too (Rom 5:8; 12:17–21). They had to realize that in being identified with Jesus in his death, they were incorporated into his body together with those from groups with which they had been hostile in a new humanity.

In other words, God had overcome all the barriers that kept these two groups apart from one another and from him and welcomed them into the fellowship of the Trinity, and thus to fellowship with one another. In this fellowship Jew and Gentile were to learn from each other; the Gentile was to learn that the Jewish heritage spoke of justification by faith, and the Jew had to learn the riches of their own heritage by seeing the Gentiles' understanding of faith. In Romans chapter 4 Paul spelt out the heritage of the Jews in terms of the salvation of Abraham by faith to show both these groups in the Roman church that they had much to learn from each other.[6]

Paul identifies that in Christ there is no Jew or Gentile, male or female, slave or free (Gal. 3:28). He also identifies that behind these divisions in our world is the work of the principalities and powers, one of which is the Jewish law, and elemental spirit of the universe (Gal. 4:8–11). As the Church demonstrates that these divisions are overcome, so it demonstrates the work of Christ who broke down these barriers on the cross which were created by these principalities and powers (Eph. 2:11–3:6). The breaking down of barriers between groups is a sign of the work of God in Christ. Christian work for peace and justice means we must take seriously that we wrestle not against flesh and blood, but against spiritual forces of wickedness that lie behind the divisions in our world (Eph 6:12).

God's love and grace are not in tension with his justice. What is due to everybody, what justice they can claim, has already been given to us in Christ – God's total acceptance in grace. Philip Wogaman writes: 'What is due to us is to belong. In the first instance it is to belong to God, the Creator and Sustainer of all. But derivatively it is also to belong to one other. No one who is loved by God may any longer be rejected by us. God's love has made us all family . . . belonging to one another in community must be undergirded by the physical, legal and institutional conditions making our participation possible.'[7]

PEACE AND JUSTICE BETWEEN RICH AND POOR

The rich can be called to peace and justice because God sets them free from rebelling against him by seeking security in their wealth. He sets them free to devote their attention and wealth to the concerns of God's kingdom, God's right relationships and especially the poor.

The gospel gives a new identity to the rich. The gospel calls them to renounce false pride and security. Extensive sections of Jesus' teaching are devoted to this (Mk. 4:19; 10:27; Lk. 14:15–24). The failure of the man who built bigger barns (Lk. 12:13–21) was in not caring for the poor. He was anxious. And he sought his security in ensuring bigger barns in which to store all his goods so that he could enjoy life. If such a person is counselled to share with the poor, the real hurdle is his anxiety about his security. Jesus assures such people that their identity and security belong in being given the kingdom and in seeking first the kingdom of God – then all the necessities of life would be theirs as well.

God's purpose for the poor is the same as his purpose for all human beings – that is that they be stewards. Behind Jesus' teaching on rich and poor is the Old Testament assumption about the calling of people to be stewards. A steward is the picture that Genesis paints of humanity. Men and women together are called the image of God. In the religions of the Ancient Near East, the image or representation of God was a statue in the temple, or perhaps a very powerful ruler. The ruler was the representative or tenant of the invisible God.

Genesis speaks of human equality when it says that all men and women, together, are the representatives, tenants of God. They are called to have dominion over the created order, to steward and manage it on God's behalf and in accountability to him (Gen. 1:27–28).

Humanity however has not lived this way. The first Adam fell. So Jesus became the second Adam. In him, the true image of God, we are restored to being the image we ought to be. We are as Paul says 'to be conformed to the image of his Son' (Rom. 8:29). This means that Jesus enables us to fulfil our role as human beings under God, as stewards of his creation. The call of both rich and the poor is to exercise this stewardship properly. The rich misuse stewardship when they keep all their resources to themselves. They are to 'help' the poor by enabling them to be stewards.

This understanding of a new basis for their identity and security as the meaning of the good news to the rich derives in part from the meaning of the good news to the poor. The good news is good to the poor in that it gives them a new identity. By defining the good news as good news for the poor, Jesus meant that the meaning of the good news for the poor who received it was to define its meaning for everybody. We see in the parable of the man who built bigger barns, how the issue of identity is critical also for the rich. It is crucial that people in separated groups such as the rich and poor experience this new identity together because both have been accepted in grace at the cross of Christ. When this understanding is lacking, a process sets in of blaming others and ignoring the sins of our own societies which contribute to the problem.

The basis for such reconciliation between races and between the rich and poor is the death and resurrection of Jesus Christ. Jesus Christ's atoning death needs to be central as the basis of forgiveness. God has forgiven us all an unpayable debt, so that we may forgive the debts that we owe one another. If a sense of Christ's death is not present, people cannot easily let go the sense of wrongs they have suffered or been party to inflicting.

Christian churches are to be signs of the new identity that God gives to people from different and hostile groups, including the poor and the rich as they express the new sharing in one community between people separated by one of the major causes of division in society – mammon.

IMPLICATIONS FOR MISSION AND EVANGELISM

The above analysis of humanity as persons-in-community means that our activity in sharing the kingdom of God in every area of life, and in specifically calling people to give their allegiance to the King of the kingdom, Jesus, must take the nature of humanity as persons-in-community seriously.

We must see people as set in a network of relationships, as members of a group in society and shaped by the factors to which that group is subject.

Bishop David Gitari writes 'To make an individualistic appeal to a Rendille or Boran community, asking people to accept Christ one by one, may be contrary to the gospel. St Paul preached and baptised in the household of Cornelius, and in that of the Philippian jailer. The gospel can also be preached in the household of a nomadic people, respecting and preserving their traditional communitarian culture . . . We are not evangelising individuals to pluck them out of their communities; but after a period of instruction, communities are turning to Christ and are being baptised and incorporated into the life of the Church.'[8]

In the gospel records Jesus related to different groups of people in different ways according to their context and situation. He challenged the Pharisees over their interpretation of the Law and the Sadducees over their understanding of power. He called the poor to have the faith that he could change things, and the rich to respond to their responsibility to the poor. He gave women new status, welcomed the children, and commended the faith of Samaritans and Gentiles.

In practical terms today, evangelical urban missiologists such as Raymond Bakke, Robert Linthicum, John Perkins and Vinay Samuel[9] stress the importance in any Christian mission or evangelism to people divided by the power structures in large cities of developing community among people.

A community is 'a group of people with a continuing experience, tradition and history, who support and challenge each other to act powerfully, both individually and collectively, to affirm, defend and advance their values and self-interest'.[10]

The process of community building includes processes which enable people to recover their identity and their roots; which network between different groups of people to build a sense of ability and mutual assistance between people otherwise divided; which build mechanisms to enable the poor to take control of their own environment and enable those with resources to make them available to poor people in ways that promote partnership.[11]

One analysis of the needs of a community looks at its 'needs' in context. Take for example a community which 'needs' water. The reason why they lack an adequate water supply may be that access to the well is tightly controlled by a powerful local landlord or slumlord. The need is a symptom of the unjust distribution of water. This unjust distribution is an expression of interests of a powerful group in relation to the control of water. This group with the power over the water perceives that control over the water to the exclusion of others is in its interest because of the value system and world view it lives by. So we need to move from needs to issues to interests to groups to values and worldviews.

The way in which we should as Christians engage with a community may not therefore be by addressing the need immediately. There may be many different needs, and those that outsiders may identify probably will not be the same as those that members of the community identify. We will need to identify the values and the worldviews of the communities we are engaging with.

This will involve drawing a 'people-profile'. A process that has emerged in Christian encounter with communities is first, to construct a profile of a people; second to discover where the life and values of the kingdom of God challenge the life and values of that community; third to discover leadership in a core-group that is looking for change; fourth to identify an event that would focus the change that is required in the life of the community; and fifth to pray. The process is to discover an event that would show the nature of the challenge of the kingdom of God to the life of the community, and then relate that event to the principal event by which we identify the work of God in the world, the life, death and resurrection of Jesus. A process of working for reconciliation of conflict between two groups would be related to the work and ministry of Jesus in bringing reconciliation.[12]

THE CONTRIBUTION OF JESUS

What then is the unique contribution that Jesus makes to issues of peace and justice?

*Jesus Christ's ministry, the ministry of the Church in the New Testament and practical ministry today shows that the fundamental process of working for peace and justice between divided groups is the process of building community, where people can belong to each other and to God. Such a community is what the Church is meant to be. This is the community we are meant to be building when we plant churches.

*Jesus Christ's death and resurrection were, and are, the means whereby the hostility between groups whether divided by race or by mammon can be broken down. Jesus' death and resurrection is the basis for community building.

*The good news about Jesus is that he is the one anointed by God to effect reconciliation between groups hostile to one another, and between such groups and God. Such reconciliation is expressed as community is built between members of such groups based in allegiance to Jesus.

*Since there is no other means in the world whereby evil is overcome than the cross, we can suggest that all efforts to break down hostility between groups and bring peace and justice are possible only because of this unique work of Jesus Christ.

*We can suggest that every effort to bring peace and justice involves a spiritual warfare which only the death, resurrection and risen power of Christ through his spirit has won. Therefore human beings need to participate in that victory to sustain peace and justice. There is a transcendant aspect to work for peace and justice which we must remember and draw people's attention to. Worship, prayer and spiritual nourishment are a vital aspect of this ministry.

*We can suggest that we, as Christians, need not be anxious about participating with groups of non-Christians in seeking peace and justice. We know that the process ultimately depends on the finished work of Christ. Without the participation of Christians and illumination by the word of God, such efforts will fail to achieve their full purpose. By our participation we can witness to the nature of Christ's salvation in the arena in which it is most fully expressed and explored in the New Testament, in building community in the arena of hostility between divided groups.

NOTES

1. Vinay Samuel and Chris Sugden, 'Evangelism and Social Responsibility' in *In Word and Deed* edited by Bruce Nicholls (Exeter, Paternoster, 1986) p. 193.

2. Vinay Samuel and Chris Sugden, 'Evangelism and Social Responsibility' in *In Word and Deed* edited by Bruce Nicholls (Exeter, Paternoster, 1986) p. 221.

3. Christopher Wright, 'The use of the Bible in Social Ethics' in *Transformation* Vol 1 No 1 1984 p. 14.

4. See further Chris Sugden, 'What is good about good news to the poor?' in *AD 2000 and Beyond – A Mission Agenda* edited by Vinay Samuel and Chris Sugden (Oxford, Regnum, 1990).

5. Brian Wren, *Education for Justice* (London SCM, 1977).

6. See Paul Minnear, *The Obedience of Faith* (London, SCM).

7. Philip Wogaman, 'The Biblical Concept of Justice' in *Transformation* Vol 7 No 2 April 1990.

8. Bishop David Gitari, 'Evangelism among Nomadic Communities' in *One Gospel Many Clothes* edited by Chris Wright and Chris Sugden (Oxford, Regnum, 1990), p. 63.

9. See for example Raymond Bakke, *The Urban Christian* (MARC, 1987), Robert Linthicum, *Empowering the Poor* (MARC 1991), John Perkins, *Let Justice Roll Down* (Word), Vinay Samuel, Maggs Lecture on Evangelism, Orebro Sweden, 1989 and *The Gospel to the Whole Person* (TAFTEE, Bangalore, India, 1982).

10. From Michael Miller quoted by Robert Linthicum *op.cit* p.101.

11. The steps involved in this process include, according to Linthicum *op.cit* p.26.

'*Networking; the [community] organizer visits and befriends the people, identifying the key issues and leaders while building trust between the poor and the churched.

*Coalition-building: The organizer gathers the poor and Christians together into coalitions to address community needs identified by the people.

*Acting/reflecting/acting: A dynamic process begins. Coalitions reflect, act, evaluate, act again and reflect more deeply. Reflection includes a freedom to look at their own sinfulness and gospel solutions. The results? Root problems are addressed, systemic action taken. Self-confidence and community trust are built. And Christians who have joined with the poor in addressing these issues can naturally share their faith.

*Leadership empowerment: Coalition leaders inevitably surface, are identified and equipped. Church leadership integrated with the community also emerges and is trained. Support networks emerge among coalitions as a vision for the birth of a community unfolds. Community-wide leadership results.

*The birth of a community: The slum people begin taking charge of their situation as the result of problem-solving coalitions. The community is organized, the church becomes integral to community life, and the poor are empowered. Under such community organizing, the slum's quality of life radically improves and the people increasingly take charge of their own lives and of their community.'

12. See further, *The Gospel to the Whole Person* (TAFTEE, 18 Hutchins Road, Cooke Town, Bangalore, India) – a 10 week practical study course based on this process. See also Christopher Sugden, 'The Impact of Conversion' in *Entering the Kingdom* edited by Monica Hill (MARC 1986).

BIBLIOGRAPHY

In addition to books cited in the footnotes:

Rene Padilla, 'The Politics of the Kingdom of God and the Political Mission of the Church' in *Proclaiming Christ in Christ's Way* edited by Vinay Samuel and Chris Sugden (Oxford, Regnum, 1989).

16

Yusufu Turaki

Dr. Turaki gives an extended outline of the biblical doctrine of Christ's universal Lordship, authority and supremacy over the whole world. He then develops both the biblical and theological basis for the Christian concept of peace and justice against the truth claims of the pluralistic world. The final focus is on what the unique Christ for peace and justice means for both the Church and the whole world.

INTRODUCTION

This paper addresses the subject. 'The Unique Christ for Peace and Justice'. This however requires us to examine critically the question of Christian value claims in our pluralistic world, especially in the light of what the unique Christ offers to the world in terms of peace and justice.

The first part of the paper focuses primarily on developing a biblical and theological basis for the uniqueness of Christ. This provides the basis for Christ's universal Lordship, authority and supremacy. It is upon this theological basis that Christian value-and-truth claims have credibility and import in the world. Thus the recognition of the unique Christ is ultimately linked to the recognition and acceptance of the authority of the Bible, without which there can be no foundation for our belief in the uniqueness of Christ.

The second and third sections of this paper focus mainly on the biblical and theological basis of the Christian conception of peace and justice. The relevance of Christian principles of peace and justice for the world are carefully defined. The unique Christ for peace and justice is presented antithetically to the value and truth claims of the pluralistic world as the one who is both the Prince of peace and the righteous Judge of the world.

The fourth section of this paper addresses partly the full implications of what the unique Christ for peace and justice means for the Church on the one hand, and the whole world on the other. Our primary focus here is upon what our Christian faith in the unique Christ achieves in both the Church and the

Rev. Dr. Yusuf Turaki is the General Director for the Evangelical Church of West Africa, with headquarters in Jos. Nigeria.

world in terms of peace and justice. This, indeed, is a practical definition of the role of the Church in world peace and justice. Furthermore, we seek also to examine the ethical implications of our Christian confession and proclamation of the universal Lordship, authority and supremacy of Christ in the whole world. The Christian values of peace and justice are rooted solely in Christ and the Bible.

However, this paper does not seek to address the full implications of peace and injustice in our modern world. The primary focus lies in the formulation of the biblical and theological basis for the concept of the unique Christ for peace and justice.

THE UNIQUE CHRIST

The question of Christ's uniqueness in our pluralistic world, especially his universal Lordship, authority and supremacy has of late assumed prominence in missiological and theological debates. These debates are pointers to the fact that there has been a significant and dangerous shift away from the teaching of the New Testament and the apostles on the subject of the uniqueness of Christ. Lesslie Newbigin in his new book, *The Gospel in a Pluralist Society (1989)*, has clearly defined this shift and its effect on biblical and orthodox Christianity. Modern secularism, pluralism, humanism, scientism and relativism have been responsible for this significant shift. In religion pluralistic value-and-truth claims are assuming a dominant role in modern world society, thus questioning the place and authority of biblical and apostolic Christianity.

Our primary task as evangelical Christians, therefore, is to set forth the case for Christ's uniqueness in our pluralistic world by continuing to affirm the historic, apostolic confession of the Lordship, authority and supremacy of Christ over the whole world. We need to establish as a biblical and theological fact that Jesus Christ is not only the Lord and Saviour of the Church but also of the whole world. Furthermore, the meaning and efficacy and scope of Christ's Lordship, authority and supremacy are of universal value and cosmic in character and not only applicable to the Church.

However, it is important that we state the case for the rejection of the uniqueness of Christ in modern pluralism and secularist and humanist worldviews.

Rejection of the Unique Christ

Our contemporary world context of multi-religious, multi-cultural and multi-value-and-truth claims demands our serious evangelical Christian reflection on the uniqueness of Christ and his universal Lordship, supremacy and authority over the whole world. It is important that we recognize the threat which the pluralistic and secular world poses for our Christian confession about Christ. Furthermore, we are also faced with the complex issues of world peace and injustice which are paramount on the agenda of national and world leaders. These issues figure prominently in both national and international forums of discussion and negotiation and bilateral relationships. In such forums pluralistic values-and-truth claims for both peace and justice have always been advanced and this has brought them into conflict with the claims of Christianity. Hence the challenge that lies before the Church is the need to present forcefully and convincingly what the unique Christ and the Christian worldview and values can offer our pluralist and secular world.

The relevance and timeliness of our Consultation cannot be overemphasized, given the rejection of the uniqueness of Christ by our pluralist and secular world. Our theme, 'The Uniqueness of Christ', indeed reflects our contemporary reaffirmation of the historic, apostolic confession and proclamation that *Jesus is Lord*. But in contrast Christianity today is facing serious questions and objections by modern religions, philosophers and even some theologians. They are raising new questions for debate and objections beyond the older, historical ones to our most basic Christian confession and proclamation about Jesus Christ.

The world of multi-religious, multi-cultural and multi-value-and-truth claims has throughout history challenged the exclusiveness of the Christian presentation of the gospel of Christ. The Christian proclamation about the uniqueness of Christ has been viewed as both objectionable and questionable. Furthermore the Christian confession and commitment to evangelize the whole world has always been viewed with great suspicion. Consequently the Church has been accused of being arrogant and lacking in a spirit of 'live and let live' or compromise. So the secular and pluralist world has always put forward many reasons why she should not accept the Church's exclusive presentation of the gospel and its absolute truth claim that Jesus Christ is the only Lord and Saviour of the whole world.

It is unquestionable that our Lord Jesus Christ and the gospel as it has been confessed and proclaimed by the Church throughout history provides a powerful negation of the secular, pluralist and relativist claims of the world of religions and cultures. The secular and pluralist world has sought, in various ways, to discredit Christianity. Students of world religions, philosophy and the social sciences view Christianity as one among the many world religions and cultures. They insist that Christianity and the truths of the Bible should be subjected to the test of rational and logical philosophy and empirical science. Their chief aim is to redefine Christianity with all its truth claims and its Lord and Saviour within the context of pluralist religions, cultures and social values. In this context Christianity and its Lord and Saviour can be neither unique nor absolute in its truth-claims. Consequently the gospel cannot be presented as absolute truth. Instead it should become a 'gospel' of accommodation to all world religions and cultures.

It is this very 'gospel' of pluralism and relativism that this Consultation seeks to counter and negate. This can be done only by presenting an exclusive gospel to the world of varying religions and cultures. Christ must be presented to the whole world as its Saviour and Lord.

The task before us as committed, evangelical Christians is to present a sound biblical and theological defence against the spirit of this world which is anti-Christ and anti-biblical and apostolic Christianity. Today we need to call all Christians to reaffirm the historic, apostolic confession and proclamation that *Jesus is Lord*. The Lordship, authority and supremacy of Christ over the whole world needs to be defended and proclaimed. It is only upon this foundation that Christ's offer of salvation, peace and justice to the whole world can be meaningful, convincing and relevant.

We now turn to setting forth the case for the unique Christ for peace and justice.

The Case for the Unique Christ

Belief in the unique Christ is grounded both in the Bible and in apostolic teaching. This is the first place to begin our discourse and the last place to end it. The uniqueness of Christ has to be derived from the Bible, without which we do not have any theological basis for presenting Jesus Christ as Lord and Saviour of the whole world. Furthermore we should lack any basis for addressing issues of peace and justice. Christ's offer of peace and justice to the whole world stands opposed to the world's spirit of pluralism, humanism and relativism. It is rooted in his uniqueness.

Unless Christ is proclaimed as the unique Lord and Saviour of the world, as attested by the Scriptures and the apostles, our offer of salvation, peace and justice to the world is meaningless and empty. Similarly, unless Christ's Lordship, authority and supremacy are of universal value as affirmed by Scripture and the apostles, then our involvement with ethical issues in the world lacks any credibility and legitimacy. Christ cannot offer to the world his salvation, peace and justice if he himself does not have any universal value and import.

Christ's cosmic nature and universal qualities are deeply rooted in both the Holy Scriptures and the apostolic teaching. His Lordship, authority and supremacy are intrinsic to him. They have not merely been conferred upon him or effected by some external factors but these qualities are self-validating. They emanate from his very being and person. Christ is what he is and no amount of human religious or philosophical artistry adds to or subtracts anything from his person. Thus it is his nature, his character and his person that radiate authority and supremacy; these are the grounds for his uniqueness in our pluralist world. Our responsibility therefore, is only to recognize him, believe him, confess him and proclaim him as such.

We now turn to the biblical and apostolic basis of Christ's uniqueness which has such implications for the whole world.

The Lordship, Authority and Supremacy of Christ

These qualities set Christ apart and make him unique. Our Christ is not only the Lord and Saviour of the Church and individual believers but also of the whole world. He is indeed the Lord of the universe, the Saviour of the world, the Prince of peace and the righteous Judge. This is what the New Testament and the apostles stood for. They fiercely proclaimed the universal Lordship, authority and supremacy of Christ over the whole world.

In the New Testament we have accounts of the apostolic teaching that Jesus Christ is both Lord and Saviour, that he is both Prince of peace and righteous Judge, that he is both unique and supreme. This is what they teach about Christ:

> Jesus Christ is the only Saviour of the whole World.
> Jesus Christ is the only Lord of the whole world.
> Jesus Christ is the only Mediator between God and men.
> Christ is supreme over the whole of creation.

Christ has authority over the whole of creation.
Christ has power over the whole of creation.

Jesus Christ as the Only Saviour of the World

Throughout the entire New Testament Jesus Christ is presented as God the Son, the Son of Man and the Saviour of the world. His saving power is rooted in his deity (Jn. 1:1–18), and God's approval of him (Lk. 9:35; Matt. 3:17; Jn. 12:23–30) and his Cross.

The apostle Matthew stated that Jesus 'will save his people from their sin' (Matt. 1:21), while the apostle Mark emphasizes the fact that 'the Son of Man has authority on earth to forgive sins' (Mk. 2:10). The apostle Luke, on the other hand, dramatizes the fact that Jesus is the Saviour of the world who has been born of human flesh, the God-Man (Lk. 2:11), and also Jesus is the One who has been seen of men (Lk. 2:30) as the fulfilment of God's Messianic prophecies and the hope and expectation of humanity. The apostle John, on the other hand, makes reference to Jesus as the 'Lamb of God who takes away the sin of the world' (Jn. 1:29).

Christ as the unique Saviour of the world has been clearly stated by the New Testament and the apostles:

> Nor is there salvation in any other, for there is no other name under heaven, given among men by which we must be saved (Acts 4:12).

This very theme of Christ's universal salvation is the central focus in the New Testament and apostolic teachings. This was summarized by the apostle John:

> But these are written that you may believe that Jesus is the Christ, the Son of God, and that believing you may have life in his name (Jn. 20:31).

Thus, Jesus Christ has been established by the New Testament and the apostles as the Saviour of the whole world.

Jesus Christ as the Only Lord of the World

The New Testament and the apostles have laid down for us in clear terms the basis of Christ's Lordship, authority, and supremacy. This is closely related to the themes of Christ's death, resurrection, and exaltation. The basis of Christ's Lordship is clearly stated by the apostle Peter on the Day of Pentecost in Jerusalem.

> (Jesus Christ) . . . being delivered by the determined counsel and foreknowledge of God, you have taken by lawless hands, have crucified, and put to death; whom God raised up having loosed the pains of death because it was not possible that he should be held by it (Acts 2:23, 24).

Thus, the death and resurrection of Jesus Christ are the prerequisites of his universal exaltation, glorification, and anointing (Acts 2:32, 33; 3:13; 4:27). 'God has made this Jesus whom you crucified both Lord and Christ' (Acts 2:36). It is quite evident that Christ's Lordship and his Messiahship, his exaltation, and glorification are grounded in his death and resurrection.

Christ after the cross was, indeed, both Lord and Saviour. He became to his apostles 'my Lord and my God' (Jn. 20:28). The entire New Testament and apostolic teachings have demonstrated the significance of the death and the cross of Jesus as God's power over death, sin, and Satan (Romans 5, 6 and 8). The apostolic teachings on the resurrection, exaltation, glorification, and anointing of Jesus were given extensive coverage by the New Testament. The apostle Paul in his writings (1 Cor. 15; Phil. 2 and Col. 1) presented in clear terms that Jesus Christ is the Lord of the whole world.

> Therefore, God also has highly exalted him and given him the name which is above every name, that at the name of Jesus every knee should bow, of those in heaven, and of those on earth, and of those under the earth, and that every tongue should confess that Jesus Christ is Lord, to the glory of God the Father (Phil. 2:9–11).

It is important to note from the foregoing that Jesus Christ is presented as the only and unique Lord and Saviour of the whole world. Salvation and forgiveness of sins are found only through the name of Jesus which is the name above every name. Homage, worship, and confession are to be make only to this name which is above every name. From this unique presentation of the gospel of Christ by the entire New Testament and the apostolic teachings, Christ is to be seen not only as the Lord and Saviour of the Church and individual believers, but of the whole world.

Jesus Christ as the Only Mediator between God and Men

The New Testament and the apostles presented Christ as the only Mediator between God and men.

> For there is one God and one Mediator between God and men, the Man Christ Jesus, who gave himself a ransom for all to be testified in due time (1 Tim. 2:5, 6).

Our Lord himself had given a similar testimony to himself as the only Mediator between God and men: 'I am the Way, the Truth, and the Life. No one comes to the Father except through me' (Jn. 14:6).

The New Testament and the apostles have clearly presented Jesus Christ as the only Mediator, the only channel and the only means of obtaining God's salvation, life eternal, truth, righteousness, forgiveness of sins, love, peace, etc. (Jn. 3:16, 36; Rom. 5:1, 2; 3:21–26; 8).

Supremacy of Jesus Christ

The New Testament and the apostles have clearly presented the supremacy of Christ over the whole of creation. The apostle John presented Jesus Christ as the Creator: 'All things were made through him, and without him nothing was made that was made' (Jn. 1:3). The apostle Paul made the same point when he states:

> He is the image of the invisible God, the first born over all creation. For by him all things were created that are in heaven and that are on earth, visible and invisible, whether thrones or dominions, or principalities or powers. All things were created

through him and for him. And he is before all things; and in him all things consist (Col. 1:15–17).

In the book of Hebrews, Jesus Christ was presented as the heir of all things and was made supreme over all things (Heb. 1–10). The supremacy of Christ over the whole of creation includes, among other things, his supremacy over all angels, all prophets, all priests, and all means of communication with God and over Moses, Aaron, and Joshua. In this book of Hebrews especially, and generally in the entire New Testament, Jesus Christ is presented as the only One approved, appointed, anointed, and exalted by God and thus establishing Christ's supremacy over all of creation.

Christ's supremacy is reflected in his deity, his person, and the exercise of his authority and power over the whole of creation.

Authority of Christ

The New Testament and apostles have affirmed the universal authority of Christ over the whole world. The apostles have clearly stated that Christ's authority has a divine source, and that it is given to him by God the Father (Jn. 3:35; Lk. 10:22). Our Lord himself confirmed this divine source and the handing over of all authority to him by God:

> All authority has been given to me in heaven and on earth. Go, therefore, and make disciples of all nations, baptizing them in the name of the Father and of the Son and of the Holy Spirit, teaching them to observe all things that I have commanded you; and lo, I am with you always, even to the end of the age (Matt. 28:18–20).

The universal authority which was handed over to Christ by God the Father was foretold by Prophet Daniel:

> I was watching in the night vision and behold, One like the Son of Man, coming with clouds of heaven. He came to the Ancient of Days, and they brought him near him. Then to him was given dominion and glory, and a kingdom that all peoples, nations, and languages should serve him. His dominion is an everlasting dominion, which shall not pass away, and his kingdom the one which shall not be destroyed (Dan. 7:13, 14).

The authority of Christ over all peoples, nations, and languages of the whole world was clearly stated prophetically by the psalmist in psalm two, and also in the visions of the apostle John in his exile on the Island of Patmos. In the Book of Revelation, Christ's universal authority was demonstrated in his worship and praise by the angelic host in heaven. As has been mentioned earlier, Christ's authority and power are rooted in his death, resurrection and exaltation. This was clearly defined by the apostle John:

> You are worthy to take the scroll and to open its seals, for you were slain, and have redeemed us to God by your blood, out of every tribe and tongue and people and nation (Rev. 5:9). Worthy is the Lamb who slain to receive power and riches and wisdom, and strength and honour and glory and blessing (Rev. 5:12). Blessings and honour and glory and power be to him who sits on the throne, and to the Lamb, forever and ever (Rev. 5:13).

From the foregoing, it has been demonstrated that the exalted Christ has authority.

Power of Christ

The narrative accounts of the miracles of Jesus in the Gospels demonstrated the power of Jesus over nature, disease, death, principalities and powers. Jesus has authority and power over Satan and demonic powers. The power of Jesus is derived from his deity as the God-Man.

In the remaining books of the New Testament, we see another kind of power which is rooted in Christ's death and resurrection. Through the death and resurrection of Jesus Christ, the evil power of Satan and all demonic powers have been broken and dethroned. Thus, Christ's power is demonstrated in his death and resurrection, in which, 'having disarmed principalities and powers, he made a public spectacle of them, triumphing over them in it' (Col. 2:15). Thus, the Cross of Christ has dealt a death blow to Satan and all his demonic powers. This fact was described by the apostle Paul:

> And what is the exceeding greatness of his power towards us who believe, according to the working of his mighty power which he worked in Christ when he raised him from the dead and seated him at his right hand in the heavenly places far above all principality and power and might and dominion and every name that is named, not only in this age but also in the age which is to come (Eph. 1:19–21).

This resurrection power has placed Christ above all other powers and these are subject to his authority.

There is another aspect of this resurrection power of Christ which is effectual only within the Church and individual believers; that is, the power of salvation in Jesus' name to everyone who believes; baptism in Jesus' name; forgiveness of sins in Jesus' name; effectual prayers in Jesus' name; faith in Jesus' name; working of miracles in Jesus' name, etc. This limited application of the power of Christ for and within the Church and individual believers was clearly demonstrated by the apostles when they called all human beings to find their salvation and God's power through faith in Jesus Christ.

> And his name, through faith in his name, has made this man strong, whom you see and know. Yes, the faith which comes through him has given him this perfect soundness in the presence of you all (Acts 3:16).

This limited application of the power of Christ is what the apostle Paul make reference to when he states:

> For I am not ashamed of the gospel of Christ, for it is the power of God to salvation for everyone who believes . . . For in it the righteousness of God is revealed from faith to faith; as it is written, 'The just shall live by faith;' (Rom. 1:16, 17).

Thus, the universal application of Christ's Lordship, authority, and supremacy becomes effectual when faith is placed in Christ. The power of Christ becomes effectual in those who believe in him. This fact is demonstrated in the close association of Christ's power with the use of and faith in his name, the name that is above every name.

This use of 'his name' derives from our faith in him.

> And whatever you ask in my name, that I will do, that the Father may be glorified in the Son. If you ask anything in my name, I will do it (Jn. 14:13, 14).

Even though the use of the power in Jesus' name is limited to his church, yet it has universal significance. That power is contrasted with his universal power over Satan, principalities and powers. It is more than just a derivative of his deity, but is rooted in his death and resurrection. God's power to grant eternal life, forgiveness, righteousness, and his love and grace to believing humanity derives from the death and resurrection of Christ. There can be no universal application of salvation, peace, and justice of God to the world without the Cross of Christ, his death and resurrection. This is what makes Christ unique and sets him apart. The New Testament and apostolic affirmation of his lordship, authority and supremacy over the whole world is rooted in his deity and his Cross. It is this that gives him victory over the world, Satan, principalities and powers.

Our subject, 'The Unique Christ for Peace and Justice,' cannot be fully understood without this biblical and theological grounding of his uniqueness. The Christ who offers and proclaims his salvation, peace and justice to the world must be seen to have authority, supremacy and power over the whole world. He must also be the legitimate Ruler and Lord of the universe for him to have any universal weight and import over world salvation, peace and justice. Christ's offer of salvation, peace and justice has been demonstrated by the New Testament and the apostles to transcend the pluralistic value-and-truth-claims. He is the ultimate source of eternal values and truth claims in our pluralistic world.

THE UNIQUE CHRIST FOR PEACE

It is only the unique Christ who is qualified to offer his peace to the world. The meaning and the significance of peace which Christ offers to the world rests upon that biblical and theological uniqueness of Christ which was defined in the previous section. 'Peace is the mission of Christ' (Augsburger, p. 149). This fact is demonstrated in his person, his character and his ministry. Peace is, indeed, the inherent quality of Christ, and the characteristic of his kingdom. The prophet Isaiah has this to say about the coming Messiah, who is Christ Jesus, the Lord:

> For unto us a Child is born, unto us a Son is given, and the government will be upon his shoulders. He will be called Wonderful Counsellor, Mighty God, Everlasting Father, Prince of Peace. Of the increase of his government and peace there will be no end. He will reign upon the throne of David and over his kingdom, to order it and establish it with judgment and justice from that time forward, even forever. The zeal of the Lord of Hosts will perform this (Isa. 9:6, 7).

The apostle Luke quoted the angels who announced the birth of Jesus by associating Jesus' birth with world peace: 'Glory to God in the highest, and on earth peace, good will toward men' (Lk. 2:14). Thus the peace which Christ offers was prophesied by prophets and announced by angels, and demonstrated in his person and effected in his Cross.

The peace of Christ has two major characteristics: the Ruler himself is the Prince of Peace; and the kingdom itself, which is his, is characterized by the reign of peace and justice (Isa. 9:6, 7). Thus, without the Prince of Peace, there can be no peace in the kingdom. Peace is what he gives; it issues from him and permeates his entire kingdom. He is the only giver of peace. Jesus made this statement to his disciples: 'Peace I leave with you, my peace I give to you; not as the world gives do I give to you. Let not your heart be troubled, neither let it be afraid' (Jn. 14:27).

Peace is the quality of the Ruler, and Prince of the kingdom, and the characteristic of the kingdom. The concept of Christian peace can be seen from these two perspectives: the Prince of peace and his kingdom; in short, Christ and the world.

We now turn to examine the biblical foundations for Christ's peace.

Biblical Foundation for Christ's Peace

Peace is often defined in the absence of many of those biblical principles which form the basis of world peace. The biblical foundations for peace are hereby presented by due considerations of some biblical principles.

The Fall of Man

Let us go back to the Garden of Eden, the origin of our humanity. Our first parents, Adam and Eve, had to make a decisive choice in the Garden of Eden. Their choice was either *God* or *something else*. As creatures created in the image of God (Gen. 1:26–27), they had the mandate to live in terms of God only (Gen. 2:15–17). God who is their Creator is ultimate and their sole object of worship and adoration (Ex. 20:1–17; Deut. 5:6–21; 6:4–9). They were to live in fellowship, union, and communion with their Creator.

But Adam and Eve were tempted to fall away from this original position (Gen. 3). They chose two things in place of God: They chose the *Self*, that is, self-autonomy and independence from God through disobedience to God's command (Gen. 2:16–17); and *Things*, that is, anything glorified by man and exalted above God.

Because of this, man throughout history has worshipped himself and things, which are creatures of God instead of their Creator. The Bible tells us that in the loins of Adam, we together with our original parents made the same choice and thereby, in consequence, fell into disunion with God, and the whole creation (Rom. 5:12).

Man's worship of *Things* is clearly denounced by the Bible, and especially in Romans 1. However, we shall deal with the other aspect of this falling away from the Origin: Man's worship of the *Self*, hence the manifestations of all aspects of his selfishness which is the root cause of human crises. Because of the sin of self-interest and greed, man has surrounded himself with many barriers and walls, separating him from the rest of his fellow men. He now lives in a cage built for and by himself, which excludes everything but himself. Since man has lost his original identity in God his Creator, he must instead create a false self-made identity. Man needs security and a home to legitimatize his identity, but does not need God to do so. Thus, the separation

of man from God has disastrous consequences for human society, hence the
lack of peace and justice.

Man's fall and sin against God, his Creator, has created a state of disunion
and chaos. Man does not live in harmony with his Creator, nor with the world
of creation, nor with his fellow man, nor even with himself. One of the most
unfortunate developments of the historical consciousness of man is that of the
transvaluation of the Self into ethic, tribal, racial, national or sectional
identity. The individual in society gradually loses his individuality to the
ethnic group, the tribe, the collective race or nation. He is no longer defined
in terms of his individuality, but in terms of what tribe, or ethnic group, or
race, or nation he belongs to. The individual selfishness has been dangerously
transvalued into ethnicity, tribalism, racism, and nationalism, etc. Racial
walls, tribal boundaries, and ethnic barriers and national frontiers have been
built to segregate and segment humanity. As a result individuals are treated
not according to their own value but in terms of their ethnic, racial, tribal or
national value. This results in chaos and crisis and in the absence of peace and
justice.

This kind of humanity creates a selfish and greedy society where peace and
harmony cannot reign. The chaos of sin and the anxiety of human selfishness
and greed make no room for peace and justice. It is the remedy for man's
disunion with God the Creator that he needs.

Individuals and groups and nations have suffered terribly in the cold and
cruel hands of others simply because they have been stereotyped. They have
been classified as 'not belonging'. Whenever a human being or a group, or a
class of people is deemed as 'not belonging', all rights are lost; freedom is
usually taken away; and equality, justice, and fair treatment are denied. The
cruelty of man against man based upon worship of the gods of selfishness,
greed, tribalism, racism, nationalism, etc., is intolerable and unimaginable.
This evil has eaten deep into the fabric of humanity and into almost every
nation and people of the world. When one takes an inventory of wars and
sufferings of the peoples of the world, most, apart from natural disasters, are
caused by the evils of tribalism, racism, nationalism, ethnicity, and human
selfishness and greed.

If we have to deal with the question of peace in the world then we must
begin with the fall of man. Sin is inherent in man (Rom. 5:12; 3:10–18; Mk.
7:18–23). Even though sin takes root in a private individual, yet it has wider
social consequences and implications. Fallen man, corrupted by his sin,
produces in turn a corrupted culture and social structures and institutions.
Whatever man touches becomes corrupted and tainted by his sin.

Peace both in individuals and society is disrupted by the social consequences
of man's fall. War, chaos and crisis are created when there is disunion with God.
Where sin reigns, there also is God's judgement and wrath which end
ultimately in death and eternal separation from God (Rom. 1:18, 6:36).

One of the major consequences of the fall of man is that the whole of
creation also fell with him (Gen. 3:17–19; Rom. 8:18–23). Thus, both man and
creation stand in need of God's redemption, recreation and reconciliation.

The uniqueness of Christ for peace is seen in his provision of an eternal
solution to man's state of sin and alienation from God, his fellow man and
creation. The peace which Christ offers has meaning and significance in this
context.

Given the state of fallen humanity and creation, what makes for peace is more important than the description of the state of peace which is, indeed, the absence of crisis. Thus, the making of peace or the conditions for peace, take prominence over the definition of peace itself.

We now turn to consider the most important biblical foundation of Christ's peace.

Reconciliation in Christ

'Peace is reconciliation' (Augsbruger, p. 138). This grounding of peace in Christ and in his Cross is emphasized by the apostle Paul (Rom. 5:8–11; Eph. 2:14–18; Col. 1:19–22; 2 Cor. 5:18–21). He relates peace to the atonement and grounds the ethic of peace in the redemptive work of Christ' (Augsbruger, pg. 138).

The apostle Paul mentions three types of reconciliation which are rooted in the Cross of Christ, namely, reconciliation between God and man, and between God and creation, and between man and man.

Reconciliation between God and man (Rom. 5:8–11; 2 Cor. 5:18, 19; Col. 1:19–22) is rooted in the redemptive work of Christ on the Cross. The wrath and judgement of God have been abolished by the Cross of Christ in that man now has peace and forgiveness from God and access to him. (Rom. 5:8–11; 5:1, 2; 8:1). Thus, the Cross of Christ has reconciled man vertically with God and horizontally with his fellow man. It is at the Cross of Christ that man is made to be at peace with God his Creator. Reconciliation was effected in the Cross of Christ when he took in the body, his flesh, our sins and God's wrath and judgement. 'Jesus actually took sin's penalty for every man, woman, and child whoever has lived or ever will live' (The Open Bible, New King James, p. 1210). Christ's atoning work on the Cross is the basis of God's willingness to make peace with rebellious humanity and to restore fellowship with man and also to restore his fallen creation.

The Cross of Christ is the starting point of man's search for peace and fellowship. Man needs to live in peace with his Creator before he can find the basis of peace with his fellow man.

The second aspect of reconciliation is found in Ephesians 2:11–22. Here the apostle Paul states that Christ in his body on the Cross destroyed the dividing wall, the enmity between the Jews and the Gentiles. The Cross of Christ has broken all walls, barriers, boundaries and frontiers which humanity has erected against both itself and God. After Christ's destruction of the walls of divisions and his abolition of all enmity, he reconciled them (both Jews and Gentiles) by making them *one* in himself.

The theological and ethical implication here is that, in Christ, there are no walls of division and no enmity, prejudice, stereotyping, discrimination, and bias, for in Christ a new humanity has been created just as we have been made anew in Christ. In this new humanity 'there is neither Jew nor Greek, there is neither slave nor free, there is neither male nor female; for you are all one in Christ Jesus' (Gal. 3:28). This is the basic state of peace in Christ.

This act of reconciliation by the Cross of Christ makes it possible for Christ to destroy barriers and frontiers created by human selfishness or greed, tribalism, racism, or nationalism, which seek to exclude others. The effectual symbol of peace in world society is the Cross of Christ. This reconciliation of humanity in the body of Christ on the Cross is the prerequisite for lasting peace in the world. It is in Christ Jesus and in him alone that we have the means of destroying human selfishness and greed and also enmity between human beings, tribes, races, nations, and classes of people. The state of war and lack of peace in the world is deeply rooted in human sin, selfishness and greed. This root cause must be dealt with, otherwise our placards for peace and justice would be without any solid ground to stand upon.

The world looks for ethical values and seeks to apply them without such proper grounding. Thus, the real issue is not the search for and the application of moral and ethical values for world peace and justice, but their grounding in the Cross and the atonement of the Prince of Peace. Peace treaties, peace conferences, and resolutions cannot replace the essential act of God in the Cross of Christ which created unity, love, and a new humanity in the Body of Christ. It is in vain for humanity to search for peace apart from Christ who is the Prince of Peace.

The new humanity in Christ is characterized by this new unity and love which are indeed the qualities of peace. The new humanity has peace in the sense that she is no longer judged by anyone or threatened by anyone or at war with someone, for all divisions, barriers and sources of enmity and prejudice and discrimination have been abolished and destroyed by the Cross of Christ. In place of war, chaos, disunity, factions, etc., there is unity and love. The making of humanity into one and its unity in Christ is the foundation of world peace and justice. 'There is one body, and one Spirit, just as also you were called in one hope of your calling and one Lord, one faith, one baptism, one God and Father of all who is over all and through all and in all' (Eph. 4:4–6).

Christianity has the capacity to offer to the world its principles of peace and justice because of the work of reconciliation in Jesus Christ.

The third aspect of reconciliation refers to the redemption or the re-creation of the fallen creation (Col. 1:19–22; 2 Cor. 5:19; Rom. 8:18–22). Even the fallen creation has been reconciled in the Cross of Jesus Christ. The prophet Isaiah describes this state of reconciliation (Isa. 11:6–9) which is a state of world peace in which both humanity and the rest of creation will live in peace and harmony. However, the apostle John describes first of all the act of re-creation and destruction of this fallen creation so as to make way for the new earth and the new heaven (Revelation). The chief actor in this act of re-creation of the fallen world is our Lord himself, who is Prince of Peace.

First of all peace is made possible between God and man, then secondly between man and man, and then thirdly between God and his Creation and man and Creation. This restoration of the state of peace is eschatological; it is a looking forward to the final day of redemption. However, it has profound ethical implications on man's relationship to creation and his environment. This restoration of both humanity and creation by Christ is not based upon his divine creative powers as the Creator of the world (Jn 1; Col. 1; Heb. 1) but upon his redemptive work on the Cross. Thus the restoration of peace for humanity and creation has its basis in the Cross of Christ.

The Signs of Christ's Peace

The Cross of Christ is the sign of his peace. There we see God's love, God's forgiveness and God's grace. We now have the reason why we should continue in God's love, forgiveness, and grace after we have been reconciled and made one in the Body of Christ.

The test of any true reconciliation in the Cross of Jesus Christ is the fruit of the Spirit, that is *love*. One of the major results of reconciliation in Christ is the out-flow of love and its manifestation. If God has indeed effected any true reconciliation in us as humanity through the Cross of Christ, then it has to manifest itself in divine love.

Peace is won by love. It is 'love acting' (Augsburger, p. 150). Love then precedes the state of peace. For this reason, it is, therefore, very important that we describe the action which brings about peace, which is divine *love*.

The biblical concept of love, especially in the New Testament, is not a human quality nor quality nor property, but purely divine. Man can only reflect what God through the Holy Spirit has give him. The divine origin of love and its divine nature was clearly defined for us by the apostle John in 1 John, and clarified and by the apostle Paul in 1 Cor. 13. Let us begin with the apostle Paul.

In his definition of spiritual gifts (1 Cor. 12–14) Paul clearly made a distinction between spiritual gifts, on the one hand, and the fruit of the Spirit, on the other. He stated clearly the supremacy of the fruit of the Spirit, which is love as the only basis of the use of spiritual gifts and of measuring the motive for their use (Chapters 12, 13). Any use of spiritual gifts without God's divine love is useless and empty. It is divine in both the source and nature. No one has such qualities of love except God himself. Hence, it is this fruit of the Spirit which Paul admonishes every Christian to have as a prerequisite to any use of spiritual gifts or in fact any action on behalf of humanity. God's divine love is the ground of the use of spiritual gifts and the means of testing their authenticity and value.

What the apostle Paul has done for us is to point us to the principle of divine love as the greatest ingredient any Christian in transaction and, indeed, even that of human society. It is the lack of this principle which has characterized and dominated human transactions, peace treaties and conferences, hence, there can be no lasting peace and justice.

The apostle John speaks directly of the source and nature of love (Jn. 4). *God is love.* God in himself is love (Jn. 4:7, 8, 16). Love is from God (v. 7), which shows that love is not a human quality or property, but comes from God. Thus, love does not originate from man, nor does he know what it is. The apostle John took time to define what love is. 'We know love by this, that he laid down his life for us' (3:16). 'By this the love of God was manifested in us, that God has sent his only begotten Son into the world so that we might live through him' (4:9). 'In this is love, not that we loved God, but that he loved us, and sent his Son to be the propitiation for our sins' (4:10).

Thus, in these verses we see that God's love is revealed to us in the Cross of Jesus Christ. It is only when we fully understand the meaning and the implications of the Cross of Christ that we begin to understand what God's love is all about. Jesus Christ is our reconciliation and peace (Eph. 2:14), so also is he our love through his Cross.

A Christian who is born of God through faith in the finished work of Christ on the Cross should be in a position to love, for the seed of God which is love, resides in him. 'Everyone who loves is born of God and knows God. The one who does not love, does not know God, for God is love' (4:7, 8). The outworking of that fruit of the Spirit is two-pronged: love to God and love to fellow man.

Our Lord Jesus Christ stated the essential nature of love to both God and man: 'You shall love the Lord your God with all your heart, and with all your soul and with all your mind . . . you shall love your neighbour as yourself' (Matt. 22:37–40).

The apostle John in 1 John 2, 3 and 4 wrote that love to a fellow human being is inseparable from one's love to God. For, according to John, any lack of love towards a fellow brother or sister is indeed a reflection of one's ignorance of God. Knowledge of God incorporates with it love to man.

This emphasis of the apostle John shows clearly that our lack of love, our divisions, quarrels, wars, prejudices and discriminations and selfishness and greed result from our lack of knowing who God is, especially his prominent character of love (1 John 3, 4). Knowledge of God is essentially our understanding of his revealed love in Christ Jesus. Our response to this revelation of love in the Cross of Christ must be manifested in its two-pronged response to both God and man if it is divine and true.

To understand the full meaning of the Cross of Christ we need also to use it as the sign of the grace of God. The grace of God has been manifested to us in the Cross of Christ. It has effected our reconciliation with God, his forgiveness and all spiritual blessings. We who were once enemies of God have been forgiven and reconciled. We who were far away and outside of God's commonwealth have been brought near and have also been made heirs together with Christ. God has lavished his love upon us in spite of our sins. All of these speak of God's grace and mercy toward us. 'While we were yet sinners Christ died for the ungodly.' We did not deserve his spiritual blessings, his love and his forgiveness, but his wrath and judgement. Instead, he showered his love and mercy upon us.

The test of whether we have been truly reconciled to God and man lies essentially in how graciously we responded to God's love as revealed in Christ Jesus on the Cross. Just as God has shown us his love and mercy, we are obliged to go and do likewise unto others and show them mercy in spite of what they are. We are to love them unconditionally. The only genuine reason why we should love others is what Christ has done for us on the Cross. 'We love because he first loved us' (1 Jn. 4:19).

Thus, the basis of our love, our forgiveness and peace lies in our understanding of the full implication of the love of Christ towards us in his Cross. Our ministry of reconciliation, love, peace and justice towards our fellow human beings has its basis in the Cross of Christ. The power of our ministry is drawn from our total faith in Christ the revelation of God's love, grace, mercy and peace.

If God has forgiven us so much in Christ, how is it that those who claim to abide in him cannot love others, even if feebly? Our lack of enthusiastic response to others who stand in need is a reflection of our own shallow understanding of God's grace. The grace of God which we have received through Christ, his love, mercy and spiritual blessings must meet with a response from us. Our response in gratitude for what God has done for us in Christ Jesus must be directed to our neighbours who stand in need of our love, forgiveness and charity. 'Owe no man anything but love' (Rom. 12:8).

God's grace toward us is immense and fathomless. No matter what we do in response to grace, we cannot outdo what God has already done for us in Christ. All our good works fall short of the value of God's grace towards us. It is that grace which is our ethical motivation.

God's grace shown in the atoning work of Christ on the Cross becomes the motivating factor for Christian social action and ultimately our spiritual service for humanity. Christian involvement in world peace and justice is first and foremost our humble response to God's grace which has been revealed in Christ. Christians must have the motivation for any social involvement and responsibility. Our vision for the world is based upon this act of God's reconciliation. And how we are to carry this out is based upon our response to God's gracious act toward us. But before we respond to the outside world, we first of all need to have a good home base, the Christian community. Does it live in reconciliation and peace?

As we measure our attitude towards our fellow brothers and sisters, we know that in most cases Christians have not been influenced by the reconciling Spirit of Christ and his love (Phil. 2:1–8), but have been influenced by the spirits of tribalism, racism, ethnicity, selfishness and greed, etc. If, indeed, Christ has accomplished all the work of reconciliation, love and grace in us, why is it that in the community of believers, many are still plagued by lack of forgiveness and peace. Prejudices, discrimination, preferential and differential treatment of one another are social ills that have become the bane of our Christian communities. Our lack of genuine love and forgiveness towards one another contradicts whatever we claim to have received from God. The true and genuine peace of God will come to us after genuine and sincere repentance and forgiveness on the one hand, and reconciliation and peace, on the other.

The quest for true and biblical Christianity in the world today calls for genuine and true repentance and forgiveness and reconciliation and peace among the tribal units, ethnic and racial groupings that form the community of world Christianity. It is only the Church in unity and love of Christ that can bring healing, reconciliation and peace to our segregated and torn societies. World Christianity needs to be converted from selfishness, greed, tribalism, racism, ethnicity and class consciousness, etc. World Christianity needs a new conscience and a new heart re-created and made anew by the Cross of Christ. It is only by this new conscience, new heart and new zeal that the Church of Jesus Christ can make any lasting contribution to world peace and justice.

If there is anything that differentiates Christianity from the attempts of the pluralistic world in issues of peace and justice, it is this biblical and theological basis. Christianity is unique not because of anything else but its biblical and theological foundations with their deep roots in the Cross of Christ and God's love and grace.

Christian justice is the making of peace in the world. We now turn to examine briefly the unique Christ for justice whose ultimate aim is to establish his justice and rule in the world.

THE UNIQUE CHRIST FOR JUSTICE

The more a Christian focuses on the Cross of Christ, the more he sees God's love, grace, reconciliation and mercy and in consequence he is constrained to work for the salvation, peace and justice of the world. His Christian convictions are directed towards works of salvation, peace and justice.

The practice of justice has its basis and motivation in the character of God and his work of redemption in the Cross of Christ. Justice then is the application of the character of God and his will to human society and the world. It is to effect the rule or reign of God in human society. In the Old Testament the books of Law and the Prophets have a lot to say about the reign of God and the demands of his justice. Yet, this divine ordering of human society after God's laws may lack any basis within the context of our pluralistic world of religions, cultures and value-and-truth claims. There is, therefore, a need to anchor God's justice in something concrete and definite. We need an anchor that transcends pluralism, relativism and multi-value-and-truth claims. That base and reference point is Jesus Christ, the second Adam who re-creates humanity and creation.

Christ the Second Adam

In the previous sections, we have already defined the fall of humanity and its reconciliation to God in Christ. However, in dealing with the modern world we must recognize that we are still dealing with the fallen world and fallen humanity. In Adam, we inherited sin, God's wrath and judgement and death, but in Christ we inherit righteousness, grace and life eternal (Rom. 5:12–21; 1 Cor. 15). Furthermore, God has reconciled all things and made them *one* in Christ. This fact is very important in our understanding of the transvaluation of all things in Christ. The second Adam, who is Christ, has transcended the first Adam who fell with creation along with him. The resurrection, the victory, the glorification and the exaltation of Christ over his whole creation relativizes and transcends all world religions, cultures and value-and-truth claims. This was effected at the Cross and will be completed when,

> in the dispensation of the fullness of times he gathers together in one all things in Christ, both which are in heaven and which are on earth. (Eph. 1:10)

Similarly, it was also stated:

> For it pleased the Father that in him all the fullness should dwell, and by him to reconcile all things to himself, by him, whether things on earth or things in heaven, having made peace through the blood of his cross (Col. 1:19–20).

Here, we see that the Cross of Christ is also central in making into *one* of all things both in heaven and on earth in Christ. Christ indeed is the *centre* of all things. This centrality took effect in his cross which in effect re-created all things in him. Thus the fallen world has been redeemed, re-created, reformed and transvalued by Christ, the second Adam. It is on this basis that Christ exercises his authority, and supremacy over the whole of creation (Col. 1:15–18; Heb. 1:2–4; Eph. 1:10–12).

Jesus Christ is both God and Creator (Jn. 1). By the act of his cross he then 'became the firstborn over all creation' (Col. 1:15), 'the appointed heir of all things' (Heb. 1:2), and the reconciler of all things (Col. 1:20). It is on the basis of the Cross that Christ could say that 'all authority has been given to me in heaven and on earth' (Matt. 28:18).

This created but fallen world has been legally handed over to Christ by God because of this victory and triumph on the cross. Thus, the Cross has become the signet of his kingdom and rule and authority and power all over the world. The Cross of Christ has dethroned Satan and all principalities and all powers and they are now subjected to him and his rule (Rev. 4:5). It is in the Cross of Christ that God is redeeming, reconciling, reforming and re-creating his fallen world and creation. The cost of doing this was the Cross of Christ. Thus, the cost of re-establishing God's rule and God's peace and justice has been paid for by the second Adam, the Firstborn over all creation. Hence this fallen world and creation are legally his. The world and creation are his purchased property and his Cross is the down-payment for that. This act of Christ establishes a new dimension to justice.

The Cross of Christ was also the means of executing God's wrath and judgement upon fallen man and the fallen world. 'For he made him who knew no sin to be sin for us, that we might become the righteousness of God in him (2 Cor. 5:21). At the Cross of Christ, God's holiness and justice were satisfied. Thus, man in Christ stands acquitted and justified before God. This justice of God was defined by the apostle Paul:

> For all have sinned and fall short of the glory of God and are justified freely by his grace through the redemption that is in Christ Jesus, whom God set forth to be a propitiation by his blood, through faith, to demonstrate his righteousness, because in his forbearance God has passed over the sins that were previously committed to demonstrate at the present time his righteousness, that he might be just and the justifier of the one who has faith in Jesus (Rom. 3:23–26).

Thus, man's justification and acquittal and forgiveness take root in the Cross of Christ. This fact has added a new dimension to our concept of justice, which is the principle of sacrifice, and propitiation. Our Lord Jesus Christ who is indeed the righteous Judge was first made sin for us and he also took the path of sacrifice and self-giving in love. True justice then is a reflection of self-sacrifice, self-giving and love and forgiveness. It is the creation of a new right standing and relationship through sacrificial love and self-giving, either with God or man.

Justice when viewed from any perspective which is not anchored in the Cross of Christ will have no basis for claiming to be unique or transcendent. However, the Cross has not in any way changed the nature and character of God but rather revealed in greater dimension who God is. The Cross has not abolished Old Testament principles of peace and justice but has fulfilled them in wider dimensions.

The Cross of Christ is the starting point of Christian conceptions of peace and justice and salvation, for herein lies the offer of the unique Christ to the whole world. The Cross is also the starting point of our new humanity and new creation and new ethical awareness and grounding. What then is the role of the church and believers who are the new humanity in world peace and justice? This is the outworking of our ethical standing based on the redemptive act of Christ.

Believers, Ethical Position in Christ

Faith in the unique Christ has both spiritual and social implications for the world. Christian faith is in the one who is the Lord of the whole world and who also exercises his authority and supremacy over it. Believers are the new humanity, the kingdom of priests and the witnesses to Christ in this fallen world. Their task is to proclaim salvation *only* in their Lord and Christ and to present him as the *only* Prince of Peace and the righteous Judge of the world. They are also to propagate and infiltrate this world with the teachings and the message of their Lord. They are to direct their efforts to redeeming and reconciling the lost humanity and the lost world. They must be up and doing to present the *unique* Christ to our pluralistic world of religions and value-and-truth claims.

The believers have already tasted the goodness of the Lord. They have experienced his love, peace, mercy and forgiveness and have been reconciled to God and to one another. So they are to display before the world, their reconciliation, unity and oneness (Jn. 17:21) and a sense of mission to the world. What God and Christ stand for as regards to justice, righteousness and holiness is what believers must also stand for. They are also called upon to be the light and the salt of the world and be peacemakers (Matt. 5:9, 13–16). Believers cannot do these things in isolation or withdrawal from the world. They must become involved and become changed agents. However, this role and this responsibility should be carefully developed and worked out by the believers.

THE ROLE OF THE CHURCH IN WORLD PEACE AND JUSTICE

Christ has entrusted this ministry of reconciliation to his Church, that is, the propagation and promotion of peace and justice in the world. The state of peace and its principles has been defined by the apostle Paul in Phil. 2:1–8:- as of consolation, love, fellowship, affection, mercy, like-mindedness, being of one accord and one mind, selflessness and humility. This state of peace has to be created, thus making peacemaking an important Christian virtue. If peace is to reign within any community, hostility has to be renounced. Augsburger makes the following important statements about peacemaking:

> Peacemaking maximizes what we have as common and minimizes our differences.
> Peacemaking emphasizes forgiveness and rejects revenge, seeking the well-being of the other person.
> Peacemaking looks beyond the issue to the person, seeking ways to resolve the problem by arbitration.
> Peacemaking means confronting in love, talking with one, rather than about one.
> Peacemaking involves a willingness to suffer loss including loss of face, for the joy of helping another to 'save face' (Augsburger, p. 135).

Peace, therefore, is reconciliation and 'harmony between God and people, between people and people, between people and nature' (Augsburger, p. 135).

The role of the Church is to promote this type of peace within Christian communities and also across the whole world. The greed and the selfishness of people and groups need to be exposed and condemned in the light of biblical teachings. The Church as a peacemaker in the world must do works of love and seek justice for everyone and do so at all costs. The Church must be compassionate in order to see and to hear the cry of the oppressed, the downtrodden, and to identify with just and righteous causes as they affect humanity.

In order for us to capture many biblical themes and principles of justice, let me summarize Augsburger's definition of peace:

> Peace is a renunciation of hostility
> Peace is a recognition of person-worth
> Peace is reconciliation, not negativism
> Peace is a positive, forgiving grace
> Peace is a refusal to accept alienation
> Peace is a rejection of violence
> Peace is the healing of brokenness
> Peace is the Shalom of God
> Peace is the mission of Christ
> (Augsburger, pp. 130–151).

This has by no means exhausted our Christian definition of peace. What matters most here lies not in its definition but its application and the making of peace by the Church in the world. We are to rely not only upon the existing churches or Christian organizations and institutions as means of promoting peace but also by developing new ones and strategizing our approach to make an impact on the world scene for peace and justice.

The Church of Jesus Christ must be ultimately concerned about matters of justice in the world and also how to promote it in the world. These issues are incorporated in this definition of justice:

> Justice is the safeguard of freedom, the maintenance of accountability, the recognition of human dignity, the equity of worth, the sanctity of humanness, the affirmation of divine purposes. Justice is the prevention of exploitation (Augsburger, p. 106).

With this background, it is important for the Church to examine critically social structures and institutions and values which are current in our world in light of the Holy Scriptures. Not all social structures and institutions and values are Christian in principle and this is what the Church is to seek to influence and change. The Church cannot sit back and allow secular and humanist values to go unchallenged, as these seek not to promote peace and justice, but the moral decay and destruction of humanity.

The uniqueness of Christ cannot be submitted to compromise, accommodation or equality of religion, value-and-truth claims, rather his uniqueness transcends and judges all these. It is this difference that makes Christianity what it is and also gives it its strength to proclaim the new value of peace and justice in Christ to the whole world. The Church should also seek creative ways and means of promoting peace and justice in the world.

CONCLUSION

This paper, in the main, focuses on the development of the biblical and theological basis of the unique Christ for peace and justice in our pluralistic world. This approach is necessary given the very serious rejection of the uniqueness of Christ in our contemporary world of religions, cultures and value-and-truth claims.

Christians must have good theological and biblical reasons to believe otherwise. This can be strengthened only by our return to the Holy Bible and the historic, apostolic confession and proclamation that Jesus is Lord and that his Lordship, authority and supremacy are over the whole world. This universal standing of Christ as Lord, both the Lord of the Church and the world, negates any claims of pluralism, relativism or secularism, etc.

The cross of Christ has effected the creation of a new humanity, and new creation that have been both reconciled to God and to one another. The cross has affected both humanity and the creation which has been redeemed, restored, and re-created. This act of restoration is a demonstration of God's love, mercy and grace which must be received with gratitude and thanksgiving. Man's response to this act of grace and mercy carries with it great spiritual and ethical responsibility and consequences. Christian social action and responsibility in society and the world are grounded in the grace of God which has made reconciliation and forgiveness possible, hence, freeing man for fulfilling his ethical responsibility in the world.

God's character and nature of justice are reflected in the divine rule and his laws which are also grounded in this victory and exaltation of Christ. God's reign, authority and supremacy are turned over to Christ, the second Adam, the firstborn of creation, and the express and invisible image of God. The ethics of peace and justice take on new dimensions and meanings in the Cross of the One who is the Prince of Peace and the righteous Judge. Believers should take their cue from him and his example and then go out to change the world for him. They are to organize and pattern their societies, institutions and life after Christ the righteous Judge. The world and humanity and all social structures and institutions and values are to be judged in the light of Christ and his word. The world is to be transformed so as to conform it to the image of Christ and his peace and justice.

What this paper was unable to do was to develop in great detail what are the implications and actual outworking of some of the ideas which were developed. The application of some of these basic ideas to world peace and justice is yet to be fully developed. However, there is enough of basic ethical principles that could be drawn for wider application in our world today. The foundation of Christian conception of peace and justice has been laid and from there on its ethical and spiritual application to the whole world.

BIBLIOGRAPHY

Augsburger, Myron S., *The Christ Shaped Conscience*. (Victor Books, 1990).
Bonhoeffer, Dietrich, *Ethics*.
Clarke, Thomas E., ed., *Above Every Name: The Lordship of Christ and Social Systems*. (Ramsey: NJ Paulist Press, 1980).
Mott, Stephen Charles, *Biblical Ethics and Social Change* (New York: Oxford University Press, 1982).
Newbigin, Lesslie, *The Gospel in a Pluralist Society* (Eerdmanns, 1989).
Webber, Robert E., *The Church in the World* (Zondervan Academic Books, 1986).

17

Bong-Ho Son

In this article Bong-Ho Son grapples with the issue of relating the exclusiveness of the uniqueness of Christ to the realities of social injustices in our society. While Christians cannot participate in Christ's work to satisfy God's retributive justice, they can and should be agents for his distributive justice in society, as seen in Christ's teachings and ministry. The author discusses the root causes of injustice and the ethical problem of motivation. His own version of 'justice and basic needs for all' calls for a Christian life-style of sacrifice and simplicity.

UNIQUENESS AND JUSTICE?

Does the doctrine of the uniqueness of Christ have any relevance to social justice? Is there any inherent relationship between them? Social justice implies a plurality of people, who enjoy equal basic rights. It seems, therefore, that to assert the uniqueness of any person is incompatible with the idea of social justice.

Worse still, is it not possible that the belief in the uniqueness of Christ is detrimental to social justice? The concept of uniqueness, whatever kind of uniqueness it may be, seems to imply an exclusive or privileged status and is contrary to the concept of social justice. Furthermore, Christian belief in the uniqueness of Christ can be misunderstood as, and is easily translated into, a unique position for Christians, and might be interpreted, wittingly or unwittingly, as a pretext for enjoying some special privileges in society. This belief may work subconsciously in the minds of some Christians in those societies where Christians occupy the majority or dominant status. In fact, some missionaries and evangelists from the West and from Korea tell unbelievers that faith in Christ will make them not only blessed in the next world but also rich and powerful in this world as well. Those who make these claims were preceded by the same Israelites who counted their status as God's chosen people as the grounds for worldly privileges.

The doctrine of the uniqueness of Christ, furthermore, can be very offensive to non-Christians who think that it is discriminatory and unfair to

Dr. Bong-Ho Son teaches philosophy at the Seoul National University, South Korea.

them. Why should, they protest, Christ alone be the Saviour and why are only the believers in Christ being singled out to be saved? In any discussion about justice, believers in the uniqueness of Christ may not be in a comfortable position to defend themselves.

COMMON JUSTICE FOR ALL

It is plain that the uniqueness of Christ is an exclusively Christian belief and that social justice presupposes a universality in recognition and application of certain values. Any kind of social justice which is so uniquely Christian that it is unacceptable to non-Christians, especially to those who are really in need of justice would be meaningless. In this discussion, we are, therefore, not primarily concerned with justice among Christians but with social justice for all, including non-Christians. Therefore, the concept of justice we are pursuing here should be of such a nature that, on the one hand, the uniqueness of Christ is relevant to it and, at the same time, it has to be sufficiently universal so that it may be acceptable and desirable to all those who are really in need of justice, including the non-Christian members of society.

At the outset, it must be made clear that social justice does not imply universalism in salvation. Those who freely refuse to acknowledge the uniqueness of Christ should not feel discriminated against when salvation through the unique Saviour is refused to them. They are refused because they regard salvation as unimportant and uninteresting to them. Furthermore, if the Christian's confession of the uniqueness of Christ also involves, as we will argue, sacrifice and suffering instead of worldly advantages, it would hardly offend those who are excluded from these disadvantages.

They would, however, feel really discriminated against if they were excluded from any social, political or economical benefits. The uniqueness of Christ, moreover, does not entail any exclusive rights of Christians in economic, political, or social realms. So it is in these areas alone where Christians and non-Christians share the same rights and where discrimination or injustice count. Salvation through Christ is primarily, though not exclusively, spiritual, but social justice is primarily secular and secondarily spiritual. The common ground for the discourse on justice for both believers and un-believers in the uniqueness of Christ is in the social, economical and political spheres of life.

When the Bible teaches that God establishes 'justice for all of the oppressed of the earth' (Ps. 76:9; cf. Jer. 9:24), it is not meant only for the chosen people of God. 'The beneficiaries are not only oppressed Israelites (or Christians). There is one God and therefore one justice for all people and for all time.'[1] The justice which God establishes is a blessing for all people and it must be acceptable and recognizable as such by all people. Justice which is not perceived as justice would be meaningless. Our concrete experiences also show that Christians and non-Christians share basically a similar understanding of justice. We all understand what John the Baptist meant when he proclaimed: 'The man with two tunics should share with him who has none, and the one who has food should do the same' (Lk. 3:11). We also understand the apostle Paul when he taught: 'Our desire is not that others might be relieved while you are hard pressed, but that there might be equality' (2 Cor. 8:13). Christ is unique, but social justice has to be universal to be meaningful.

The fact that Christians and non-Christians share the same understanding and desire for social justice, however, does not yet prove conclusively that the uniqueness of Christ is relevant or inherently related to social justice. We may assume only that in God's government of the world there must be some organic relationship between the two important concepts. In what sense, then, is the uniqueness of Christ relevant to social justice?

JUSTICE IN RELATION TO BASIC NEEDS

Before we proceed to attempt to explicate the relationship, we should be clear about the kind of justice which is desirable for societies today and at the same time practically realizable. Theories related to social justice are not of much value unless they are practically applicable and helpful to meet the actual needs of those who suffer from injustices. A theory of social justice which is related to the doctrine of the uniqueness of Christ is apt to fall into abstract words. Justice is, however, a practical subject and the need of it is real and urgent.

The kind of justice which is particularly needed today is not so much retributive or non-comparative justice as distributive or comparative justice. It does not mean, however, that retributive justice is unimportant or the need for it has been sufficiently met. On the contrary, in many parts of the world today, even the minimum of retributive justice is not satisfied. Further, distributive justice is not entirely separated from retributive justice. Distribution without any consideration of desert would not be a complete justice. It is the fatal weakness of Marxistic socialism that it stressed distributive justice too much and retributive justice too little.

Nevertheless, more attention is paid today to social or distributive justice. In many cases, deficiency of retributive justice turns out to be the consequence of inadequacy in distributive justice. A proverb circulated recently in Korea illustrates this relationship: 'Have you money? Not guilty! No money? Guilty!'

The formal principle of comparative justice, i.e., like cases to be treated alike and different cases to be treated differently, is not very useful in practical applications. The likenesses and differences of cases should be relevant so that the principle may have practical value. The criteria of relevance for various contexts of justice, or material principles of justice, have to be supplemented to the formal principle.[2] And the criteria of relevance for just distributions are much more difficult to agree upon than commonly supposed. Nonequalitarians hold that one should be rewarded according to one's deserts such as contributions, achievements, efforts, etc. Equalitarians insist that distribution of social goods should be made according to one's needs. Strict equalitarianism recommends that social goods be distributed to everyone equally for the simple reason that one is a human being, but Marx and Lenin envisioned a society in which the ideal, 'From each according to his ability, to each according to his need' would be realized.

Simple as they may seem, both views raise a host of difficulties when they are applied to concrete situations of society. For the nonequalitarian position, the following questions must be answered. Which among one's native abilities, acquired skills and abilities, family, race, colour, education, efforts, contributions, achievements, etc., or which combinations of these should be counted as one's desert so that reward for them is said to be fair and just? Further, how can one's merits, achievements, contributions, or efforts be measured? For the equalitarian, the questions are just as complicated. Should one's needs be met regardless of one's efforts or contributions? How can one's needs be measured? Would a society be able to sustain itself if the needs of all of its members are met equally without considering their contributions? Given the incontestable fact that the majority of people are selfish in most circumstances in their daily lives, is it truly responsible to distribute social goods to everybody equally? Even if it is, is it practically possible to do so? The recent collapse of Communism in Eastern Europe is a clear proof that the equalitarian principle is neither possible nor even desirable.

As an alternative, I would like to propose what I call the justice of basic needs. It is a proposal to distribute social goods in such a way that basic needs such as the necessary amount of food, clothes, health care, and education may be provided for each individual simply because he or she is a human being, while luxuries, which go beyond the basic needs, be rewarded to each according to one's desert, i.e., one's contributions and achievements. It goes without mentioning that the provision of basic needs should take priority over the division of luxuries, and as the social wealth increases, the limit of the basic needs should be extended so that what have been formerly regarded as luxuries and distributed according to one's desert may now be distributed according to one's need.[3] It is a mixture of equalitarian and nonequalitarian positions in social justice, or of the merits of both capitalism and of socialism.

The justice of basic needs has several advantages over other positions. It is, first of all, realistic in view of the given fact that most people are selfish, a general fact which socialism and other optimistic visions of society have overlooked too readily. It, further, is not only concerned with equal division of a given pie but also with enlarging, or at least not reducing, its size by providing certain incentives for efforts in terms of luxuries, without sacrificing the basic necessities of the least advantaged. But by widening the scope of basic needs gradually as the social wealth grows, the poor are not left forever bound by the bare necessities of life. This would also encourage them to make greater efforts to increase the social wealth because an enlarged pie means greater possibility to share more.

Another advantage of the view is that it helps save social or personal resources available for justice by concentrating them on those who most need them. Attention is paid not so much to the general equality of all members of the society as to the protection of the basic rights of its members. It would be nice if distribution of luxuries among the privileged is also fair and just. But to be concerned with such a matter is itself a luxury which many societies today cannot afford.

This conception is so practical and reasonable that many governments are in fact making use of it in defending their concrete social policies. Free food, free medication, free compulsory education, cheap housing for the poor are common practices in many countries. In fact, it appeals so strongly to our general intuitive sense of justice that governments do not need any particular apologies for it.

The biblical teachings on justice are also primarily concerned with the least advantaged in the society. The God of Israel is the one 'who executes justice for the oppressed: who gives food to the hungry. The Lord sets the prisoners free; the Lord opens the eyes of the blind. The Lord lifts up those who are bowed down; the Lord loves the righteous. The Lord watches over the sojourners, he upholds the widow and the fatherless; but the way of the wicked he brings to ruin' (Ps. 146:7–10). The parable of the Good Samaritan teaches not only sympathy toward the others but also love toward the abused.[4] 'The Scriptures do not allow the presupposition of a condition in which groups or individuals are denied the ability to participate fully and equally in the life of the society. For this reason, justice is primarily spoken of by the biblical writers as activity on behalf of the disadvantaged'.[5]

Karl Barth said, '. . . the human righteousness required by God and established in obedience – the righteousness which according to Amos 5:24 should pour down as a mighty stream – has necessarily the character of a vindication of right in favour of the threatened innocent, the oppressed poor, widows, orphans and aliens. For this reason, in the relations and events in the life of His people, God always takes His stand unconditionally and passionately on this side and on this side alone: against the lofty and on behalf of the lowly; against those who already enjoy rights and privilege and on behalf of those who denied and deprived of it.'[6]

The Bible does not present any abstract and general principle of justice. It starts from the plain fact that human society has never been completely just. And it never envisions a man-made utopia which is both completely just and prosperous. Being basically sinful and selfish, the best man can hope for is to reduce the inequalities and sufferings due to human selfishness as much as possible.

The biblical teachings on justice are not only realistic but also practical. Its way of accomplishing justice is rather simple. The Bible does not recommend the abolition of all private properties or the introduction of a graduated taxation system. We are asked simply to find out who are the least advantaged in the society and to uphold them either directly or indirectly. One important way to help them indirectly would be by instituting structural changes so that the justice of basic needs may be met. The justice of basic needs in principle agrees with the biblical teachings on justice. Thus protecting and upholding the basic rights and needs appeals to everyone's intuitive sense of justice and is also supported by biblical teachings.

ROOT OF INJUSTICES

Injustice is one of the main causes of mankind's sufferings, and this is why injustice should be corrected. As far as our recognition is concerned, anything which gives us pain or makes us suffer either directly or indirectly is evil. Suffering or pain,[7] one of the primordial experiences of mankind, causes us to recognize negative realities for what they are. If there were no experience of pain, all those realities which we know to be evil would have not been disliked and treated as something to be avoided.

Some of the pains we suffer are caused by nature and cannot be prevented by human efforts. But according to Lewis, perhaps four-fifths of man's sufferings are caused by man.[8] Lewis is not exaggerating in view of the fact that, for instance, more than 90% of the physically handicapped find the causes of their invalidities in human faults such as accidents, negligence, misuse of drugs, environmental pollution, etc. It is undeniable that the majority of human suffering has social origins, and a great many of them stem from social injustices. Injustice produces suffering in any place and at any time. But it is particularly the case today as society becomes increasingly complex and the lives of individuals depend in growing measure upon the structures of their society.

The root of injustice is, of course, man's sins against God. In Genesis 4, we see how sin against God develops into social injustices. Alienated from God, Cain, the prototype of sinners, feels insecure. Driven from the presence of God, Cain complains, 'Today you are driving me from the land, and I will be hidden from your presence; I will be a restless wanderer on the earth, and whoever finds me will kill me' (Gen. 4:14). Interestingly, what he fears most is not natural disaster or God's punishment but his fellow men (perhaps Abel's relatives). The fact that he and his children built a city (apparently surrounded by walls) and forged weapons out of bronze and iron (v. 22) expresses their sense of insecurity and reveal the objects of their fear. The fear of Cain is really unfounded. God promised that 'if anyone kills Cain, he will suffer vengeance seven times over' (v. 15), but Cain could not trust the Lord. The real root for man's insecurity is not so much the deficiency of God's protection as his disbelief in God's promise of protection, a typical characteristic of sin (cf. 16:9).

Human history consists mainly in man's frantic struggles to safeguard his security by means of his own power and ingenuities. It is also the root cause of all the competitions and conflicts within and between societies. If the threats to life and happiness which men have to face were from the forces of nature alone, protection from them would have certain limits. But when the threats are from the power of other men, there is never sufficient defence. We witness one absurd consequence of such competition in the stockpiling of weapons which together are capable of destroying the entire world several times over. The gaining of new power by one person or by a group means new threats to other persons or groups, and reciprocally competitive accumulation of worldly powers inevitably produces situations of injustice for some persons or groups. The strong possess too much, while the weak have too little and starve. Yet neither feels entirely secure and their enjoyment is short-lived.

Group egoism especially has debilitating effects on social justice. The fact that greater power can be secured even for individuals when they are united in a group and the necessity of protecting collective interests over against competing groups strengthen the cohesion of the group. Furthermore, individuals within the group lose moral inhibitions which might exercise a moral restraint on an individual outside the group, thereby strengthening the concessive power of the group.[9] It is primarily the group egoism expressed either in its naked force or in terms of social structures which create circumstances for major injustices in almost all societies. Any group, whether of priests, military, higher castes, landowners, capitalists, etc., occupying the position of power, enjoys special privileges and an undeserved share of social goods while refusing outsiders their legitimate rights. Power corrupts, and big powers corrupt more easily than small powers. But the power of a group, not only because it is big but also because it lacks the moral inhibition of individual conscience, tends to corrupt still more easily. And every corruption of power produces some forms of injustice directly or indirectly.

The most powerful and most egoistic among all human groups is the modern state.[10] This ancient leviathan is still very alive and even stronger than it used to be. Originally instituted to preserve order and justice within the boundary of national territory, the state has now turned into a primarily economic interest group and become the major obstacle of international justice. For the economic benefits it brings to its citizens, the cohesive powers of modern states have become greater than those of any other kind of institution in history. Modern states have created a world in which only the rule of the jungle prevails. The degree of suffering a nation unjustly inflicts upon the people of other nations is proportional to its economic strength.

The secularization of culture aggravates the moral situation of modern societies and the multiplication of injustices. Having lost sight of the next world and transcendental values, modern men seek to find the meaning of life and the basis of security solely in the things of this world. This necessarily intensifies competitions and conflicts between individuals and groups because the values they seek after are mainly relative and quantitatively limited so that if one possesses much, others necessarily have less. Material possessions and political powers have become the supreme values of secular society.

Fortunately, not every individual and not every group of individuals is always so egoistic and inimical to justice. Men are capable of sympathy and moral indignation in response to violations of justice. Mencius counted sympathy, or the feeling of commiseration (*ts'e yin*), as one of the four basic good qualities with which all men are endowed by nature (beside the feeling of shame and dislike (*hsiu wu*), the feeling of modesty and of yielding (*tz'u jang*), and the sense of right and wrong (*shih fei*).[11] The problem is, according to Mencius, that the good qualities are not fully cultivated or are polluted by the senses.[12]

For most people, however, their sympathy or indignation at injustices is not strong enough to compel them to remedial actions, especially when their own pleasures or interests are at stake. Rationality, natural sympathy and moral indignation, although they are the most precious moral resources men have, are not sufficient guardians of social justice.

Even intuitive desires for justice and rationality, important though they are for social justice, are not entirely free from human selfishness. It is not utterly cynical to interpret them as the expressions of the subconscious fear of being unjustly wronged coupled with the principle of reciprocity, which again can be explained in terms of probability calculation.

UNIQUE IN SACRIFICE

What relevance, then, does the uniqueness of Christ have to do with these circumstances of social justice? The confession that Christ is our only Saviour is one of the fundamental elements of the Christian faith. Regardless as to whether or not it is palatable to modern men and acceptable to the people of other faiths, it is not to be compromised. If the confession of the uniqueness of Christ contradicts our efforts for social justice, we may have to give up the latter, because otherwise, it would be no longer a 'Christian' effort for social justice.

Simply claiming that 'there is no other name under heaven given to men by which we must be saved' beside the name of Jesus Christ of Nazareth (Acts 4:12), at the first hearing, certainly sounds very arrogant and unfair to many people. The fact that Christ is the only incarnate Son of God appointed to die to redeem his people is not something which every human being has agreed upon or which has any direct bearing on social justice. This rather formal understanding of Christ's uniqueness appears to be inimical or, at most, indifferent to social justice.

But the biblical teachings concerning Christ are rich with contents which together constitute inalienable aspects of his uniqueness as Saviour. His being and person, his coming in the flesh, his ministry and teachings, his death, resurrection, ascension and his second coming are not to be considered apart from his being unique Saviour and Redeemer. Every aspect of these teachings shares the uniqueness of his whole person and ministry.

Yet the uniqueness which each aspect carries should not be of such a character that it is incomprehensible and thus incapable of being communicated. In the history of Christian theology, negative theology or existentialism has stressed the characteristics of incomprehensibility and incommunicability of God's self-revelations. But biblical teachings do not seem to support such extreme theories. We are commanded to love each other as God loves us. Perhaps God's love is not identical with our love, but it must be sufficiently similar to ours or, at least somewhat analogous to ours so that God's will can be communicable to us.

Paying due remuneration for services rendered is taken for granted as justice in the Bible and justice is also a chief attribute of God (Ps. 103:6).[13] It is also what our intuitive sense of justice demands. We understand and believe that the vicarious death of Christ satisfies the demand of God's retributive justice. He died to pay the price of death for all those who have sinned against God. Jesus Christ was crucified not only 'for our sins' (1 Cor. 15:3), but also 'for the sins of the world' (1 Jn. 2:2).[14]

However, God's retributive justice is extended to distributive justice through the redemptive ministry of Christ.[15] Jesus made it very clear that his saving ministry is the fulfilment of Isaiah's prophecy that the good news of salvation was particularly directed to the poor and oppressed (Lk. 4:18–20). He died for all who believe in him, but especially for the poor and oppressed who are wronged in unjust societies. They are mostly victims of, and easily victimized by, social injustices. It is true that his salvation is open to all, but it is presented in such a way that the poor, the prisoners, the blind, the oppressed may easily accept it as theirs, for they can be poor in spirit more easily than those who are rich in the things of the world. Salvation implies being content and there can be no contentment and peace where there is no justice.[16]

Christ suffered and died not for his own salvation or reward but for the salvation of sinners. And he did this as a victim of social injustice, identifying himself not only with sinners but particularly with other victims of social injustices. He went through a legal process which totally violated retributive justice, the sinless one being sentenced to the most cruel death men had ever contrived. He humbled himself in order to lift the lowly: 'But God chose the foolish things of the world to shame the wise; God chose the weak things of the world to shame the strong. He chose the lowly things of this world and the despised things – and the things that are not – to nullify the things that are' (1 Cor. 1:27–28). This aspect of his redemptive ministry is an essential constituent of his uniqueness. The uniqueness of Christ does not imply privilege but rather sacrifice, and in this respect, his uniqueness is unique. And uniqueness in sacrifice is not offensive to man's intuitive sense of justice but rather can be auxiliary to social justice.

CHRISTIAN EFFORTS FOR SOCIAL JUSTICE

A theoretical argument on an ethical subject is meaningless unless it is practically useful. We have stated that the doctrine of the uniqueness of Christ is not only relevant but also auxiliary to establishment of social justice. But how can it be concretely made relevant to and contribute to social justice, while it is not accepted by all those who are involved in social justice?

We believe, of course, that God is able to work mysteriously so that social justice is directly affected by the sacrificial death of Christ. 'The judge of all of the earth' (Gen. 18:25) is right, and the final judgement of the righteous Lord must be just. But as far as we know, the present world is still full of injustices, and we see little clear indication that there is a progressive development toward greater justice. It seems, rather, that the uniqueness of Christ is related to social justice only through the mediation of Christians, who confess their unique Saviour on the one hand and are chosen and commanded to work for justice in societies on the other hand. The uniqueness of Christ as personal Saviour is confessed by the church in faith, but the uniqueness of Christ as the final judge of the world 'ought' to be realized by his followers through their labours for social justice. 'People are God's channels of justice, as well as of proclamation.'[17]

As a medium of blessing, however, Christians are to be agents of justice rather than its beneficiaries. As members of society, they can also benefit when society becomes just, but they stand primarily on the side of the benefactor, i.e. of Christ, rather than on the side of the beneficiaries.

If justice is a blessing to a society, Christians who work for justice are the medium of the blessing: 'All people on earth will be blessed through you' (Gen. 12:3; 18:18). Believers are 'a chosen people, a royal priesthood, a holy nation, a people belonging to God' (1 Pet. 2:9), called to be the salt and the light of the world, and to make the uniqueness of Christ concretely discernible by upholding the disadvantaged in society.

Christ died for the sake of sinners, thereby satisfying the retributive justice of God. But he died also to lift up the oppressed so that distributive justice for them may be satisfied. Those who are willing to sacrifice themselves for Christ, therefore, sacrifice also for the oppressed in society. Christians cannot participate in Christ's work to satisfy God's retributive justice in society. Redemption is to liberate sinners from the bondage of sin. So Christian efforts for social justice are human endeavours to liberate those who suffer under unequal and unjust social structures, which are a prominent conse- quence of the selfishness and insecurity of sinful men. Followers of Christ can contribute to social justice, at the least, by withdrawing themselves partly from the struggles of all against all for survival and for greater power. Those who are committed to the unique Christ and are assured of eternal security may, in principle, relinquish some of their legitimate rights and pleasures for the sake of social justice more easily than anybody else could.

It is true this approach to promoting justice is not sufficient, but it is, nevertheless, by no means easy to put into practice in this secularized world where the gods of mammon and pleasure reign. The effects of the self renunciation of believers are not to be underestimated either. Fewer competitors mean diminished competition and if one possesses less, others will get more. A simple life style and temperance in acquisition of worldly goods contribute, among other things, to the promotion of social justice. In those societies where Christians are minorities and enjoy no sizeable social influence, this may be their best and only way to contribute to improving the state of social justice.

It is important for Christians to realize that they, as citizens of a state, participate inevitably in the national interest. This should be a burden to the conscience of Christians in relatively rich nations because they are most likely enjoying undeserved benefits which their nations have gained by exploiting people of poor countries. The undeserved prosperity of individuals in rich countries may mean undeserved poverty of individuals in poor countries. To be consistently Christian, one should be able to give up much of the unjust benefits one enjoys beyond the average, and those who are living reasonably well in today's world community should realize that others are being victimized for their benefit. To live simply is, therefore, not a benevolent gesture but one way of reducing one's debt to others who are unjustly victimized. Further, Christians in stronger nations should be ready to fight nationalism, which today is motivated predominantly by economic interests.

This negative approach, however, may not be uniquely Christian. In fact ascetic religions may do better. Yet temperate living by Christians is unique in the sense that their relinquishment, like that of their Lord, is not primarily for the purification of their own souls, as a part of earning salvation, but a loving sacrifice for the sake of others. It is this element of self-sacrifice purely for the sake of others which should characterize all Christian efforts for social justice in distinction from other approaches, including socialist ones.

Personal sacrifices should, therefore, accompany all Christian undertakings for social justice. No attempt to improve social justice will be both genuinely Christian and truly effective unless those who are involved are ready to renounce their worldly pleasures and possessions.

Believers, however, cannot be satisfied with this negative approach alone, especially where they are a social majority or in influential positions in terms of social, political or economic power. Unless special measures are taken, the surpluses Christians have created by their sacrifices may not be given to the least advantaged but may be appropriated by the strong of the society, and consequently widen the gap between the rich and poor still further. In many cases, the simple good will and sacrifices of Christians are effectively exploited by those in power and worsen rather than improve the status of justice. To leave all the consequences to God's wise hands and to be satisfied with acting out of good motives, – a common attitude found among evangelical Christians all over the world – very often works counter effectively.

We are called not only to do good to others, but also to act responsibly so that evil may not be further strengthened by our good intentions. To obey the commandment of love and to work for justice, we must mobilize not only our will but also our entire faculties and abilities including our trained reason and experiences. To be satisfied with acting out of good motives and not to take full responsibility for the consequences is a sign not of true faith in God but of laziness, as exemplified in the parable of talents by the man who returned only one talent to the master.

Christians are servants of God, but in regard to others in society they are also stewards in charge of distributing God's bounty to all people fairly at the proper time (Lk. 12:42). To provide for everyone what is most needed is the task of wise stewards of God. For a few to enjoy luxuries, while others are destitute of basic necessities for survival and human dignity constitutes abuse of God's property. To be faithfully economical with God's treasure, one has to have some basic knowledge of and influence on structures by which selfish human beings manage society.

Experiences throughout history and analyses of social scientists have clearly shown that human evils manifest themselves not only in actions of individual persons but also through social structures. Christians, therefore, are not necessarily forbidden *a priori* from changing them. There is no reason why changing social structures should be the monopoly of socialists.

In changing social structures, however, political means are neither the only nor the most desirable way for Christians, even though they need not be excluded in principle. The surest way is to educate individuals to respect the basic rights of all people, particularly of the weakest members of society. Christians can organize social movements to raise, first, the consciousness of fellow Christians on issues of justice and together with them conscientize the rest of the people by teaching and practising.

In some grave circumstances of injustice, concerted actions may be necessary in order to put some moral and political pressure on official or civilian organizations to be fair and just in their actions. This cannot be done without costs and risks on the part of Christians. As exemplified in the well-known case of Kitty Genovese,[18] average citizens try as much as possible to avoid meddling with affairs of others unless they directly interfere with their own interests. Few in modern societies are really concerned with social injustices unless they themselves are directly hurt by them. It is in this situation that Christians should take the trouble to initiate movements to change the structures or values which cause the injustices. Unless one believes in an impersonal law of historical development and waits for an automatic self-correction of social evils, somebody should start corrective actions, and Christians are responsible to do it in order to protect the rights of the oppressed.

But it is only in extreme situations that Christians can appeal to violence for social changes. Unless they are absolutely certain that there is no other door open beside violence and that the sufferings in the present structures clearly exceed possible damages produced by the violence, they should avoid it. We have also learned valuable lessons from the failure of Communist experiments in Eastern Europe. Violent revolutions have not paid off so far. Yet, there can be occasions where the use of violence is the only possibility open even to Christians and sometimes it is not only permissible but also responsible. Men can be exceedingly evil when their greed is masked by social structures which insure their collective interests.

Last but not least, evangelism and mission ministries are among the most important agents for improving social justice.[19] If the Kingdom of God is the only state of complete justice, recruiting one more person to it means ensuring justice to one more person. More concretely, more justice ought to be found in Christian communities than in society at large, and the growth of Christian communities implies more justice for more people. But above all, evangelism and mission ministries increase the number of the agents working for social justice. Christians are God's channels of justice, and greater justice is expected in society when more channels come into operation.

In reality, however, the numerical increase of believers has not necessarily secured greater justice in a society. More often than not, Christians have turned oppressors rather than liberators of the oppressed. Evangelism and missions which are really meaningful for promoting social justice, therefore, have to be coupled with sound biblical nurture. The new converts should grow to become mature followers of Christ willing to give up their possessions and pleasures for the sake of their disadvantaged neighbours. Evangelism, missions and nurture are the essential elements of the church's ministry. When the church grows as its Head wills, it will form a unique community where justice reigns within and which creates an invaluable condition for social justice. The Church faithful to its Master, therefore, is God's uniquely chosen people, through whom all people around them will be blessed.

NOTES

1. S.C. Mott, *Biblical and Social Change*, New York/Oxford: Oxford University Press, 1982, p. 61.

2. cf. Joel Feinberg, *Social Philosophy*, Englewood Cliffs: Prentice-Hall, 1973, p. 100.

3. John Rawls' so-called difference principle says that 'Social and economic inequalities are to be arranged so that they are both (a) to the greatest benefit of the least advantaged and (b) attached to offices and positions open to all under conditions of fair equality of opportunity' (*A Theory of Justice*, Cambridge, Mass.: Harvard University Press 1971, p. 83). Especially point (a) above is similar in intention to the justice of basic needs principle, even though in method of implementation it may be a little different.

4. I will not here go into the controversial question of the relationship between love and justice, but be satisfied with understanding that justice is one fundamental element of love. God's love never contradicts justice, but goes beyond it. Christ's vicarious death is the supreme example of God's love which at the same time satisfies the demand of God's justice. The Lord's summary of the commandments in terms of love (Mt. 22:34–40) is another proof.

5. Mott, *Biblical Ethics and Social Change*, p. 65.

6. Karl Barth, *Church Dogmatics*, trans. T.H.L. Parker, et. al., vol. 2: *The Doctrine of God*, 1, Edinburgh: T. & T. Clark, 1955, p. 386. Requoted from N. Wolterstorff, *Until Justice and Peace Embrace*, Grand Rapids: Eerdmans, 1983, p. 73.

7. Pain and suffering are not to be sharply distinguished as generally known. Of the two, I think pain is still more primitive than suffering. cf. Bong-Ho Son, 'Phenomenology of Pain,' in *Phenomenology of Life-World and Hermeneutics* (in Korean), Seoul, 1992.

8. C.S. Lewis, *The Problem of Pain*, New York: Macmillan, 1962, p. 89.

9. Group egoism and the cohesive power of groups have been persuasively analyzed by Reinhold Niebuhr in his *Moral Man and Immoral Society*, London: SCM, 1932.

10. cf. Bong-Ho Son, 'The Power and Egoism of the Modern State', *Transformation*, vol. 5, No. 3 (July/Sept. 1989): pp. 1–5.

11. Fung Yu-Ian, *A History of Chinese Philosophy*, vol. 1, *The Period of the Philosophers*, trans. D. Boddle, London: Allen & Unwin, 1952, pp. 120–121.

12. *Ibid.*, p. 123.

13. Mott, *Biblical Ethics and Social Change*, p. 60.

14. cf. K.G. Howkins, 'Christianity, Truth and Dialogue' in *Jesus Christ, the Only Way*, ed. P. Sookhdeo, Exeter: Paternoster, 1978, p. 45.

15. Mott calls God's retribution as justice, while distributive justice as righteousness. Love is involved in extending retributive justice to distributive righteousness (Mott, *Biblical Ethics and Social Change*, p. 62). But God's justice is not confined to wrathful judgment, and love includes righteousness and justice.

16. Wolterstorff, *Until Justice and Peace Embrace*, p. 71.

17. Mott, *Biblical Ethics and Social Change*, p. 112.

18. At 3 a.m. a young woman named Kitty Genovese was brutally assaulted in front of the Kew Garden housing complex. Thirty eight of the residents of Kew Gardens heard her crying out in terror, and they came to their windows to look. Not only did no one come to her aid, but no one even notified the police. For half an hour the scene continued, and finally the assault succeeded in killing Kitty Genovese. Yet the police had not been notified. See Gregory Mellema, *Individuals, Groups, and Shared Responsibility*, New York: Peter Lang, 1988, p. 57.

19. cf. Mott, *Biblical Ethics and Social Change*, p. 109ff.

18

David S. Lim

The author writes from the context of the injustices and violence of the Philippines. In this abridged chapter he maintains that justice is the basis of peace and that only biblical Christianity offers a coherent framework for people to work for the social transformation of our one world.

In his theses he expounds the uniqueness of Christ's understanding and self-giving to bring the Kingdom reign of peace and justice upon earth through the agency of his Church.

FIFTEEN THESES FOR JUSTICE AND PEACE

Does biblical Christianity have anything to offer to the modern world order in terms of justice and peace?[1] In the context of longings for tolerance and acceptance of pluralism, the claims of biblical Christianity to the uniqueness of Christ and his teachings is clearly being challenged.

This chapter presents fifteen theses which highlight various aspects of the claim to the uniqueness of Christ regarding justice and peace.[2] At the close of each thesis, some of the practical implications for the church's witness are also offered, so that we may be able to contribute positively to the working out of a 'new world order' (especially in the political sphere) that humanity has been longing for. This is because it asserts that only biblical Christianity offers a coherent framework by which the peoples of the world can work and struggle for true 'social transformation', which is used interchangeably with 'justice and peace' in this chapter.

THESIS ONE: THE UNIQUE AUTHORITY FOR CLAIMING CHRIST'S UNIQUENESS FOR JUSTICE AND PEACE IS THE BIBLE

Christ's uniqueness in the area of justice and peace is an absolute claim based on biblical revelation. There needs to be some reliable authority for objective standards by which we can judge whether the efforts for justice and peace are

---

Dr. David Lim taught at the Asia Theological Seminary, Manila and is now engaged in research and writing with the Oxford Centre for Mission Studies, U.K.

really helping to lessen the degeneration of societies into worse oppression and violence. As evangelicals, we begin with God's revelation in the Holy Scriptures. In them, we know of Jesus Christ who claimed to be the unique Son of God, the personal revelation of God who is his Father and the creator of the world. This God has revealed himself clearly, and people can know his will through his word revealed in the Bible. Jesus himself and the early church held the highest view of the authority of the Scriptures.

In affirming the revelational nature and scriptural authority of biblical Christianity, we claim not only the uniqueness of Christ, but also the universal normatives of his teachings on justice and peace. Those who deny the normative authority of the Bible, if they are consistent, will be lost in various relativisms. With no absolute norms, they would have no moral grounds by which to critique theologies, ideologies and structures that dehumanize people, and/or develop those which truly benefit humankind. Relativism or normlessness defeats the very purpose for advocating social transformation, since it doubts the reality of any claim to truth and justice.

Only revealed faith can offer the absolute basis for the pursuit of justice and peace. References to natural law, human reason, human rights, or human aspirations for happiness or freedom are good reasons but inadequate foundations, for pursuing these values.[3]

THESIS TWO: THE UNIQUE REVELATION OF GOD AND HIS WILL FOR JUSTICE AND PEACE IS THE HISTORICAL JESUS

The Bible reveals that Christ claimed that he was the unique Son of God who came to bring a definitive revelation of the character and will of God. His life, death and resurrection, as well as his teachings provide the central focus of God's redemption history. Thus he offers the historical and normative foundation for doing God's will. Most religions, philosophies and ideologies do not allow truth to depend on the events of history. Biblical Christianity contends that biblical events are placed in the continuum of world history. This is in striking contrast to the indifference which is generally seen in other religions' low regard for the significance of particular events even in secular history.[4]

Jesus Christ claimed that God himself was uniquely present in him, and thus the origin, meaning and destiny of all things were being revealed in and through him. He was not just a model (or even the best model) of Gods will. His life was the story of events by which the human situation was being concretely and irreversibly transformed by God himself, particularly to fulfil his redemptive will.

In the historical Jesus, the promises of God's redemption declared in the Old Testament were fulfilled and demonstrated in reality. The Old Testament looked forward to the arrival of a Messiah-king who would come to do perfect justice and thereby bring in peace or *shalom* (Isa. 11:2–5; 61:1f; Ps. 72:1–4, etc.). God created the human race to obey his will, so that they might give him free obedience and love. But they chose to disobey, and thus developed into a multitude of selfish, unjust and warring peoples, instead of a multicultural community of love, justice and peace. To redeem them out of this tragedy, God came on earth in Jesus Christ who lived out and taught about

God's love, justice and peace (cf. Lk. 1:68–79; Ac. 10:36,38; Eph. 2:17). People are now being called to believe and follow this Christ who will liberate them from their sins, so they may be transformed to love God and their neighbours (cf. Col. 1:19–23; Eph. 2:11–18).

Without this normative revelation of God in the historical Jesus, we would lack the intellectual, moral and spiritual resources to deal with the multiplicity of exploitation and conflict in the world. There are no other absolute norms by which social orders in history can be evaluated and judged as to whether or not they truly reflect justice and peace.

THESIS THREE: CHRIST'S UNIQUE GOAL IS PEACE ON EARTH

Called the Prince of Peace (Isa. 9:6; 11:1–8, cf. Lk. 1:79), Jesus came making and preaching *shalom* or peace (Ac. 10:36; Eph. 2:15–17). Peace, the kingdom of God,[5] the age-to-come, new heavens and new earth, eternal life, new humanity are the principal names and images in the Scriptures for the ultimate goal of world history. It is not just an eternal or heavenly goal of world history. It is not just an eternal or heavenly peace, nor an interior or inner peace, but an earthly peace – 'peace on earth' (Lk. 2:14). It is the condition of full harmony in humanity's relationships with God, neighbours, nature and within themselves (cf. Isa. 11:6–8), which the Creator originally intended, but which has not been realized because of sin.

The Jews in Jesus' time knew of two ages: 'this age' which referred to present history, full of sin, evil, suffering, oppression and violence; and 'the age to come', the future era of universal redemption where people will experience freedom, love, justice and peace in all its fullness. For example, the book of Isaiah envisioned a new world where people plant crops and raise livestock in abundance and safety (32:20), and the same farmer will eat what he plants (65:21–23).[6] Jesus did not alter this vision of his contemporaries, but rather urged his followers to be concerned with history and so participate in shaping it towards the kingdom of God.

In this age, the kingdom of *shalom* includes sight to the blind, healing of the sick, bread to the hungry, justice to the prisoners, forgiveness of sinners, freedom for the oppressed, and preaching to the poor right here on earth (cf. Lk. 4:18f; 7:22). The King of the peaceable kingdom has come; his kingdom is not just the eternal heaven where souls will go after death, but is to be found also in the models and partial concretizations of that future world order which can be experienced through human actions in history. The final and definitive world peace will be fully realized at the end of this on-going history, but its blessings of abundant life become realities in partial yet real ways now, just as they did in the life of Jesus.

THESIS FOUR: CHRIST'S UNIQUE WAY TO ATTAIN PEACE IS IN AND THROUGH SOCIAL JUSTICE

Jesus' and his contemporaries' view of *shalom* included all humanity living in harmony, not just with their Creator, but also with their fellow human beings. This original intention of God was marred by human sin, and its main manifestation is injustice, where the strong take advantage of the weak. *Shalom* will be established to the degree in which justice is achieved: 'And the fruit of justice will be peace, and the result of righteousness, quietness and trust forever' (Isa. 32:17). So those who desire peace must work for justice (cf. Isa. 58:6f).

This was also clearly taught in the wisdom literature of the Old Testament: 'By justice a king gives stability to the land, but one who exacts gifts ruins it' (Prov. 29:4), and 'If a king judges the poor with equity, his throne will be established forever' (v. 14). Justice brings in the benefits of *shalom*, such as joy (10:28; 11:10,18; 29:2), life (11:4,19,30; 12:28; cf. 10:2,11), honour (11:11,20; 13:9; 16:31), freedom (11:21), goodness (11:23; 12:12; cf. 16:7), and prosperity (13:21f; 14:11; 15:6; 16:12). In preaching peace, Jesus understood that his messianic mission included the proclamation of freedom to the prisoners . . , the release of the oppressed . . .' (Lk. 4:18; cf. Isa. 61:1f). To work and struggle for justice is the way to attain *shalom* (cf. Lk. 1:46–55; 6:20–26; 7:22; 10:30–36).

Although *shalom* goes beyond justice, there can be no *shalom* without justice. In *shalom*, each person experiences and enjoys justice. This is because *shalom* is experienced in an ethical community. Wolterstorff writes: 'If individuals are not granted what is due to them, if their claim on others is not acknowledged by those others, if others do not carry out their obligations to them, then shalom is wounded . . .'[7] So *shalom* exists as a characteristic of a responsible community in which God's will (even in the form of human rights and just laws) for his people is obeyed.[8]

Hence the 'liberation mandate' to work for social justice is part and parcel of Jesus' promise of *shalom* to those who will follow him. To attain peace, we must struggle for justice.

THESIS FIVE: CHRIST'S UNIQUE PERSPECTIVE IS THAT THE LACK OF JUSTICE AND PEACE IS DUE TO THE REALITY OF SOCIAL SIN

Jesus Christ taught that the root of all injustices and disruptions of peace is sin, which emanates from the human heart (Mk. 7:21–23). Yet it was manifested in the various social institutions of his day, such as the temple, the sabbath laws, the Sanhedrin, and the Roman state (Mt. 15:1–13; 21:12f; 22:15–22; 23:1–39; 26:3–5, 57–67; Mk. 8:15; 2:21–3:6; Lk. 11:37–54) which were controlled by satanic forces (Mk. 3:22–30; Lk. 13:31–33). Because of these social evils,[9] justice and peace will always remain an eschatological hope until injustice is eradicated by his return. Meanwhile, his followers will suffer persecution from these ungodly structures, including the most basic, the family (Mt. 10:17–39; 24:9; Lk. 12:11f; 21:12–19; J. 15:18–25; 16:20).

In his ministry, Jesus highlighted the oppressive nature of these institutions. Standing before Pilate, Jesus declared that his kingdom transcends the worldly power structures, and that it can not be reduced to the power plays and struggles of human social orders. It is God, the absolute king who gave Pilate his position, and who will take his position away.[10]

Hence the early church viewed the world order as basically evil (Rom.

12:12), characterized by sensuality, materialism, naturalism, hypocrisy and egoism (1 Jn. 2:15f). In relation to what Jesus did on the cross, Paul considered that the 'rulers of the age' were either the human agents of spiritual powers or the powers that worked through human agents, or most probably both (I Cor. 2:8; cf. Col. 2:14f).[11] It seems clear that biblical references to the 'powers (that be)' have double or bipolar referents, i.e., including both spiritual and institutional forces.[12] They promote oppression rather than justice, war rather than peace. They are often firmly approved by the individual members of society, allegedly for their common welfare, survival or security. Hence Christ's redemptive mission to bring in justice and peace had to reckon with and struggle against these social evils.

Hence the unique Christ calls for the desacralization of power and the relativization of political systems. All claims to authority of any kind, which demand obedience, some even total obedience, tantamount to 'worship' from its subjects have to be relativized by the biblical claim that 'only Jesus is king'. Historically, biblical Christianity has been a desacralizing force in the world. Much of the sacral prestige (even divine rights of kings) attached to ancient rulers has been forsaken; but sadly, the secralization of power has taken on new forms. Secular versions of the old sacral power structures continue to surface, even in the modern post-technological world of democratic states. These include commercialism, tribalism, racism, militarism, national security states, developmentalism, etc.

Christians should find their identity in the kingdom and thus resist being coopted by the ungodly values of the present order. Recognizing the reality and pervasiveness of social sin should lead to a basic stance of non-conformity to the world, so that one becomes a signpost pointing to Christ's uniqueness.

THESIS SIX: CHRIST'S UNIQUE BASIS FOR PURSUING JUSTICE AND PEACE IS GOD'S GRACE

Biblical Christianity grounds the responsibility for seeking justice and peace in the grace of God, as revealed on the cross. On the cross, God's grace was poured out on all people, regardless of their status. Jesus spoke of God's love for all sinners, including those who have consciously disobeyed God and become his enemies. Thus the fullest expression of God's grace is non-discriminatory love that even extends to the ungodly (cf. Mt. 5:43–47),[13] which should serve as the basis for Christian ethics (v. 48).[14] 'Whatever you wish that others should do to you, do so to them' (Mt. 7:12) serves as the basis of justice, for there is no discrimination based on any social status (cf. James 2:1–7).

'Hence 'the cross is the heart of grace which confers worth', for God is able to love even those who have demerits.[15] Grace confers worth before people have the opportunity to gain merits. Thus one's worth is a status that God confers, not something that one intrinsically has. People can partake of this grace only when they abandon all considerations of the worth of the objects of their love. This they can do, but only in Christ and the cross. Only in the unique crucified Christ can people find God's grace revealed, and their own self-worth as children of the God who loves them and who desires justice and peace for them.

Hence biblical Christianity should live out this hope, based on the reality of God's grace. Anyone, anywhere, at anytime may be able to experience the reality of God's grace in Christ. We can invite and challenge people to receive the world order that God intended for all to experience. All people regardless of their backgrounds can avoid being trapped in the perennial terrors and sufferings of oppression and violence. So we must not only dissect and proclaim God's judgement on false powers and hopes; we must also provide the vision, relationships and structures that are so inviting for people to see God's grace coming into their midst in freedom, justice and peace, even while not putting an absolute value on these efforts. We should build alternatives that demonstrate to all that God's love is for all, for each can choose to live according to his gracious and loving terms rather than their own self-determined terms.

THESIS SEVEN: THE UNIQUE RESPONSE THAT GOD'S GRACE REQUIRES IS FAITH IN JESUS CHRIST

The only hope for justice and peace to be realized in our fallen planet by God's grace is for people to be empowered by God's Spirit through conversion to faith in Jesus Christ. The problem of sin, both individual and social, demands that people need not only guidance and vision, but also redemption and power to pursue the vision. Jesus called people to repent from their sins and to follow him in realizing God's kingdom (Mk. 1:15; Lk. 9:23–27; 14:26–33; Mt. 7:21–27; 10:37f; Jn. 7:37–39; 16:7–11). In working for social transformation, especially during times of crisis and persecution, it is the Spirit of Christ who will provide the wisdom, strength and perseverance to overcome the tensions, discouragements and defeats of the struggle (cf. Mt. 10:17–20; Lk. 12:11f; Jn. 15:26–16:15). Thus the early church taught that spiritual conversion is necessary for the new order to be realized (cf. 2 Cor. 5:17).

Many cultures today have accepted Christian standards of justice and peace, but have rejected or neglected the only source of power to attain and maintain them. The result is an increasing decline from those values and norms in which conformity to them involves spiritual strength for self-discipline and perseverance. Moreover, many efforts for social transformation have failed because of dishonesty, greed, power struggles, corruption and conflicts. Human nature is stained with sin and social structures are distorted by injustices and power play. They need spiritual transformation beginning in individuals and extending to the whole society. As people turn to the unique Christ and are transformed by his Spirit, their individual lives and social relationships will improve substantially, liberating them to live more fulfilled lives and build better structures.

Education may lessen the selfish expressions of sin by broadening people's horizons and influencing them to pursue nobler goals. But substantial and definitive deliverance from sin can be effected only by turning their devotion to full obedience to God. This is not to say that people are totally bad, or that they are more bad than good, but that even their goodness is infected by sin, which exposes them to temptations when they gain wealth or power. This does not mean that wealth and power should not be given them, for God desires that people should have freedom even if they abuse it. They will surely abuse it (as history shows), unless they have a higher loyalty which is established only by a sense of contentment and gratitude for God's grace in Christ.

Many evangelistic messages are found wanting. They call only for belief but not for obedience, pointing people to knowledge *about* Christ, but not to forsake all to follow him. Obedience to the unique Christ has been compromised by easy believism, resulting in the preaching of 'cheap grace'. At the same time the kingdom of God emphasized by Jesus and the message of Christ as the king who brings a new order is almost excluded from modern evangelism.

THESIS EIGHT: THE CHURCH IS CHRIST'S UNIQUE INSTRUMENT TO EXTEND JUSTICE AND PEACE ON THE EARTH

Jesus called people to follow him and his socio-political option by joining his church, a unique community whose relationships are marked by justice and peace and whose mission is to spread the good news of justice and peace on earth. He called them as salt and light (Mt.5:13–16), sowers (Mt. 13:3ff, 24ff), leaven (v. 33), and witnesses (Acts 1:8) – all of which implies that their task is the outward expansion of his kingdom on earth. He commanded them to go into all the world to make disciples, teaching them to obey all that he has taught them (Mt. 28:19f).

The early church slowly yet increasingly obeyed. But soon, the Church lost and only sporadically recovered this social transformation dimension of his teaching and their mission. Yet generally throughout history, the Church has had a positive socio-political impact on the world. The more closely she called people to follow the way of Jesus, the more positive has been that impact in creating forms of socio-political life that ensure power-sharing and enhance community harmony, social justice and world peace.

A good example is the rise of modern democracy and its attendant freedoms. The so-called Western democratic ideals are not indigenous to the Western cultures, but arose primarily through the West's encounter with Christian values. The concepts of freedom, human rights,[16] political pluralism (multi-party systems), and greater tolerance of opposing views come basically from Christian teaching. Because of secularization, most people are not aware that these democratic values and institutions have come from Christian roots, especially in the Reformed tradition.[17] Tragically, the reactionary roles of many churches have contributed to this lack of appreciation, and even to the constant suspicion that biblical Christianity is somehow indifferent or retrogressive and unhelpful in tackling the modern issues of social justice and world peace.

An informed historical perspective, however, would also attribute the most significant transformations of unjust relationships and power structures, such as racism, class and caste systems,[18] subordination of women, domination of elites, and unequal trade treaties, to the influence of Christianity. We hope that churches today will recover this sense of transformative mission – that they are called by Christ to bring more freedom, justice and peace in this world.

THESIS NINE: CHRIST'S UNIQUE MODEL FOR JUSTICE AND PEACE IS THE CHURCH

The main way by which Jesus commanded his Church to serve his kingdom is for her to demonstrate the reality of his transformative power right in her midst: 'By this shall all people know that you are my disciples, if you love one another' (Jn. 13:35). This was exemplified by Jesus and his twelve disciples as they shared a common purse (Jn. 12:6; 13:39), and by the earliest house-churches in Jerusalem as they pooled their resources together (Ac. 2:42–45; 4:32–37).

Such groups of peace based on sharing were formed with the basic understanding that God's grace produces relatively egalitarian communities of love and justice (cf. 2 Cor. 8:14f). God's grace brings forth 'creative justice' which reaches out and accepts the unworthy, the unlovely, the weak, the outcasts and the unprivileged into communities where every one receives his/ her rightful share in God's loving provision for their basic needs (Mt. 23:23; Mk. 10:17–31; cf. Lk. 1:52f; 3:10–14; 12:13–34; 14:12–14).[19] They are to serve each other in a loving community of peace, sharing their faith, problems, possessions and even their own lives together. Each would contribute according to his/her Spirit-endowed gifts, and each would receive according to her/his needs.

'Christ is our peace' is revealed in the Church as she breaks down all barriers, particularly the wall between Jews and Gentiles (the ultimate aliens to the Jews). The Church is the sign of barriers being broken down between people of different ethnic, cultural and even religious backgrounds (Eph. 2:14–19).

Hence churches should be communities where just and harmonious relationships abound, where people from different backgrounds (racial, social, educational, economic, political and religious) are accepted 'as they are', and where *agapē* love is extended even to the unlovely. Sadly, most churches fall short of this model. We need to develop new models of communal life – in smaller groups.[20] where love, freedom, justice and peace can be lived out as mini-democracies of God's people.[21] Thus will the churches be in a good position to bring people-groups into better democracies in the world of tomorrow.[22]

THESIS TEN: CHRIST'S UNIQUE LOCUS FOR JUSTICE AND PEACE IS AMONG THE POOR

Jesus 'preached good news to the poor':[23] They will live in *shalom* as they obtain justice, for they will be delivered from poverty and oppression. Jesus associated with the poor and outcasts, defending against the religious, economic and political elites of his day.[24] In siding with the poor,[25] he criticized the religio-political establishment, earning mortal enemies who succeeded in plotting to kill him (cf. Mt. 12:9–14; Mk. 12:1–40; Jn. 11:45–53). The elite of his time felt threatened, for he chose to give dignity to the marginalized 'sinners' (e.g. tax collectors, prostitutes, drunkards) and the deprived poor (women, children, the sick, lepers, Samaritans). He crossed social barriers, thus provoking hostility, and challenged the social order of his time.[26]

The historical reason for Jesus' death was his prophetic critique of the temple-state and state-religion and their political guardians (the high priests, the Sadducees, and the Pharisees). The theological significance of his death was its sacrificial atonement for the sins of the world.[27] Both the historical events and the theological meaning converge to give the full interpretation of Jesus' death on the cross. And his resurrection from the dead reveals God's vindication of this peace-making 'servant of the Lord'. Having risen and ascended, he pours out his Spirit on all, so that somehow and in various ways, humankind, especially the poor, may experience the blessings of his kingdom.

Thus, Jesus' option will cause discomfort and upheaval in any social order for it is 'good news to the poor', who are the victims and marginal peoples of society. Those who represent the status quo will respond in indifference, mockery or even hatred. The new order he prescribed involves a break from the established idolatries and prevailing assumptions of the present world. This implies that God is against those who live affluently at the expense of the poor. Sadly, many modern Christians have accepted uncritically the dominant values and structures of injustice and violence today.

The emergence of 'theologies of the poor', especially in Asia,[28] has opened up new areas of encounter between Christians and their non-Christian neighbours. Christian encounters with Asian cultures have been dominated by understanding the great religions on intellectual and doctrinal levels. This should remain our important concern. But these developing theologies have helped bring the churches closer to the 'difficult to reach' peoples on the level of folk-religion and folk-culture.[29] The writings, cultus and traditions of Asia's religions have been dominated by the concerns of the religious and social elite. It is popular history in the form of legends, music, poetry and religion which provides insights into the worldview and needs of the masses of ordinary people. As poor Christians interpret their faith in dialogue with their traditional folk spiritualities, they will enrich our understanding of Christ's uniqueness.

THESIS ELEVEN: CHRIST'S UNIQUE RATIONALE FOR IDENTIFICATION WITH THE POOR IS THE BIBLICAL CONCEPT OF 'THE IMAGE OF GOD'

Jesus and the early Christians preached good news to the poor because of their underlying concept of human dignity and sense of self-worth based on the Old Testament. They perceived that the identity of every human being is by virtue of his being created by God in his image, and thus being objects of God's grace. Human merit does not contribute to human creation and worth, and their demerits do not deprive them of redemption and worth: 'Grace confers identity.'[30]

Since human dignity is gained by grace, and not merited by status or works, each person (even the poorest of the poor) can and should freely decide to use his/her God-given talents or gifts for serving others. Each person and group has gifts to contribute to the whole community which others need.

Human dignity is more than 'human rights', the rights of individuals before the law in modern jurisprudence. It is the right to the basic necessities for a decent life in the context of a caring community, 'the right to be human'.[31] This includes 'sustenance rights': if we do not care for the poor, we are violating the God-given rights of the poor.[32] Biblical Christianity relativizes all the perceived and man-made inequalities between peoples by stressing their common dignity as creatures of God.

This calls the world Church to empower the poor,[33] not only by sharing with the poor, but also by becoming advocates for the poor who are struggling against economic injustice and political oppression. The church should be sympathetic with revolutionary movements.[34] In the past, this has led to the liberation of low castes in India, slum-dwellers in Chile, and blacks in U.S.A. and South Africa.[35] She should act with those who desire to allow every level of society to exercise local democratic power, promote equal rights, and throw off any oppressive structure.

THESIS TWELVE: CHRIST'S UNIQUE APPROACH TO BRING FORTH JUSTICE AND PEACE IS SUFFERING SERVANTHOOD

Jesus taught that we attain greatness not through the exercise of political authority and military might, but by our willingness to serve others even at great personal cost and sacrifice, contrary to the 'way of the Gentiles' (Mk. 10:42–44). He also set himself as the model, the servant-king who calls his people to be a servant-people (v. 45). When he said, 'My kingdom is not of this world' (Jn. 18:26), he did not mean it was not geographically located in the world, but that his rule is qualitatively different from that of the world.[36]

Jesus combined the concepts of leadership and servanthood: whereas the common understanding of leadership calls for an arrogant display of power to satisfy the desire for personal glory and fame, Jesus' way of leadership calls for self-sacrifice, giving up one's life to serve others. The Jesus-way is not domineering nor self-pleasing, but rather redemptive and serving: 'for Christ did not please himself' (Rom. 15:3).

The central message of biblical Christianity is Christ and him crucified (1 Cor. 2:2). His power was demonstrated and ennobled by his voluntary death on the cross. His way to bring heavenly peace was not by exalting himself, but by humbling or denying himself to the point of dying an unjust and violent death. Such 'non-dominating power' is to use power to forgive, not to retaliate; to suffer injustice, not to inflict suffering; to care, not to hate; to serve, not to dominate. Thus the world of power struggles is scandalized by Christ's sacrificial servanthood.

So the view that Jesus was politically neutral or other-worldly is false: the authorities saw him as a threat and had him killed as a political criminal. Jesus offered a unique political option in his time. The Sadducees and Herodians used pragmatism and expediency to preserve their religion by collaborating with the Roman invaders. The Zealots wanted to drive away the Romans by violent force. The Essenes chose to withdraw from society to keep their religious life. And the Pharisees were preoccupied with their religiosity and segregated themselves from politics. But Jesus heralded a unique approach to handling power: through engagement or involvement marked by sacrificial love to offer justice and peace to all.

Justice and peace can emerge only when people are willing to pay the price of building relationships. The price is high for relationships are not built from positions of power. They are most effective and most facilitative when built from positions, of vulnerability.[37] Hence some kind of 'downward mobility' to identify with the poor is necessary for effecting true justice and peace.

Perhaps the church should also be transforming herself into a more humble and servant-like structure, away from her Christendom complex. Happily there seems to be a growing movement towards basic Christian communities, house-churches, covenant or intentional communities, and other forms of smaller Christian groupings that form loose networks for mission and social transformation. Each of these small Christian communities accepts the principle of servanthood, for the benefit of its own members and also for the larger community. They should nurture more Christian business-people and politicians who will use their power to serve God. This servant-church structure may be the best way forward for the world-wide Church in organizing herself for extending the unique Christ's kingdom on earth.

THESIS THIRTEEN: CHRIST'S UNIQUE METHOD FOR JUSTICE AND PEACE IS NON-VIOLENT, FORGIVING LOVE TOWARD ALL, INCLUDING OPPRESSORS

Jesus rejected violence as a mean of extending the kingdom. The use of arms and military force will never be able to usher in the kingdom. The way of Jesus is the way of servanthood and non-violence, not the sword. He taught that we are to love our enemies, because God does (Mt. 5:45; Lk. 6:35). The basis for his non-violence is not the effectiveness of non-violent strategies, nor the survival of the human race, but the very nature of God.

The command to love our enemies shows that our first duty towards oppressors is pastoral: to help them recover their humanity. Non-violence opens the way for both the oppressed and the oppressors to rise above their present condition to become more of what God intended them to be. The spirit of forgiveness is willing to submit to injustice and violence. It is not cowardly fear of reprisals, but hope that faith in God may be awakened in the other's life.[38] For 'we fight not against flesh and blood, but against the powers and principalities . . .' (Eph. 6:12). Oppressors who 'know not what they do' are also victims of the delusion-system that evil spiritual forces use to thwart God's purposes. Wars and revolutions will fail to bring true justice and peace, because they rely on the same means as the system that they seek to change.[39] One has to use spiritual weapons (prayer, fasting, forgiveness, etc.) against the system itself and those who carry out its dictates. It may seem impossible, but it can be done. God's grace is revealed immediately and concretely when we let go our hatred and vengeance and rest on God's love and justice. This witness can be uniquely Christian in our time.

Yet at the same time, it must be clear that although Jesus did not join the Zealots, he was clearly on the side of the poor and oppressed and against the power structures of his time. While he was wrongly accused of assuming the role of the Messianic leader of an armed revolution, he was rightly accused of taking the side of the poor against the established authorities. Thus, our non-violence must be equally credible and revolutionary: if our non-violence is being ideologically used against the poor to accept peacefully the violence of the oppressive order, or if we benefit from the sufferings of others while we preach non-violence, then we contradict the pattern and spirit of Jesus. To follow Jesus and give our non-violence integrity, we must be sure that our decisions and actions will set us on the side of the poor, and that they be so clearly made that we are likely to be convicted of subversion by the established order. 'In Christ there is a necessary relationship between non-violence and suffering . . .'[40]

THESIS FOURTEEN: CHRIST'S UNIQUE ATTITUDE TOWARDS PEOPLE OF OTHER PERSUASIONS ON JUSTICE AND PEACE IS OPEN AND NON-EXCLUSIVE

When his disciples reported other people doing the same works that they were doing, Jesus replied that 'those who are not against us are for us' (Mk. 9:40; Lk. 9:50).[41] He treated people from various religious and ideological backgrounds – Jew, Samaritan, Roman or Greek, and Pharisee, Sadducee, Zealot or Herodian – with an attitude that was open and inclusive rather than exclusive. Having a humble servant-spirit, he was tolerant of diverse and even dissenting views, without losing his convictions.

So in the New Testament, Jesus and the early Church shared the gospel primarily through 'attracting evangelism', through building friendships and provoking questions through words and works that evidenced the presence, love, power, justice and peace of God and his kingdom. The responsibility rests on the Christian – what he must be and do in order to effect questions in people to which Jesus is the answer. Being a witness is not developing good sales techniques and gimmicks, but quality discipleship, both personal and corporate. The witnesses should be Christ-like so that their lives are so attractive, that they elicit such searching questions as 'Why are you like this?'

The pluralist ideology of our times calls for tolerance of various loyalties. Affirming the uniqueness of Christ has been seen as offensive narrow-mindedness; but pluralism has not explained away the validity of holding universal convictions. Nevertheless, it should help Christians to develop a more sensitive and non-triumphalistic attitude towards other religions and ideologies.[43]

Exclusive claims for Christ often go with exclusivist attitudes towards others, yet we need to accept the integrity of others, build friendships with patience, and allow ourselves to be vulnerable and open.

This also means that we can cooperate with people of other religions and ideologies in social movements and projects that move towards justice and peace. As we engage in dialogue, we can expect and welcome different signs of God's grace working in the lives of non-Christians. Situations may arise that turns this dialogue into witness, where basic differences have to be clarified. We know we need to aim prayerfully at conversion for a holistic witness. But such witnessing need not always be explicit; sometimes implicit ways may be more effective.

THESIS FIFTEEN: CHRIST'S UNIQUE BASIS FOR NON-EXCLUSIVISM IS GENERAL REVELATION

The basis for Christ's non-exclusivistic approach is the concept of common grace and general revelation. Jesus taught that the Holy Spirit works in the world (Jn. 16:8–11), and the New Testament teaches that he is 'the true light that gives light to every person' (1:9). The work of the Holy Spirit is clearly discerned in the activities where Christ is explicitly mentioned (1 Cor. 12:3; 1 Jn. 4:3f; cf. Rom. 8:10f). and linked integrally with the church and her ministry (1 Cor. 3:16f; 12:4–13; Ac. 1:8; Eph. 2:21f). There is also another work of the Spirit among all people, convicting them and opening them to God in their movements toward freedom and love (2 Cor. 3:17; Rom. 5:5). Both these movements in the Church and in the world will converge in the realization of the future new world order. The criteria for discerning the Spirit's work in all social and religious movements must include openness to Christ and acceptance of his eschatological vision.[44]

Evangelical theology has developed mainly on salvation history that starts with the Fall. We need to set our witness on the common ground that we all share as God's created beings, so that we can stand and act in solidarity and live in peaceful harmony with our non-Christian neighbours and friends. Fall-based theology has tended to separate Christians from their neighbours, but a creation-based theology will build on various commonalities that will allow for a more positive witness in the world. Human beings are sinful, but as God's created beings they retain the capacity and desire no matter how faint, to seek him and his will.[45] We cannot deny that there are many morally upright and peace-loving non-Christian people today. They need to be viewed as sincere seekers after truth, justice, peace and even salvation, rather than only as miserable sinners.

By 'general revelation' is meant not a universal availability of the knowledge of God's salvation and will, but a universal possession of some aspects of the knowledge of his will (Rom. 1:18–2:16). God has not forsaken the world that he created; he continues to love the world. Though sin restricts people from the full knowledge of truth, general revelation provides the basic foundation for people to appreciate the unique revelation of Jesus Christ.

Human quests for justice and peace can be good and sincere efforts to work out the innate human impulse to know God, and thus may lead towards the truth, including salvific truths which can be found ultimately in the unique Christ. Non-Christian religions and ideologies represent humanity's sincere longing for God and his peace, so they should not be rejected totally as false or demonic. They could be used as 'bridges', so that the gospel can be seen as a continuity with God's creation-plan (cf. Ac. 14:15–18; 17:22–32).[46] The uniqueness of Christ should therefore be seen not as an isolated event in the history of God's dealings with humankind, but as a continuity of blurred interconnecting seed-events which reveal God's will to human beings in their varied cultures. Other faiths and ideologies contain 'elements of continuity'[47] which Christ fulfils and realizes.

This attempt to build bridges on 'common grounds' will bring the gospel into a closer relationship with people. Rather than condemning people who seek after justice and peace, even in ways different from ours, we should patiently start from where they are and find more effective ways of showing them the finality of Christ and his kingdom. It is possible that the Holy Spirit uses the experiences of other cultures, religions and ideologies to show us how to draw closer to Christ.[48]

CONCLUSION

As the world stumbles into the twenty-first century in search of a new world order with secular concepts of justice and peace, it is our hope that biblical Christianity will be able to serve the world's best interests. Let the relevance of Christ be shown through a clear witness, in life and thought, so that we can evolve those social conditions most conducive to the fullest development of the human family. Let the Church serve not as another self-serving religious institution, but as a movement rooted in the biblical vision of the kingdom of God and the unique Christ, so as to transform the secularized and semi-Christianized versions of the new world order.

We need to develop mission programmes which integrate social transformation with religious creativity in building communities of justice and peace. Over the centuries, the Church has had no consistent theology of power by which Christians were to function in the political and economic spheres and contribute positively to world justice and peace. Often Christians have entered the public arena with naivety, fascinated by the splendour of power and easily serving as agents of the status quo. Church growth has not always led to more justice or more peace. It is when the Church has stood nearest to and advocated most clearly the biblical vision of justice and peace that her witness has produced less starvation and more bread, less exploitation and more justice, less wars and more peace.

It is not biblical Christianity that has failed, but its adherents who failed to understand and live according to its standards. Those who lived consistently have received its blessings and have helped the world to see a better tomorrow based on the unique Christ's option of freedom, justice and peace. Perfect obedience to the unique Christ is not possible in this life, except for God's grace working to set people free from sin and to offer their lives to contribute to society's welfare. Therefore, we cannot hope to see perfect peace in this life. But since it is our eternal goal, we have to do all we can to turn history into a movement in the direction of justice and peace that the unique Christ offers to all humankind.

NOTES

1. This paper puts 'justice' before 'peace' for it avers that the former is the basis of the latter: there can be no peace without justice. See Thesis Four below.

2. Though Christians may never come to full agreement on their interpretation of biblical revelation, the writer believes that further reflection and discussion will lead by 'progressive illumination' towards, and not differ much from, the 'biblical theology of justice and peace' presented in this work.

3. Cf. Wolterstorff, 18f.

4. Cf. Newbigin, 50ff.

5. On the Kingdom of God, cf. Samuel & Sugden, *CRHN*, 128–150; Mott, 82–106; and Ellul, 160–162.

6. Note that the conditions envisioned were not the final state of the new earth: people still sin and die, serpents still eat dust. It hopes that the vision will be attained in this life, to a certain degree, even before the eternal state begins.

7. Wolterstorff, 70.

8. Cf. ibid., 69f.

9. On social sin, cf. Mott, 3–21; and Sider, 117–60.

10. Wright, 15.

11. Ibid., 14.

12. Ibid., 15.

13. Mott, 39–42, 59–81.

14. Ibid., 23, cf. 22–38.

15. C. Sugden in Samuel & Sugden, *AD*, 69.

16. Though the terminology of 'human rights' is Stoic in origin, the motivation for its development is Christian; the modern concept of rights comes from early Protestantism, esp. Puritanism; cf. Mott, 52.

17. Wolterstorff, 3–41; cf. Moberg, 17–53; and D. Little, *Religion, Order and Law: A Study in Pre-Revolutionary England* (New York: Harper & Row, 1969).

18. On the impact of biblical Christianity on the caste system, cf. V. Mangalwadi, *Truth and Social Reform* (Delhi: Nivedit, 1989), and V. Samuel & C. Sugden, *The Gospel Among our Hindu Neighbours* (Bangalore, 1983).

19. Mott shows that 'creative justice' goes beyond human rights – relationships are based not just on equity and reciprocity, but also unilateral and self-sacrificing acceptance of the marginalized (pp. 64–67). 'Needs become rights under the provisions of the covenant because the basic needs of all are to be met by the whole community' (cf. Lev. 25:35f), which implies that each member of the community should be strong enough to maintain her/his position in relation to the other members (p. 67).

20. Cf. Sider, 179–190; and 'Thesis Twelve' below.

21. Wallis states, 'In the face of a society whose affluence keeps others in hunger and misery, the church must become poor. In the face of a world-system embroiled in a violent striving for power, the church must become a suffering servant. In the face of a society of mass alienation and fragmenting isolation, the church must be a healing community of reconciliation. In the face of a social order dependent upon docility and conformity, the church must become an agent of resistance and change' (p. 37).

22. Wolterstorff notes, 'Our deepest dilemma today, causing deep rifts within our world-order, is our inability or refusal to devise a social system that comes at all close to satisfying both of these deeply human motivations. The West grasps freedom at the cost of inequality, thereby consigning the economically impoverished to all the constraints of poverty. The East grasps equality at the cost of freedom, thereby consigning the politically powerless to all the inequities of tyranny' (p. 39).

23. In OT, *'Anawim* or *'aniyim* refer to the deprived, needy, oppressed in economic terms.

24. Whereas the people in biblical times defined their identity mainly in religious terms, people in today's secular world find their identity through the material possessions or living standards they have gained.

25. On God's special concern for the poor, cf. Mott, 64ff; Sider, 53–78; and Samuel & Sugden, *AD*, 59f.

27. Isaiah 53's suffering servant has been used as the biblical basis for this interpretation.

28. These 'liberation theologies' tend to perceive Christ in lines of liberal theology, which actually undermines the richness, power and even absoluteness of their claims.

(They have been influenced by the dichotomistic tendencies of Western theology, which have been predominantly docetic). Evangelical 'transformation theologies,' with balanced biblical Christologies should be able to enrich this kind of growing hermeneutic and understanding of Jesus Christ, and also strengthen these theologies, with definite claims to normativeness and finality of our struggles for justice and peace.

29. There are evidences that expatriate missionaries and local church leaders in the past have discouraged evangelism of the poor for fear that their conversion would hinder the evangelism of the higher classes: the poor can be an 'embarrassment to the church'. Cf. J. Massey, 'Christians in North India: Historical Perspectives with Special Reference to Christians in the Punjab,' *Religion and Society*, XXXIV, 3 (September, 1987), 88ff; cited in Nazir-Ali, 17ff.

30. C. Sugden in Samuel and Sugden, *AD*, 58, cf. 58–61.

31. Ibid., 59.

32. Wolterstorff, 81ff.

33. The modern concept of 'people empowerment' includes all such projects that enhance the ability of the marginalized and oppressed masses (they are 'powerless' in terms of economic, political and military power) to take their destiny into their own hands so as to create a better future for themselves and their children.

34. Cf. Nazir-Ali, 170–181. Wallis avers, 'Though the church rejects the revolution-aries' new myths and idolatries, refuses their ideological visions based upon false human hopes, and regards their means of violence and death as signs of their conformity with the world, it keenly feels the oppression and aspirations of those who revolt against the established order of things. The church has the unique and crucial role in history of viewing the systems and institutions of the world through the eyes of the *victims* . . . The church must serve, stand with, plead the cause of, and defend the life and value of all those who have been victimized for ideological, economic and political reasons' (p. 98).

35. Cf. Sugden, op. cit., 61–65; p. 63 cites L. Newbigin: 'The Gospel was doing [in India] what it has always done, making possible for those who were formerly "no people" to become God's people.'

36. Cf. Wright, 12f.

37. V. Samuel in Samuel & Sugden, *AD*, 163.

Wallis comments, 'While the world rushes to take up sides and define "the other" as the enemy, Jesus readily associated with all manner of men and women, Zealot and publican, sinner and priest, Jew and Roman, poor and rich. In doing so, he made enemies into friends, and by being obedient unto death, he accomplished the great work of salvation, transforming those who have made themselves "enemies" of God into the children of God, reconciled and made new . . .' (p. 88).

39. Wallis notes that violence just perpetuates the spiral of violence: using violence is not radical enough, 'not that it changes things too much, but that it does not change things enough' (p. 85).

40. Ibid., 87.

41. This may seem to contradict his statements in Mt. 12:30; Lk. 11:23, but these were given in the context of stubborn refusal by the Pharisees to recognize his exorcisms to be the work of God.

42. Cf. Carr, 242–247.

43. V. Samuel in Samuel & Sugden, *AD*, 162f.

44. Ibid., 161f.

45. On the universal recognition of moral law and justice in human conscience, cf. Nicholls, 13f.

46. One ancient religion in Asia may have produced the magi of the East who followed the star to Bethlehem to worship the Christ-Child.

47. L. Newbigin cited in N. Anderson, *The World's Religions* (Grand Rapids: Eerdmans, 1975), 236f.

48. V. Samuel, op. cit., 163.

BIBLIOGRAPHY

Buhlmann, Walbert. *The Church of the Future*. New York: rbis, 1986.

Carr, Dhyanchand, 'Social Action and Communicating Christ,' *Evangelical Review of Theology*, XV, 3 (July, 1991) 233–250.

Demarest, Bruce A. *General Revelation*. Grand Rapids: Eerdmans, 1982.

Ellul, Jacques, *The Meaning of the City*. Grand Rapids: Eerdmans, 1970.

Moberg, David. *Wholistic Christianity*. Elgin: Brethren Press, 1985.

Mott, Stephen C. *Biblical Ethics and Social Change*. New York: Oxford University Press, 1982.

Nazir-Ali, Michael. *From Everywhere to Everywhere*. London: Collins, 1991.

Newbigin, Lesslie. *The Finality of Christ*. London, 1969.

Nicholls, Bruce, J., 'The Salvation and Lostness of Mankind,' *E.R.T.*, XV, 1 (January, 1991) 4–21.

Samuel, Vinay & Sugden, Christopher (eds.). *A.D. 2000 and Beyond*. Oxford: Regnum Books, 1991.

———. *Evangelism and the Poor*. Exeter: Paternoster, 1986.

———. *The Church in Response to Human Need*. Grand Rapids: Eerdmans, 1987.

Wallis, Jim. *Agenda for Biblical People, New Ed.* San Francisco: Harper & Row, 1984.

Wolterstorff, Nicholas. *Until Justice and Peace Embrace*. Grand Rapids: Eerdmans, 1983.

Wright, N. T., 'The New Testament and the "State",' *Themelios*, XVI, 1 (October–November, 1990) 11–17.

Part Six

The Unique Christ as the Hope and Judge of the World

19

Dr. Isaac Zokoue

In this chapter Dr. Zokoue lays the biblical foundation for theological reflection on Christ as the only hope and judgement of the world. He focuses on Christ who is to come rather than things to come. He shows that the incarnation, death and resurrection of Christ make him a unique person and the hope of the world. The judgement of Christ includes both the elect and the ungodly, the present and the future and will be executed with justice.

This subject is expressed with an eschatological perspective in view. Christ as the hope and judgement of the world is the one who is coming again. Biblical eschatology is not primarily the announcement of a series of events – though it does also include that – but it concerns itself above all with the second coming of Jesus. We might ask ourselves if we do well to place the emphasis on '*things* to come', as in the title of Dwight Pentecost's book[1], rather than emphasizing *He* who is to come. Concern for developing a doctrine, sometimes to the detriment of developing a living relationship with Christ, can push us to put the emphasis on the events surrounding his return, instead of on his person.

Biblical eschatology expects a person, the Christ who is coming back to fulfil the hopes of mankind and to execute final judgement on the world.

I. BASIS

The affirmation of the unique Christ as the hope and judgement of the world has its basis in the very history of salvation. We would do well to remember, before going any further, that the eschatological Christ is the very one who was announced by the prophets, was born in Palestine, was crucified under Pontius Pilate and rose again on the third day. We will come back later to the trans-historical character of the person and work of Jesus, but for the

---

Dr. Isaac Zokoue is Principal of the Evangelical Theological Seminary at Bangui, Central Africa Republic.

moment, this brief reminder of the elements of the creed will suffice to establish our starting point, for it is necessary to have a basis.

Hope and judgement refer to future realities. Hope means that one is living in the expectation of the fulfilment of the promises of God. As far as judgement is concerned, it is announced by the Bible for the end times. But these realities are not without a link to the present, for the future is built upon the present. In fact, hope is rooted in the work that has already been accomplished by Christ. Peter says it this way: God 'has given us new birth into a living hope through the resurrection of Jesus Christ from the dead' (1 Pet. 1:3). Paul declares that 'God raised us up with Christ and seated us with him in the heavenly realms in Christ Jesus' (Eph. 2:6). Right now, in the present, we are already in Christ by virtue of our union with him by faith; therefore our hope for what God has promised to give us with Christ is a firm assurance (Heb. 11:1).

The judgement also is rooted in the work already accomplished by Christ. For Jesus, in speaking of the significance of the cross, declares, 'The ruler of this world has been judged.' The verdict has already been pronounced by Christ himself; the judgement has already begun at the cross (Jn. 16:11). Paul confirms the fact that Christ has already 'disarmed the principalities and powers and has made a public spectacle of them, triumphing over them by the cross' (Col. 2:15). Therefore, we can base our thinking on the following thesis: The unique Christ is the hope and judgement of the world because of his death and resurrection. We take our departure from the heart of salvation history. It is this central event of salvation which has its consequences in the future and which determines the future. Salvation history is the history of God's working among men. Eschatology is part of this history, even though, in this case, it is a question of history in the making. This fact is made clear in the light of what has already happened. And the whole of this history is dominated by one unique character: Christ. He, and not another, is the hope and the judgement of the world, because he alone, and no one else, stands in the centre of ALL human history.

II. THE UNIQUE CHRIST

To say that Christ is unique as an historical figure does not cause us to fall into 'that Christian "atheism" which refers only to the Son and eliminates the Father' as Gounelle fears.[2] The person of Christ is present throughout human history from beginning to end.

He is there when the first human couple is created. Blocher agrees with Clines' explanation of the plurals in the verse, 'Let us make man in our image' (Gen. 1:26). The plurals 'let us make' and 'our' mean that 'God speaks to himself, but He can do that only because He has a Spirit, who is one with Him and, at the same time is distinct from Him. First glimmers of the trinitarian revelation.'[3] However, this interpretation acknowledges only two persons of the Trinity – the Father and the Holy Spirit, leaving the Son out of the activity of the creating of man. Obviously, the text cannot be forced to say more than ~tually says, but it is permissible to look for scriptural support in other ;. I would like to refer to the narrative of the birth of Jesus in Luke and note that this account involves the three persons of the Trinity. It is the Son who is incarnated, but the Father and the Holy Spirit are there at work, as this verse shows (underlinings are mine): 'The *Holy Spirit* will come upon you, and the power of the *Most High* will overshadow you. So the holy one to be born will be called the *Son of God*' (Lk. 1:35). There is certainly a parallel between the creation of the first Adam and the incarnation of the second Adam with respect to the join work of the Trinity. At crucial moments in the existence of man (his creation into the world and his re-creation in Jesus), the Trinity is revealed. Therefore, it is fitting to say that Jesus is, with the Father and the Holy Spirit, Co-Creator of man. In other words, he is involved in the origin of mankind. As the producing cause, he is not only distinct from but also different from humanity. This is the starting point!

But immediately after the fall of man, the solidarity of the Creator with fallen man is signalled by the announcement of the redemption of which Christ will be the author. Of course, it is an announcement in veiled terms (Gen. 3:15), but the seed (take note of the singular, cf. Gal. 3:16) of the woman (who here represents all of humanity) is Christ, the Creator. This is the announcement of the incarnation. Of the three persons of the Trinity, only Christ will take upon himself the condition of man: in that respect he is unique.

As to the woman, God predicts the victory of her seed over that of the serpent. Note the relationship between the strength of the two antagonists: the seed of the serpent will be satisfied with crushing the heel of his enemy, while the seed of the woman will crush the head of his enemy; he is the one who will come out victorious from this battle. Adam and Eve have yielded to the temptation and are henceforth under the domination of Satan. According to the divine verdict, they are even dead, and with them, all their descendants. However, Christ will come forth from within humanity to overcome the tyrant and give back to man his liberty: in this he is unique.

So then, whether Christ is considered from the point of view of his divinity or from that of his humanity, he is indeed unique from the very beginning and he will always remain so. Moreover, if Genesis 1:26 gives the first glimmers of the trinitarian revelation, Genesis 3:15 brings the first glimmers of human hope. Already at this point, Christ is announced as the hope of the world. He is thus the hope of the world not only in an eschatological sense; he has always been the hope of the world ever since the world lost hope and he always will be as long as the fallen world endures.

Thus, the coming of Christ is announced from the very beginning, it will be carefully *prepared* right up to his birth. A general declaration will suffice here, if we say with Luther: 'In truth, the entire Bible relates to Christ'.[4] So the same thing is said in both Testaments, and particularly in the Old Testament: everything relates to Christ. As to details, the revelation was progressive, culminating in Christ; and Christ was the object of the prophecies. God, who is the Master of history, could not send his Son incognito into the midst of humanity. Christ came 'in due time' or 'at the right time'. This mastery of time makes Christ singular. Never again would the birth of a man be announced and expected for millennia, an expectation which would become more and more precise as the event drew near. In this respect, Brunner says with reason that this coming was prepared for not only in the midst of Israel, by the biblical revelation, but also in the history of the entire world. Here is a resumé of the elements of this preparation that the theologian of Zurich identifies:

(a) The military career of Alexander and the *imperium romanum* put an end to the obstacles created by the national religions which formerly separated peoples and would have created insurmountable difficulties for any mission coming from the exterior.

(b) Greek philosophy and Roman civilization slipped an uneasiness and a secret trouble into the midst of the religious systems which up to then were closed, causing an acutely felt need for redemption.

(c) The development of Diaspora Judaism: Paul went initially into the synagogues, creating there the first followers.

(d) Facility of universal communication that the Roman civilization and empire created.

(e) Jesus was fully a Jew of his time.[5]

More recent studies of the New Testament period add other clarifications to this preparation.[6] From all that is above, let us draw the following conclusion: so-called secular history and sacred history converge toward Christ. He is the figure who dominates history, even if spiritual blindness has often hindered man from seeing this fact.

The incarnation, death and resurrection made of Christ a unique person. Receiving Jesus into his arms, the elderly Simeon declared, 'This child is destined . . . to be a sign that will be opposed' (Lk. 2:34). 'Opposed' because, with Christ's coming into the world, God intervenes in history in a decisive way to change the course of events. Mary realized this when she sang, 'The Mighty One . . . has scattered those who are proud in their inmost thoughts. He has brought down rulers from their thrones but has lifted up the humble. He has filled the hungry with good things but has sent the rich away empty' (Lk. 1:51–53).

For King Herod, 'opposed' when he learns that another 'king of the Jews . . . has been born'. 'Opposed' for the religious leaders who could find no further argument to confound the powerful Teacher. For Pilate, the highest political authority in the country, representing the primary power of the world, 'opposed' when he publicly and three times in a row gives a verdict that he does not uphold, notably this: 'I have found no basis for your charges against him. Neither has Herod, for he sent him back to us; as you can see, he has done nothing to deserve death. Therefore, I will punish him and then release him' (Lk. 23:14–16, 22). Nevertheless, Pilate himself delivered Jesus to be crucified. 'Opposed' when the religious and political authorities learn that the body of the one with whom they were infuriated is no longer in the tomb.

It is true that all the Jews were waiting for the coming of the Messiah, but the idea of God's becoming incarnate was intolerable to them. Cohen explains that in its interpretation of the sacred texts, 'Judaism did not allow the concept that the infinite could be enclosed in a body, in a limited space; it did not accept the idea that God could be divided into several parts of which one would appear to the eyes of mortals, while the other would remain invisible, and still infinite in the depths of the heavens, although divided.'[7]

Christ is condemned to an odious death for having declared that he, Jesus eth, is equal to God. However, in that ignominious death is hidden, the divine omnipotence, since 'God has raised this Jesus to life' (Acts 2:32). The Holy Spirit reveals to the first Christians that the whole world is implicated in the event that has just shaken Jerusalem. For behind this crowd which cries, 'Put him to death! Crucify him!' is all of humanity, which demanded the death of the One who came to save them. The church in Jerusalem prayed, 'The kings of the earth take their stand and the rulers gather together against the Lord, and against his Anointed One. Indeed, Herod and Pontius Pilate met together with the Gentiles and the people of Israel in this city to conspire against your holy servant Jesus, whom you anointed' (Acts 4:26–27). Once again, Christ is at the very heart of human history.

However, he is the risen Christ, not only in the hearts of his disciples, as Bultmann claims[8], but in the history of mankind (cf. 1 Cor. 15:5–7). Before going back to be seated at the right hand of his Father, he gives his disciples the Great Commission; they receive the mission to go to 'all nations', and Christ says, 'Surely I am with you always, to the very end of the age' (Matt. 28:19–20). Christ is with his disciples no matter where they are; he is present everywhere. Notice this unique fact: Christ does not merely command the disciples to propagate his ideas and his teachings throughout the world, as do the cults, but *he himself* is with them every day and always will be. There is no one like Christ! Moreover, as the risen One, he has 'all authority' (Matt. 28:18). We see, then, that in his incarnation, his death, and his resurrection, Christ remains unique.

The heavenly session also makes a unique person of Christ. In his dual nature as God and man, Christ sits at the right hand of the Father: he is *the* representative of humanity before the Father. 'Such a high priest meets our needs – one who is holy, blameless, pure, set apart from sinners, exalted above the heavens' (Heb. 7:26). Christ is exalted above the heavens; thus there is no one, either on earth or in heaven, who is better able than he to plead man's cause before the Father. His priesthood is universal. Paul says of Christ that 'God exalted him to the highest place and gave him the name that is above every name' (Phil. 2:9). Christ's exaltation is in relation to his creatures and not to God. Moreover, the right hand of God is a symbol of power and authority. It is the Father who says to the Son, 'Sit at my right hand until I make your enemies a footstool for your feet; (Ps. 110:1; Matt. 22:44; Heb. 1:13). The context in which this prophecy was given was that of judgement, for it is written, 'The Lord is at your right hand; he will crush kings on the day of his wrath. He will judge the nations . . . crushing the rulers of the whole earth' (Ps. 110:5–6). The announcement of the final judgement can be read between the lines here. In sitting down at the right hand of the Father, Christ also takes the position of judge. And just as in his heavenly session his priesthood is universal, so also his judgement will be.

Up to now we have placed the emphasis on Christ's connection to the history of men, for he who is the hope and the judgement of the world is the Son of Man. It is well known that 'Son of Man' was Christ's favourite title for himself during his earthly ministry. He constantly wanted to highlight his solidarity with the human race. He is 'the first-born from among the dead' and as such, he is the hope of the world. Moreover, God would not appoint someone alien to this world to judge it; instead, the judge is his Son, our brother.

III.   THE UNIQUE CHRIST AS HOPE OF THE WORLD

It is by virtue of his death and resurrection that Christ is the hope of the world. By his death, he suffered the judgement of God; by his resurrection, he re-endowed men with life. Christ's substitutionary death is an event that does not fit into the framework of human logic, and the apostle Paul observes this when he writes, 'Very rarely will anyone die for a righteous man, though for the good man someone might possibly dare to die' (Rom. 5:7). However, Christ 'died for the ungodly' (v. 6). Therefore, he died a death which was not his own; nevertheless, it was not an accident. Paul said to the Romans, 'At just the right time, Christ died for the ungodly' (Rom. 5:6). The right time was not simply an historical sequence nor a certain season of the year or a particular time during the week. The very hour of the death of Jesus had been chosen. Three arguments corroborate the fact that Jesus himself decided on the precise moment of his death:

(a) He died at the ninth hour, a symbolic hour,[9] for this was the traditional hour for the slaying of the Pascal lamb (Ex. 12:6; Lev. 23:5; Num. 9:3, 5, 11). The others who were crucified with him died later (cf. Jn. 19:31–35).

(b) Pilate's surprise: 'Pilate was surprised to hear that he was already dead. Summoning the centurion, he asked him if Jesus had already died. When he learned from the centurion that it was so, he gave the body to Joseph' (Mk. 16:44–45).

(c) The centurion: when he 'saw how he died, he said, "Surely this man was the Son of God!"' (Mk. 15:39), attesting to the fact that Jesus died exactly when he wanted to die.

At the cross, he had refused the drugged wine that was offered to him (Matt. 24:37) and in full lucidity and voluntarily, he took the place of men in death. Christ's substitution in our place is not just a theological idea; it is an experience that was lived by our Saviour at the cross. The intensity of the suffering that is predicted in Isaiah 53 and was experienced by Christ at the cross conveys the severity with which God judged the sin. God did not attenuate his judgement of sin because it was the Just One, his very own Son, who was offering himself in the place of the sinner. On the contrary, 'God did not spare his own Son' says Paul (Rom. 8:32).

Jesus truly did die, and this was an inescapable necessity, for in the last cry at the cross – 'It is finished' – is also found the execution of God's verdict pronounced in the Garden of Eden: 'You are dust, and to dust you shall return' (Gen. 3:19). This verdict sends man back in non-existence. There is an echo of this verdict in Genesis 6:3, where God says, 'My spirit will not remain in man forever, for he is mortal.' (Though this reading does not follow most English translations, it is a marginal reading in NIV and follows closely the French translations which were used in the preparation of this article.) It seems almost as if God is threatening to take from man his status as creature in God's image. However, he does not go to this extreme: man will not return to non-existence, and the human race will not disappear with the flood. God arranges a way out in expectation of the death and resurrection of Jesus. However, the Christ who, at the cross, takes the place of man, must take upon himself the effects of this verdict to their full extent – that is, he must ⸱⸱ die.

⸱ath is both physical and spiritual. The physical death of Christ was established: seeing that Jesus was already dead, 'one of the soldiers pierced Jesus' side with a spear, bringing a sudden flow of blood and water' (Jn. 19:34). This was the sign of the decomposition of his body. On the spiritual plane, Christ, in his passion, went to the breaking point. 'Why have you forsaken me?' This is how far Jesus went: taking the place of man, he was 'made to be sin' (2 Cor. 5:21), and since God's eyes are too pure to look on sin (Hab. 1:13), he turned his face from this scene. His turning of his face from Jesus marks the consummation of God's judgement of man.

By his resurrection, Christ gives life. The hope of which the Scriptures speak is that of eternal life, and also of the glory that accompanies his life (cf. Rom. 5:2; 8:21; 2 Cr. 3:12; Col. 1:27; Tit. 2:13; 1 Pet. 1:13, 21; 1 Jn. 3:2–3). To say that Christ is the hope of the world means two things, both of which are attested by scripture. First of all, the resurrection of Christ guarantees the resurrection of all men – believers and unbelievers. Without the resurrection of Christ, no human being could aspire to an eternal existence. Paul draws a parallel between the imputation to all men of Adam's sin and the imputation of Christ's righteousness to men. He writes: 'Consequently, just as the result of one trespass was condemnation for all men, so also the result of one act of righteousness was justification that brings life for all men' (Rom. 5:18).

This verse should not be understood in a universalistic sense. Paul means that by Christ's resurrection, God gives life to all men. In Adam, all men died; in Christ, all men live again. In Adam, all men return to non-existence by the judgement of God; in Christ, all men regain existence. In Adam, the sentence of death struck all men, but since Christ has fulfilled the righteousness of God, that sentence has been annulled, and God has effaced it by the blood of His Son. Consequently, the righteousness of Christ – meaning here, the gift of life – extends to all men. However, as Daniel affirms, 'Multitudes who sleep in the dust of the earth will awake: some to everlasting life, others to shame and everlasting contempt' (Dan. 12:2; cf. Matt. 25:46). Consequently, it is on the basis of the gift of life to men by God, through the resurrection of Christ, that the issue of salvation is raised. Salvation is eternal life.

The second meaning of Christ as the hope of the world is that he is the only one in whom eternal life is found. Having eternal life is not simply the fact of having an existence. This is the error that the universalists make, in particular Tillich, who teaches this: 'To one degree or another, all men participate in the power of the healing of the New Being. If it were not so, they would lose their being: the self-destructive consequences of the alienation would have destroyed them.'[10] Moreover, this quotation from Tillich is consistent with the title of his book: *Existence and Christ*. His concept of the existence of man corresponds to the idea expressed in the previous paragraph.

However, biblical salvation is more than the enjoyment of existence. Biblical salvation is conditional on the acceptance or the rejection of the risen Christ. In this regard, one must understand the scriptural term, 'the second death' because, in the first place – and that is the first death – all men have died in Adam (Eph. 2:1). However, God has brought all men back to life in Christ. Henceforth, all men have access to salvation. As Paul explains, 'salvation is in Christ Jesus' (2 Tim. 2:10). In other words, outside of Christ Jesus, there is no possibility of salvation. Nevertheless, certain individuals will refuse this offer of life in Christ; they will alienate themselves from God for the second time and permanently exclude themselves from fellowship with him; this is the second death. Having been resurrected in Christ, they will renounce this privilege and plunge themselves into death for the second time. On the other hand, the elect will retain this privilege forever, and this is eternal life. In this respect, Christ is both the hope and the judgement of the world: hope for those who by faith have tasted eternal life and are expecting his return, but judgement for those who have refused the free gift of God; for it is the refusal to believe in Jesus which brings judgement (cf. Jn. 3:19; 5: 24; 12:48). This is why the Bible says that unbelievers are 'without hope' (Eph. 2:12; 1 Th. 4:13). Christ is the only hope of the world.

IV. THE UNIQUE CHRIST AS JUDGEMENT OF THE WORLD

This declaration is to be understood as having a double meaning. Some passages (Matt. 25:31ff; Jn. 5:24) seem to indicate that the judgement will apply only to the ungodly, whereas other passages (Rom. 14:12; 1 Cor. 3:13; 2 Cor. 5:10; 1 Pet. 4:17) show that the elect also will be judged. The truth is that there will be two judgments. The two types of judgement are certainly in view in the passages that declare that Jesus is the judge 'of the living and the dead' (Acts 10:42; 1 Pet. 4:5). This means that the prospect of the judgement is a simultaneous summons for both believers and unbelievers. Consider the principal characteristics of this judgement.

The Judgement Will Be Executed By Christ

The intra-trinitarian relationship is respected: The Father entrusts *all* judgement to the Son. However, this is more than a simple appointment. It is by virtue of the redemptive work of Christ that the Father gives the work of judgement to him (Jn. 5:22, 27; Acts 10:42; 17:31). Acts 17:31 places the emphasis on Christ's humanity: God is going to judge the world by 'the man he has appointed'. This appointment is made in a unique way: the man appointed is the one that he has raised from the dead. But how is Christ's resurrection a proof of the divine choice? How is his resurrection a unique event, since history had already known other resurrections (2 Ki. 4:35; Matt. 9:25; Lk. 7:14–16; Jn. 11:44)? It is in the light of Christology as a whole that the answer to these questions can be found. Since this resurrection is considered as the 'proof' that God has appointed this particular person raised from the dead, and not another, let us simply say this: Christ died as a convict, and the principal accusation against him was that he declared himself to be the Son of God. In raising the one whom the Jews have judged in the name of the Law, the one considered to be a blasphemer, the one whom the world, by its representatives at Jerusalem, has condemned and executed as a criminal (Acts 4:26–27), God re-establishes the truth in the eyes of all: Jesus of Nazareth *is* the Son of God, a just and righteous man, whose teachings and works among the people came from God. Psalm 2:2 specifies that it is 'against the Lord and against his Anointed One' that the kings and rulers of the earth have gathered together. The rejection of the Son was also the rejection of the ⸻ʳ. and Psalm 2:1 registers surprise at this attitude: 'Why do the nations ⸻ and the peoples plot in vain?' In the face of mankind's vanity, God demonstrates his righteousness by raising Christ from the dead and appointing him as the judge of all.

The Judgement is Both Present and Future

With the fall came the first judgement, and by his death, Christ satisfied the conditions demanded by divine justice so well that in him man is no longer under the first judgement. It may be said that this first judgement, the judgement that Jesus suffered in our place, corresponds to the first creation and first humanity. Therefore, a new creation and a new humanity, of which Christ is the Head, began in him; and with him, another judgement, which will be the last, also began. Just as salvation is caught in the tension between the 'already' and the 'not yet', so the final judgement is in this tension of the 'already and the 'not yet'. Jesus' teaching, passed on by the apostles, is that God has appointed a DAY when he will judge the world, and that day has not yet arrived. The final judgement, then, is indeed an eschatological event. However, the Bible tells us elsewhere that judgement has already begun: the prince of this world, Satan, has been judged (Jn. 16:11), and anyone who refuses to believe in Jesus has been judged already (Jn. 3:18). The 'already' and the 'not yet' of divine judgement should be considered as God's grace to man, for God reveals to the unbeliever that he has already been judged, but that this judgement has not yet taken effect; therefore, he can escape by turning to Christ. It is when he will have refused God's grace up to the very end, 'at the last day', that the judgement will be executed, for there will be a last day (Jn. 12:48), marking the end of the time of man's disobedience. The fall, with death following in its train, is like a large parenthesis in God's plan for humanity. God did not create man for judgement, and Jesus discloses the fact that the 'eternal fire' was not prepared for men but 'for the devil and his angels' (Matt. 25:41). God will put an end to his creatures' rebellion so that the new creation, of which Christ is the author, may be completely harmonious.

The Judgement Will Be Executed with Justice

Christ is the just judge (Jn. 5:30; Acts 17:31; Rom. 2:5; 2 Th. 1:5; 2 Tim. 4:8; 1 Pet. 2:23; Rev. 19:2). This declaration of Christ's righteous judgement highlights man's guilt. His judgement of non-Christians is just, for Christ came the first time, not to judge, but to save (Jn. 3:17). Thus, he offered to all the possibility of being saved. The one who refuses salvation is altogether responsible for his choice, and the judgement that comes with that choice will only be just. In formulating this thought in this manner, we are conscious of the fact that it does not agree with the third of Calvinism's five points (limited atonement), but that is another issue. Christ's judgement will be just, because he will judge each one according to his works, taking into account also the possibilities that were offered to each one (2 Cor. 5:10; 1 Pet. 1:17). This means that man is fully responsible for his actions. Christians are responsible to the same degree, for 'his divine power has given us everything we need for life and godliness' (2 Pet. 1:3). Furthermore, in Christ, Christians are 'dead to sin' (Rom. 6:11), and since they have the advantage of the Holy Spirit's help, they have everything they need to lead a holy life and produce the fruit of the Spirit. If the Christian leads a carnal and sterile life, it is totally his own responsibility. Of course, such a statement is not pleasing to the ears of modern man, who would like to lead a dissolute life and still have the privilege of salvation without judgement. He would like God to issue a decree of general amnesty. However, the fundamental reason for the inevitability of the judgement lies in the fact that God's creatures (first Satan and then man) have sinned, and that without reason. The entrance of sin into the world is inexplicable. Man can lay claim to absolutely no attenuating circumstances; he is exposed to all the pernicious results of the evil that he unleashed against himself and that he cannot control. Christ's judgement is according to justice, because, in all areas of life, he re-establishes the order that has been unreasonably perturbed. This justice in Christ's judgement will be acknowledged by all when his lordship is universally recognized and confessed (cf. Phil. 2:10–11).

In closing, let us quote once more the elderly Simeon, a man of hope, who 'was waiting for the consolation of Israel'. He is the one who said, 'This child is destined to cause the falling and rising of many in Israel' (Lk. 2:34). In pronouncing these words over the baby Jesus, Simeon was a visionary, for not only in Israel, but also in all nations and until the end of time, the Christ who is unique in his person and his work, will remain the hope and the judgement of the entire world.

NOTES

1. Reference to the book of J. Dwight Pentecost, *Things To Come.* (Grand Rapids: Zondervan, 1974).
2. André Gounelle, 'Le Salut', in *Etudes theólogiques et religieuses* (1978/2): 236.
3. Henri Blocher, *Révélation des origines* (Lausanne: PBU, 1979), 77.
4. Martin Luther, *Ouvres* (Genève: Labor & Fides, 1963), III:72.
5. Emil Brunner, *La dogmatique chrétienne de la création et de la rédemption* (Genève: Labor & Fides, 1965) II: 264.
6. Cf. Gerd Theissen, *The First Followers of Jesus* (London: SCM, 1988), and Derek Tidball, *An Introduction to the Sociology of the New Testament* (Exeter: Paternoster, 1983).
7. J. Cohen, *Les déicides* (Paris: Michel Lévy Frères, 1861), 110.
8. Rudolf Bultmann, *Foi et compréhension* (Paris: Ed. du Seuil, 1970) I: 231–233.
9. The chronology of Jesus' death in relationship to the Jewish Passover is a debatable issue. However, allusion is made here only to the symbolic character of the hour of his death.
10. Paul Tillich, *L'existence et le Christ* (Lausanne: L'Age d'Homme, 1980) 197.

20

Ken R. Gnanakan

The focus of this chapter is on the theological significance of the biblical revelation on the resurrection of Jesus Christ, the promise of his return to reign and the future state of the world and of humankind. He critiques both liberal and evangelical theologians for their limited and often one-sided perspective on these issues, and gives credit to insights of biblical truth wherever they are found. Dr. Gnanakan deals creatively with several tensions in the relationship of eschatological judgement and hope, including the end of the world and the presence of the future in Jesus; the scandal of the Cross as believed to have universal validity; the nature and extent of rejection and hell, with comments on John Stott's exploratory views. Above all he emphasizes that the unique Christ is Lord of all things.

Hope and judgement are aspects of the Christian faith that have been for a long time looked upon as something so other-worldly that any critical approach to the Bible demanded that they be set aside. Interestingly, the first use of the word eschatology (in 1844) is said to have had a disparaging connotation. This was purely because liberal attitudes to eschatology did not see any connection with Jesus' immediate relevance to the Christian. Any reference to Jesus' knowledge of the future by means of divine foreknowledge was set aside as untenable.

However, the questions were soon to arise – How do we handle Paul's overwhelming concern for the 'parousia'? What precisely did Jesus mean by the Kingdom of God, a theme that so dominated his message and his ministry? Liberal scholarship dismissed these purely as remnants of the overwhelming apocalyptic preoccupations within which early Christianity was formed, and which could be discarded once the Jesus of history was discovered.

In recent times eschatological themes have been restored to their central place in the entire Christian message and with it there is a renewed interest in the subject at all levels of scholarship. Future hope and judgement, the

---

Dr. Ken Gnanakan is General Secretary of the Asia Theological Association, based in Bangalore, India.

doctrine of 'last things' was for a long time relegated almost to irrelevance, but hardly so today. As Jürgen Moltman put in his 'Theology of Hope' – 'From first to last, and not merely in the epilogue. Christianity is eschatology, is hope, forward looking and forward moving, and therefore also revolutionising and transforming the present.'[1]

While Evangelicals and other conservative Christians have held on to the biblical teaching, although differing drastically in interpretations of millenarian details, liberal scholarship has seen drastic changes and a brief survey is instructive. It was Ernst Käsemann who first aroused popular interest in apocalyptics through his essay 'The beginnings of Christian Theology'.[2] His claim was rather provoking – 'Apocalyptic was the mother of all Christian theology, since we cannot really class the preaching of Jesus as theology'.[3] He explained, 'Even if the validity of the judgement were challenged and it was desired to associate Jesus more closely with the beginning of Christian theology than seems to be justifiable, those who took this view will still have to recognize in post-Easter apocalyptic a new theological start; they would have to give some reasonable account of a situation in which dogmatics no longer begins with the problem of eschatology but, according to the traditional pattern, makes apocalyptics the subject of the last chapter.'[4]

For Käsemann, even the inclusion of eschatology as one of the several themes within theology is taking the issue far too casually, and treating it in a 'cavalier fashion'.[5] Theology cannot survive without adequate consideration of the apocalyptic issues which 'sprang from the Easter experience and determined the Easter faith'.[6]

Till then, liberal biblical scholarship had accepted apocalyptics as something of a periphery of the Old and the New Testaments, but with reminders such as Käsemann's it was thrust right into the centre. Moltmann, and Wolfhart Panneneberg just as importantly picked up the growing attention focused on the subject and gave it a very prominent place in their theologies. Both Moltmann's theology of hope with its heavy emphasis on the future and Pannenberg's universal horizon of history with its end perspective utilize biblical eschatology to the maximum, giving to Christology some fresh and helpful insights for the debate today.

Moltmann wrote – 'The eschatological is not one element of Christianity, but it is the medium of Christian faith as such, the key in which everything in it is set, the glow that suffuses everything here in the dawn of an expected new day. For Christian faith lives from the raising of the crucified Christ, and strains after the promises of the universal future of Christ. Eschatology is the passionate suffering and passionate longing kindled by the Messiah.'[7]

The eschatological distinctive of biblical Christianity is aptly introduced into the pluralistic debate as it is here that we will be able to underline clearly the uniqueness of Jesus Christ and his universal significance. The relevance of the end time events as recorded in the Bible to history, the Second Coming of Jesus Christ and all its implications, the significance of the future kingdom to our present reality, and the finality of Jesus' revelation as the hope and judgement of the world will powerfully distinguish the Christian claims from rather nebulous concepts of the future in other religions. Whether it be concepts of the salvific experience or the understanding of the coming ͺᴖm, or even the understanding of the ultimate God in the future, there ᵈ contrast that highlights the fact and significance of Jesus Christ.

I. JESUS CHRIST AND ESCHATOLOGY

With the resurgence of a concern for restoration of the centrality of the eschatological theme in Christianity it was proper that attention be paid to Jesus' message itself. Soon, it was beginning to be confirmed that far from being in the background, eschatology had to be seen as the very essence of Jesus' life, ministry and message. Wolfhart Pannenberg emphasizes the centrality of the future in Jesus' message – 'Jesus thought and spoke within the context of apocalyptic expectations. Thus one cannot remove Jesus' words from this context in the history of thought without eliminating their historical particularity.'

Even more crucial to Pannenberg's discussions is the remarkable tension between the futurity of the end of the world and the presence of the future in the person of Jesus. The tension between the present and future in Jesus' proclamation makes apparent, what Pannenberg refers to as 'the proleptic character of Jesus' claim', an anticipation of a confirmation that is to be expected only from the future.

Wolfhart Pannenberg's distinctive understanding of the 'proleptic' structure of Jesus' claim, lays heavy emphasis on the anticipation of the future. 'Jesus' claim through its proleptic structure corresponds to the apocalyptic vision's relation to history, which in turn goes back to the relation of the prophetic word of God to the future. The prophets received words that must be confirmed by their future fulfilment, and thereby must be shown to be Yahweh's words.'[8] The apocalyptic view of history was unique in the sense that it grasped future events before they occurred. Yet this required confirmation by the actual course of the history of the events themselves.

This is how Jesus offers future salvation in the present. For instance, while in the Baptist's call to repentance only judgement was present, in Jesus' activity eschatological salvation also had already made its appearance. 'Not merely the expectancy of ultimate salvation on the basis of repentance – that may also have been the case with John the Baptist – but salvation itself was present. For this reason, the future participation in salvation was decided by the attitude taken toward his person; for this reason, Jesus' own person, in distinction from the Baptist's stands in the centre.'[9]

Pannenberg's distinctive emphasis on the proleptic nature of Jesus' revelation surfaces as he proceeds on to assert that '. . . with Jesus the end is not only as in the apocalyptic writings – seen in advance, but it has happened in advance. These observations indicate profound differences between the activity of Jesus and that of the apocalyptic prophet, differences which also make it understandable why in Jesus, as probably earlier in John the Baptist, apocalyptic pictures and the end events recede into the background. Apocalyptic remains, nevertheless, the intellectual context of the Baptist's preaching of repentance as well as of the proleptic occurrence of God's rule through Jesus.'[10]

II. THE RESURRECTION AND ESCHATOLOGY

We have been so caught up in attempting to establish the historicity of the resurrection that its eschatological significance has been overlooked. Paul suggests in his letter to the Corinthians (1 Cor. 15) that the resurrection of Jesus Christ is the beginning of the resurrection of all humankind. It is the climax of God's revelatory acts and the beginning of the eschatological reality of the hope and judgement of the world.

Pannenberg's conclusions are significant as he stresses the event as being integral to the whole eschatological future which has appeared in the present. For one thing, he was writing at a time when the resurrection was looked upon as merely a matter of faith with nothing much to do with history. The scientific and positivistic concepts of history had allowed no room for any such 'miraculous' event which had to do with God's revelation. Not only was he proposing that the event was actually historical, but the even more distinctive stress is its connection to the climax of history and the final revelatory manifestation of God himself.

Pannenberg points out first – 'If Jesus has been raised, then the end of the world has begun.'[11] And with this the universal resurrection of the dead and the judgement is imminent. The connection here is that which Paul makes so clearly – the expectation that the resurrection of believers, will immediately follow that of Jesus.[12] Jesus is 'the first-born among many brethren' (Rom. 8:29). Christ is raised as the first fruits of those who have fallen asleep (1 Cor. 15:20). In Colossians 1:18 Jesus is called the first-born of the dead.

The eschatological stress in Pannenberg's thesis on the resurrection also links the ultimate revelation of God inseparably with this event. 'If Jesus having been raised from the dead, is ascended to God and if thereby the end of the world has begun, then God is ultimately revealed in Jesus.' This is so because in Jesus' resurrection the end of all things, which for us has not yet happened, has already occurred. In Jesus the ultimate is already present in him, and God himself, has manifested his glory in Jesus, in a way that cannot be surpassed. Only because the end of the world is already present in Jesus' resurrection is God himself revealed in him.[13]

Proceeding further, Pannenberg develops his understanding of the significance of this event. Israelite prophecy expected the self demonstration of God, which it proclaimed, as an event that would take place before the eyes of all peoples. Not just Israel but all nations were to recognize from this future event the exclusive divinity of Israel's God. The exilic prophets Deutero-Isaiah and Ezekiel especially preached in this way. The same proclamation occurs repeatedly in the Psalms. This expectation corresponds to the hope, rooted in the Jerusalem tradition of the election of David and Zion, that in the end time all people would submit themselves to the Lordship of Yahweh and his Anointed One.

However, we will need to ask whether the hope of the Gentiles means that everyone will automatically be saved. Paul stresses that every knee will bow and every tongue confess that Jesus is Lord but does this presuppose a universalistic conclusion? Even the inclusivistic position similarly avoids the reality of the biblical understanding of God's judgement. The resurrection, the Second coming, the climactic end of history, while signifying the fulfilment of hope must also emphasize the severity of God's judgement. There tends to be a minimizing of this fact both in Pannenberg and Moltmann.

Pannenberg states that 'in contrast to apparently widely held conceptions of Jewish contemporaries, Jesus did not predict divine vengeance on the Gentiles for the eschaton, but the participation of many of them in eschatological salvation, while he threatened the impenitent Israelites with wrathful judgment.' While this is true in the sense that Jesus' immediate judgement was on the narrowness of the Jewish perspectives, there is hardly any justification for us to dismiss judgement of sin as foreign to Jesus' message.

III. THE UNIVERSAL AND THE PARTICULAR

The main question confronted by those wanting to resolve the pluralistic predicament is the fact of the particular event of Jesus Christ, the scandal of the cross which is believed to have universal validity. The central message of the Christian faith and essentially the heart of the good news is that there is hope for everyone who believes on grounds of the reality of the biblically attested resurrection event. This particular event has universal validity and is the basis of our hope. Moltmann's stress on 'promise' and 'hope' came at a time when theology itself was going through a depression. He, like Pannenberg, developed his theology on the basis of the event of the resurrection within the eschatological horizon of this event. Moltmann affirms – '. . . to recognize the resurrection of Christ means to recognize in this event the future of God for the world and the future which man finds in this God and his acts'.[14]

Moltmann wants to underline also the fact that the resurrection event is not merely one among all the events of world history. Rather, it examines the inner tendency of the resurrection event, asking what rightly can and must be expected from the risen and exalted Lord. It inquires about the mission of Christ and the intention of God in raising him from the dead. It recognizes as the inner tendency of this event his future lordship over every enemy, including death. 'For he must reign . . .' (1 Cor. 15:25). It recognizes as the outer tendency, or as the consequence of this tendency, its own mission: 'The gospel must be published among all nations' (Mark 13).

Strangely, Moltmann continued in a Barthian frame to minimize the historical value of the resurrection. 'Christian eschatology speaks of the future of Christ which brings man and the world to light. It does not, on the contrary, speak of a world history and a time which brings Christ to light, not yet of man whose good will Christ brings to light. It is therefore out of the question to classify the resurrection event among the events of world history and apocalyptic and to give a date for his future or his coming again;. While attempting to protect eschatology and the resurrection event from human concepts of 'time' and 'history' he could be surrendering the factuality of the hope within the concreteness of historical experiences. Pannenberg on the other hand leaves too much for history, minimizing the fact of God's Lordship over history itself.

The primary fact to underline is the universal significance of Jesus Christ through the eschatological demonstration of his Lordship over all of God's creation as well as sin, Satan and death. The universal validity of this event is historically demonstrated but with an eschatological thrust.

IV. RESURRECTION AND WHOLENESS

One of the chief distinctions of the hope in the resurrection is a hope of wholeness. It is not immortality, at least in its Greek and Hindu understanding of the soul, where only one aspect of man is seen to live on with God. This platonic dualism needs to be discarded as we draw out more and more of the wholeness of the biblical understanding of everlasting life. The ultimate hope of a person in Christ is the confidence of a spiritual body 'raised imperishable', 'raised in glory' and 'raised in power' (1 Cor. 13:42f.).

This wholeness is also a confirmation of the present experience of salvation. We evangelicals have grown out of the unhealthy dualism that restricted our mission, thinking we were to avoid the material and stress the spiritual. Salvation is a body/soul experience which brings back to humankind what was lost in the fall, making us even more human than we have ever been.

Another vital aspect of our salvation is to do with our relationship with Jesus Christ. Paul's stress on Jesus being the 'first fruits' in relation to our eschatological relationship with him confirms his emphasis on this relationship with his Saviour. Paul's relationship with Jesus is powerfully portrayed in his frequent emphasis of being 'in him'. Salvation then is a relationship rather than an experience. Our material tendencies force us into an experience in terms of individual benefits rather than looking at the ultimacy of our being with the Saviour himself. It is interesting to note that the prophets expressed the hope of a New Israel by means of the picture of a new relationship. Hosea speaks of this in terms of the true and faithful relationship between a husband and wife.

In fact the concept of the covenant involves a relationship. The prophets Jeremiah and Ezekiel speak about the new covenant and the new relationship that will exist between God and his people. Undoubtedly, this is the imagery that Jesus utilizes when he speaks of his relationship to his followers not only in the coming kingdom but even now. Paul develops this relationship to the fullest in his concept of being in Christ.

The fact of our relationship with God through our Lord Jesus Christ is one that will need to be underlined heavily in our discussions on the uniqueness of Jesus Christ alongside other claims. Hinduism for instance lacks the idea of any real relationship particularly when it comes to a hope for the future. Rather than any idea of a living presence of the individual there is the idea of being submerged into the absolute God, a total loss of any identity of the individual. In contrast, the hope of humankind in Jesus Christ is a restoration of total humanity, a wholeness as creation dwells in the eternal presence of the creator.

V.   HOPE AND JUDGEMENT

There is sufficient validation within the New Testament – Jesus Christ's words, the disciples' testimony and Paul's teaching – to confirm the centrality of the Second Coming of Jesus to usher in the eschaton. I do not go into a treatment of the Second Coming mainly because there is so much already said in relation to the event. The linking up of the resurrection with the ushering in of the eschaton should in no way diminish the importance of the Second Coming of Jesus Christ. However, what needs to be given some attention is the fact of judgment.

With the Second Coming there is a manifestation of the Lordship of Christ so that men and women will acknowledge what has already been displayed at the resurrection – Christ's Lordship over everything. The resurrection has already signalled this victory, but with the Second Coming this will not only be demonstrated but actualized through his final role as judge. Judgement is one of the main roles ascribed to him in his Second Coming. That will be the time for those who believe in him to be blessed with eternal life in the Kingdom and those who have rejected him to be condemned to eternal death, punishment and hell in whatever way this will be experienced.

Some study on judgement in its biblical perspectives will be helpful. Right from its background in the Old Testament, God very commonly appears in the role of 'Judge of all the earth' (Gen. 18:25) or more generally as the 'God of Justice' (Mal. 2:17; Ps. 9:8, 94:2, 97:2; Ezk. 7:27;). The judgement of God is the working out of the mercy and wrath of God in history and in human life and experience. Thus the judgement of God can bring deliverance for the righteous (Dt. 10:18; Ps. 25:9–10) as well as doom for the wicked (Ex. 6:6; Num. 33:4; Dt. 32:41; Is. 4:4; Jer. 1:10, 4:12; Ezek. 5:10, 23:10, 28:22).

The hope of the resurrection comes clearly in Daniel 12:1–3 and offers the promise that many who have died will awake, some to everlasting life, some to everlasting condemnation. The emerging idea is that people will be judged individually in the age to come or perhaps after death and consigned to their everlasting destinies. As the O.T. draws towards its close the thought of God's judgement, of the coming 'Day of the Lord' (Joel 2:1f; Am. 5:18f; Ob. 15: Zp. 1:7, 14f.; Mal. 4:1f.) is emphasized.

The New Testament continues the O.T. stress upon judgement as belonging to the nature of God and as part of his essential activity (Rom. 1:18; Heb. 12:23; 1 Pet. 1:17; 2:23; Rev. 18:8). As in the O.T. God's judgement is already at work in man's life in the present age (Jn. 8:50; Rom. 1:18, 22, 24, 26, 18; Rev. 18:8). However, this cannot be taken to mean that future judgement has been spiritualized or already taken place in the present. There is sufficient stress on the coming judgement for us to be able to agree that 'future eschatological judgement is not converted into present spiritual judgment'.[15]

In the New Testament there is a bold underlining of the judgement to come, a future and final judgement which will accompany the return of Christ (Matt. 25:31–46; Jn. 5:22, 27f.; Rom. 3:5f.; 1 Cor. 4:3–5; Heb. 6:1f). 'This is the coming day of judgement' (Jn. 6:30; Rom. 2:15f; 1 Cor. 1:8; 5:5; Eph. 4:30; Phil. 2:16; 2 Thess. 1:10; 1 Pet. 2:12; 2 Pet. 3:12; 1 Jn. 4:17; Jude 6; Rev. 6:17, 16:14). Christ himself will be the Judge (Jn. 5:22; 12:47d; Acts 10:42; 17:31; 2 Tim. 4:8). All men will be judged, none will be excused (2 Tim. 4:1; Heb. 12:23; 1 Pet. 4:5). Even the angels will be passed under more judgement (2 Pet. 2:4; Jude 6). Every aspect of life will come into account, including the 'secrets of men' (Rom. 2:16), 'the purposes of the heart' (1 Cor. 4:5), and every careless word (Matt. 12:36). Judgement will not be confined to unbelievers. Christians too will face a judgement (Matt. 7:22; 25:14–30; Lk. 19:12–28; 1 Cor. 3:12–15; 2 Cor. 5:10; Heb. 10:30; Jas. 3:1; 1 Pet. 1:17; 4:17; Rev. 20:12f.). There can be no avoiding this coming judgement (Heb. 9:27), it is as certain as death (Rom. 2:3, Heb. 10:27). Nowhere is this fact more clearly asserted than in the teachings of the parables of Jesus (Matt. 13:24–30; 36–43; 47–50; 21:33–41; 22:1–14; 25:1–13; 31–46).

Linked to our discussion on judgement is also Paul's very vivid term 'wrath,' primarily an eschatological demonstration of God against sin (Rom. 2:4 and 1

Thes. 1:10, 2 Thes. 1:8, 9). As G.E. Ladd reminds us the concept cannot 'be reduced to a natural impersonal interaction of cause and effect'.[16] In Paul, Ladd points out, 'the wrath of God is not an emotion telling how God feels, it tells rather how he acts toward sin – and sinners'. Sometimes we have tended to regard the judgement of God as the revenge of God settling score with those who have offended him. On the other hand even this emotionless judgement can be taken to the other extreme where God is seen to judge anyone who is outside our pre-set criteria for a relationship with Jesus Christ.

Romans 2.5 graphically pictures men and women 'storing up wrath' through their stubbornness and unrepentant heart. It is the person who stores this up not God! John Murray sums up – 'There is no wrath of God except as the reaction of his justice and truth against sin. Hence there is no increment of wrath, no addition to the pile of wrath stored up, except as sin on the part of man provokes and evokes wrath.'[17] Hence wrath is pictured as something we store up ourselves.

Judgement is linked with God's revealed will and humanity's response to that which is revealed. It will therefore include the entire range of human experience, thoughts, words and deeds and will be such that account is to be taken of different degrees of knowledge of God's will and hence of different degrees of ability to fulfil it (Matt. 11:21–24; Rom. 3:12–16). In our categorical conclusions we may tend to use the criteria of Jesus Christ to such an extent that even those who have not had an opportunity to respond to him will be taken to be condemned. The following conclusions may be drawn to assist us in our discussions:

1.   All people will be judged, both the living and the dead (Acts 10:42), both Christians and non-christians (Rom. 14:10–12). This future judgement is associated with Christ's final coming (Matt. 8:38; 1 Cor. 4:5; 2 Thess. 1:5–10). The Lord Jesus coming in power and glory will act as saviour and judge.

2.   Judgement will be according to works (Matt. 16:27; Rom. 2:6; Rev. 22:12). At the final judgement, a person's work will be the evidence of whether a living faith is present in him or not. Yet, those who truly belong to Jesus Christ will be exempted from the severity of this judgement.

3.   The final judgement will be a moment of division between those who are revealed truly to belong to Christ and those who do not. There will be some surprises – Some who even refer to him as 'Lord' will be condemned to hell.

4.   Salvation and condemnation for those outside of Jesus Christ is to be considered on terms of response to or rejection of that which is revealed to them of God. The criterion by which people's destiny will be determined is manifold – a failure to worship and serve the God who is generally revealed in the created order, the basis of their works in conformity to the witness of God already within them.

5.   For those who have had an opportunity to encounter Christ, it is clearly seen that their hope or judgement is on the basis of their having responded to the claims of Christ. However, there is a degree of judgement even for them.

Who Will Be Rejected?

Despite the references to scripture above, there is still an openness to the fact regarding who will be saved and who judged. On the one side we have tendencies towards universalism which gloss over sin and judgement and seem to indicate a hope for everyone. On the other hand there are those that will accept and reject people on the basis of narrowly formulated criteria either from denominational or even limitedly biblical perspectives.

Lesslie Newbigin calls us rightly 'to hold firmly together both the universalist perspective of the Bible and the clear teaching about judgement and the possibility of rejection'.[18] Newbigin is careful and offers the clarification – 'We must reject the kind of rationalistic universalism which argues from the omnipotence of God's love to the necessary ultimate salvation of every soul.'[19] He thinks that this kind of universalism does not give serious attention to the freedom and responsibility which God has given to the human person as indicated in the Bible. However, on the other side he is equally concerned that we must refuse to engage in speculation about the ultimate salvation of other people. 'In the many references to final judgement in the teaching of Jesus, the most characteristic feature is the emphasis on the element of surprise. Normal expectations will be proved completely wrong. Those who were sure of their acceptance will find themselves rejected. The last will be first and the first, last. The righteous will be shocked by the generosity of the Lord to other people (Matt. 20:1–16) and by his severity to themselves (Matt. 7:1–5). It is in line with this that when the disciples ask 'Lord, will those who are saved be few?' Jesus swiftly replies with a direct warning to the questioners 'Strive to enter by the narrow door; for many, I tell you, will seek to enter and will not be able' (Lk. 13:23–30).[20]

The reminder is needed as we have made the evangelistic enterprise a manipulative numbers game and with the pressure on statistics we ourselves must stand in judgement. There is an element of surprise, perhaps mystery in the prerogative of God that we have all but discarded with our categorically judgmental attitude towards the 'saved' and the 'lost'. As Newbigin so aptly sums up. 'The question of eternal salvation and judgment is not for speculation about the fate of other people; it is an infinitely serious practical question addressed to me.'

Very interestingly, study of the references in the teaching of Jesus to the possibility of rejection at the final judgement shows that the prime target of his warning is the people who are sure of their own salvation, not to the outsider but the insider, even those who confidently cry out 'Lord, Lord' who will find themselves rejected. This need not be taken to mean that there is no judgement for the outsider, for the sinner or for the godless, but is a forceful warning for our own caution.

Newbigin comments – 'It is the "sons of the kingdom" who will be cast out. It is the branches of the vine which will be cut off and burned if they do not bear fruit. As always in the Bible, it is the elect who come under severe judgement. The one who is appointed steward is tempted to think he is master and so falls under judgement . . . God's saving purpose works by way of election means that those who are chosen and called fall into the temptation of imagining that they have a claim on God which others do not. God must destroy this claim, otherwise the sovereignty of grace will be undone. So the warnings of judgement are addressed primarily to the elect.'[21]

In our enthusiasm to maintain the centrality of Jesus Christ, we may glibly ascribe judgement on religion, and peoples of other religions. Jesus was accusing the pharisaical Jews of an attitude that could be characteristic of some evangelicals today. The uniqueness of Jesus Christ certainly must be stressed in relation to all other religions particularly in the context of its decisive claims to be the climax of all of humankind's hopes. But that is no license for us to take up the task of judgement on ourselves lest we ourselves be judged.

VI. WHAT IS HELL?

Evangelicals have been accused of taking the biblical passages referring to hell and judgement far too literally, although noting that there are varying degrees of this acceptance. Much of our preaching of the gospel has dwelt heavily on the negative aspects and consequently incurred the criticism of the liberal scholars. In a recent publication, John Stott expresses his cautions 'with great reluctance and with a heavy heart'.[22] Dealing with the question, 'What is Hell?' he suggests that 'we need to survey the biblical material afresh and to open our minds (not just our hearts) to the possibility that Scripture points to the direction of annihilation . . .'[23] He offers four arguments.

First, Stott reminds us about the language utilized by NT writers. The vocabulary of 'destruction' is often used in relation to the final state of perdition. The commonest Greek words are the verb *appolumi* (to destroy) and the noun *apolcia* (destruction). When the verb is active and transitive, 'destroy' means 'kill'. (Matt. 2:13; 12:14; 27:4). Jesus himself told us not to be afraid of those who kill the body and cannot kill the soul. 'Rather,' he continued, 'be afraid of the One (God) who can destroy both soul and body in hell' (Matt. 10:28; cf. Jam. 4:12). Stott concludes – 'If to kill is to deprive the body of life, hell would seem to be the deprivation of both physical and spiritual life, that is, an extinction of being.'[24]

He surveys various other scripture passages to show us that hell is seen to be deprivation of both physical and spiritual life, extinction of being, destruction, etc. 'It would seem strange, therefore, if people who are said to suffer destruction are in fact not destroyed.' Stott is not saying that death is itself the end. '. . . everybody survives death and will even be resurrected, but the impenitent will finally be destroyed.'[25]

Stott's second argument concerns the imagery used in Scripture to characterize hell. Particularly referring to 'fire' he points out that Jesus spoke of 'the fire of hell' (Matt. 5:22; 18:9) and of 'eternal fire' (Matt. 18:8; 25:41), and in the Revelation there is reference to 'the lake of fire' (20:14–15). He suggests 'It is doubtless because we have all had experience of the acute pain of being burned that fire is associated in our minds with conscious torment.' But the main function of fire is not to cause pain, but to secure destruction, as all the world's incinerators bear witness.'[26]

John Stott's third argument utilizes the concept of God's justice to underline the possibility of annihilation – the belief that God will judge people 'according to what they (have) done' (e.g. Rev. 20:12); which implies that the penalty inflicted will be commensurate with the evil done. He argues – 'Would there not, then, be a serious disproportion between sins consciously committed in time and torment consciously experienced throughout eternity? I do not minimize the gravity of sin as rebellion against God our Creator, and shall return to it shortly, but I question whether "eternal conscious torment" is compatible with the biblical revelation of divine justice, unless perhaps (as has been argued) the impenitence of the lost also continues throughout eternity.'[27]

The final argument deals with passages used as the basis for universalism. Stott clarifies 'I am not a universalist . . . So there is no need for me to say more than that the hope of final salvation for everybody is a false hope, since it contradicts the recorded warnings of Jesus that the judgment will involve a separation into two opposite but equally eternal destinies. My point here, however, is that the eternal existence of the impenitent in hell would be hard to reconcile with the promises of God's final victory over evil, or with the apparently universalistic texts which speak of Christ drawing all men to himself (Jn. 12:32), and of God uniting all things to himself through Christ (Col. 1:20), and bringing every knee to bow to Christ and every tongue to confess his lordship (Philp. 2:10–11), so that in the end God will be "all in all" or everything to everybody' (1 Cor. 15:28).[28]

John Stott has definitely opened himself to much criticism. However, even more than that he has provided room for a closer look at scripture with a mind that should not be coloured by traditional attitudes to eschatological themes. We need not go completely along with Stott's proposals as he himself is honest enough to offer them tentatively. However, the reminder is for us to develop the positive side of the gospel even more – the hope of an eternal relationship with Jesus Christ.

Our material ideas of salvation as discussed earlier have led to even more material ideas of hell and judgement. My advice will be not to get sidetracked with the discussion as all that can be said about the future this side of heaven will need to be tentative with the purposeful silence we confront in scripture. The more valid reminders that we will need to underline are as follows. First, while Jesus himself confessed ignorance on certain issues related to the future, it is required that we accept an even greater measure of ignorance. Second, God's prerogative will need to be affirmed even alongside a significant dimension of mystery in relation to the future. The future is in God's hands and if we know all the details we will have exhausted the transcendent nature of God which certainly involves a great measure of unknowability.

Third, and even more relevant to the discussion – whatever heaven or hell is in their material aspects the emphasis ought to be on our relationship to Jesus. Hope and judgement are directly connected with the presence or absence of Jesus Christ. As discussed earlier even our present salvation is to be seen on these terms. Our emphasis on the future could avoid material conceptualizations of hell and heaven. When Sadhu Sundar Singh said – 'I'd rather be in hell with Jesus than in a heaven without him,' he said it all. Our hope in the future is not merely a heaven that is distinct from hell materially, but the joy of being continually in the presence of Jesus Christ himself.

VII.   THE PARABLES OF JESUS

The universal validity of Jesus Christ comes through clearly when we consider some of the parables of Jesus, while at the same time stressing the particularity of Jesus Christ. For instance, in the parable of the Wedding Banquet (Matt. 22:1–4), there is practically the entire plan of God summarized within the span of a few terse verses. The restricted invitation in the beginning is undoubtedly the election of Israel and the privilege they had enjoyed as the initially invited ones. But then the parable goes on to depict the opening out of the invitation to everyone, only as the result of the initial refusal to heed to the call. This need not be taken to mean that the universalizing of the gospel occurred only because of the stubborn refusal of the Jews to obey God. Even the book of Acts depicts this kind of sequence – the initial lack of response of the Jews and then the opening out of the opportunity for the Gentiles. Jesus himself instructed his disciples to preach first to the Jews as is clear in the command.

A parable must be looked at for its central message and very clearly the emphasis in this parable is the making available of the invitation to the banquet to everybody. The stubbornness of Israel is already evident. Jesus is now disclosing the fact of God's plan for making salvation available to everybody through his sacrifice on the cross soon to be accomplished. However, the universal availability does not mean an availability with no personal cost involved, neither an anonymous entity that gets one into the wedding feast regardless of one's identity. The second round of invitations still requires men and women to be dressed appropriately. To think that the universality of the availability of salvation implies an entry into the kingdom regardless of the way one chooses to enter is contradictory to the central message of Jesus and the development of this message in the rest of the New Testament.

In yet another parable, in the parable of the sheep and the goats (Matt. 25:31–46), Jesus stresses the universality of his ministry as he refers to the last judgment when all the nations will be gathered. However, the problem is to do with the criteria the parable depicts as valid for the separation of the two different kinds of people – one commended to eternal life and the other condemned to eternal punishment. The problem that arises is whether Jesus here speaks of the anonymous Christians, men and women saved on grounds of whatever light is made available to them, on grounds of their own goodness.

Some comments will need to be made. First, if this parable is looked at in isolation from all the other teaching of Jesus Christ, there should be no doubt that the only criteria for salvation is human compassion and generosity. But surely that is not what the rest of the Bible affirms. Having to hold this parable alongside all else that Jesus has said, we must first note that Jesus certainly expects his people not to neglect their Christlike acts of mercy and compassion to a world that will continue to be in need because of the sin of humankind. Greed and covetousness will always leave some men and women deprived and the Christian must respond as Christ would.

However, the other point that will need to be admitted even more is that there appears to be the possibility of men and women being saved on grounds of their sincerity, where they operated within a limited knowledge of God's salvation having been deprived of the opportunity to know Jesus Christ in this world. This is a rebuke to the neat formulas we have developed to distinguish the saved from the unsaved, and the cocksure arrogance that we display in rejecting those whom God may have already received. This does not mean there are no external signs which will enable us to distinguish those who are in Christ from those who are not, but rather it challenges the false certainty based on the static formulated approaches to a conversion event, with little concern for God's hand in the conversion process drawing men and women to himself.

The question often arises in relation to the sincerity and the outward goodness of many men and women, devout and dedicated – will they be saved despite their lack of any observable commitment to Jesus Christ. The standard reply is 'No', the reason being men and women are saved only through Jesus Christ. While this is true, are we really in a position to make such judgements ourselves? Commenting on the kind of attitude with which Christians make claims that pre-empt the final judgement of God, Lesslie Newbigin points out that 'it is the wrong question, because it is a question to which God alone has the right to give an answer'.[29] In keeping with his comments earlier, he comments – 'Nothing could be more remote from the whole thrust of Jesus' teaching than the idea that we are in a position of know in advance the final judgement of God.' Judgment day will be a day of surprises, of reversals, of astonishment. 'In his most developed parable of the last judgements, the parable of the sheep and the goats, both the saved and the unsaved are astonished. Surely theologians at least should know that the judge on the last day is God and no one else.'[30]

Evangelicals have privatized the gospel to such an extent that statements are made on behalf of God from limited interpretations of a few verses of the Bible. Even the verses chosen are those that seem to emphasize individual benefits rather the richer dimensions of salvation and what it means to God himself and his kingdom. Once again on the question – 'who will be saved?' Newbigin makes his dissatisfaction known because 'the question starts with the individual and his or her need to be assured of ultimate happiness, and not with God and his glory.'[31] He correctly complains that 'Christians have privatised the mighty work of grace and talked as if the whole cosmic drama of salvation culminated in the words "For me, for me." '[32]

This is a timely reminder when we find ourselves in our pluralistic predicament. The privatization of the gospel has reached such frightening proportions that we seem to be launching out on an updated version of the older colonial mission, claiming converts into the Kingdom merely on grounds of their 'yes' or 'no', or in some cases the signing of a card that is stacked away in our files once they have found their place in statistics for our reports. One must not discard the personal emphasis of the gospel as that is part of the uniqueness of Jesus' relationship to his followers. What Newbigin is concerned about, and what should be our concern too, is that the emphasis has shifted to so much of what we have made the gospel to be, an over emphasis on human efforts that there does not seem to be any room for God's prerogative, his miraculous outworking anymore.

The point that Jesus makes in his parables is that the universal scope of his eschatological influence within the particular plans for God for his world are much broader than we can comprehend. The grace of God is unreachably beyond our conceptualizing, even more beyond our attempts to press it into predictable actions. Even the observable seeds we plants are those that will grow into infinitely greater proportions than we can at present speculate. It is within such an unpredictable and unmeasurable dimension that our finitude finds its meaning and significance both now and in the kingdom to come. There is a greater measure of the transcendent mystery of God when it comes to our final hope and judgement than what has been revealed. This is Paul's emphasis when he speaks of the future of the believer in God.

CONCLUSION

We have surveyed a small range of theological and biblical material which although limited draws us towards the emphasis on the uniqueness of Jesus Christ. One point that will come through clearly is that his uniqueness is powerfully highlighted in the finality of the revelation of Jesus Christ rather than drawing out distinctions at present. The end-perspective of the revelation of Jesus Christ is that which we will need to underline even more.

Our discussions have also dealt with some aspects of the future. What is heaven? What is hell? Although I have cautioned that we do not get side-tracked by material speculations of these facts, the one powerful distinctive of a future with Jesus Christ is in a reality that can be contrasted with the abstractness of Hindu or Buddhist concepts, or even the over emphasis on the material in Islamic concepts of heaven. There are two aspects that may be highlighted.[33]

First, 'the overwhelming reality will be God himself – God in his totality as Father, Son and Spirit.'[34] The Book of Revelation abounds with pictures of this reality – 'I heard a loud voice speaking from the throne: "Now God's home is with mankind! He will live with them, and they shall be his people. God himself will be with them and he will be their God"' (Rev. 21:3). Jesus in his parables relates our destiny in terms of this relationship – a wedding feast where God is the host (Matt. 22:1–10), a household where the master graciously serves his servants (Lk. 12:35–38). This overwhelming reality is not the sense of God consuming our identity but one where it flourishes to the fullest.

Secondly, the future with God is a future in community. This is the community that lives in the 'Shaloam' of God, as the people of God living for the purpose they were created. We certainly ought to say that 'heaven is other people'. This is one reason why we shall have bodies – resurrection bodies. 'To have resurrection bodies implies that we shall be distinct persons, with our own identity, able to relate to others and to God.'[35] It is the reality of individuals bound together in community under one Lord that is the uniqueness of the Christian hope made available through the redemptive work of the unique Saviour and Lord Jesus Christ.

NOTES

1. Moltmann, Jürgen, *Theology of Hope* (London: SCM Press Ltd., 1967), p. 16.
2. Käsemann, Ernst. *New Testament Questions of Today* (London: SCM Press Ltd. 1969), p. 82.
3. *Ibid.*, p. 102.
4. I*bid.*
5. *Ibid.* p. 107.
6. *Ibid.*
7. Moltmann, Jürgen. *Theology of Hope* (London: SCM Press Ltd., 1967), p. 16.

8. Pannenberg, Wolfhart. *Jesus God and Man* (London: SCM Press Ltd., 1968), p. 60–61.

9. *Ibid.*, p. 61.

10. *Ibid.*

11. *Ibid.*, p. 67.

12. *Ibid.*

13. *Ibid.*, p. 69.

14. Moltmann, *Theology of Hope*, p. 194.

15. Ladd, G.E., *A Theology of the New Testament* (London: Lutherworth Press, 1974), p. 307.

16. *Ibid.*, p. 407.

17. The Epistle to the Romans. *New London Commentaries*. Marshall Morgan & Scott. London 1974. p. 61.

18. Newbigin, Lesslie. *The Open Secret* (Eerdmans, 1978), p. 88.

19. *Ibid.*

20. *Ibid.*, p. 88.

21. *Ibid.*, p. 89.

22. Edwards, David L. with Stott, John, *Essentials* (London: Hodder & Stoughton, 1988, p. 312).

23. *Ibid.*, p. 315.

24. *Ibid.*

25. *Ibid.*, p. 316.

26. *Ibid.*

27. *Ibid.*, p. 318–319.

28. *Ibid.*, p. 319.

29. Newbigin, Lesslie, *The Gospel in a Pluralist Society* (London: SPCK, 1989), p. 177.

30. *Ibid.*

31. *Ibid.*, p. 179.

32. *Ibid.*

33. Travis, Stephen H. *I Believe in the Second Coming of Jesus* (London: Hodder & Stoughton 1982), I have drawn from Travis' discussion on pp. 177–181.

34. *Ibid.*, p. 177.

35. *Ibid.*, p. 179.

21

Stephen T. Franklin

This thought-provoking analysis of the theological foundations for our under-standing of and witness to the unique Christ deserves careful reading. The author argues that the uniqueness of Christ does not rest primarily in any doctrine, image or symbol, for they have analogies in other religions and belief systems – for example, the doctrine of incarnation. Nor does the uniqueness of Christ reside in our Christian religious experience, for there too there are parallels – for example, the experience of salvation by grace alone. Rather, he argues, the uniqueness is found in the 'historical–factual' meaning of events in biblical history – for example, the Exodus and the Resurrection. These are God's actions. Jesus Christ is the unique action of God. He distinguishes this evangelical understanding from the secular view of history as in liberalism and the mythological interpretation of John Hick and company. Further, the author's understanding of our 'existential-universal' experience of the historical-factual enables us to relate the present to the past and to the future. His treatment of the use of analogy, especially when it becomes idolatrous, brings a wholeness to the discussion. Some reflection on the way God interprets his acts in history in verbal revelation – for example, the meaning of the Cross, would have been helpful and necessary to the doctrine of the unique Christ.

For many Christians, a reference to 'The Unique Christ as the Hope and Judgment of the World' arouses vivid images of the end times: the day of resurrection and the final judgement. As evangelicals, we believe that the final resurrection and the final judgement will be actual events in (a perhaps profoundly altered) time and space. We also believe that the primary actor in these events will be Jesus of Nazareth – not as a generalized image nor as a symbol, but as the specific God-man in all his individual personality.

These *future* events, however, do not exhaust the Christian meaning of either hope or judgement. Judgement is also a *present* reality. John 3:18–12 teaches that those who do not believe on Jesus Christ are judged already. What we hope for, must, by definition, be in the future, but the possession of hope can be a present blessing. Peter describes Christian existence as

Dr. Stephen T. Franklin is Professor of Philosophy and Theology at Tokyo Christian University, Japan.

characterized by faith, joy, love, and hope, all of which come from God through Jesus Christ (1 Pet. 1:3–9). In addition, judgement and hope are also linked to *past* history because they are based on God's previous actions – above all, on the death and resurrection of Jesus Christ outside the city gates of Jerusalem early in the first century.

The Bible teaches that hope and judgement, whether past, present, or future, depend on the unique, specific individual whom we know as Jesus of Nazareth, as Jesus who is the Christ. The unqualified, unapologetic, joyful confession of the uniqueness, supremacy, and centrality of Jesus Christ marks evangelicals. Most of us reject any attempt to limit or reduce the claim that Jesus is the only way to God. For example, we reject the notion that Jesus is supreme *for us* when that is taken to imply that other roads, other saviours, other practices may legitimately be supreme for other people. Another example: while judgement itself belongs in God's hands and not ours, daily life among non-Christians forces us – whether we like to or not and whether we try to avoid it or not – to evaluate the actions, practices, and beliefs of other people. In doing so, evangelicals take Jesus Christ to be the standard by which to make such evaluations. Such an appeal to Jesus Christ may offend not only non-Christians but even other Christians who have internalized the pluralism of our age. But, because Jesus Christ is supreme and unique, we have no other option. And as evangelicals, we steadfastly (but gently, kindly, and politely, I would hope) point all people to Jesus Christ as the universally and supremely valid way, truth, and life.

What I have written thus far is confession: the unique Jesus Christ is the final hope and judge of the world, both of the individual people in the world and of our social, political, economic, and cultural institutions. But in what does this uniqueness rest? It is, after all, an empirical fact that most religions – maybe all of them – offer some sort of hope and teach some sort of judgement. Islam is nothing is not adamant about the coming judgement (in which Jesus is said to have a major role!). And Buddhism, in addition to its final liberation, offers innumerable heavens, hells, and judgements and not just the one heaven, one hell, and one judgement heralded by Christianity and Islam. Next Sunday, most people sitting in the pew, even in so-called Christian countries, will have a friend or co-worker who accepts one of these alternative, non-Christian views. Our evangelical churches may confess the uniqueness of Jesus Christ as the world's hope and judge, but the everyday life of most members of those churches will challenge that confession. Our historical situation urgently demands that we demonstrate just how and why Christ is unique. We must make this demonstration not only to the larger world but for our own people as well.

THE UNIQUENESS OF CHRIST DOES *NOT* RESIDE IN DOCTRINES, IMAGES, OR SYMBOLS

Let me mention several places where the uniqueness of Christ does *not* reside. First, the uniqueness of Christ does not rest primarily in any doctrine, image, or symbol. Any important Christian doctrine or symbol will have analogies in other religions and belief systems.[2]

Individual Doctrines

Scholars of comparative religions commonly apply the notion of incarnation not just to Jesus but to many other figures and even to inanimate objects in other religions. The Shiite Muslims have their imams who are said to carry in themselves the full divine presence. While one might make the case that this Shiite teaching historically derives from the Christian model, it is harder to argue that the Hindu avatars of Vishnu stem from Christian models. Of course, the Hindu avatars are not exact parallels to orthodox Christianity because most Hindu intellectuals would have a docetic understanding of them. That is, it is less significant whether or not there really was a fish swimming in the ocean in whom Vishnu dwelt than that we have the story or image of such a fish. In the case of Krishna, however, it does seem important to some worshippers that such an individual actually existed historically.[3] As a high school boy living in the country of Panama, I made friends with a family who had emigrated from India to Panama. They had a poster, whose meaning at the time I did not grasp but whose incongruity even then was fully apparent. This poster included pictures of the traditional avatars of Vishnu (the boar, the fish, Krishna, etc.), but in addition, the poster had pictures of Jesus and, if I remember correctly, the Virgin Mary. Here Jesus and Mary had been absorbed into a pastiche of Hinduism and Roman Catholicism as incarnations of Vishnu.

The notion of incarnation can be extended – perhaps 'stretched' would be a better word – even farther. Inside certain traditional Japanese Shinto shrines, there is a 'Holy of Holies' holding a special object such as a mirror, or sword, or stone-jewel. This object is called the shintai which can be translated as 'Divine Object'. The Divine Object provides a place for the presence of the Sacred. In a very general sense, one may say that most religious traditions – certain forms of mysticism, gnostic traditions, etc., may be exceptions – apprehend the divine presence through some very concrete object or person. The absence of such a concrete object/person may even signal a turn toward philosophy and away from religion. Thus, considered as a theme, incarnation, far from being unique to Christianity, seems to be a universal possession of the religious heritage of mankind.

Combinations of Doctrines and Combinations of Images

This same logic could be extended to every other doctrine concerning Jesus Christ and the Christian religion. Creation, fall, sin, atonement, propitiation, resurrection, church, sanctification, the rule of God, and hope and judgement – these all have analogues in other religions. It must be immediately added that no analogy is exactly perfect. But every Christian doctrine has a counterpart in at least one other religion which is remarkably close – close enough to cause considerable uneasiness when our North American students and parishioners encounter them for the first time. And if we accept somewhat weaker analogies, then we will find almost endless parallels in other religions to each Christian doctrine.

It must also be added that the various Christian doctrines fit together to form an overall pattern, a gestalt, and an ethos. While at a rather abstract level, other religions exhibit analogies to the general gestalt of Christian doctrine, at a more concrete level, the gestalt of Christianity gives it a unique 'feel' or 'tone'. At the abstract level, one can make a good case, for example, that all religions have some vision of the ideal state of affairs (their version of creation), some statement of a deviation from that idea state of affairs (their version of the fall), and some statement of how to cope with those deviations (their version of salvation). Yet Christianity – and every other religion as well – fleshes out this abstract pattern in its own unique way. The world view presupposed by Christianity (with its creator God) and that presupposed, for example, by Zen Buddhism (with its stress on ultimate Emptiness (are clearly contradictory.

In addition, there is a middle zone between the meaning of a particular doctrine and the gestalt of the entire religion. In this middle ground, several doctrines in a non-Christian religion may combine in pattern that are hauntingly parallel to Christianity. A good example comes from the True Pure Land Religions of Japan. The Buddhist saint Shinran (1174–1268) despaired of ever working his way to salvation, and came to depend totally on the mercies of Amida. Amida had made a vow to bring all sentient creation into enlightenment even if this took countless eons of reincarnations, each reincarnation bringing greater perfection and merit. Shinran taught that faith in Amida allowed one to appropriate the infinite merits that Amida had build up through these endless reincarnations. Amida asked only that people should trust him to provide this salvation. Shinran clearly understood that if 'faith alone' counts, then his efforts as a monk were meaningless. So he gave up his monk's status, married a former nun, and began preaching his message to the common people. The common people, who had neither the financial resources nor the social freedom to pursue the rigours of monastic meditation, could surely place their trust in Amida. Shinran, it should be added, had no desire to create a new Buddhist sect, but opposition from the established Buddhism along with the commitment of his followers resulted in a new Buddhist sect.

The parallel with Luther is astonishing. Certainly Shinran taught a Pauline-like doctrine of salvation by grace through faith. When, however, we expand the parallel between Shinran and Luther/Paul to other doctrines, some profound differences emerge. For example, there is no clear doctrine of creation, and there is no notion of an atonement through a vicarious death that pays the penalty of our sins. And Amida is neither the creator of the universe nor the incarnation of the creator-god. However much, and however appropriately, one may wish to speak of the Christ-figure in Amida-Buddhism, the entire gestalt of ideas differs dramatically between the two religions.

Conclusion

The conclusion I wish to draw is that doctrines, ideas, symbols, or images do not, by themselves precisely distinguish the special character of Christ from other figures in world religions. Of course, the total gestalt of ideas concerning Christ is different from the total gestalt of beliefs in other religions (except at a highly generic level). Every other religion, however, can make the same claim for the uniqueness of its own pattern of beliefs. The specialness of Christianity, in short, is not special, if we attend solely to the ideational or symbolic structure of Christianity.

THE UNIQUENESS OF CHRIST DOES *NOT* RESIDE IN RELIGIOUS EXPERIENCE

Let me turn to a second area where the uniqueness of Christianity does not reside. The religious experience of Christians does not decisively distinguish between Christianity (or Christ) and other religions (or other saviours). I do not dispute that experience has a profound role in Christianity. Christians get experientally involved with their religion in many ways, some appropriate and some inappropriate – for example, in revivals, in worship, in sacramentalism, in mysticism and in commitments to serve as clergy, missionaries, and lay leaders. Evangelicals in particular would not dismiss the role of experience. We are known for our emphasis on a 'personal relationship with' or a 'commitment to' Jesus Christ – which surely has an experiential dimension. It should also be noted that quite beyond the evangelical world, Christians generally have emphasized the role of experience. The name of Schleiermacher comes immediately to mind. For Schleiermacher the primary meaning of a Christian doctrine as well as the norms for its truth were to be found in Christian experience. He argued that Christian doctrine must explicate the structure of Christian experience. Many, many theologians have followed in Schleiermacher's footsteps, arguing that the Christian religion has first and foremost to deal with our human experience of the divine, or, to phrase it differently, with the divine dimension in our experience.

Most theologians today, evangelical or not, would affirm the role of experience in Christianity. Nonetheless, the uniqueness of Christ cannot be established on the basis of our Christian experience. To whatever experience we might turn, we can find a similar experience in other religions. For example, other religions can certainly match the intensity of Christian commitment. Consider the depth of conviction that motivates many Muslims to holy battle or the passion that enables certain Hindus to walk on fire. Yoga, meditation, and mysticism (no matter how defined) can produce deep and powerful forms of ecstacy. Love for a god, for the ultimate, for a saviour can be found throughout the world. Nearly every religion has some parallel to glossolalia. The same is true of the experiences of atonement, forgiveness, and reconciliation. To take one example, sacramental experience extends far beyond Christianity. I have observed a ceremony at the Shinto shrine in Izumo in which the priests made offerings of cooked rice and sakè (rice-wine) to the gods of Japan, and then the believers ate the rice and drank the sakè as gifts in which the gods made themselves available to those believers. And when visiting in India, I noticed that some of the ceremonies of worship ended with meals of divine-human communion.

It is sometimes said that (in non-Christian religions) men reach out to God, whereas God in Christ reaches out to men. It would follow that only Christianity offers the experience of grace, of being found by God. While this may be true as a Christian evaluation of the real nature of other religions, it is not true as a phenomenological or empirical description of the religious experiences to be found in these other religions. Many forms of bhakti in Hinduism as well a the True Pure Land sects in Buddhism claim to experience grace and to taste salvation as a gift.

In summary: our claim that Jesus is the unique judge and hope of the world cannot be rooted merely in Christian experience or in Christian doctrine.

HISTORICAL EVENTS AND THE CHRIST

Where then can we find the uniqueness of Christ? To move our discussion towards an answer, I wish to repeat a comment made earlier. Every religion has its own gestalt, its own ethos, and its own feel and tone. It is certainly permissible, therefore, to explore the specificity of any religion. To search for the specificity of a religion is to search for those factors, if any, which drive the religion towards its characteristic dogmas, rituals, theologies, ethical systems, and attitudes.

The Old Testament Events: Historical and Mythical

It is a well-worn but important observation that biblical religion emerges out of particular historical experiences. In the Old Testament, the Exodus stands as the great event of salvation, which is not to deny God saved Israel from her enemies many other times as well. The Exodus so overwhelms later Hebrew experience that most scholars, even on secular assumptions, hesitate to dismiss its historicity entirely.[5] Gerhard von Rad, hardly an evangelical, goes so far as to argue that the Old Testament's formulation of its doctrine of creation – as a specific, one-time event – emerged out of Israel's profound reflection on those specific historical events in which she experienced salvation from her enemies.[6] The important point to notice is this: when Israel experienced salvation, as in the Exodus, she experienced God's action. The focus is always on what God has done.[7]

Israel has to defend her historical foundations against the mythically oriented religion of her Canaanite neighbours.[8] The great scholar of comparative religions, Mircea Eliade, has taught us that a fundamental function of the myths of most early religions, including Canaanite religion, was to structure the current experience of the worshipper and put him into contact with the Sacred.[9]

The myths of Baal were not intended to give historical information about what happened at one particular time, but were intended to put us into contact with what is true at all times. The mythic 'time' of the stories of Baal is really the sacred dimension of reality that is equally present at all 'historical times'. The same applies to the sense of space in mythic religions. There is no contradiction between a myth which pictures creation as beginning in the centre of my city, making it the centre of the universe, and another myth which states that creation began in the centre of your city, making it the centre of the universe. The respective myths function to place the believers in contact with the mythic 'space' which is equally present in all spaces, not to provide a factual account of particular occurrences at specific locations.

The early prophets – Elijah is the paradigm, but Samuel, Amos and others may also be mentioned – forced Israel to confront the Canaanite religion. Who is the God of Israel – Jahweh or Baal? On what did the existence of Israel depend – the historical Exodus and Covenant or the experience of the omnipresent, omnitemporal, true time and true space offered by the myths and rituals of Baal? Four hundred priests of Baal lost their lives at Mt. Carmel in conflict with Elijah precisely over this issue. The Old Testament records the growing awareness of Israel that her destiny depended on Jahweh alone.

Israel's Incorporation of the Mythic Dimension[10] into Her Religion

Yet Israel could not entirely avoid the mythic dimension of religion. Canaanite myth and ritual apparently focused on the land, on sexuality and fertility, and on the seasons – on what we would call nature. Israel had to ask herself this question: if Jahweh's role is limited to past historical events (escape from enemies), then can he really be adequate to sustain the continuing existence of Israel? Did not Israel also need saving from droughts, famines, and infertility as well as enemy nations? Israel had to learn that Jahweh can be Israel's true saviour only if he is also the creator and, thus, master of heaven and earth. It is fascinating to observe how many of the stories about Elijah focus on Jahweh's capacity to control rain, famine, lightning, thunder, fertility, food, health, and even life and death, where such concerns were the special province of Baal. In short, Jahweh must be present, not just in history, but in nature as well, shaping our experience of the Holy in nature. That is, there must be a mythic dimension to Hebrew religion as well as a historical dimension.

There is, however, another and perhaps equally important reason why Hebrew religion had to incorporate the mythic dimension into its own religious consciousness. The prophets taught that Israel could expect Jahweh to continue to provide salvation from her enemies because God had brought Israel out of Egypt and because he had made a Covenant with Israel at Sinai. Somehow, therefore, the Exodus and the Sinaitic Covenant had to be made a part of the living experience of later generations of Hebrews. In short, the Exodus and Sinai stories had to be given a mythic dimension for later generations lest their significance be lost. The Hebrew community did this in various ways. One was by having later generations periodically renew the Covenant (Deut. 30:15–20, Josh. 24:1–28, 2 Kings 23:1–3, etc.). Joshua's covenant renewal ceremony at Shechem is particularly fascinating because in the ceremony Joshua has God saying 'I brought you out [of Egypt],' 'I brought you to the land of the Amorites', etc. By the time of Joshua's renewal ceremony, however, only Caleb and Joshua himself had been adults at the time of the Exodus. Some of the oldest of Joshua's listeners may have been children, but most had not yet been born when the Exodus occurred. Yet Joshua's speech views all his listeners as if they had been full participants in these historical events. The Exodus and Sinai have become contemporaneous for the hearers, and these stories now have the role of structuring the hearers' present existence, and of putting them into contact with God's sacred power. In short, Joshua's speech focuses on the present availability of the Exodus and Sinaitic Covenant for the new generation.

The Historical-Factual and Existential-Universal Dimensions of Events, Stories, and Doctrines

I wish to introduce some technical terminology at this point. On the one hand, insofar as they are particular, factual occurrences in history, the Exodus and the Sinaitic Covenant have a 'historical-factual' significance.[11] On the other hand, insofar as they are present realities in the lives of later generations of Hebrews, the Exodus and the Sinaitic Covenant have an 'existential-universal' meaning.[12] And, of course, stories about the Exodus and the Sinaitic Covenant may be used to structure the experience of later generations and to put these later generations into contact with the sacred power of Jahweh; such stories may then be said to have an 'existential-universal' dimension of meaning.

The terminology of 'historical-factual' and 'existential-universal' can be expanded to include all the major doctrines of Christianity. Thus the historical–factual resurrection is nothing less than God's act of raising Jesus from the dead, outside the city gates of Jerusalem approximately 1,960 years ago. Yet the resurrection must also be made present to the later generations of Christian believers. In the words of an American spiritual, 'Were you there when God raised Jesus from the tomb?' The resurrection, through the power of the Holy Spirit, shapes our current experience of salvation, of self-understanding, and of access to God's presence. Similar analyses could be made of doctrines such as incarnation, atonement, Pentecost, crucifixion, and even creation and judgement.

My basic theory is that the specific character of biblical religion and, thus, of Christianity stems from the priority given to the historical-factual dimension of the Bible's basic teaching and doctrines. The basic content of the doctrine of the Exodus, for example, is God's action of saving Israel out of Egypt. And if we want to know the fundamental meaning of the incarnation, we must appeal to God's act in which he took on flesh in Jesus Christ. Both of these are particular events, located in the temporal sequence of history. In addition, the Exodus and incarnation also have an existential-universal dimension. The Exodus is a part of the contemporary, living experience of every later generation of Christians as, for example, they experience Christ through the physical bread and wine of the Lord's Supper, as they express practical compassion for physical suffering, and as they take joy in the physical aspects of their marriages. Nevertheless, neither sacraments nor ethical action nor Christian marriage carries any normative weight in itself; the actual historical and factual incarnation that began in Mary's womb provides the basic meaning of the incarnation and serves as the norm for all the other experiential and universal meanings of incarnation. In short, because biblical religion is rooted in specific historical events, and because the religious experiences of later generations are normatively grounded in the specificity of these events, it follows that a biblically based religion will emphasize its unique and particular characteristics and will resist the universalization of this historical specificity into mythic patterns whose truth-value is determined by the experience of the contemporary believer.

The Historical-Factual Priority of Jesus Christ

The New Testament presents Jesus Christ as God's action. That is, the Christ-event is something that God did. In the Old Testament, God acts in, and as the cause of, certain events, such as rescuing Israel out of Egypt and of constantly refilling the jar of flour and jug of oil for the widow of Zarephath during the drought (1 Kngs. 17:7–16). In the New Testament, those sorts of divine actions continue to occur. But, in addition, there is a new form of divine action – the life and teachings of a particular man, Jesus of Nazareth, are proclaimed to be the very action of God. ('God proves his love for us in that while we were yet sinners, Christ died for us', Rom. 5:8, and 'Anyone who has seen me has seen the Father', Jn. 14:9b).

The Christian emphasis on the specific individual Jesus Christ and, thus, on his uniqueness, has several roots. First, insofar as God has acted in Jesus Christ, we have another case of God's action at a particular time and place in history. Therefore, in doctrines connected with Jesus Christ (incarnation, resurrection, atonement, etc.), the primary emphasis will be on the historical-factual foundation of those doctrines – that is, on Jesus Christ himself. Of course, somehow, the events in the life of Jesus must be made available for the experience of later Christians; that is, they must have an existential-universal function as well. Nonetheless, as part of the heritage of Hebrew religion, priority must be granted to the historical-factual event of Jesus Christ. The historical and factual Jesus of Nazareth, who is God's action, must be the norm by which we give content to all our Christological doctrines and by which we evaluate the appropriateness of our existential-universal appropriations and applications of these doctrines.

Second, some weight must be given to the fact that in the New Testament, God's supreme action did not merely take place through a prophet or other person, but that God's supreme action was (and is) nothing less than a person. Particular, historical persons who actually lived have a specificity and power which is possessed by no other kind of event or object. They have, to use Martin Buber's classic phrase, an unrepeatable identity as a particular 'thou' that cannot be reduced to a fully describable and analysable 'it'.

Even the Exodus, while it certainly was a particular and specific event, was also an example of a class of events – namely, escapes from slavery or divine rescues. Fictional characters can often leave an impression of great specificity and uniqueness, but that is a by-product of the much greater specificity and unrepeatability of genuine, individual human beings. Of course, people can be put into various classifications of age, rank, sex, nationality, personality, occupation, residence, etc. But these categories, whether considered one-by-one or as an entire group, somehow miss the essence of the actual, individual, human being as he exists in time and space. To the extent, therefore, that Christianity rests on God's action in a person – and not just in a dramatic rescue out of slavery or even in raining fire down from heaven to consume Elijah's sacrifice on Mt. Carmel – we have an additional basis for expecting Christianity to focus on the specific, unique, unrepeatable Jesus of Nazareth who is God's own action.

The Bible provides a number of other avenues for approaching the figure of Jesus. We could, for example, trace the implications of the various titles and roles for Jesus Christ – Messiah, Son of Man, Saviour, Lord, eschatological prophet, etc. And we could trace the New Testament's application to Jesus of various Old Testament passages which, in their original context, referred to Jahweh. In each case, we find that the New Testament roots its message in the historical-factual figure of Jesus Christ in all his specificity, idiosyncrasy, particularity, and individuality.

It may be worth noting that the later Christological and Trinitarian controversies are both a natural and a necessary continuation of the biblical emphasis on the historical Jesus of Nazareth. Modern advocates of pluralism – such as John Hick – are quite correct to attack both the notion of God-Incarnate and the related doctrine of the Trinity if they wish to undermine the notion of Christian uniqueness or normativity.[13] Hick and company have reversed the priority of the historical-factual over the existential-universal;

they have reversed the priority of God's specific action at a particular time and place over God's mythic presence at every time and place.

Let's look briefly at some of the implications of calling the incarnation a myth, as Hick would suggest. It implies [a] the devaluation of the actual occurrence in Mary's womb as normative. God's presence in Mary's womb is 'just a myth' in the negative sense of myth – as a story about something that did not actually happen in real history. But, more positively, to call the incarnation a myth also implies [b] that it is a story which can be used to interpret and structure Christian experience. It can open up to our experience that sacred place, which being at no particular place is at every place, and that sacred time, which being at no particular time is at every time. Lastly, to call the incarnation a myth is to recognize the possibility that other myths might also provide an access, a window to the divine. Other myths might connect the believer with the same aspects of the Sacred Mystery or with other aspects of the Sacred Mystery. In either case, since myths do not make any normative appeals to the history of God's actions, they do not necessarily conflict with each other. In short, to call the incarnation a myth is to imply that there is no place for Christian triumphalism nor for any claim that Jesus Christ is the norm by which to test all other claims to religious or ethical knowledge.

It is no accident, therefore, that evangelicals have maintained their commitment to a high Christology and to the doctrine of the Trinity. Both doctrines refer us back to the historical-factual ground of our Christian religion, to God's act in Jesus of Nazareth. We would affirm, of course, that Christological and other Christian doctrines also have existential-universal meanings; but these existential-universal meanings are secondary and under the norm of God's action in the specific, historical Jesus Christ. This return to the historical-factual foundations of our faith is a characteristic mark of biblical religion and provides the underlying explanation for the specific and idiosyncratic form of Christian doctrines, rituals, theologies, ethical systems, and attitudes. This priority of the historical-factual Christ-event over its existential-universal dimensions may be called the 'Christian *a-priori*'.[14]

THE CHRISTIAN *A-PRIORI*

In the previous section we sought those factors that drive Christianity towards its distinctive forms. We found that underlying biblical religion is a commitment to the radical priority of the historical-factual character of God's actions over the existential-universal appropriation of those actions by later generations. This we called the Christian *a priori*.

There is nothing in principle, however, to prevent other religions from searching for their own *a priori* – for searching for those factors which give the religion its characteristic doctrines, rituals, etc. As each religion finds its own *a-priori*, its own structure, we should expect to find both differences and similarities with Christianity, probably more differences than similarities. The significance of those difference/similarities for a particular religion will be determined by the character of that religion's *a priori*.[15]

If we know the *a priori* that gives a religion its gestalt and ethos, we can make some educated guesses about its likely responses to the existence of other religions. Many religions, both in practice and in theory, give priority to the existential-universal dimension. This would be true of those religions with an orientation to the mythic (in Eliade's sense). A mythically oriented religion would, most likely, try to find some way of accommodating Christianity. A mythic religion can be quite accepting of other religions – at least as 'lesser' or preliminary religious paths. For example, Buddhism, which is strongly oriented to the existential-universal side of religion, actually needs other religions to co-exist with it. The myths, rituals, and meditational techniques of Buddhism are intended to provide insight into one's own ultimate identity. But for the full round of human existence – birth, marriage, fertility, etc. – Buddhism has little to offer and has no objection to the simultaneous practice of other religions.[16] It must also be stated that most of the advanced mythic religions – Buddhism, Hinduism, gnosticism, etc. – perceive themselves as quite tolerant, although most of them also perceive themselves as the final or highest stage of religious truth. Such religions will certainly view Christianity as intolerant with its stress on particular divine actions – above all, the incarnation in Jesus Christ – as the norm for all religious claims. Advocates of such religions are likely to feel more comfortable with a mythic reinterpretation of Christianity in which the Christ-motif takes priority over the historical Jesus. Such a mythic Christ, then, would become just one more way of encountering the divine.

In theory, it is certainly possible for another, non-Christian religion to give priority to the historical-factual dimension, just as Christianity does. In that case, there would be a professed set of special events on which the religion would be based, where these events were divine actions or otherwise revealed the Sacred Power of the universe. This would create a very sharp conflict with Christianity. In principle, however, it would be impossible for both sets of events to have occurred as reported by the respective religions. Thus, historical investigation of the professed events would be quite relevant in deciding between the two religions.[17] In fact, it might even happen that historical investigation could actually settle the disagreement between such a religion and Christianity, because proof of the non-occurrence of one of the central 'events' on which the religion was founded would decisively count against the truth of that religion. Any religion founded on historical-factual events runs a risk – namely, that the events did not occur or that they occurred in significantly different ways than reported by that religion. Finally it should be observed that such attention to historical facts simply is not relevant when interacting with religions that give priority to the existential-universal dimension.[18]

An Extension of the Existential-Universal Dimension of Christian Doctrine

The Christian faith begins with God's historical-factual acts, supremely Jesus Christ. It makes those past actions available in the present, which is the existential-universalism dimension of Christianity. Stories, creeds, rituals, etc., can be used either historically-factually or existentially-universally, that is, to point to the original actions or to open up their present significance and presence.

The Bible, it should be noted, contains literature that does not directly fit into the scheme of historical-factual and existential-universal meanings as it has been developed thus far. The wisdom literature, for example, does not normally refer to God's saving acts in history, nor does it apply those acts to the present, nor does it tell stories (as myths do). The Book of Proverbs, for example, provides guidance for daily living and Job and Ecclesiastes challenge the standard wisdom of the people of Israel. The guidance is intended to enable one to live well before Jahweh, in short to connect us with Jahweh in our everyday life. In that sense, the wisdom literature may be said to have an 'extended' existential-universal meaning.[19] I would argue, however, that even the wisdom literature functions only within the context of a primary Hebrew commitment to God's historical-factual actions as the foundation of Israel's existence.

It possible to expand the existential-universal dimension of Christianity to an even broader horizon. Scholars of, for example, literary analysis often find Christian categories, such as sin, redemptive suffering, atonement, etc., useful tools for analyzing fiction, even fiction from non-Christian cultures. Anthropologists have found parallels to Christian categories in many cultures. We have already mentioned that each doctrine of Christianity has a close analogue in one or more non-Christian religions. And an entire discipline, the theology of culture, has used Christian categories to understand cultural phenomena.

I believe that these uses of Christian categories simply extend their existential-universalism meaning. To be sure, such highly extended applications of the existential-universal meaning of Christian doctrines no longer function to put the hearer into direct contact with the historical-factual acts of God that originally gave these doctrines their normative meanings within Christianity. But neither can the applicability of Christian categories outside the Christian religion be dismissed as accidental coincidence.

There are a number of places in which we might look to explain the applicability of Christian doctrines outside of Christianity. The doctrine of creation tells us that God is the maker of heaven and earth. If God is personal, as evangelicals surely believe, then we would expect his creation to exhibit characteristic traces of his individual character. Since God's character is supremely, normatively, and foundationally revealed in his historical-factual acts culminating in Jesus Christ, we should expect to find parallels or analogies between God's specific actions (which ground Christian doctrine) and his acts in creation. Another place we might look at is the doctrine of the Logos, especially in the light of the claim that it was the Logos who became flesh in Jesus Christ. One might also point to general revelation or to the doctrine of common grace. If all human beings have an innate – albeit perhaps subconscious – awareness of God, then the character of the true God should have some impact upon all human religion, culture, and consciousness. Sin might distort this impact, but we should not expect it to be missing.

The Doctrine of Analogy and Christ as Hope and Judge of the World

Assuming that our argument has thus far been correct, it seems plausible to expect that certain analogies should hold between Christianity and other religions, other ideologies, other world views, and other value systems. I would like to use the analysis of analogy and metaphor offered by Ian Barbour.[20] According to Barbour, when I say that 'Jane is a tiger,' there are three different aspects to this metaphor. First, there is the positive anology – areas in which Jane is quite explicitly like a tiger. For example, Jane is assertive and strong. Second, there is the negative analogy – areas in which Jane is quite obviously not like a tiger. For example, Jane does not have a furry tail or large fangs. And third, there is the open area – areas in which it is neither explicitly affirmed nor denied that Jane is like a tiger. This is the area for exploration, development, and creativity. Perhaps Jane is somewhat dangerous, or cunning, or has the capacity to move silently and gracefully, appearing where we do not expect her. Every powerful anaology has a large open space.

My suggestion is that the use of analogy and metaphor has an essential role in the development of Christian doctrine. The bedrock of Christian doctrine is, of course, the actual divine events in history, as recorded in scripture. From that bedrock, we enrich our doctrines through a series of analogies. First, there is the analogy between the historical-factual event (such as Christ's incarnation as reported in scripture) and its existential-universal appropriation in the Lord's Supper, in our attitudes towards our bodies, etc. The foundation is the historical-factual incarnation in Mary. Insofar as later Christian experience is explicitly like that incarnation, it must be accepted. For example, we must be open to God's presence in concrete persons, such as one's neighbour or one's pastor. Insofar as later Christian experience is explicitly unlike the historical incarnation, that later experience must be rejected. For example, Christians are not physically born of virgins without a human father,[21] nor has the Logos assumed the flesh of anyone but Jesus. In addition, however, there is a broad open area in which we may explore the analogy between the historical-factual incarnation and our existential-universal application of it. As the church explores this open area, we gradually gain a richer and more nuanced understanding of the doctrine of the incarnation. Roman Catholics and Protestants alike agree that the extension of the incarnation to include icons (in the technical sense) is inappropriate; and Protestants would also hold that the use of the incarnation to justify the doctrine of transubstantiation is also inappropriate. This much we have learned from history. On the other hand, it does seem appropriate to appeal to the incarnation to justify Christian art and concern for human social welfare.

The second analogy holds between Christian events, doctrines, stories, etc. and their existential-universal echoes that we find throughout the world. Thus, to the extent that there is a 'positive analogy' between the presence of the Divine Object in a Shinto shrine and the Christian doctrine of incarnation, it should be affirmed. At the very least, the Christian is obligated to accept the focus on the concrete as the locus of the divine presence. To the extent that there is negative analogy, however, that aspect of Shinto must be denied. God's presence in Jesus Christ is, for example, infinitely richer than a mere rock or sword; and Christians should certainly reject the Shinto tendency to perceive, not the God who created that rock, but local powers who have chosen to inhabit that rock. And to the extent that the Divine Objects in Shinto shrines serve to legitimate the divinity of the Japanese emperors and the sacred character of the emperor system, there is another negative analogy that must be vigorously rejected. Lastly, however, there is the open area, neither affirmed nor denied in the analogy between the Christian incarnation and the Shinto Divine Object. Here is the area for exploration.

God's actions in history, recorded in scripture and culminating in Jesus Christ, constitute the cornerstone in this series of analogies. Direct agreement implies acceptance by Christians. Here Christ functions as a positive norm. Direct disagreement implies rejection by Christians. Here Christ functions as a negative norm.[22] In the third case, the open area, Christ functions as an invitation for and guide to inquiry. This last area implies that Christianity can be enriched as it meets new cultures, new historical eras, and even other religions. This enrichment requires judgement and wisdom because there are no mechanical decision procedures guaranteeing a correct and proper evaluation of the open areas. It also takes time, even generations, to come to a decision. Each theologian and cross-cultural expert will have his own preferred areas and skills for exploration. I am personally interested in the Buddhist theme of Emptiness as a way of enriching our understanding of the kenosis (Phil. 2:5–6) and of the Cross.

It is important that we acknowledge the existential-universal application of Christian themes beyond the borders of Christianity for two additional reasons. First, it makes missions and evangelism possible. We sometimes talk of *pre-evangelism* or that pre-understanding necessary before the gospel can be a real option. In the deepest sense, God himself has done that pre-evangelism. By providing echoes of Christian themes in every culture and in every religion, he has given the entire human race some 'handles' that allow them at least a preliminary understanding of the gospel when it is preached.[23] Without these 'handles' – these echoes, these existential-universal applications of Christian themes – the Gospels would come as something totally incomprehensible to the non-Christian and, therefore, never as a true option.[24] One of the most extraordinary outcomes of the Christian missionary movement is the demonstration in actual practice that the gospel can be understood, at least to some extent, by members of every known culture, era, and religion. Second, the existence of these existential-universal themes throughout all cultures and religions is important evidence for the truth of Christianity. We hold that the same God whom we meet as Saviour in Jesus Christ is also the Creator. Since we also hold that the Exodus, the Christ event, etc., as recorded in scripture most fundamentally reveal the nature of that Creator-Saviour God, we should expect to find analogies to those divine actions distributed throughout all the world. Of course, because of sin, we should also expect those analogies to have limitations (negative analogical content). But a complete lack of existential-universal echoes throughout all history and all cultures would be convincing evidence that Christians have erred in identifying the Saviour God with the Creator of God – if, indeed, there should be any 'god' at all.

Beyond Analogy: the Future Judgement and Hope as History

The Christian *a priori* rests in the historical-factual acts of God in which he saves his people – supremely his act in Jesus Christ. The Bible extends this emphasis on specific actions both backward to creation and forward to the eschaton. Of course, creation and the eschaton also have profound existential-universal applications to our current experience, both to specifically Christian experience and to generically human experience. But this existential-universal dimensions do not exhaust the meanings of either creation or the eschaton. Creation is an event at the beginning of time. And the judgement and perfect reign of God will come at the end of history. Because our language is constructed to deal with events and objects within history, within the stream of time, we should be quite humble when dealing with events at the beginning or end of history as we have known it. Nevertheless, the fundamental structure of Christian belief – that God reveals himself primarily through his historical-factual deeds – leads to the expectation that both the beginning and the end are genuine events. And indeed, this is precisely what the Bible teaches.[25]

Christians believe that the historical-factual Jesus is God's act. Jesus is not just an existential-universal image. Jesus is also unique, even among God's actions, for he alone is truly a person. As a person, he is a 'thou' with all the individuality and personality that only true, actually existent persons possess. This individuality and personality reveal the character of God, who is also personal, also a 'thou'. Because of the deep sense of individuality that the Bible attaches to a person, to a 'thou', only one human 'thou' could manifest the full presence of the divine 'thou'.[26] If the unique person Jesus truly reveals the personhood of God, then we should find the Bible connecting Jesus of Nazareth with all of God's other actions. And indeed this is exactly what we do find.

God's act of creation is attributed to the pre-incarnate Christ – that is, to the logos (Jn. 1:1–5). Because of the Bible's deep sense of temporality, there is no hint in scripture that the humanity of Jesus was involved in that act of creation, only the logos. However, once the incarnation has occurred, then the actions of the logos never take place apart from the historical-factual Jesus. Having taken on flesh in Jesus Christ, God never shuffles off that flesh. Even now God is the incarnate God. Thus the final judgement is both God's act and at the same time, Christ's act. The deep-level structure of the Christian faith implies that the incarnate Christ is indeed the judge of the world. In addition, the final kingdom, the final eschaton, the final harmony has Jesus at its very centre. Paul says, in Ephesians 1:9–10, that the historical Christ unfolds the divine mystery that all things will someday be united under one head, even Christ. And Revelation 22:1 says that at the centre of the New Jerusalem will be a single throne, which is 'the throne of God and of the Lamb'.

The Christian *a-priori*, the deep structure of the Christian faith, declares the unique Christ to be both the hope and the judge of the world.

NOTES

1. The organizers of this consultation chose the term 'The Unique Christ'. By this phrase, I understand the special character of Jesus that justifies the biblical claim that Jesus is the way, the truth, and the life, such that no one comes to the Father except through him. Because of his unique (special, foundational, and particular) character, he is the unique (one and only) way to the Father. The purpose of this paper is to search for that unique (special and particular) foundation of Christianity that leads us to say that Jesus is the unique (one and only) way to the Father. It should be clear from the context, when I am using 'unique' in the sense of 'one and only' and when I am using it in the sense of 'special, particular, and peculiar'.

2. I would affirm that the ideational content of Christianity *ultimately* is special and particular. But, to jump ahead to my conclusion, the uniqueness of Christianity stems

from 'facts' (God's actions in history) and not from 'ideas' (such as doctrines, images, etc.). Given the specificity of the facts, we can move to the special and unique character of Christian doctrine, but we cannot proceed the other way around.

3. The story of Krishna's dancing with the milk-maids would seem calculated, however, to encourage a docetic interpretation even of Krishna. In the story, a very handsome Krishna has attracted a group of admiring milk-maids, each wanting to dance with him. The story continues by telling us that each girl does dance with Krishna and that this dance creates an overwhelming ecstasy in her. Moreover, the girls were all dancing simultaneously! This is possible because the girls were 'really' dancing with each other. The ecstasy had turned each girl's consciousness away from normal sense perception so that she did not notice her 'real' – that is, her *external* – partner. And yet at a deeper level, each girl really – that is, *internally*, the true reality for which no quotation marks are needed – did dance with Krishna. I think it is fair to say that the story suggests that the Krishna in our souls is the important Krishna and that any external figure must be considered secondary.

4. The common meanings of the terms 'shin' and 'tai' are 'god' and 'body'.

5. For example, John Bright in his *A History of Israel* (Philadelphia: The Westminster Press, 1959) argues that at least some portion of the people who later identified themselves as Israel experienced an actual escape from Egypt. His argument, at least in intention, seems to be based on secular standards of historiography.

6. See his *Old Testament Theology*, vol. 1, *The Theology of Israel's Historical Traditions*, trans. D.M.G. Stalker (New York and Evanston, Ill.: Harper and Row, Publishers, 1962), 136–39.

7. Modern secular historical-consciousness differs radically, at this point, from the Hebrew sense of history which focused on God's actions. Consider the Exodus as an example of a biblically important event. Contemporary secular scholarship tends to separate the 'real' Exodus from its 'interpretation' as God's action. The secular sciences of history, sociology, etc., can investigate the Exodus only insofar as it is a factor in human experience with observable causes such as the character of Egyptian slavery, the local geography, the wind, tides, etc. These historical, scientific, and academic perspectives, thus, encourage us to think of the observable (i.e., available for observation by any appropriately situated observer) aspects of the Exodus as the 'real' occurrence and to consider the claim that the Exodus is God's action as a secondary 'interpretation' or a 'religious addendum'. For the Bible, in contrast, the Exodus is both divine action and human experience; but the divine action is the primary factor and the human experience of the Hebrew nation, while obviously necessary, is nonetheless the secondary or derivative factor. (This raises some serious methodological issues concerning the extent to which the modern sciences – and in particular the social sciences – have the resources to deal appropriately with the biblical record of God's actions in history.)

8. In its mythic orientation, Canaanite religion resembles much of Indian religion, Greek religion, gnostic Christianity, etc.

9. Of Eliade's many words, a good starting point is *The Sacred and the Profane*, trans. Willard R. Trask (New York: Harcourt, Brace and World, Inc., A Harvest Book, 1959). Another useful book with which to begin is *Cosmos and History: The Myth of the Eternal Return*, trans. Willard R. Trask (New York: Harper & Row, Publishers, Harper Torchbooks, The Bollinger Library, 1959).

10. See footnote 12 for a discussion of the meaning of 'mythic dimension' when applied to biblical religion.

11. Because of the tendency mentioned in footnote 7 – that is, the tendency of the modern social sciences, including historiography, to restrict the terms 'factual' and 'historical' to what is available to secular observation – I wish to emphasize as strongly as possible that I am using the term 'historical-factual' to refer to God's action. Without doubt, God's action in the Exodus was experienced by the original human participants. I am not, however, restricting the term 'historical-factual' to what the

contemporary discipline of history or the modern social sciences can ascertain about the Exodus or Mt. Sinai.

It may help to clarify this issue by reference to the 'historical Jesus'. There are three possible meanings to this term: (a) the Jesus who is God's action in space and time, who is proclaimed in scripture, confessed in the creeds, and believed by the faithful; (b) the Jesus insofar as the modern disciples of history, sociology, etc., can recover information about him; and (c) the actual Jesus who really existed. It is the conviction of evangelicals that (a) and (c) are identical – that is, that the Jesus who is God's action in space and time is the Jesus who truly and actually existed. At best, the historical Jesus as recovered by the modern social sciences – option (b) – is part of the real event, of what actually happened; and at worst, the historical Jesus of the modern historians is a fabrication that has nothing to do with what actually happened and may even falsify what actually happened. When I say that the deep structure of Christianity – what gives it its characteristic shape, doctrine, rituals, ethical stance, etc. – centres on God's actions in history, and especially on Jesus Christ. I have in mind the combination of (a) and (c).

12. All existential-universal language shapes the experience of the contemporary person and brings that person into contact with the Divine or the Holy. There is, however, more than one kind of existential-universal language. In the case of full-blown, genuine myth, a story is told. This study may or may not have actually happened. But even if that story is historically accurate, its connection with history is logically independent of its 'truth' and of its capacity to structure our experience and to place us in contact with the Holy. In the case of Hebrew religion, in contrast, the function of existential-universal language is precisely to elicit God's past saving acts into present significance and even into a kind of present reality. Thus the existential-universal language of the Hebrews contâins a necessary link to historical actuality and differs profoundly from the existential-universal language of myth. When comparing Israelite with Canaanite religion, or Christianity with Indian religion, we must remember both the similarities and the differences of the different forms of existential-universal language. The existential-universal language of the Hebrews is sufficiently like that of the religions oriented to myth that it is proper to speak of a mythic dimension to the Hebrew religion. At the same time, we must also keep in mind the profound difference between the Hebrew existential-universal language that is logically tied to history and the existential-universal language of the myth that has no essential connection to history.

13. See John Hick, ed., *The Myth of God Incarnate* (Philadelphia: The Westminster Press, 1977). 'The Non-Absoluteness of Christianity', in *The Myth of Christian Uniqueness*, ed. John Hick and Paul Knitter (New York: Orbis Press, 1987). And *An Interpretation of Religion* (New Haven, Conn.: Yale University Press, 1989).

14. Many theologians – including Schleiermacher, Ritschi, Troeltsch, Bultmann, Tillich, and Meland – who have placed a high emphasis on the existential-universal dimensions of Christian doctrine – have also wished to affirm the origin of Christianity in a particular event. The tendency, however, of such thinkers is to emphasize Christian origins as available to the social sciences, that is, a part of human experience and insofar as they are available to secular modes of understanding human experience. They downplay the notion of a knowable act of God as the norm of our theological commitments.

I appreciate the contributions of each of these theologians. And they are indeed sensitive to many of the themes that I have stressed. Nevertheless, I would argue that their analyses of 'history' actually focus more on the existential-universal side of Christian doctrine than on what I have called the historical-factual.

For example, Schleiermacher often rejoices in the presence of God in Christ – which sounds like what I have been stressing. But the presence of God in Christ, for Schleiermacher, seems basically to mean Jesus' possession of a 'God-consciousness' insofar as historical science can recover the human experience of God-consciousness.

Since Schleiermacher has begun with human experience, we will not be surprised to hear that the God-consciousness in Jesus is the perfect development of a capacity that is potentially available to all human beings. The issue at stake is this: Schleiermacher's fundamental theological interpretation of the presence of God in Jesus emerged out of his analysis of the religious experience of Jesus and Christians generally. Evangelicals begin by accepting the Bible's proclamation that God has acted decisively in Jesus Christ.

Of course, the divine action in Christ has impacted human experience in many ways. This impact means that the Christ event *is*, in part, intertwined with every other event in history, and, thus, modern historiography and the social sciences may undertake a legitimate but *partial* and *secondary* investigation of the Christ event. Indeed, because of this interweaving of God's action in Jesus into human experience, it is possible for Christian doctrine to possess an existential-universal side. Unlike Karl Barth, therefore, I would *accept* the analyses of Shcleiermacher and company as profound investigations of the existential-universal dimension of Christian doctrine – which dimension, although secondary, is an important and necessary aspect of our Christian teaching and preaching. I would also *reject* these same analyses when understood as giving us the *basic* meaning of Christian doctrine (as Schleiermacher intended).

15. It is not a part of this paper to engage in apolgetics. However, this would be the location, in terms of the paper's structure, to present a defence of the truth of Christianity. If my argument thus far is correct, then it should be possible to give good reasons which add up to a 'cumulative case argument' for Christianity. This may not be an incontrovertible 'proof' for Christianity, but it would indicate that Christianity is at least as reasonable an option as any other (including agnosticism) and perhaps the most reasonable option.

In outline, my case would run like this: I would presuppose that religious language can have meaning and that God or a Sacred Power of some sort exists. If these two factors are not granted then we would have to deal with those issues first. In the case of discussion of religious pluralism, however, I would think that we could assume that religious language has meaning and that God or the Sacred is real. Assuming that there is no argument about those two claims, then the rest of my argument would run as follows.

(a) When one considers a religion, one enters into it and accepts, at least provisionally, its basic orientation. In the case of Christianity, this would be a provisional acceptance of the Christian *a priori*, of the Christian commitment to God's acts in history. (b) If these events really did occur, then they would have had an impact on human experience. (c) Thus if there were good evidence that no such impact occurred, we would have to reject the Christian claims. For example if the Jewish leaders or Roman authorities had produced the body of Jesus, sometime after his alleged resurrection, then Christianity, at least in its classical, orthodox form, would be false. It is important to note that apparently no one every produced the corpse, and later anti-Christian polemic does not claim that the corpse was produced. (d) I would further expect the social sciences to be able to confirm that some aspects of these events did occur – specifically, those aspects which are a part of human experience and publicly observable. I would expect, for example, the balance of historical evidence to show that it is probable that there was a man named Jesus and that his disciples truly thought that they had seen him after his death. (e) The Christian faith, based on the acceptance of the Bible's presentation of God's acts, claims to make those acts available to me now, as part of my current experience – for example, in the Lord's Supper, or in a personal encounter with Christ, or in having a purpose for living, or in experiencing the forgiveness of sins. Since (1) there is no good evidence that these events did not occur; since (2) the original historical-factual events, if they did occur, had an impact on human experience, and since (3) there is good historical evidence for that impact, we may conclude that it is likely that our existential-universal experience of those events is veridical. (f) Given these foundations, the coherence of Christian doctrines, and the ability of the Christian faith to provide a coherent world-view becomes highly relevant evidence. (g) Analogies to Christian doctrine throughout other religions and in a wide variety of cultures become additional confirming evidence. Taken together, we have good reasons by which to justify a commitment to the Christian faith. Nonetheless, we must remember that it is the Holy Spirit who truly unites to Jesus unto salvation, and not logic nor historical evidence.

16. Those forms of Buddhism stemming from Nichiren (1222–82) preach that, at least in Japan, Buddhism should be the only religion. So far as I am aware, however, Nihiren's Buddhism seems to be the only significant exception to the general Buddhist practice of friendly co-existence and division of labour with other religions.

Anyone who has lived in a Buddhist culture quickly becomes aware of Buddhism's mixing with other religions. For a sociological analysis of this phenomenon in a Theravadan setting, including certain limits to multiple religious participation, see S.J. Tambiah, *Buddhism and the Spirit Cults of North-east Thailand* (Cambridge, Cambridge University Press, 1970).

17. As an illustration of the relevance of historical investigation to a certain type of religious dispute, consider that the Koran teaches that Jesus did not die on the cross, while the Bible teaches that he did. Historical evidence for the crucifixion of Christ, therefore, counts in favour of Christianity and against Islam, whereas any evidence that Jesus was not executed would tend in the opposite direction. Fortunately for Christianity, the evidence that Jesus was executed is quite compelling.

18. For example, Buddhists have invested considerable labour trying to uncover 'the historical Buddha'. And some Buddhists, when they 'take refuge in the Buddha' have in mind the historical Siddhartha who lived in India. Nevertheless, suppose that it could be shown that the Buddha never existed or that his actual teachings were quite different from those we now know under his name, this would not undercut the foundations of Buddhism since the image of the Buddha is what counts more than the details of history. One of the most radical traditions of Buddhism states that 'if you meet the Buddha, kill him!'

19. There are some religions that do not seem to centre on divine actions, nor on the application of those divine actions to the present, nor on mythic stories. For example, Confucianism, at least in some of its early variations, centres on wisdom and the ideal of the sage. Confucianism thus stresses the existential-universal side of religion, but this seems to be a different type of the existential-universal from those found either in Christianity or in the mythic religions.

20. *Myths, Models, and Paradigms: A Comparative Study in Science and Religion* (New York: Harper & Row, Pub., 1974), 44.

21. It is traditional, however, to see an analogy between Christ's Virgin Birth and our spiritual rebirth. According to John 1:12–13, people who believe in Jesus 'become children of God – children born not of natural descent, nor of human decision or a husband's will, but born of God'.

22. At times the negative analogy can consist of mere mistakes and errors. At other times, the negative analogy seems to stem from sin. Negative analogy in the area of incarnation (God's presence in the concrete) is particularly open to idolatry. As we observe sin and idolatry in the negative analogical content of other religions and world-views, however, we must not overlook our own sinful tendency to misappropriate and to misue Christian doctrines, rituals, and symbols.

23. In his book, *Peace Child* (Glendale, California: G/L Regal Books, 1974), Don Richardson has written a fascinating account of a custom among certain non-Christian tribes that profoundly echoed the Christian doctrine of the atonement. As an evangelical missionary, Richardson used that custom as a point of contact between those tribes and the gospel. I would consider this custom to be an existential-universal echo of the historical atonement on the cross – an echo that made available to those tribes the preunderstanding which they needed to hear the gospel as a live option, but also an echo deeply distorted by sin.

24. Langdon Gilkey has shown in his *Naming the Whirlwind: The Renewal of God-Language* (Indianapolis: The Bobbs-Merrill Company, 1969) that the death of God movement of two decades ago arose, in part, out of Karl Barth's theology. By denying any point of contact – to use Emil Brunner's phrase – Barth effectively divorced Christianity from the general life of mankind. The gospel came as a 'bolt from the blue' and, therefore, as something inherently incomprehensible and isolated. As the Death of God theologians clearly and correctly saw, an incomprehensible and isolated 'God' is a dead god indeed. My argument is that the existential-universal echoes of the Christian faith to be found throughout the world function as the context that allow the gospel to be understood and appropriated as it moves into new situations or even into new generations.

25. To claim that the eschaton will be an actual event (or series of events) does not imply that every biblical description of these events must be taken literally. We can use symbol, code, and metaphor to describe actual events. The language, for example, describing the New Jerusalem as 'made of pure gold, as pure as glass' (Rev. 21:18) seems to me to be metaphor and should be taken as such. Many of our problems in interpreting scripture, when dealing with the creation and the eschaton, stem from our failure to realize that an event can be described symbolically without thereby compromising that event's character as something that actually happens (or did happen or will happen).

26. At this point, we have another approach for understanding the Trinity. The full presence of God in Christ is the Word. The full presence of God here and now is the Holy Spirit. More specifically, only the Holy Spirit can unite me, here and now, with the historical-factual Christ. It is the work of the Holy Spirit that creates a distinction between those existential-universal applications of God's actions that provide salvation (above all, creating a union between the believer and the historical-factual Jesus) and those existential-universal myths, themes, and images that do not convey salvation.

22

Roger Kemp

Dr. Kemp writes as a missiologist who seeks to relate theology and missiology in issues of the Mission of the Church. In this chapter he relates hope to the goal of the covenant relationship and the Kingdom of God, and judgement to the integrity and humility of those who make judgements. He argues for dialogue that expounds the Lordship of Christ and does not delete it.

The Christian faith is by nature dogmatic and is therefore considered by many to be critical and judgmental of any other system of beliefs. Indeed the manner in which some Christians have expressed a critical and judgmental spirit in the past has in many ways countered the very objective of Christianity – viz. to share the good news of the gospel and to bring the world to Christ. Of course even in such a judgmental spirit a message of hope was expressed.

I believe therefore that in discussing the uniqueness of Christ as the hope and judgement of the world I must do so with sensitivity and humility.

In this paper I write as a missiologist rather than a systematic theologian. I have not discussed the theology of hope or the theology of judgement in the way which would satisfy the theologians in the audience. I have endeavoured to cover the material from a missiological perspective. I make no apology for that because to be properly missiological one must also be theological, and to be truly theological one must be missiological.

While it is true that Christianity has always existed in a pluralistic world, it is commonly accepted that in these days in which we live, there is a more intense awareness of the plurality of beliefs. As Newbigin says,

> During recent years, however, new perceptions of this milieu have emerged, and pluralism is fast assuming the character of an ideology. Hence the need to understand afresh the nature and role of the church's mission in today's pluralistic world.[1]

This is certainly true in the area of the world from which I come. In a recent report published in a Sydney newspaper it was noted that 'Australians are

---

Rev. Dr. Roger Kemp is Director of the International Council of Accrediting Agencies and teaches at the Baptist College of NSW, Sydney, Australia.

turning away from most mainstream religions . . . non-Christian gods attracting support from every increasing numbers'.[2] The article went on to report that the support for non-Christian religions grew by almost 150% during the period 1976–1986, while the mainstream Christian churches either barely maintained numbers or in fact dropped in numbers.

As if to forecast this increased interest in non-Christian religions, at least in Australia, was the inaugural conference of the Australian Association for the Study of Religions (AASR), in Adelaide South Australia in 1976. It was reported that the conference 'generated a new and exciting sense of corporate adventure into a subject field of fundamental importance and endless spirit'.[3]

The phenomenon reported in Sydney above is surely not isolated simply to Sydney but must be true for many other cities around the world. We are living in a period when Christianity can no longer be taken for granted even in so-called 'Christian' countries. Christianity must stand up and be counted. Its tenets must be proclaimed with clarity and conviction. It is to two of those tenets – hope and judgement – that this paper addresses itself.

Christianity must come to terms with the increased awareness of plurality for it to maintain its integrity. Donald Dawe stated it well when he wrote,

> It is not simply that the Christian church is one religious community among others, with its own particular faith, cultus and institutional forms. The problem for the Christian is that he or she is committed to a very particular faith that claims universality for its vision of God and God's purposes in the world . . . The question that presses upon the Christian community is what faithfulness to that confession means in a world where the overwhelming majority of humankind lives by other faiths and ideologies.'[4]

Christians cannot escape dialogue with people of other faiths, so I address something of the principles involved as I discuss hope and judgement. The dilemma facing Christians in this area has been highlighted by Bosch in referring to Hans Küng when he says, '. . . today's Christian is confronted with the question whether Christianity is indeed something essentially different, something special'.[5]

First then I look at the concept of hope as the Christian Scriptures in general understand it, including the basis for hope and its relationship to the Kingdom of God. The concept of judgement is discussed – again using scripture as a basis, but also examining a methodological framework for relations with other faiths.

I. HOPE

The word 'hope' is used in the Scriptures to translate a variety of Hebrew and Greek words, hence it has a wide range of meanings. Understanding the word is made more complicated by the fact that often the contexts are theological rather than narrative, and need to be read carefully to discover the implied meanings.

A brief study allows us to make some generalized statements as to its meaning.

*It can be said that hope is bound up with the covenants made by God with his people. Hope links the two parties of the covenant – God is man's hope so man hopes in God. Divine action and human response is an essential part of hope. This becomes significant in the context of the theme of this paper.

*Hope depends very much on God. The Old Testament recognizes God as the hope of Israel (Jer. 14:8). It is he alone who makes man dwell in safety. The future is assured when hope is exercised in God. Hope is therefore based upon the character and essence of God. He is a rock (Deut. 32:14, Ps. 18:2, 31, 46), a refuge and fortress for the poor and righteous in the midst of affliction (Ps. 14:6; 61:3).

In scripture man's response to God is varied. The article in the Interpreter's Dictionary of the Bible on hope mentions four responses which are appropriate for our discussion. They are:- (a) trust in God for peace and protection (Ps. 9:10); (b) eagerness to take refuge from one's enemies (Ps. 5:11); (c) confident expectation of good which results in rejoicing (Ps. 13:5); (d) a patient waiting for the Lord to bring salvation (Ps. 31:24).

In the New Testament the emphasis is similar. Hope centres around God. '. . . hope is God-grounded, God-sustained, God-directed, hope is a reality within which man may dwell . . . hope is expectation expressed in faith, confidence, patience, endurance and eagerness.'[6]

What this says to us is that for Christians hope is not a matter of chance. Nor is it a matter purely of activity on man's part, stirring up positive action in order to feel secure for the future. It is, rather, a confident trust in the eternal God – a confidence which rests in the eternal character of God himself. The Christian can feel secure for the present and the future because things do not depend on the fickleness and uncertainty of mankind. This is an important point to make in the context of a pluralistic society.

The evidence for such hope – if evidence is needed – is found in the resurrection of Jesus Christ. Jesus Christ has conquered sin and death which, when considered in the light of the certainty of death for all humankind, is a truly hopeful fact. 'When there is the certainty and assurance that through this particular person death has lost its hold on life, there is the alternative of hope in the midst of death.'[7]

All faiths must endeavour to answer the question of what happens to man in the end. Christianity is no exception. 'While recognising the plurality of these answers, Christians believe that in Jesus Christ the Ultimate has become intimate with humanity, that nowhere else is the victory over suffering and death manifested so decisively as in the death and resurrection of Jesus Christ, and that they are called upon to share this good news humbly, with their neighbours.'[8]

It is not possible for a Christ to talk about hope without at the same time making reference to the kingdom of God, for it is the kingdom to which we longfully look for life after death (Heb. 13:14) recognizing that there is an existential component involved as well (Eph. 1:11–14).

Peter Beyerhaus sees a need for a greater emphasis by evangelical Christians on eschatology.

. . . our evangelical eschatology makes the gospel a message of hope to those who hear it. Outside of Christ, people are 'without God and without hope in the world' (Eph. 2:12), although they might live with various illusions of hope that are bound to end in disappointment and despair. Often, these people lack a sense of history and therefore they find it hard to find a purpose and meaning.'[9]

It is not enough however simply to talk about the kingdom. Christians must have some definite way of showing what this is all about. Beyerhaus goes on to describe such signs. 'Such signs are first of all the renewed lives that show something of the glorious liberty of God's children . . . It is not only the work we do as Christians which counts in relation to other religions but we ourselves.'[10]

In all this it is important for evangelicals to confirm their relation to God through Christ; to have an aim of bringing people of other religions to the same relationship.

> The Christian faith cannot surrender the conviction that God in sending Jesus Christ into our midst, has taken a definitive and eschatological course of action and is extending to human beings forgiveness, justification, and a new life of joy and servanthood, which, in turn, calls for a human response in the form of conversion.[11]

The hope of the Christian is based on the firm belief in Jesus Christ as Lord. Christians then, whether as individuals or together as community, must hold out by any and every means possible, such a hope to people of all other faiths. 'We do this, however, not as judges or lawyers, but as witnesses; not as soldiers but as envoys of peace; not as high pressure salespersons, but as ambassadors of the Servant Lord.'[12]

II. JUDGEMENT

To have such hope is very satisfying for a Christian. However, it is not difficult to act as judges, soldiers or high pressure salespersons. In fact some may well expect it of Christians given the tremendous message of the Christian gospel, to want by all means possible to bring other people to a similar belief.

However, I do not believe that is the biblical way. Certainly there is a tension here which needs to be recognized. The tension comes about when comparing the *methodology* of proclamation – something which requires humility – with the *fact* of the proclamation – the uniqueness of Christ as Lord of all. Christians face the problem of how to tell others about the Lordship of Christ without doing so in an attitude of selfish pride. In a sense, the claim of Christ to be Lord of all is a judgmental statement on all other lords. Yet there is no ground for Christians to be judgmental in a condemnatory way in evangelism. There are several matters to be considered from scripture here.

(a) First it is quite clearly pointed out that Christians can never act as judge or lawyers on the matter of belief, because Christians themselves are under judgement. It is not a matter of Christians judging the world, but God judging all. Unfortunately, the way Christians sometimes act, appears judgmental and starting from an elitist position. Christianity is a message about the cross of Christ, and that is a message of judgement upon sin and the sinner. It was D.T. Niles who said that evangelism is one beggar telling another beggar where to find bread. Donald Dawe refers back to the covenant people of God in the Bible. In explaining what it means to be a covenant people he makes the point that judgement is upon them as much as it is upon the rest of the world. 'They are not free of judgement, while other people receive judgement. Instead, paradoxically, they receive "from the Lord's hand double for all her sins" (Isa. 40:2). When they are saved it is to allow them to carry on their work of witness to God' (Isa. 55:5).[13]

(b) That work must be carried out with an attitude of humility, 'because such an attitude of humility is intrinsic to an authentic Christian faith'.[14] However it is not a humility which denigrates the Christian experience for fear of embarrassing someone of another faith. 'We delude ourselves if we believe that we can be respectful to other faiths only if we disparage our own.'[15]

(c) We proclaim the Lordship of Christ in an attitude of humility but we do so with the authority not of ourselves but that of Christ himself (Matt. 28:18). This is at the very heart of mission thinking. Bosch in his exposition of 'the Great Commission' in Matthew 28:16–29 says that the authority had always been with Jesus. What is new here is the *universal extension* of that authority. Verse 18 in Matthew 28 is an important precursor to verse 19. It is precisely because the risen Christ has universal authority that the disciples are able to move out on mission into the world. 'The universal mission flows from Jesus' universal authority. The proclamation of the gospel is the proclamation of his lordship; mission is the manifestation of his universal dominion.'[16]

Throughout its history Christianity has not always exhibited the above-mentioned humility. The pendulum has swung from love to aggression, from humility to hatred – perhaps indicating the tension between knowledge of truth and the expression of such knowledge. There are too many examples which could be cited that make Christians feel uncomfortable, ranging from the crusades in the 12th and 13th centuries to the racism in some quarters today. Missionary methodology in the past days was often based on a sense of superiority which expressed itself in judgmental terms on the beliefs of other people. Hendrik Kraemer's concept of 'radical discontinuity' is in effect an expression of this. It has been argued that that concept meant Christians were ignorant of developments in other faiths because they (the Christians) had deliberately cut themselves off from contact with other people of other faiths. This was judgement by avoidance of contact.

For many centuries Christians have taken the view that their Christian faith (or indeed their particular aspect of Christianity) is the only way to salvation, so conquest and displacement is the essence of methodology. 'Christianity was understood to be unique, exclusive, superior, definitive, normative, and absolute. The only religion which has the divine right to exist and extend itself.'[17]

Fortunately, this attitude has changed for the better. An 'enlightenment paradigm' has taken place whereby Christians have begun to realize that it is not as clear cut as previously expressed. The Christian cannot stand aloof from, and make judgements on other faiths, and still be listened to seriously. 'Serious Christians have . . . discovered that those "other" religions are incongruously, both more different from and more similar to Christianity than they had thought.'[18] The dilemma then remains – how to maintain an attitude of humility and openness to the world with the knowledge of truth, without being seen to be hypocritical and judgmental.

III.   TOWARDS A SOLUTION

Bavinck discusses two method which Christians can use in their relationship to other faiths which he believes to be worthy of our attention. Time doesn't permit an extensive study of them here so I mention the main thrust of each.

The confrontational approach is indirect in that a Christian does not make any outward judgement of another person's beliefs but rather endeavours to begin where the other person is, and understand that person's thoughts, beliefs and practices. This is to make a 'point of contact'. Once contact has been made the Christian moves on by expressing and explaining the Christian gospel using the context of the receptor, eventually leading the person to a point of commitment.

The direct approach is simply to proclaim in a direct manner the message of the gospel. This method is based on the fact that the gospel can speak for itself in convicting and convincing of sin, and then of the need of salvation through Christ. No attention is given to the context of the hearer. Bavinck sees advantages and disadvantages in both methods, and indeed sees a combination of the two as a way ahead for Christians in mission.

Bosch outlines several approaches which have all been part of the Christian attitude to other faiths – including exclusivism, fulfilment and relativism, none of which he sees as being satisfactory. Bosch makes eight observations in his attempt to answer the dilemma. I mention them briefly to stimulate our thinking.

i) Being willing to accept the coexistence of different faiths. In other words we ought not to resent the presence of people with other views but recognize their right to exist as we expect others do for us.

ii) Commitment. Witness to our deepest convictions while listening to those of others.

iii) Believe that we will meet God who prepares people within their context and convictions.

iv) An attitude of humility. This, as mentioned earlier, is an essential characteristic of Christianity.

v) Each faith has its own structure and context and so the Christian gospel will relate differently to each one.

vi) Mission is at the heart of the Christian faith and cannot be substituted by other activities.

vii) Christianity is holistic and the Christian endeavours to bring about change in other people in all aspects of life, although central is a change of allegiance to Christ as Lord.

viii) Recognize the tension between having the knowledge of the only way of salvation, and humility.

CONCLUSION

I conclude with a quotation from David Hesselgrave.

In a world of religious pluralism, evangelical witness, preaching and teaching should become increasingly dialogical – answering those questions and objections raised by non-Christian respondents rather than simply answering questions of the evangelicals' own devising. In the words of my colleague and friend, Carl. F.H. Henry 'the only adequate alternative to dialogue that deletes the evangelical view is dialogue that expounds it. The late twentieth century is no time to shrink from that dialogue.'[19]

NOTES

1. Newbigin, L., *The Gospel in a Pluralistic Society*, Grand Rapids; Eerdmans, 1990.
2. *Sydney Morning Herald*, 11th January 1992.
3. V. Hayes, *Australian Essays in World Religions*, Adelaide; Australian Association for the Study of Religions, 1977, p. 5.
4. Anderson & Stransky, *Christ's Lordship and Religious Pluralism*, Maryknoll; Orbis, 1981, p. 1.
5. D. Bosch, *Transforming Mission*, Maryknoll; Orbis Books, 1991, p. 477.
6. P.S. Minear, 'Hope', in the *Interpreter's Dictionary of the Bible*, Nashville; Abingdon Press, 1962, p. 641.
7. Anderson & Stransky, p. 26.
8. Anderson & Stransky, p. 36.
9. P. Beyerhaus, 'Eschatology: does it make a difference in missions?', in *Evangelical Missions Quarterly*, October 1990, p. 371.
10. P. Beyerhaus, E.M.Q. p. 371.
11. D. Bosch, p. 488.
12. D. Bosch, p. 488.
13. D. Dawe and J. Carman (eds.), *Christian Faith in a Religiously Plural World*, Maryknoll; Orbis Books, 1978, p. 211.
14. D. Bosch, p. 485.
15. D. Bosch, p. 485.
16. D. Bosch, 'The Structure of Mission: An exposition of Matthew 28:16–20', from Schenk, W.R. (ed.) *Exploring Church Growth*, Grand Rapids: Eerdmans, 1983.
17. D. Bosch, *Transforming Mission*, p. 475.
18. D. Bosch, p. 475.
19. D. Hesselgrave, *Theology and Mission*, Grand Rapids; Baker, 1978, p. 238.

BIBLIOGRAPHY

G.H. Anderson & T.F. Stransky, *Christ's Lordship and Religious Pluralism*, Maryknoll; Orbis, 1981.
J. Bavinck, *An Introduction to the Science of Missions*, Phillipsburgh; Presbyterian and Reformed Publishing Company, 1979.
P. Beyerhaus, 'Eschatology: does it make a difference in missions?, in *Evangelical Missions Quarterly*, October 1990, pp. 366–376.
J. Blauw, *The Missionary Nature of the Church*, London; Lutterworth Press, 1964.
D. Bosch, *Transforming Mission*, Maryknoll; Orbis Books, 1991
    The Structure of Mission: An exposition of Matthew 28:16–20, from Schenk, W.R. (ed.), *Exploring Church Growth*, Grand Rapids; Eerdmans, 1983.
A. Bouquet, *Comparative Religions*, London; Penguin Books, 1964.
D.G. Dawe & J.B. Carman, *Christian Faith in a Religiously Plural World*, Maryknoll; Orbis Books, 1978.
N. Goodall, *Christian Missions and Social Ferment*, London; Epworth Press, 1964.
V. Hayes (ed.), *Australian Essays in World Religions*, Adelaide; Australian Association for the Study of Religions, 1977.
D. Hesselgrave, *Theology and Mission*, Grand Rapids; Baker, 1978.
P.S. Minear, 'Hope,' in *Interpreter's Dictionary of the Bible*, Nashville; Abingdon Press, 1962, p. 641.
S. Neill, *Christian Faith and Other Faiths*, London; Oxford University Press, 1970.
L. Newbigin, *The Gospel in a Pluralist Society*, Grand Rapids; Eerdmans, 1990.

Index